DATE DUE

BRODART, CO.   Cat. No. 23-221

D1208213

LIBERATING JUDGMENT

LIBERATING JUDGMENT

FANATICS, SKEPTICS, AND JOHN LOCKE'S POLITICS OF PROBABILITY

Douglas John Casson

PRINCETON UNIVERSITY PRESS   PRINCETON AND OXFORD

Copyright 2011 © by Princeton University Press

Published by Princeton University Press, 41 William Street,
Princeton, New Jersey 08540
In the United Kingdom: Princeton University Press, 6 Oxford Street,
Woodstock, Oxfordshire OX20 1TW

press.princeton.edu

Library of Congress Cataloging-in-Publication Data

Casson, Douglas.
  Liberating judgment : fanatics, skeptics, and John Locke's politics of
probability / Douglas John Casson.
      p.   cm.
  Includes bibliographical references and index.
  ISBN 978-0-691-14474-0 (hardcover : alk. paper) 1. Locke, John, 1632–1704.
2. Political science—Philosophy—History—17th century. 3. Judgment (Logic)
I. Title.
  JC153.L87C38 2011
  320.01—dc22   2010018916

British Library Cataloging-in-Publication Data is available

This book has been composed in Sabon

Printed on acid-free paper. ∞

Printed in the United States of America

10 9 8 7 6 5 4 3 2 1

Just as you do not know how the breath comes to the bones in the mother's womb, so you do not know the work of God, who makes everything.

—Ecclesiastes 11:5 (NRSV)

Contents

Acknowledgments

ONE OF THE MOST IMPORTANT LESSONS I have learned while studying John Locke and his predecessors is that intellectual labor is never a completely solitary affair. While researching and writing this book, I have benefited from the work of innumerable scholars. My greatest debt, however, is to Ruth Grant, without whom this project would never have been completed. Her unwavering support and stubborn common sense first convinced me to reevaluate the prevailing critiques of classical liberalism and to take a closer look at the complexities of Locke's thought. Throughout this process, she provided me with a living example of how a scholar can be intellectually rigorous, academically generous, and profoundly humane.

I am also happy to recognize a debt to my other teachers, especially Michael Allen Gillespie, Timothy Fuller, Sanford Kessler, Thomas Spragens, Jr., Alasdair MacIntyre, Rom Coles, and Peter Euben. Although their approaches vary significantly, they have all shaped the way I think about the questions raised in this book. In the early stages of this project, many friends and colleagues, including Thomas Merrill, Craig Borowiak, Tania Roy, Johnny Goldfinger, Matthew Specter, and John Zachman, provided invaluable friendship, criticism, and encouragement. I presented some of the ideas that eventually found their way into this book in a number of contexts, and I thank the members of panels and audiences for helping me to clarify my views. I am especially grateful to Bryan Garsten, Steven Forde, and Peter Josephson for stimulating conversations and thoughtful advice. My colleagues at St. Olaf College, including Sheri Breen, Christopher Brunelle, Tony Lott, Kathy Tegtmeyer Pak, Dan Hofrenning, Greg Walter, Jeanine Grenberg, and Anthony Rudd, provided support and a bit of prodding during the final stages of writing. I am also thankful to Shawn Paulson and Emily Tremblay for reading through parts of the manuscript in its final form.

The Earhart Foundation provided generous support for the final stages of this project. I would also like to thank Ian Malcolm and all of the helpful people at Princeton University Press. I would especially like to express my gratitude to Barbara Shapiro and an anonymous reviewer for their close reading of my manuscript. Their thoughtful comments and criticisms spurred me to make much-needed changes to the original manuscript. Any infelicities and oversights that remain are my own.

I owe a greater debt to my extended family than I can articulate here. My parents and siblings have encouraged me to pursue my intellectual interests while making sure that I did not take myself too seriously. The Stromberg family has been unwavering in their patience and encouragement, especially when I needed it most. My children, Martha Grace, Alexander, and Claire, continually remind me to delight in the unpredictable. Finally, my wife, Kathleen, has patiently tolerated the musings and complaints involved in producing this book and responded with good humor, unflagging support, and sound judgment. I dedicate this work to her.

The Great Recoinage

THE ACHIEVEMENT OF LIBERAL SELF-GOVERNMENT is by no means inevitable. It is a complicated, contingent, and ultimately provisional undertaking. This observation might seem commonplace, yet it is also commonly ignored. Enchanted by the belief that liberal democracy is the result of the effortless proliferation of universally accepted principles, its supporters have underestimated the difficulty of fostering stable and just communities both at home and around the world. They have failed to see that government based on free and equal participation cannot simply be decreed, and have thus overlooked the many ways in which such polities can falter. Perhaps such overconfidence was predictable. In the wake of international liberal ascendancy, it has been tempting to assume that everyone embraces the same political aspirations.

Yet this costly self-assurance is not only the result of the proliferation of regimes claiming to be liberal democracies. It also stems from the way in which modern liberalism has come to understand itself as primarily a set of political axioms that can be universally endorsed. All rational individuals, it is assumed, can agree on a set of basic commitments: a hostility toward tyranny, a faith in toleration, an insistence on representative government and the separation of powers, a commitment to free inquiry in the arts and sciences, a conviction that the common good is served through regulated private ownership, and most importantly, the belief that governments are human creations that derive their legitimacy from the consent of the governed. These commitments seem so familiar that it is difficult to imagine that anyone could object to them. In the context of such a consensus, it would seem that liberal democracy could be justified and sustained simply by the articulation of its principles.

By assuming that political justification rests solely on abstract principles, however, we have tended to overlook the dangers and excesses to which liberalism is especially vulnerable. We have ignored the ways in which liberal institutions can foster the very conditions that threaten their continued viability—conditions characterized by isolating egoism, thoroughgoing materialism and secularism, and the uncritical pursuit of a narrowly self-interested freedom. Such conditions can undermine shared political commitments, breeding both debilitating skepticism and violent fanaticism.

The liberal emphasis on intellectual and moral autonomy can make citizens especially susceptible to the perils of radical subjectivity and disconnectedness. Cut off from a shared sense of place or tradition, they risk stumbling into the Tocquevillean nightmare in which "each man is narrowly shut in himself and from that basis makes pretense to judge the world."[1] Modern liberalism seems to foster a skepticism concerning the possibility of genuinely shared standards of judgment. This type of skepticism isolates citizens from one another and undermines their ability to form stable and lasting communities. Given the capacity of liberalism to fracture and isolate individuals, it is not hard to understand the continuing allure of religious and ideological movements that promise to clarify political ambiguities by offering members a sense of certainty that transcends the doubts and disagreements that pervade liberal culture. These movements cannot simply be dismissed as the last gasps of an atavistic faith or the predictable symptoms of socioeconomic deprivation. They continue to appeal to individuals living in a world shaped by liberal institutions and practices because they respond to an inextinguishable desire for transcendent assurance, a desire that liberalism often seems to suppress or ignore. In fact, the restlessness and uncertainty that characterizes liberal democratic culture seems at times to nurture a type of fanaticism that promises clarity by imposing uniformity.

The assumption that liberalism consists of a set of unassailable political axioms obscures the fragile and tentative character of self-government. The specters of skepticism and fanaticism that haunt modern liberal society cannot simply be exorcized by the incantation of abstract principles, regardless of how universally acceptable they might seem. Liberal democracy rests on the character, dispositions, and capacities of those who sustain it. Citizens must be able to think and act in ways that foster self-government. They must be able to evaluate their leaders and hold them accountable if they rule in ways that are harmful to the people as a whole. The establishment and maintenance of liberal institutions relies upon the judgment of the governed.

The problem of judgment lurks at the very center of the tradition of liberal theory. Here we find a seemingly contradictory view of human reasonableness. The plausibility of consensual government rests on faith in human judgment, trust that those around us will make more or less reasonable judgments concerning the common good. Yet it also relies on widespread suspicion of the ways people arrive at and defend their judgments. On one hand, human beings are regarded as naturally free, equal, and rational. We are capable of forming sensible judgments that ensure

---

[1] Alexis de Tocqueville, *Democracy in America*, ed. J. P. Mayer, trans. George Lawrence (New York: Harper, 1969), 394.

our peaceful and prosperous coexistence. On the other hand, human beings are identified as slavish, domineering, and irrational. We are partial in our judgments, clinging to indefensible opinions, and pursuing reckless desires even when our actions lead to misery and conflict. Human beings, it would seem, experience a dual nature: although capable of recognizing the prudence of mutual preservation, we have a troubling tendency to dupe, kill, and enslave one another.

This tension—between the potential dignity and potential barbarism of human judgment—animates the familiar defense of constitutional government, rule of law, and individual rights. In the *Second Treatise*, John Locke argues that it is the failure of individuals to make predictable and accurate judgments in their natural condition that necessitates civil society and the establishment of a public, authoritative judge. "The inconveniences of the state of nature," he writes, "must certainly be great, where men be judges in their own case" (2T 13).[2] The volatility of our judgment makes unregulated interactions not only inconvenient but ultimately unbearable. The primary problem of human association is the potential transgressiveness of private judgment.

Yet Locke appeals to this same faculty in order to establish a practical standard of political authority. As naturally free, equal, and rational individuals, Lockean agents are called on to remain vigilant judges of whether existing institutions are worthy of continued allegiance. The judgment of individuals serves not only as a practical check but also as an ethical benchmark for any political regime. Legitimate political authority rests on the consent, that is, the considered judgment, of those who are being governed. The answer to his oft-repeated question, "Who shall be judge?" is unmistakable: the Lockean agents themselves are to discern whether a regime should be obeyed or resisted. It is by exercising their judgment that individuals experience self-government and dignify themselves as free, equal, and rational beings. Thus for Locke, as well as for the tradition of consensual government that he inspired, the faculty of judgment plays an ambiguous role. It is celebrated as a sign of our individual freedom and equality and appealed to as a guarantor of legitimacy. Yet it is also viewed with suspicion as a source of disorder and conflict, an unpredictable faculty that must be tutored and constrained if it is to resist its own tendency toward excess. Locke does not resolve this tension. Instead, his political thought is best understood as an attempt to respond to its political consequences. It is the determined effort to provide a

---

[2] John Locke, *Two Treatises of Government*, ed. Peter Laslett (Cambridge: Cambridge University Press, 1988). Locke's *First Treatise* will be cited throughout as 1T and the *Second Treatise* as 2T followed by paragraph number. I have modernized spelling and followed modern practices of capitalization.

political solution to the problem of judgment that unifies his various writings into a single, comprehensive project. This solution involves intellectual and cultural transformation. Locke sought to shape the way his readers form judgments and deliberate over matters of public importance.

Toward the end of his life, Locke wrote several pamphlets in response to a looming monetary crisis that he believed would cripple the economy of England and destabilize its political institutions. Deceptive merchants were clipping the edges of sterling crowns, half-crowns, and shillings, smuggling the bullion out of the country, and then passing the clipped coins off for their original value. This type of fraud was devastating for the emerging economy. The problem was not only that unscrupulous bankers and tradesmen were slowly siphoning off silver bullion from the national treasury, but more importantly that the recognized and accepted value of the common currency was being undermined. For Locke this crisis was primarily an epistemological one. The coin-clippers were unsettling the settled and established meaning of money. They were breeding uncertainty and confusion in order to achieve short-term gain and expand their own economic power. They were tearing down the trust between citizens by debasing the coin of the realm. Without a trustworthy currency, it was feared, individuals would have difficulty conducting trade or entering into contracts since they could not be sure that others were assenting to the same terms of exchange. Locke echoed many of his contemporaries when he insisted that a Great Recoinage was needed immediately to preserve the possibility of commerce and sustain a peaceful and prosperous society.[3]

Although Locke's reply to the coin-clippers took shape within a particular economic context, his discussion of the currency crisis mirrored his diagnosis of a more profound and far-reaching political predicament. His condemnation of those who would undermine the common currency and his work to stabilize that currency at the end of his life reflected in small scope his political project as a whole. His worries over debased currency parallel his worries concerning the collapse of a common language of public judgment. Locke himself draws this connection in his writings on money as well as in his treatment of language and politics. He recognizes that the tools and institutions that human beings use to bind themselves to one another and improve their lives, whether they are coins or words, are uniquely vulnerable to manipulation and abuse. Those capacities that make us capable of living together in a peaceful and mutually beneficial

---

[3] P. H. Kelly has collected Locke's policy proposals concerning money in a single volume. For a thorough discussion of the debates that took place during the currency crisis of 1695 and the Great Recoinage of 1696 as well as an account of Locke's important role in shaping policy during these years, see Kelly's excellent introduction in Locke, *Locke on Money*.

manner are the same capacities that enable us to perform acts of unsettling deception and shortsighted cruelty. By utilizing monetary and linguistic currencies, we facilitate social interaction. Yet at the same time, we open ourselves up to a whole range of social dangers.

This often-overlooked connection between coins and words provides us with a clue to both Locke's diagnosis of political disease and his remedy for it. Locke took the economic possibilities and the dangers of money to be analogous to the political possibilities and dangers of language generally. Coins and words are uniquely human tools of social unity and interaction; both can assist us in forming lasting bonds with one another. Yet they can also undermine the very conditions for the formation of such bonds. For Locke, the money used to enable commerce is akin to the language used to form and sustain communities. Just as coins serve as a durable measure of physical labor, words serve as a common standard of intellectual labor that can be accumulated, stored, and traded. Our acquired capacity to use coins allows us to prosper beyond mere subsistence because it provides us with an authoritative standard that facilitates a nonviolent exchange of goods and fosters cohesive communities. Our acquired capacity to use words sets us apart from other animals because it enables us to speak and reason and form lasting attachments with one another. It enables us to enter into political contracts. Just as a recognized unit of currency makes it possible for individuals to bind themselves to each other over time through financial agreements, an accepted and stable vocabulary serves as "the great instrument and common tie of society" (E III.i.1; see also III.x.13).[4]

Yet the uniquely human capacity to use coins and words carries with it significant dangers. The practices that draw us together can also tear us apart. This is because individuals not only *use* these tools to craft stable and prosperous societies, but they also *abuse* them. And the abuse of words unsettles society in the same way that the abuse of coins does. "It is no wonder," Locke writes in *Further Considerations on Money*, "if the price and value of things be confounded and uncertain, when the measure itself is lost. For we have now no lawful silver money current amongst us; and therefore cannot talk nor judge temporality right, by our present, uncertain, clipped money, of the value and price of things" (FCM 158).[5] If we are to "talk and judge right," we need to maintain a common

---

[4] Locke, *An Essay Concerning Human Understanding*, ed. P. H. Nidditch (Oxford: Clarendon Press, 1975). The *Essay* will be cited throughout as E followed by book, chapter, and section.

[5] Locke, "Further Considerations on Money," in *Locke on Money*, ed. P. H. Kelly (Oxford: Clarendon Press, 1991), 158. Locke's economic tract "Further Considerations on Money" will be cited as FCM, and "Some Considerations on Lower Interest and Raising the Value of Money" as SCM followed by page number.

understanding of the value of money and a stable consensus surrounding the meaning of words. It is for this reason that Locke inveighs against the "shameful and horrible debasing" of coins that "disorders trade and puzzles accounts" (SCM 127; FCM 189) and also derides scholastic philosophers as "mint-masters" and ridicules religious fanatics for "coining" their own private languages (E III.x.2, and II.xiii.27, IV.xix). Counterfeiters, Scholastics, and religious sectarians all destabilize the conventions that are necessary for peaceful coexistence.

In the same way that it is an abuse of the common trust to debase the currency, "'tis plain cheat and abuse" to make words "stand sometimes for one thing, and sometimes for another; the willful doing whereof, can be imputed to nothing but great folly, or greater dishonesty" (E III.x.5). "For words," Locke writes, "especially of languages already framed, being no man's private possession, but the common measure of commerce and communication, 'tis not for any one, at pleasure, to change the stamp they are current in" (E III.xi.11). For Locke the clipping and counterfeiting of words is worse than the abuse of money: "to me it appears a greater dishonesty, than the misplacing of counters, in the casting up a debt; and the cheat the greater, by how much truth is of greater concernment and value, than money" (E III.x.5; see also I.vi.23). The clipping of coins is certainly devastating to the economy, but it is nothing compared with the abuse of language, an abuse that threatens to impede the free and dependable exchange of ideas that provides the "comfort and advantage of society" (E III.i.1).

Locke viewed the monetary crisis of the 1690s as a symptom of a deeper social and political crisis. He believed that a stable and reliable mode of discourse constitutes a unifying authoritative language through which norms of law and justice can be articulated. It does not guarantee universal agreement on every particular, but it does allow for the possibility of a makeshift consensus within which political deliberation can take place. It is for this reason that he insists in the *Essay* that "the discourses of religion, law and morality" are of the "highest concernment" (E III.ix.22). When a shared vocabulary deteriorates or is undermined, common experiences are suddenly susceptible to systematically different interpretations. Public judgment collapses into private opinion. Formulas that had once served as unambiguous explanations and unquestionable justifications suddenly appear controversial. Distinctions suddenly seem spurious. When matters of public importance can no longer be publicly evaluated, mutually beneficial communal practices fracture and fall apart.[6]

[6] Hannah Dawson has recently argued that Locke's insight into the instability of language threatens to undermine his political project. Hannah Dawson, "Locke on Language

In many ways Locke's experience of cultural fracturing and cognitive instability is similar to our own. Like us, Locke found himself in a world of religious conflict and social upheaval. Yet the brutality that he experienced was much closer to home. He was ten when Civil War broke out in England, sixteen when the king was beheaded next to his school, and twenty-six when Oliver Cromwell's death brought about two years of political chaos that eventually led to the Restoration of Charles II.[7] As a student at Oxford, Locke described England as a "great Bedlam" of "hot-headed" sectarians and "mad" zealots. He observed men and women, especially religious men and women, asserting their moral and political claims without bothering to articulate them in terms that might be discernible to others. They justified the most preposterous statements and rationalized the most vicious and violent actions by appealing to the subjective guidance of their own divine inner light, a light only comprehensible to those who were similarly illumined. For Locke, such appeals were not only perplexing; they were insane.[8] He believed that the widespread rejection of a stable and common language of justification represented an epidemic of madness. The violence and turmoil in the years prior to the Restoration only confirmed his view. Invocations of reason or reasonableness seemed to have no meaning. In 1659 he wrote to a

in (Civil) Society," *History of Political Thought* 26, no. 3 (2005), 397–425, and *Locke, Language and Early-Modern Philosophy* (Cambridge: Cambridge University Press, 2007). Since the publication of de Man's influential essay "The Epistemology of Metaphor," it has been common to deride Locke as naively ignorant of the metaphors and slippages that take place in his own attempt to achieve clarity. As Dawson shows, however, Locke is perfectly aware of the slippery character of language. Yet he remains much more optimistic than most of his commentators about the potential for humans to understand each other. For Locke, language may be philosophically deficient and descriptively approximate, but it is still a crucial medium of exchange. It can still bind people together in community.

[7] John Marshall, *John Locke: Resistance, Religion and Responsibility* (Cambridge: University of Cambridge Press, 1994), 8. J.G.A. Pocock writes that "seventeenth-century men were still pre-modern creatures for whom authority and magistracy were part of a natural cosmic order, and ... the starting point of much of their most radical thinking was the unimaginable fact that, between 1642 and 1649, authority in England had simply collapsed." *Virtue, Commerce, and History: Essays on Political Thought and History* (Cambridge: Cambridge University Press, 1985), 55.

[8] One of the most conspicuous features of Locke's early correspondence is his repeated employment of medical or psychological terms such as "distempered," "mad," and "hot-headed" to describe the political and religious actors of his day. See John Locke, *The Correspondence of John Locke*, ed. E. S. De Beer, 8 vols. (Oxford: Clarendon Press, 1976–80), 1:30, 43, 59, 82, 91. For a provocative account of the role that madness plays in Locke's thought, see Uday Singh Mehta, *The Anxiety of Freedom: Imagination and Individuality in Locke's Political Thought* (Ithaca, N.Y: Cornell University Press, 1992). For a general discussion of the relationship between madness and religious fanaticism among Locke's contemporaries, see Michael Heyd, *"Be Sober and Reasonable": The Critique of Enthusiasm in the Seventeenth and Early Eighteenth Centuries* (Leiden: Brill, 1995).

friend in exasperation, "Where is that Great Diana of the world, Reason? Everyone thinks he alone embraces this Juno, whilst others grasp nothing but clouds. We are all Quakers here, and there is not a man but thinks he alone hath this light within and all besides stumble in the dark."[9]

These are the words of an eyewitness to an epistemological crisis. Appeals to reason, which had once appeared to hold a generally accepted and assessable meaning, suddenly seemed like nothing but smoke and mirrors. The common language that had once sustained rational deliberation in matters of public importance was breaking down. This cognitive instability was intensified by the discovery of new worlds—some suspended in the heavens, others across vast oceans, and still others within the body itself. Assumptions that had once served as a stable framework within which individuals understood themselves and their relation to others no longer seemed plausible. The collapse of a common mode of discourse left people feeling profoundly isolated from one another. The absence of a shared understanding of the individual's place within a unified whole endangered the stability and coherence of civil society.

This anxiety about the political consequences of a deteriorating common language was certainly not unique to Locke and his contemporaries. Long before him, Thucydides worried about words' loss of meaning in the chaos that arose in Greece during the Peloponnesian War.[10] And long after him, George Orwell argued passionately that the abuse of language is the first step toward totalitarian government.[11] The importance of a common political vocabulary among those who aspire to self-rule has long been recognized. Many have also noted that these vocabularies are among the most fragile and least durable of human innovations. The loss of a shared moral language of judgment represents the loss of community and the collapse of a common world. "In the whole conduct of the

[9] Locke, *Correspondence*, 1:81. For a brief overview of Locke's views of the political unrest in the years before the Restoration, see Roger Woolhouse, *Locke: A Biography* (Cambridge: Cambridge University Press, 2007), 35–38; Maurice Cranston, *John Locke: A Biography* (London: Longman's, Green, 1966), 40–46; and Marshall, *John Locke*, 25–32.

[10] Thucydides, *History of the Peloponnesian War*, trans. Richard Crawley (New York: Modern Library, 1982), III.82, 198–200.

[11] See George Orwell, "Politics and the English Language," in *Shooting an Elephant, and Other Essays* (New York: Harcourt Brace, 1950), and, of course, his haunting depiction of "doublespeak" in the novel *1984* (San Diego: Harcourt Brace Jovanovich, 1984). Similarly Hannah Arendt worried that "we have ceased to live in a common world where the words we have in common possess an unquestionable meaningfulness, so that short of being condemned to live verbally in an altogether meaningless world, we grant each other the right to retreat into our own worlds of meaning, and demand only that each of us remain consistent within his own private terminology." Hannah Arendt, *Between Past and Future* (New York: Penguin, 1968), 95–96.

understanding," Locke writes, "there is nothing of more moment than to know when, and where, and how far to give assent, and possibly there is nothing harder. . . . Some admit of certainty, and are not to be moved in what they hold: others waver in everything, and there want not those that reject all as uncertain" (CU 33).[12] Locke recognized that the temptation of fanaticism and skepticism is a constant threat to the possibility of public deliberation. Yet he did not only diagnose the problem, he also went to great lengths to remedy it. Locke's solution to the deterioration of a common vocabulary of rational appraisal parallels his solution to the monetary crisis. He sought to institute a Great Recoinage of language. He wanted to establish and defend a stable mode of public judgment that could serve as an authoritative and communal standard for judging the legitimacy of political claims.

Undoubtedly, Locke shared this project with many of his contemporaries who also recognized the political implications of the collapse of a common vocabulary of judgment. He is exceptional, however, in that he saw that a Great Recoinage of language could not simply be imposed by an absolute monarch or powerful political regime; he knew that a shared vernacular must emerge into general use from the bottom up.[13] A common language of judgment would have to be renewed and maintained by the people themselves. Locke aims to establish a regime dedicated to both popular sovereignty and individual rights, committed to both consent and reason. For this reason Locke's primary political task can only be accomplished in a somewhat indirect way. By convincing his readers to accept a new vocabulary within which they could govern their political opinions and regulate their political judgments, he hopes to cultivate a new type of reasonableness. Throughout his various writings on religion, law, and morality, Locke seeks to disseminate a vocabulary of judgment that can sustain public deliberations over matters of public importance and provide for the establishment of an entirely new type of political authority.

---

[12] Locke, *Some Thoughts Concerning Education* and *Of the Conduct of the Understanding*, ed. Ruth W. Grant and Nathan Tarcov (Indianapolis: Hackett, 1996). *Of the Conduct of the Understanding* will be cited by CU and *Some Thoughts Concerning Education* will be cited as STCU followed by paragraph number.

[13] To a great extent Locke's view of the importance of a stable political language and the many threats to such a language echoes a view that Hobbes articulated before him. The "tongue of men" Hobbes writes, "is a trumpet of war and sedition." Thomas Hobbes, *Man and Citizen: De Homine and De Cive*, ed. Charles T. Wood (Indianapolis: Hackett, 1991), 168–69. The solution that Hobbes proposes, however, differs from the one that Locke offers. Hobbes insists that the purification of language can only be achieved through the declaration of an all-powerful sovereign. Locke's approach is much more pragmatic and indirect. He seeks to help his readers arrive at judgments so that they can come to an agreement over political authority in the absence of a single, unlimited sovereign power.

Locke responds to the problem of multiple and contending authorities not simply by offering abstract principles of political justification, but by working to transform his readers into the type of citizens who are able to think, judge, and act in ways that are conducive to self-government. In a short essay written late in life Locke explains, "Politics contains two parts very different the one from the other. The one containing the original or societies, and the rise and extent of political power, the other, the art of governing men in society."[14] Locke recognizes that the project of defining institutions and articulating principles is only one side of the story. The other, equally important aspect of politics involves "the art of governing." Some commentators have interpreted this famous passage to show that Locke limited his writing to the elaboration of abstract demonstrations concerning rights and obligations and that he was relatively uninterested in the "art of governing."[15]

Yet what is striking about Locke's division of politics into the theoretical and the prudential is that he did not collapse it into either part. Locke did not believe that politics could be reduced to a science. Nor did he think that it must be abandoned completely to the prudential manipulation of power. Politics certainly includes formal arguments for Locke, yet it is not limited to an articulation and defense of abstract rights and institutions. Politics is not exhausted by the attempt to provide a demonstration of morality, since our political lives cannot be reduced to scientific certainties. Locke recognized the inescapability of contingency and uncertainty, and his political project involves the "art of governing" insofar as he seeks to shape the way his readers make judgments. He wants to convince his readers to conduct their lives properly and reasonably within the limitations of this "state of mediocrity" (E IV.xiv.2). Locke's argument concerning "the true original, extent, and end of civil government" is couched in a larger polemical, one could even say rhetorical, framework. The coherence of his narrow argument relies on the persuasiveness of a much larger formative vision.

We can best appreciate the mixed quality of Locke's political project by looking closely at his attempt to transform the way in which his contemporaries make judgments. It is here that we see the intersection between the explication of political power and the art of government. Judgment, as he tells us in the *Essay*, is required in matters in which absolute certainty cannot be attained (E IV.1.3). These are the matters of disagree-

---

[14] Locke, "Some Thoughts Concerning Reading and Study for a Gentleman," in Locke, *Political Essays*, ed. Mark Goldie (New York: Cambridge University Press, 1997), 351.

[15] Pocock points to this distinction to argue that Locke took the "high road of right and authority," articulating abstract, juridical theories while all but ignoring the art of government. J.G.A. Pocock, "A Discourse of Sovereignty," in *Political Discourse in Early Modern Britain*, ed. Nicholas Phillipson and Quentin Skinner (Cambridge: Cambridge University Press, 1993), 394–95.

ment and contingency that make up our political lives. "Man would be at a great loss," Locke writes, "if he had nothing to direct him, but what has certainty of true *knowledge*. For that being very short and scanty ... he would be often utterly in the dark, and in most of the actions of his life, perfectly at a stand, had he nothing to guide him in the absence of clear and certain knowledge" (E IV.14.1). Since most of the matters that we face in our lives cannot be resolved in any final and absolute sense, it is of great importance to Locke that we learn to govern our judgments in ways that are conducive to rational deliberation.

It was this practice of reasoning, the hard labor of judgment, that became Locke's primary interest in his final years. By placing judgment at the center of this study of Locke's thought, I hope to show that he was involved in something deeper and more complex than is usually recognized. Locke's epistemological, political, and religious writings should not be read as philosophical discourses in the narrow sense, but rather as "civil" discourse.[16] Locke is not simply offering his readers a formal argument in defense of a particular set of institutions; he is not simply laying out a theoretical account of legitimate political organization. Instead, he is attempting to foster the development of a certain type of intellectual conduct, which could in turn hold a constitutional regime together. In his philosophical as well as his explicitly political writings, Locke is setting the boundaries of reasonable judgment in order to foster the possibility of public justification and rational self-government.[17]

The Allure of Certainty

Given the centrality of the problem of judgment for Locke and the importance that he places on instituting a common language of judgment, it might seem surprising that so few scholars have embarked on a sustained analysis of the role it plays in his work. One of the reasons for this neglect

[16] For the distinction between philosophical and civil discourse, see E III.ix.3. Michael Zuckert offers an important account of the importance of this distinction for interpreting Locke in "Fools and Knaves: Reflections on Locke's Theory of Philosophical Discourse," in *Launching Liberalism: On Lockean Political Philosophy* (Lawrence: University Press of Kansas, 2002), 107–28.

[17] Although most commentators emphasize Locke's abstract, theoretical arguments concerning rights and obligations and neglect the way he helps cultivate dispositions that sustain liberal government, there are important exceptions. See Mark E. Button, *Contract, Culture, and Citizenship* (University Park: Pennsylvania State University Press, 2008); Peter Josephson, *The Great Art of Government: Locke's Use of Consent* (Lawrence: University Press of Kansas, 2002); Duncan Ivison, *The Self at Liberty* (Ithaca, N.Y.: Cornell University Press, 1997); James Tully, *An Approach to Political Philosophy: Locke in Contexts* (Cambridge: Cambridge University Press, 1993); and Nathan Tarcov, *Locke's Education for Liberty* (Chicago: University of Chicago Press, 1984).

is Locke's own tendency to present his arguments, especially his political arguments, as if they were incontrovertible. Although he comes to focus his attention on the importance of probable judgment, he also seems to want to establish his claims in a way that transcends the vicissitudes of political contingency. At many points in his writings, Locke appears to be captivated by the possibility of achieving a type of demonstrative certainty in political and moral affairs. He seems more interested in establishing abstract truths that are irrefutable than in worrying about the vagaries of practical reasoning. In fact, Locke repeatedly asserts in the *Essay* that morality could be just as capable of demonstration as mathematics (E III.xi.16, IV.iii.18, IV.xii.8). In the *Second Treatise*, moreover, he presents his case with such methodical self-confidence and rigorous argument that judgment, at first glance, seems unnecessary.

In spite of his explicit appeals to intellectual modesty, Locke often appears supremely confident that divisive questions concerning morality and divine command can be answered with absolute certainty. He seems to think he can resolve disagreements concerning religion, law, and morality by appealing to an independent source of reason that lies beyond the empirical divisions and competing claims present in society. James Boyd White describes Locke's voice as "a voice of certainty, telling his readers how things are. . . . This is the mind that will tell you its first principles, then show you what flows from them, all as though this were an automatic process."[18] His arguments compel the reader to submit to them—not only in substance, but also in tone and style. We encounter a writer who seems breathtakingly optimistic about the political possibilities of rational inquiry, confident that he will be able to replace the diversity and disagreement that he encounters in the political sphere with the universally acceptable deliverances of reason.[19]

---

[18] James Boyd White, *Acts of Hope: Creating Authority in Literature, Law and Politics* (Chicago: University of Chicago Press, 1994), 149.

[19] This view of Locke is most clearly developed in the work of Peter A. Schouls, *The Imposition of Method: A Study of Descartes and Locke* (Oxford: Clarendon Press; New York: Oxford University Press, 1980) and *Reasoned Freedom: John Locke and Enlightenment* (Ithaca, N.Y.: Cornell University Press, 1992). Yet many influential commentators have focused on Locke's failure to provide the type of unassailable philosophical system that he promises. John Dunn depicts Locke as a sincere yet somewhat befuddled thinker who retreats to Scripture when his demonstrative proof fails to materialize. Leo Strauss portrays Locke as a cunning philosopher who artfully offers his readers inadequate demonstrations in order to usher in a new age of egoism and acquisition. Both of these readings begin with a view of Locke as an unsuccessful system builder. John Dunn, *The Political Thought of John Locke* (Cambridge: Cambridge University Press, 1969), chaps. 8–9. See also Dunn's article "Measuring Locke's Shadow," in John Locke, *Two Treatises of Government and a Letter Concerning Toleration*, ed. Ian Shapiro (New Haven: Yale University Press, 2003), 257–85; Leo Strauss, *Natural Right and History* (Chicago: University of Chicago Press, 1957), 202–51.

Thus Locke, as the founder of modern liberalism, is seen as an abstract, normative theorist who sets down a line of reasoning akin to a geometric proof in order to establish the legitimacy of certain abstract institutional arrangements. His arguments compel the reader to submit to them—not only in substance, but also in tone and style. Faced with the logical demonstrations that Locke offers, it would seem that there is no need for us to utilize our faculty of judgment. We simply assent to that which is undoubtedly true, an assent that Locke describes as almost involuntary (E IV.vii.14). This is a picture of a thinker who is breathtakingly optimistic about the political possibilities of rational inquiry, confident that he will be able to replace the diversity and disagreement that he encounters in the political sphere with the universally acceptable deliverances of reason.

With this view in mind, commentators have sought to uncover the foundations of Locke's philosophical edifice. They have wrestled with his cryptic appeals to natural law and struggled to understand how he could argue that this law provides the basis for a logically compelling demonstration of both the content and the obligations of a system of moral injunctions. Some have attempted to explain Locke's position by placing it within the context of the notion of moral science discussed in the *Essay*.[20] Others have sought to supplement this view of science by locating the true foundation of his moral and political argument in his appeal to the self-evident or intuitive character of certain propositions.[21] And still others have insisted that the basis of Locke's philosophical demonstration is found in his understanding of the necessary relationship between creator and creature.[22] Although these interpretations have brought to the fore important aspects of Locke's thought, the search for a freestanding, foundationalist argument yielding incontrovertible ethical conclusions has come up short. Some have pointed out that Locke's notion of demonstrative moral science is trivial, a process that cannot

---

For a recent example of this approach, see Michael S. Rabieh, "The Reasonableness of Locke, or the Questionableness of Christianity," *Journal of Politics* 53 (1991), 933–57.

[20] Ruth Grant, *John Locke's Liberalism* (Chicago: University of Chicago Press, 1987), 27–39. See also John Colman, *John Locke's Moral Philosophy* (Edinburgh: Edinburgh University Press, 1983); J. W. Gough, *John Locke's Political Philosophy: Eight Studies*, 2nd ed. (Oxford: Clarendon Press, 1973).

[21] John Yolton points to Locke's scattered references to self-evidence as well as his assertion that certain moral propositions are "writ in the Hearts of all Mankind" in the *Two Treatises* (2T 4, 5, 11) to argue that the basis of his political argument is a species of innatism. John Yolton, *Locke and the Compass of Human Understanding: A Selective Commentary on the "Essay"* (Cambridge: University Press, 1970).

[22] The most thorough account of Locke's "workmanship" argument is found in James Tully, *A Discourse on Property* (Cambridge: University of Cambridge Press, 1980), 3–4, 34–51.

yield much more than clarified definitions.[23] Others have shown that his scattered appeals to self-evident truth contradict his forceful and tireless attack on similar arguments based on innate moral ideas in the first book of the *Essay*.[24] And still others have attacked Locke's theological argument for its failure to demonstrate the actual existence of effective moral commands enforced by divine sanctions.[25] Yet Locke himself seems to have recognized these shortcomings. He also repeatedly voiced concerns about the limits of human reason. Toward the end of his life he wrote that "it is plain, in fact, that human reason unassisted failed men in its great and proper business of morality. It never from unquestionable principles, by clear deductions, made out an entire body of the 'law of nature'" (RC 241).[26]

Faced with these difficulties, many commentators have understood their task as either to help clarify and perfect Locke's rationalist project or to expose his failure to do so. The assumption that underlies these approaches, however, is that Locke's primary purpose was to offer a demonstrative proof. Given this assumption, some commentators present Locke as a sincere yet somewhat befuddled theorist who is unable to supply the type of argument that he promises.[27] In the absence of demonstrative proof, he appeals to the guidance of Scripture, but his confident claims concerning politics and morality take on the hollow ring of dogmatic assertion. Other scholars view Locke as a cunning philosopher who recognizes the gaps in his own demonstrations. By feigning adherence to a traditional notion of natural law as the manifestation of the divine will and then offering a perplexing and ultimately contradictory argument in its defense, he artfully reveals that this notion is implausible.[28] In much of the literature, therefore, Locke is seen as either a muddled thinker, a man too caught up in his own historical con-

---

[23] R. S. Woolhouse, *Locke's Philosophy of Science and Knowledge* (Oxford: Basil Blackwell, 1971).

[24] Peter Laslett is among many Locke scholars who have pointed out this difficulty. See his notes to 1T 86 and 2T 11 in *Two Treatises of Government*, ed. Peter Laslett (Cambridge: Cambridge University Press, 1988).

[25] Thomas L. Pangle, *The Spirit of Modern Republicanism: The Moral Vision of the American Founders and the Philosophy of Locke* (Chicago: University of Chicago Press, 1988), 199–201; and Strauss, *Natural Right and History*, 203–4. See also Peter C. Myers, *Our Only Star and Compass: Locke and the Struggle for Political Rationality* (Lanham, Md.: Rowman & Littlefield, 1998), 42–49.

[26] Locke, *The Reasonableness of Christianity as Delivered in the Scriptures*, ed. George Ewing (Washington, D.C.: Regnery Gateway, 1965). Cited throughout as RC followed by page number.

[27] Dunn, *Political Thought of Locke*.

[28] Pangle, *Spirit of Modern Republicanism*; Strauss, *Natural Right and History*; Zuckert, *Launching Liberalism*.

text to recognize his obvious mistakes, or a crafty schemer, a context-transcending philosopher who purposely misleads his less philosophically acute readers.

Yet I believe that this stark choice is an artificial one. It rests on assumptions that have more to do with our preconceived notions of what Locke *should* be arguing than with what he *actually* says. It stems from a particular understanding of what philosophical activity entails, and this understanding leads us to search for something in Locke's writings that is simply not there and neglect aspects of his thought that are deemed inconsequential. This desire to isolate an abstract and logically compelling rationalist system from Locke's various tracts, essays, and letters can obscure the original meanings and purposes of these texts. As Eldon Eisennach has pointed out, this method can become a bloodless procedure in which scholars effectively sterilize Locke's texts against infection from their local contexts and then perform "analytic operations" on them.[29] The result is the discovery of confused and contradictory claims that must be modified or discarded in order to salvage the unity of his system.

It is worth remembering that Locke was aware that he had not supplied his readers with the type of comprehensive and demonstrative account that he said was possible.[30] Yet he seemed genuinely unconcerned with this fact. It is telling that modern commentators have fretted far more about this supposed failure than the author himself. Of course, it is undeniable that Locke was enamored with the possibility of producing a mathematically certain demonstration of our moral obligations. Yet he also seemed to understand that the success of his political project somehow stood apart from his ability to provide a logically compelling demonstration of the content and obligation of natural law. He recognized the ambiguous relationship between abstract reason and public life. Locke believed that properly governed judgment accords with nature. It is not entirely conventional. Yet he understood that our access to this

[29] Eldon Eisenach, "Religion and Locke's *Two Treatises of Government*," in *John Locke's Two Treatises of Government: New Interpretations*, ed. Edward Harpham (Lawrence: University Press of Kansas, 1992), 50. This criticism is most plausibly leveled against the decidedly ahistorical and analytical works of Peter Schouls and John Simmons. See Schouls, *The Imposition of Method* and *Reasoned Freedom*; and A. John Simmons, *The Lockean Theory of Rights* (Princeton: Princeton University Press, 1992), and *On the Edge of Anarchy: Locke, Consent, and the Limits of Society* (Princeton: Princeton University Press, 1993).

[30] When Locke's contemporary Thomas Burnet criticized him for failing to provide a mathematical demonstration of morality or the natural law, Locke shot back, "I have said indeed in my book that I thought morality capable of demonstration as well as mathematics. But I do not remember where I promised this gentleman to demonstrate it to him." Thomas Burnet, *Remarks Upon an Essay Concerning Humane Understanding in a Letter Address'd to the Author* (London: Printed for M. Wotton, 1697), 34.

natural standard is always tentative and probable, especially in matters of public importance. Locke saw that it is *reasonableness* and not *reason* that ultimately binds civil society together.

The Pedagogy of Probable Judgment

In a sense Locke is a theorist of "public reasonableness." He does not simply appeal to an abstract conception of public reason, as some contemporary liberal theorists tend to do. Instead, he actively strives to generate and shape what constitutes reasonableness by persuading his readers to internalize a particular notion of judgment. His political project can thus be seen as a type of political pedagogy. Locke recognizes that the widespread acceptance of a common language of justification is a precondition for the acceptance and preservation of social contracts. It is only by teaching his readers to accept a more or less common notion of reasonable judgment that he will be able to foster the conditions that would enable constitutional self-rule. Locke is not simply defending an abstract theory of legitimate political institutions; he is promoting and encouraging the rational development and intellectual discipline of those who would inhabit such institutions. Locke recognizes that just and stable institutions require more than the articulation of what liberal theorists call public reason. Liberal democracy depends not just on articulation of principles, but also on the cultivation of virtues that sustain public reason.

The idea of public reason originates with Thomas Hobbes, who insists in chapter 37 of *Leviathan* that individual deliberation in the public sphere should be supplanted by a single, unified judgment or "publique reason." Faced with the political instability brought about by the religious civil wars, Hobbes points out the difficulty of adjudicating between the opinions concerning miracles and insists that the stability of the state requires a common, authoritative view. Matters of public importance should be decided not by private opinion but by public reason, articulated and enforced by the sovereign. In place of irreconcilable private judgments, the sovereign can provide a judgment that applies to everyone equally. In contrast to private judgments, which often lead to conflict and disagreement, public reason can serve as a common standard in the midst of profound disagreement.[31]

Although subsequent liberal theorists rejected Hobbes's notion of an unlimited sovereign, they often returned to his conception of public rea-

---

[31] For an influential explanation of the importance of public reason in Hobbes's political theory, see David Gauthier, "Public Reason," *Social Philosophy and Policy* 12, no. 1 (1995), 31.

son as a way to ameliorate (if not to resolve) the tension between individual liberty and the necessary preconditions for establishing and sustaining liberal institutions. In the context of consensual government, public reason is invoked in order to place limits on private judgment, defining what counts as a legitimate basis for deliberation in the public sphere. Often the appeal to public reason has been a strategy to avoid the contingencies and uncertainties of politics by securing an external standard of judgment that exists beyond or above the actual opinions of citizens in communities. Thus Immanuel Kant argues that the social contract is best understood as a pure idea of reason, a regulative or "eternal norm" that can be used to judge laws and institutions regardless of whether that norm has any resonance with people inhabiting political institutions.[32] By presupposing a conception of practical reason or human will as the source of universal law, Kant presents a categorical, apodictic morality that hovers above political contestation.[33] The Kantian view of liberal theory as an *a priori* standard of right largely does away with concerns about equipping citizens with the types of capacities and dispositions that sustain political society.[34]

Insofar as contemporary liberal theorists, such as John Rawls, embrace the Kantian aspiration to articulate universal principles of right, they overlook the importance of moral and intellectual transformation. In his early work, Rawls derives "principles of justice" by exploring "the choice rational men would make in a hypothetical situation of equal liberty."[35]

---

[32] Immanuel Kant, "On the Common Saying: 'This May Be True in Theory, but It Does Not Apply in Practice,'" in *Political Writings*, ed. Hans Reiss, trans. H. B. Nisbet (New York: Cambridge University Press, 1991), 79–81.

[33] Patrick Riley points out that unlike other liberal thinkers such as Locke or Rousseau, "Kant does not have to struggle [to get his subject] to think as a citizen and not as a man, because consent can be treated as a standard." Patrick Riley, *Will and Political Legitimacy* (Cambridge: Harvard University Press, 1982), 127.

[34] The most famous example of this is Kant's assertion that "the problem of setting up a state can be solved even by a nation of devils (so long as they possess understanding)." Kant, "Perpetual Peace," in *Political Writings,* 112. In recent years, however, Kant scholars have sought to provide a broader view of Kantian ethics and politics in response to criticisms of his thought as overly formal, abstract, and individualistic. They have sought to balance his *a priori* argumentation with his anthropological and political writings. The result is a view of Kantian politics as more provisional and attuned to social conditions than has been previously recognized. See Elizabeth Ellis, *Kant's Politics: Provisional Theory for an Uncertain World* (New Haven: Yale University Press, 2005); Jeanine Grenberg, *Kant and the Ethics of Humility* (Cambridge: Cambridge University Press, 2005); Mika LaVaque-Manty, *Arguments and Fists: Political Agency and Justification in Liberal Theory* (New York: Routledge, 2002); Henry E. Allison, *Kant's Theory of Freedom* (Cambridge: Cambridge University Press, 1990); and Onora O'Neill, *Constructions of Reason* (Cambridge: Cambridge University Press, 1989).

[35] John Rawls, *A Theory of Justice* (Cambridge: Harvard University Press, 1971), 11.

These principles are arrived at only by setting aside the actual values and aspirations of the individuals who would inhabit his political institutions. In his later work, Rawls seems to move away from an explicitly Kantian approach, yet he continues to seek a "free-standing" criterion for judging the legitimate exercise of political power.[36] His effort to define the social institutions and moral principles that free and equal agents would endorse focuses on the articulation rather than the formation of public reason. Insofar as he neglects or downplays the importance of cultivating liberal capacities and dispositions, Rawls's later work retains a decidedly Kantian character.

The project of securing liberal democracy, however, is never merely a matter of defining abstract principles that can be accepted by hypothetical agents under certain specified conditions. It always involves the cultivation of citizens so that they are able to embrace a certain ethical sensibility and political self-understanding. Liberalism relies on the presence of citizens who possess particular capacities, dispositions, and virtues.[37] A stable and just regime based on consent requires subjects who are able to sustain a social compact or political agreement. These citizens must possess the moral and intellectual ability to evaluate and uphold such agreements over time. As Benedict Spinoza recognizes, "the preservation of the state depends mainly on the subjects' loyalty and virtue." Yet he adds that "the means whereby they should be induced to persevere in their loyalty and virtue are not so readily apparent."[38] Liberal citizens must somehow

---

[36] John Rawls, *Political Liberalism* (New York: Columbia University Press, 1993), and "The Idea of Public Reason Revisited," in *The Law of Peoples* (Cambridge: Harvard University Press, 2001), 129–80.

[37] The debate over virtue and character in liberalism has been a result of the powerful challenges posed by Alasdair MacIntyre, *After Virtue* (Notre Dame, Ind.: University of Notre Dame Press, 1984); Michael Sandel, *Liberalism and the Limits of Justice* (Cambridge: Cambridge University Press, 1982); and Charles Taylor, *Sources of the Self: The Making of the Modern Identity* (Cambridge: Harvard University Press, 1989). Those who defend the cultivation of virtue within liberal political theory include Peter Berkowitz, *Virtue and the Making of Modern Liberalism* (Princeton: Princeton University Press, 1999); Richard Dagger, *Civic Virtues* (New York: Oxford University Press, 1997); Ronald Beiner, *What's the Matter with Liberalism?* (Berkeley: University of California Press, 1992); William Galston, *Liberal Purposes: Good, Virtues, and Diversity in the Liberal State* (Cambridge: Cambridge University Press, 1991); and Stephen Macedo, *Liberal Virtues* (Oxford: Clarendon Press, 1990). Those who have resisted this renewed emphasis on virtue include John Gray, *Two Faces of Liberalism* (New York: New Press, 2000); Richard Flathman, *Reflections of a Would-Be Anarchist: Ideals and Institutions of Liberalism* (Minneapolis: University of Minnesota Press, 1998); and Douglas B. Rasmussen and Douglas J. Den Uyl, *Norms of Liberty: A Perfectionist Basis for Non-Perfectionist Politics* (University Park: Pennsylvania State University Press, 2005).

[38] Spinoza, *A Theological-Political Treatise*, trans. Samuel Shirley (Indianapolis: Hackett, 1991), 193.

develop the capacity for fairness, sociability, and foresight. They must cultivate a shared capacity for political judgment; they must come to accept a moral and intellectual currency of justification.

Locke remains important for contemporary liberal theory because he shows us that the liberal subject is not simply an unencumbered, originating source of political legitimacy, but rather an uncertain, incomplete, and fragile achievement. Locke helps us reconsider the type of intellectual cultivation necessary for sustaining meaningful commitments to liberty within the constraints of political order. By emphasizing the importance of a new type of probable judgment, Locke recoins a political vocabulary that enables citizens to agree on the terms of their relationship with government and to hold that government accountable when it fails to live up to those terms. Such a shared vocabulary is a prerequisite to self-rule. Howard Schweber writes, "Consent to the creation of a juridical language is what calls a sovereign 'people' into being in the first place . . . a group of people constitutes itself as a self-sovereign People by an act of political will exercised over the field of discourse."[39] The possibility of legitimate constitutional rule, for Schweber, relies on the willingness of citizens "to translate private thoughts and opinions into an appropriate artificial language of constitutional discourse."[40] The point of Lockean reasonableness is not to eradicate disagreement, but to ensure a common vocabulary within which disagreement can take place. A common language of judgment serves as a homogenizing agent that allows heterogeneity to arise without disaster. Even a regime that self-consciously avoids organizing itself around a single substantive purpose or good requires a particular shared understanding of what constitutes legitimate public justification.

Just as successful currency reform must avoid being either too lax or too austere, Locke's successful reform of judgment has to restrain radical subjectivity without imposing an artificial uniformity upon his readers. As Mark Button puts it, Locke seeks "to shape and govern individual judgment from the inside out."[41] Locke recognizes that his ability to promote limited, consensual government is intimately tied to his ability to persuade his fellow subjects to internalize a new vocabulary of judgment. By coming to view their own intellectual faculties in a new way, Locke's readers can learn to resist the spurious claims of religious authoritarians and tyrannical monarchs. In this way Locke aims to effect a cultural and intellectual transformation through which a common mode of probable

---

[39] Howard H. Schweber, *The Language of Liberal Constitutionalism* (New York: Cambridge University Press, 2007), 78.
[40] Ibid.
[41] Button, *Contract, Culture, and Citizenship*, 132.

judgment can take root. Only then can political authority be rightfully established and maintained "by the people."

In order to understand Locke's project as a Great Recoinage of language, however, we must first come to terms with the collapse of public judgment in the late medieval and early modern world. In the first chapter, I trace the breakdown of the medieval vocabulary of justification that was characterized by certain knowledge on one hand (*scientia*) and probable belief on the other (*opinio*). Terms associated with *scientia* such as "certainty" and "demonstration" came under intense attack by nominalists such as William of Ockham in the fourteenth century, and these nominalist suspicions were reinforced by the discovery and dissemination of ancient skeptical writings a century later. The unsettling of the medieval understanding of knowledge, we will find, was accompanied by an unsettling of opinion. Terms associated with *opinio* such as "probability" and "authority" were battered by the forces of the Reformation and the Counter-Reformation. In the place of a shared language of cognitive appraisal, Europeans encountered multiple and contending methods of justification. The collapse of the epistemological framework of the medieval world brought about a profound crisis of authority.

In the second chapter, I describe how this crisis led some to abandon the possibility of public justification altogether and others to seek out a type of knowledge that would be invulnerable to skeptical objections. Michel Montaigne and his popularizer, Pierre Charron, argued that in the absence of universally acceptable standards, wise men should defer to established traditions and reigning authorities. In stark contrast, René Descartes sought to resolve the problem of multiple authorities once and for all by erecting a new, apodictic science built on unassailable foundations. Although he hoped that his project would eventually yield absolute certainty in the contested realms of morals, politics, and religion, Descartes nonetheless counseled his readers to follow the customs and laws of their localities until such certainty could be achieved. Thus both the skepticism of Montaigne and the foundationalism of Descartes led to a kind of political quietism. Here we see that the fanatical longing for certainty and the skeptical rejection of public reason are two sides of the same coin. It is in this context that we can best understand the early writings of John Locke. As a student and teacher at Oxford, he expressed a deep anxiety concerning the inability of his countrymen to arrive at a shared understanding of their moral and political obligations. Although he explored possible ways in which such a consensus could be established, he ultimately embraced the sovereign power of the magistrate as the only trustworthy source of public order. Locke's first response to the crisis of authority brought about by the collapse of the medieval language of justification was a decidedly illiberal appeal to the unrivaled and unlimited command of an established sovereign.

Yet Locke did not remain a skeptic and absolutist. In the third chapter I show that Locke's gradual move away from his early political positions parallels his encounter with a new notion of reasonableness based on probable judgment. This shift took place as Locke became involved with a group of researchers surrounding Robert Boyle who were adopting a "new probability" linked to the evidential testimony of natural signs or nondemonstrable facts. Although their vocabulary grew from medieval notions of probability, these experimentalists unwittingly secularized practical rationality in a way that transformed scientific, religious, and political justification. They offered a notion of judgment authorized by God's utterances through natural signs. This shift hinged on an assumption that evidence presented to the senses can be seen as a natural deliverance emanating from an ultimately inaccessible, yet divinely ordained structure of order. The accessible world of sensory perception could then become a public standard of warranted judgment, a type of public reasonableness that remained open to interpretation and debate.

The purpose of Locke's *Essay*, seen in this light, was to teach readers the proper way to govern their faculties and constrain their intellectual yearnings in accordance with this new standard of public reasonableness. In the fourth chapter, I argue that Locke's goal in turning to epistemology was not simply to engage in abstract speculation about philosophical difficulties, but to instruct his readers in the proper way to govern their limited faculties and take on the burdens and responsibilities of judgment. Locke's philosophical investigations aim at a type of civic education; he seeks to teach his contemporaries the intellectual virtues of a properly governed mind. Although Locke continues to appeal to the traditional vocabulary of knowledge and opinion, he carefully shifts his readers' attention away from abstract, speculative reasoning and toward the importance of the faculty of judgment, which can attain degrees of probability but not certainty. In our "fleeting state of action and blindness," he insists, carefully regulated judgment is sufficient "for all our purposes" (E IV.xvi.4, I.i.5).

This teaching is not meant to guide a select group within society, but rather to transform society as a whole. In the fifth chapter, I explain that for Locke our capacity to experience freedom is tied to our capacity to make probable judgments. Although Locke joins Hobbes in arguing that liberty is a type of self-expression through action, he insists that it also requires a type of self-transcendence through judgment. Locke argues that our "reasonableness" cannot simply be measured by internal coherence, but must always be gauged by our conformity to that which lies outside of us. It is our ability to adjust our behavior to the authoritative signs of nature that ultimately makes us free selves capable of self-governance. By learning to make judgments based on nature's probable deliverances, individuals become both reasonable and free.

It is this same appeal to reasonableness that runs through Locke's more explicitly political works. In the sixth chapter, I explain that Locke's extensive attack on Robert Filmer in the *First Treatise* is of a piece with his larger political project of recoining a language of probable judgment. The particular arguments that Filmer advances and the conclusions that he reaches are not as threatening to Locke as Filmer's general appeal to a type of divine certainty based on Scripture. Locke is at pains to show that Filmerian certainty is both rationally groundless and politically disastrous. His sustained effort to discredit the patriarchal defense of absolutism is part of an attempt to supplant Filmer's method of justification with a new vocabulary of judgment. By insisting on the distance between the mind of God and the minds of men, Locke can transform Filmer's appeal to divine providence into a call for active and industrious application of limited human faculties in order to bring about the prosperity and order that characterizes "God's great design" (1T 41).

In the seventh chapter, I show that Locke's *Second Treatise* can be read as a revolutionary call for subjects to employ this new notion of probable judgment. In order to teach his readers to be active, critical, and at times even revolutionary members of the polity, Locke sets out to convince them not only that they are capable of making crucial determinations concerning the limits of political power, but also that they are obligated to do so. His account of the state of nature is not simply a heuristic device illustrating an abstract theory of government, but an attempt to provide tangible support to his contention that individuals have a natural right of judgment. Along the way he seeks to guide his readers in the proper exercise of this capacity by showing them the reasonableness of limiting their judgment to the concrete, visceral experiences of neediness and injury. By presenting the state of nature as one in which virtue and convenience are initially in agreement, Locke can also reassure his readers that an appeal to the judgment of the people will not necessarily entail the anarchic assertion of subjective will. Whether exercised by individuals in the state of nature, the executive in established government, or the body of the people during a constitutional crisis, the faculty of judgment based on visible and tangible experience ought to be the animating force of our political life. By teaching his readers to internalize the constraints of a new conception of probability, Locke hopes to enable them to take up the great task of self-government.

I

Unsettling Judgment

KNOWLEDGE, BELIEF, AND THE CRISIS OF AUTHORITY

JOHN LOCKE AND HIS CONTEMPORARIES were very aware that they were living in an age of intellectual and moral crisis. "The rules that have served the learned world these two or three thousand years," Locke writes in the *Conduct of the Understanding,* "are not sufficient to guide the understanding" (CU 1). In the sixteenth and seventeenth centuries, traditional modes of ordering experience were breaking down throughout Europe. The interpretive frameworks that had once served to explain and justify theological systems, political arrangements, and ethical imperatives were appearing increasingly inadequate. In the wake of the Reformation and subsequent struggles over religious, political, and moral authority, the available languages of justification ceased to constitute a unifying authority through which norms of law and justice could be articulated. Appeals to traditional vocabularies could not be the basis for publicly reliable judgments. A once common mode of discourse had fractured into mutually exclusive interpretive camps all claiming authority. Those who continued to utilize earlier languages of justification appeared increasingly untrustworthy. Their arguments smacked of partisan interest, corrupt habit, or personal passion. This collapse led to intellectual stalemate, as rival factions hurled incompatible assertions at each other. Without a shared language that could sustain public deliberation, irreconcilable arguments often gave way to brute force.

This crisis and the responses that it brought about gave shape to Locke's modes of discourse and our own. If we are to understand Locke's concern with the language of justification and his attempt to provide a remedy, we must first grasp the interests and purposes that led him to write down his thoughts. We must place his project in a context of inherited vocabularies, persistent difficulties, and available solutions. From what traditions of discourse did Locke draw his vocabulary? To what difficulties or collection of difficulties was he responding? With what alternatives should his response be compared? Answers to these questions will not only help us understand Locke as a historical figure. They will also help us evaluate how his proposal for a new language of justification might inform our own religious, political, and ethical modes of discourse.

Locke was clearly troubled by what he saw as the poor health of intellectual discourse, yet he was not the first to diagnose the intellectual
maladies of his day. As early as the sixteenth century, observers such as
Michel Montaigne and his admirer Pierre Charron had noted that the traditional epistemic categories could no longer sustain public deliberation.
With heartfelt concern and scathing wit, they documented how debate
between factions had slid from vigorous argument into shrill assertion.
They unmasked the confidence of religious and political leaders as nothing more than dimwitted dogmatism and self-interested obstinacy. Montaigne and his followers artfully pointed out the absurdity of flamboyant
claims to certainty in the midst of profound disagreement and bloodshed.

One response to the collapse of traditional modes of discourse was
to conclude that rational argument had no place in the political sphere.
Those who took this path turned the moribund languages of judgment in
on themselves in order to point out the futility of public justification. If
the categories and distinctions that had once been accepted as invulnerable could be shown to be suspect, then it would seem that any framework
of interpretation would be vulnerable to similar attacks. For these keen
observers of the shifting sands of history, the ancient teachings of skepticism gained a new plausibility. The criteria of truth, intelligibility, and
rationality were themselves put into question. Any attempt at public justification could be faulted for either vicious circularity or infinite regress.

Yet not everyone responded to the epistemological crisis by turning to
radical skepticism. Some, led by Descartes, moved in the opposite direction, setting out on an unprecedented search for unshakeable foundations. In the face of pervasive doubt and uncertainty, these revolutionary thinkers sought to construct a new and indestructible fortress of
certainty. They believed that if rational judgment was to withstand the
forceful attack of radical skepticism, it must be built on the firm and
unquestionable foundation of apodictic science. In the absence of a stable
and consistent language of justification, the revival of ancient skepticism
seemed sufficiently threatening to these thinkers to warrant a rationalist
response.

In the following chapters, we will see that Locke's thought is haunted
by the specters of both radical skepticism and dogmatic rationalism. At
times he seems to endorse one or the other as a suitable response to the
collapse of traditional modes of justification. Yet ultimately his answer
to the epistemological crisis is neither radically skeptical nor wholly
rationalist. Following the lead of a host of practitioners of law, natural
philosophy, and theology, he neither rejects the possibility of reasonable
discourse nor insists that warranted judgments must somehow involve a
God's-eye view of the moral universe. His proposal for a renewed lan-

guage of judgment sits uneasily between these alternatives. The type of judgment that Locke advocates—the judgment that lies at the heart of the Lockean regime—involves the widespread acceptance of a renewal of probable reasoning. This new emphasis on probable judgment is meant to serve as a standard of public reasonableness. The widespread acceptance and habituation of this type of probability is a necessary prerequisite for accurately assessing the legitimate exercise of political power. This standard, we will discover, proves politically useful yet philosophically problematic. Before we can situate Locke's proposal, however, we must first understand how traditional discourse deteriorated in the late medieval world to such an extent that skepticism and rationalism were seen as plausible responses.

Certain Knowledge and Probable Belief

When individuals in the medieval and early modern periods discussed the truth of religious, political, and ethical claims, they employed a vocabulary dominated by the categories of knowledge and belief. A claim could either be *known* with certainty by demonstrative proof or *believed* for good reason according to authoritative sources and experience. Or it could fall short of both of these criteria. Although some claims, such as those concerning religious practices and beliefs, sat uncomfortably between these categories, the two distinct realms of inquiry provided a framework through which speakers could communicate levels of epistemological confidence and listeners could justify or criticize those claims. The realm of certain knowledge was known as *scientia* and involved logic and mathematics, whereas the realm of probable belief, or *opinio*, concerned dialectic and rhetoric. These cognitive categories served as a type of framework, a shared vocabulary, through which judgments could be made and assessed publicly. Yet this framework did not simply appear; it was not spontaneously invented. It emerged out of a long tradition of deliberation and practice concerning what constitutes rational justification.

One of the most enduring images in this tradition comes from Plato's account of the process of enlightenment. In the sixth and seventh books of the *Republic*, Plato describes the stages of human cognition in various ways as an ascent from darkness into light. As we approach what is fully real, we move out of ignorance, through the murky shadows of belief (*doxa*) and toward the clarity of knowledge (*episteme*). These accounts seem to teach that genuine philosophical fulfillment cannot to be found in the contingent and uncertain realm of belief; it is only achievable through the contemplation of knowledge, which is necessary, eternal, and immutable. As we strive toward *episteme*, we liberate ourselves from the triviality and illusion of *doxa*.

Of course Plato recognized that most of our interactions with others, that is, most of our social and political interactions, take place in the realm of appearance or belief. Most of the claims we make before a court of law or in deliberation with fellow citizens are more or less probable rather than certain, eternal, and necessary. Plato and his contemporaries used the term *pithanon* to describe statements or opinions that are not demonstrable but nonetheless plausible or persuasive. In the *Laws,* Plato has Clinias speak of what is "plausibly true" or "easy to credit" (*Laws* 782d, 839d). Similarly he uses the word *eikos* (literally "like") to denote that which is likely (*Crito* 45d; the term is often used in this way in *Republic* as well). Although Plato recognizes the usefulness of referring to plausible or probable belief, he is careful to distinguish between those who are content with deliberating about opinion and those who seek certain knowledge. Only the pursuit of knowledge is philosophy; deliberation about the plausibility of opinions remains in the lesser realm of rhetoric. Thus he can denounce rhetoricians such as Gorgias and Tisias for claiming that "likelihoods (*eikota*) are more to be esteemed than truths" and for making "small things seem great, and great things small by the power of their words" (*Phaedrus* 267a; see also *Gorgias* 464b–465d). Plato insists that those seek truth must transcend the illusory character of opinion and free themselves from its deception.

To a great extent medievals shared this Platonic ideal. They believed that the goal of human understanding was the contemplation of the eternal and necessary, and for them that meant the contemplation of God. Yet they also recognized that *doxa* plays a crucial role in the way human beings rationally evaluate the world around them. They believed that their limitations as imperfect creatures forced them to make daily decisions about the world based on opinion and belief. So they sought both certain knowledge of the divine as well as probable opinion concerning the contingent world around them. As with many aspects of medieval thought, this twofold view of human understanding had first been carefully delineated by Aristotle and then reiterated by Roman, Islamic, and Christian readers. Although medieval and early-modern thinking was by no means monolithic, it tended to follow the basic categories laid out in Aristotle's *Organon*.[1]

---

[1] The *Organon* includes six works on logic, *Categories, Prior Analytics, On Interpretation, Posterior Analytics, Sophistical Refutations,* and *Topics*. In these works, Aristotle distinguishes between demonstrative, probabilistic, and fallacious reasoning.

It was Thomas Aquinas, however, who set out to clarify and disseminate a common vocabulary of justification for the medieval world. He
embraced the categories of certain knowledge and probable opinion as a
way of organizing contested claims. In his commentary on Aristotle's *Posterior Analytics*, Aquinas explains that both knowledge and belief, what
he calls *scientia* and *opinio*, are integral to human thought.[2] Rational
justification can generally be divided into these two categories, each one
involving its own particular objects and methods of inquiry.

Here Aquinas follows Aristotle's categorical distinction between
demonstrative arguments and dialectical ones.[3] For Aristotle, a demonstrative argument is one in which necessary truths follow from necessarily true premises, as in geometry. A dialectical argument, on the other
hand, is one in which probable conclusions are reached from generally
accepted opinions (*endoxa*), that is, opinions that are "agreed to by all or
most of the wise" (*Topics* 100a30–b25). Aristotle likens dialectical argument to rhetoric in that they both trade in propositions of "good repute"
that are not demonstrable (*Rhetoric* 1354a). For Aristotle, *endoxa* are
ultimately grounded in experience or *empeiria*, which is why he can also
sometimes refer to them as *phainomena*, or "things which appear to be
the case" (*Topics* 104a12). In contrast to Plato, Aristotle placed special
emphasis on the importance of dialectical and rhetorical argument and
the probable assurance that it provides. Although he viewed certain
knowledge as the ideal, demonstrative proof was not easy to come by in
everyday affairs. For Aristotle dialectical and rhetorical arguments were
central to political, legal, and moral deliberation since such deliberation
involves human actions, actions that are by their very nature contingent
and subject to debate. He offered elaborate procedures for scrutinizing
and evaluating commonly held opinions in his *Rhetoric* and *Topics*, texts
that were seminal to the medieval and early-modern study of rhetoric.
For Aristotle the realms of certain knowledge and probable belief are
both important categories of cognitive evaluation.

[2] Thomas Aquinas, *Commentary on the Posterior Analytics of Aristotle*, trans. Fabian R.
Larcher (Albany, N.Y: Magi Books, 1970); and Aristotle, *Posterior Analytics*, trans. Jona-
than Barnes (Oxford: Clarendon Press, 1994). See E. F. Byrne, *Probability and Opinion:
A Study in the Medieval Pre-suppositions of Post-medieval Theories of Probability* (The
Hague: Martinus Nijhoff, 1968). Aristotle makes a similar delineation between scientific
knowledge, or *episteme*, and prudence, or *phronesis*, in *Nicomachean Ethics*, trans. Terence
Irwin (Indianapolis: Hackett, 1985), 1139b15–1140b25.
[3] For example, see *Topics* 100a30–b25; *Prior Analytics* 70a4–7; *Posterior Analytics*
90a5–23, 93a30–b15; *Rhetoric* 1402b20–1403a1. See Larry Arnhardt, *Aristotle on Political Reasoning: A Commentary on the "Rhetoric"* (DeKalb: Northern Illinois University
Press, 1981).

Cicero transported this Greek distinction into the Roman world.[4] Although he dabbled in the philosophical quest for certain truths, he championed the art of rhetoric as the public discipline needed to address the contingent sphere of law and to sustain republican self-government. Cicero employed the Latin terms *probabile* (credible) or *veri simile* (like truth) for the Greek *pithanon*, emphasizing that probable opinion or belief is the most appropriate standard for matters of rhetoric, politics, and law.[5] The rhetorician Quintilian further codified the division between certain knowledge and probable belief, adding gradations of probable opinion.[6] This distinction was also embraced by Islamic and Jewish commentators. The great Muslim polymath Al-Farabi in the ninth century, and later Ibn Sina (known in the West as Avicenna) and Ibn Rushd (Averroës), emphasized the role of logic in establishing demonstrable truths and of rhetoric or dialectic in establishing probabilities.[7] A Jewish contemporary of Ibn Rushd and fellow inhabitant of Cordoba, Maimonides, also embraced these Aristotelian categories. A long line of Roman, Islamic, Jewish, and Christian commentators defended and refined Aristotle's schema, helping to establish a widely embraced distinction between philosophy/science and dialectic/rhetoric in the late medieval and Renaissance world.

Working in this Aristotelian tradition, Aquinas uses the term *scientia* to refer to knowledge of truths that are universal, necessary, and certain. In order to be deemed *scientia* a proposition must be demonstrated as such by means of a syllogism that begins with first principles. Different scientific disciplines have separate and distinct first principles, so a demonstrative proof can only be carried out within the confines of that particular science. A geometric proposition can be included within *scientia* if it can be deduced from the first principles of geometry. Similarly, the articulation of causes (formal, final, efficient, and material) involves reasoning from particular first principles and thus falls within the sphere of *scientia*. At times, Aquinas argues that first principles of particular disciplines can be abstracted from concrete perceptions by the active intellect. At other times, he seems to imply that they are intuitive or innate.

[4] For examples of the distinction between certain knowledge and probable opinion, see Cicero, *De inventione* I.46–48; *Ne Natura Deorum* 1.12; *Tuscalan Disputations* 1.17, 2.5; and *De Officiis* 2.7–8.

[5] For example, Cicero, *Contra Academicos* 2.1.26. See also John Glucker, "*Probabile, Ver simile*, and Related Terms," in *Cicero the Philosopher*, ed. J.G.F. Powell (Oxford: Oxford University Press, 1995), 115–44.

[6] Quintillian, *Institutio oratoria* 5.9.8–12, 5.10.15–17. On the continued use of *probabilitis and versimilis*, see D. Garber and S. Zabell, "On the Emergence of Probability," *Archive for History of Exact Sciences* 21 (1979), 35–53.

[7] Deborah Black, *Logic and Aristotle's Rhetoric and Poetics in Medieval Arabic Philosophy* (Leiden: Brill, 1990), chaps. 1–2.

For Aquinas, philosophy aims at *explanation* of what is generally assumed, rather than discovery of new phenomena. He seeks to offer an account of *why* things are the way they are. Following Aristotle, Aquinas is not satisfied with presenting a description of the properties of an object, because such a description would still lack an explanation that could rise to the level of certain knowledge, or *scientia*. It would still fail to explain *why* it is the way it is. However, this emphasis on abstract explanation does not mean that the senses are completely ignored. In fact, for Aquinas, knowledge is always derived from experience or sensory awareness. Yet this sensory awareness does not involve the observation of single events in the context of a controlled experiment. Sensory awareness is knowledge acquired through the habitual experience of a phenomenon, such as the sun rising each day or heavy objects falling downwards. So when Aquinas appeals to experience as the basis of *scientia*, he is appealing to experiences of the "ordinary course" of nature that he assumes his audience will have shared. Experience is always embedded in a community of people.[8] The most trustworthy sources of "experience" are preeminent authorities who have articulated phenomena that are, literally, *data*, "givens." Aquinas relies on a type of universalized awareness, or "common knowledge," in order to offer an explanation of phenomena that are, in an important sense, *already known*. Peter Dear's description of Aristotle applies equally to Aquinas—they both provide "a natural history of knowledge rather than a critical epistemology."[9] For Aquinas each particular field of inquiry has its own set of first principles that are not themselves demonstrable yet make demonstrative reasoning possible. If a proposition can be shown to follow necessarily from principles that are taken to be ineluctable, then that proposition can qualify as knowledge. Following Aristotle, Aquinas restricts the realm of knowledge to those areas of inquiry in which uncontroversial premises can be abstracted from the contingencies of daily life.

Opinion, for Aquinas, consists of beliefs or doctrines that are not arrived at by demonstration, either because they are accepted prior to being demonstrated or because they cannot be demonstrated. Although he sometimes distinguishes between *opinio* (beliefs that result from reflection, argument, or disputation) and *aestimatio* (beliefs that result from sensation), he generally refers to both types of beliefs as *opinio*. In contrast to *scientia*, opinion cannot ever be certain, only more or less probable.

---

[8] Peter Dear, *Discipline and Experience* (Chicago: University of Chicago Press, 1995), 21–25.

[9] Peter Dear, *Revolutionizing the Sciences* (Princeton: Princeton University Press, 2001), 5.

When inquiring into human activity, especially the contested realms of politics and law, probable assurance is the best we can achieve. Demonstrably certain knowledge remains beyond our grasp. Aquinas writes that in the "affairs of men there is no such thing as demonstrative and infallible proof." In the midst of the contingencies of human experience, "we must be content with a certain conjectural probability, such as that which an orator employs to persuade."[10] In another passage, Aquinas cites Aristotle's dictum that "we must not expect to find certitude equally in every matter," adding that, when we consider human actions, "it is impossible to have demonstrative certitude, because they are about things contingent and variable. Hence the certitude of probability suffices, such as may reach the truth in the greater number of cases, although it fail in the minority."[11] Yet how can "the certitude of probability" be achieved? What makes a claim more or less probable?

When Aquinas uses the term "probable," he is referring to approval or acceptability by the respected, the wise, or the many. For the Scholastics who followed him, the probable is the best of what the best men think. The tradition of ancient texts is seen as the most trustworthy source of wisdom when scientific, logical, and demonstrative knowledge cannot be achieved. For Aquinas, this authoritative tradition rests on the writings of the church fathers, but he also frequently defers to Maimonides and, of course, Aristotle.[12] Since the term is tied to the reputation and wisdom of revered textual authorities, it carried with it the sense that is preserved in our words "probity" and "approbation." Just as certainty is an attribute of knowledge for Aquinas, probability in this sense is an attribute of opinion. Byrne points out that probable opinion has several connotations. In the first place, probability refers to "the authority of those who accept the given opinion; and from this point of view 'probability' suggests *approbation* with regard to a proposition and *probity* with regard to the authorities who accept it." In the second place, the term "probability" refers to "the arguments which are presented in favor of the opinion in question; and from this point of view it suggests *provability*, that is, capacity for being proven (though not necessarily demonstrated)." Finally, "probability" takes on "a somewhat pejorative conno-

[10] Thomas Aquinas, *Summa Theologica*, trans. Fathers of the English Dominican Province (New York: Benziger Brothers, 1948), I-II q. 105 art. 2 ad 8.

[11] *Summa* II-II q. 70 art. 2. See also Byrne, *Probability and Opinion*, 203–5.

[12] Aquinas sees divine revelation as distinct from these authoritative sources, referring to it at one point as "incontrovertible proof" (*Summa* I q. 1 art. 8). Yet he also recognizes that Scripture is "veiled in metaphor" and has depth of meaning that cannot be contained in one single sense or reading (*Summa* I q. 1 arts. 9–10). Aquinas insists that careful reading of Scripture must take place within the apostolic community or church (see *Summa* II-II q. 1 art. 9).

tation precisely insofar as the proposition in question is *merely* probable; for from this point of view the proposition is only *probationary* and not strictly demonstrated as are propositions which are properly scientific."[13] Thus we see that Aquinas separates the language of justification into two distinct epistemic categories. On one hand we find *scientia*, consisting of certain knowledge, the result of demonstrative proofs based on first principles. On the other hand we have matters of *opinio*, consisting of probable beliefs grounded in authoritative approbation.

Aquinas recognized that many of the probable suppositions that help us navigate through our common lives cannot be found in any clear or unproblematic form in authoritative sources. He was keenly aware that even the best opinions of the best men occasionally come into conflict. For that reason he argued that just as *scientia* is governed by demonstration, *opinio* should be governed by what he referred to as dialectical reasoning. When authoritative sources reveal tensions between various opinions, we need a way to decide why we should adhere to one opinion and not the other. "Dialectical disputation," Byrne explains, "takes as its very point of departure the question that is raised by opposite opinions."[14] The dialectical investigation of authoritative sources sought to uncover what should be accepted and what should be rejected in the seemingly conflicting opinions of the wise. Since Aquinas assumed that all authoritative opinions are at least partially true, he understood dialectical reasoning to be a process by which we can sift out what is valid in each opinion and arrive at a synthesis of what is most convincing in the authoritative sources without categorically rejecting any particular belief. The dialectic proceeds from puzzles or questions (*quaestio*), to the views pro (*videtur quod*) and con (*sed contra*), to the author's own conclusion (*responsio*). The goal of this process is to achieve right opinion or *ortho-doxy*. Insofar as these beliefs remain beliefs and not knowledge, they reside within the realm of probable opinion. Although the appropriation of the textual tradition through dialectic can be a preparation for the practice of *scientia*, Aquinas repeatedly insists that dialectical reasoning cannot yield certain knowledge, regardless of how persuasive its findings might be. A prudent man, he teaches, is someone who is able to arrive at good judgment about opinions—those claims that cannot be demonstrated but are open to deliberation and debate. This type of practical rationality is dependent on a body of authoritative opinion, a collection of reasonable standards, that make up the *sensus communis*, or communal sense, of what is good and right in matters that cannot be demonstrably resolved.

---

[13] Byrne, *Probability and Opinion*, 188.
[14] Ibid., 141.

The categories of knowledge and belief and their distinct methods of inquiry thus served as an interpretive framework through which generations of thinkers made sense of their traditions and deliberated over religious, legal, and ethical issues. The general acceptance of these two interrelated categories offered a shared cognitive space within which individuals could weigh arguments and determine the level of assurance that a claim might yield. Demonstrative syllogism based on first principles on the one hand and dialectical inquiry into authoritative texts on the other provided the broad intellectual structure within which reasons could be given for adhering to particular claims and rejecting others.

This distinction was integrated into the "trivium" of medieval education. The trivium consisted of three areas of study: grammar, logic, and rhetoric. While grammar served as a preliminary study for the identification and right ordering of words, rhetoric came to be associated with oratory and persuasion, and logic with sound reasoning. The three were followed by a "quadrivium" comprised of the mathematical subjects of geometry, arithmetic, astronomy, and music. Together these areas of study were known as the "the seven liberal arts." As students pursued this course of study, they would ideally become conversant in assessing truth claims in the realms of *opinio* as well as *scientia*. Some studies, such as rhetoric, would be entirely within the realm of *opinio*, while others such as logic and geometry would aspire to *scientia*.[15]

Integrated into the standard course of education, the distinction between certain knowledge and probable belief shaped the language of justification for hundreds of years. It made its way into European vernaculars and was employed well into the sixteenth and seventeenth centuries. As we will see, Montaigne and Descartes made use of these Latin terms and their French cognates throughout their writings, and Locke structured his study of human understanding around the distinction between certain knowledge and belief or opinion. These terms continued to be passed down from century to century and appeared in subsequent modes of discourse, including our own. Yet the categories of *scientia* and *opinio* faced profound challenges in the early modern era.

The careful integration of knowledge and belief that Aquinas advocated began to break down as the authoritative tradition or *sensus communis* that he relied upon came to be seen as problematic or ambiguous. Subsequent thinkers sought to adjust to these changes by emphasizing

---

[15] The term "dialectic" was seen as a probabilistic subset of logic that was taken to include both probabilistic and demonstrative reasoning. Later, because of a humanist rejection of distinction between these types of reasoning, the terms became conflated. See E. J. Ashworth, "Traditional Logic," in *The Cambridge History of Renaissance Philosophy*, ed. C. B. Schmitt, Q. Skinner, E. Kessler, and J. Kraye (Cambridge: Cambridge University Press, 1988), 143–72.

one category at the expense of the other or by reorganizing the categories completely. Bolstered by newly discovered Aristotelian texts, Scholastics tended to focus on logic as the most important part of the trivium, neglecting grammar and rhetoric. They were intrigued by the possibility of certain knowledge and attempted to construct *scientia* through the careful definition of terms. For later critics, this explanatory strategy based on definitions seemed nothing more than verbal trickery. Renaissance humanists, on the other hand, turned their attention to the areas of study that the earlier Scholastics neglected.[16] They argued that a study of *opinio* was much better training for active, responsible citizens than the hairsplitting logic of scholasticism. Yet in contrast to the classical tradition of probable reasoning, the study of rhetoric came to focus primarily on style and ornamentation. A number of influential humanists, such as Rudolph Agricola, Phillip Melancthon, and Peter Ramus, had already begun to break down the scholastic distinctions between logic and rhetoric. They tried to simplify the curriculum by placing both demonstrative and probable reasoning under the heading of logic. Rhetoric was reduced to elocution, the art of using tropes to persuade an audience. Yet probable reasoning as well as rhetoric remained dependent on the authoritative testimony of ancient sources, testimony that was increasingly recognized as potentially dubious.[17]

Nominalism, skepticism, and religious conflict began to erode the notion of a unified and authoritative tradition even further and the already contested notions of *scientia* and *opinio* no longer seemed to serve as reliable vehicles for justifying public commitments. Neither the scholastic focus on logical demonstration or the humanist reform of rhetoric and logic could salvage the medieval vocabulary of justification. In fact, the epistemic crisis that unsettled so many thinkers in the early modern era consists of the simultaneous deterioration of these two basic categories.[18] Both *scientia* and *opinio* were discredited; the traditional notions of knowledge and belief were undermined.

---

[16] The concepts of "scholasticism" and "humanism" are, as Hannah Dawson argues, "to a great extent confused and modern fabrications, and often cannot be pulled apart." The term "scholasticism" includes the culture of the "schools" or universities, which at times were influenced by humanism. Yet as Dawson concedes, scholasticism has come to connote "a particular preoccupation with logic, and especially with Aristotle and his tradition." On the other hand, "humanism" represents the "championing the *studia humanitatis* (grammar, rhetoric, poetry, history and moral philosophy) and thus focuses on argument, probability, and the citizen orator. Dawson, *Locke, Language*, 13.

[17] R. W. Serjeantson, "Testimony and Proof in Early-Modern England," *Studies in the History and Philosophy of Science* 3, no. 2 (1999), 195–236.

[18] This point is developed in somewhat different ways in Shapiro, *Probability and Certainty*; Jeffrey Stout, *Flight from Authority* (Notre Dame, Ind.: Notre Dame University

Unsettling Knowledge

Several factors conspired to undermine the notion of *scientia* in the late medieval world. One crucial factor was the unprecedented expansion of its application. In an attempt to carve out a space for demonstrative proof, Aquinas had insisted that scientific propositions must be deduced from a particular set of first principles. For him, every science has its own first principles, which are the axioms upon which truths are based in that particular science. Aquinas emphasized that those seeking to provide a demonstrative proof can not dispute *scientifically* with someone who "denies principles" and "concedes nothing."[19] Demonstration begins with the acceptance of certain principles as self-evident (*per se notum*). These principles themselves cannot be demonstrated. However they are limited to their particular science. It would simply be a mistake to appeal to the first principles of one discipline in another discipline or in defense of scientific inquiry in general. It is in this sense that Aquinas could assert that the various sciences, as limited and distinct arenas of inquiry, are rationally ordered and humanly accessible.

Yet this carefully restricted view of scientific demonstration gave way to a much more ambitious aspiration for certainty. Dazzled by newly discovered Aristotelian writings on logic, Scholastics following Aquinas sought to apply demonstrative reasoning to all areas of human endeavor.[20] Sweeping changes in the structure and aims of university life in the fourteenth and fifteenth centuries transformed the nature of intellectual inquiry and altered the context of *scientia*. A growing educated laity demanded more from centers of education that had once limited their intellectual discussions to members of religious orders. Monarchs, princes, and wealthy merchants created new universities and colleges where nonclergy not only attended as students but also served as faculty. Between 1300 and 1500, the number of European universities rose from twenty to seventy, while sixty-six new residential colleges were built in France, twenty-one in England, fifteen in Italy, and sixteen in Germany.[21] The growing number of laymen in these new universities encouraged an expansion of the realm of *scientia*. They began to construct elaborate arguments based on carefully posited definitions. This type of theorizing

---

Press, 1981); and Nicholas Wolterstorff, *John Locke and the Ethics of Belief* (Cambridge: Cambridge University Press, 1996).

[19] Aquinas, *Summa* Iq. 1 art. 8.

[20] Aristotle's writings on logic were traditionally known as the *Organon*, Greek for "tool," because logic was seen as an instrument that could be used in all subjects.

[21] Steven E. Ozment, *The Age of Reform, 1250–1550: An Intellectual and Religious History of Late Medieval and Reformation Europe* (New Haven: Yale University Press, 1980), 201.

was uniquely secular in the sense that it was directed toward explicating the *seculum*, the world as it appears in the interval between the Fall and the end times. They began to lean heavily on premises concerning experience of the natural world that they assumed were universal and certain. They based their syllogisms on what they believed to be "common knowledge" concerning the "ordinary course" of nature. Lured by the possibility of certain knowledge, these university men sought to integrate the entire world into a formal and codified system of *scientia*.

This optimism concerning scholastic demonstration led to the breakdown of distinctions between disciplines, as the first principles of mathematics were introduced into physics, ethics, and theology. In spite of the Aristotelian-Thomist emphasis on separate and distinct fields of inquiry, this new generation of Scholastics sought to extend the notion of *scientia* beyond the boundaries of delimited sciences. The new outward-looking university took the techniques of demonstrative reasoning that had been developed and employed within relatively isolated religious communities and extended their application. Faced with growing theological and ecclesiopolitical controversies, these thinkers turned to the demonstrative proof of *scientia* for unprecedented answers. Although Etienne Gilson has characterized the fourteenth century as one of "speculative lassitude" and the fifteenth century as one of further decline, recent scholars have pointed out that the era was actually one of ambitious expansion and unprecedented intellectual growth.[22] However, the bold extension of the application of *scientia* went hand in hand with its intellectual collapse. As Gordon Leff puts it, "This change denotes an almost naïve confidence in the intelligibility of the world and the capacity of reason to discern it." The seemingly limitless extension of *scientia* "inaugurated a new path

[22] Much of the scholarship in medieval intellectual history in the last fifty years has sought to refute or defend Gilson's view of the late medieval world as a long, slow decline from the great synthesis of the thirteenth century. According to Gilson, Thomas Aquinas avoids the extremes of fideism or "theologism" on one side and rationalism on the other. Tertullian, Bernard of Clairvaux, Peter Damian, and the Spiritual Franciscans are examples of theologism, and the pure Aristotelanism of the Islamic philosopher Averroës represents rationalism. See Etienne Gilson, *Reason and Revelation in the Middle Ages* (New York: C. Scribner's, 1938), *The History of Christian Philosophy in the Middle Ages* (New York: Random House, 1955), and *The Christian Philosophy of St. Thomas Aquinas*, trans. L. K. Shook (New York: Random House, 1956). Franciscan, Augustinian, and Protestant scholars have responded by seeking to show that their traditions contain other candidates who should be placed at the "summit of medieval thought." Yet some moderate and thoughtful revisionist scholars have rejected these polemics. Accepting much in Gilson's depiction, they argue that the period following the "great system-builders" of the thirteenth century was in fact a very fertile intellectual time during which thinkers confronted the contradictions within the theological systems they had inherited, reexamined their historical sources, and critiqued the theoretical cogency of their arguments. See also Heiko Augustinus Oberman, *The Harvest of Medieval Theology* (Cambridge: Harvard University Press, 1963).

of inquiry which ... in the context of the fourteenth century ... could only be destructive of the existing modes without being comprehensive enough to substitute a new outlook."[23]

This increased use of *scientia* in more and more areas of inquiry placed a new strain on old tensions within the Christian-Platonic tradition. The aspiration for certain knowledge rested on the assumption that the world itself was logically ordered and that order was discernible. It also assumed that certain axiomatic principles are universally recognizable and eternally applicable. Yet the idea of a creator God in the Judeo-Christian tradition had always fit uncomfortably within the Greek understanding of the universe as an ordered, intelligible, and eternal system. Ancient thinkers such as Plato and Aristotle had spoken of a demiurge who endowed an eternal cosmos with order; they did not imagine a God who could create the world according to his own boundless will and then stand outside of its laws. The notion of God as an infinite being utterly free of limitation who created the world out of nothing would have been mind-boggling to them. As early as the second century, Greek Neoplatonists had argued against early Christians that a God of harmony and order would never interrupt the perfect motions of creation. Celsus ridiculed the notion of a God who would disrupt the harmonious order of the world to attend to the desires of a small, dirty, and provincial people.[24] Early defenders of Christianity responded to these arguments with vehemence, but they did not answer the charges directly. They refused to accept the opposition between divine freedom and divine order that their Greek critics urged on them. Instead they sought to provide a moderating mode of discourse that could simultaneously embrace the seemingly contradictory claims of omnipotence and order.

It was Augustine who was most influential in combining the biblical God of Abraham, Isaac, and Jacob who created the universe out of nothing with the deity of the Greek philosophers whom he encountered in "the books of the Platonists."[25] The long and complex history of philosophy throughout the Middle Ages may be read as a series of attempts to reconcile the biblical God of power upon whose will the universe is contingent with the characteristically Greek intuition of the divine as existing within a necessary and rational order of the eternal cosmos. Most of the hereti-

[23] Gordon Leff, *The Dissolution of the Medieval Outlook: An Essay on Intellectual and Spiritual Change in the Fourteenth Century* (New York: New York University Press, 1976), 15–16.

[24] These are some of the arguments made in *Alethes logos*, written in 178 AD. The actual text has been lost, but we know about this work from Origen's response. Origen, *Contra Celsum*, trans. Henry Chadwick (Cambridge: Cambridge University Press, 1953).

[25] Augustine, *Confessions*, trans. Gillian Clark (Cambridge: Cambridge University Press, 1995), VII, 9, 20, 21.

cal movements of the third and fourth centuries can be seen as attempts to resolve these and related mysteries. The Pelagians, Donatists, Arians, and various Gnostics sought to put an end to these tensions by adhering to one side and rejecting the other. The early church, led by Augustine, was determined to defend a way of speaking about God and the created world that could incorporate these tensions into a unified church. The church would maintain a common language of justification, a language that would embrace both mystery and order, by insisting on both the unlimited power of God and the rational order of creation. Those who refused to embrace these tensions would be excluded from the linguistic community, or *excommunicated* from the church's language of justification. Nicholas of Cusa depicted the contentious and often tenuous unity of the medieval world as an ongoing struggle to maintain the "coincidence of opposites."[26]

In an attempt to elucidate these tensions but not to resolve them, Origen formulated a distinction between that which God does by means of power and that which God does by means of justice. Similarly, Aquinas sought to preserve this tension by maintaining that every order God creates is contingent, that is, dependent on God's unfathomable and free power. Yet once an order has been created, it is at least partially accessible to human reason. In this way, Aquinas could vindicate the order, rationality, and intelligibility of the universe. He could emphasize an "eternal law" that governs "the whole community of the universe."[27] In spite of these formulations, the tensions between divine freedom and divine order remained a stumbling block for many late medieval thinkers. In the century following Aquinas's death in 1274, many of the aspects of his synthesis were rejected for being too rationalistic and thus threatening the freedom and omnipotence of God.

However, it was the attempt to broaden the Thomistic category of *scientia* and apply it to growing theological and political difficulties of the fourteenth and fifteenth centuries that ultimately unsettled this fragile synthesis. William of Ockham, one of the most perceptive thinkers of the late medieval period, saw that the epistemic category of *scientia* just couldn't sustain the types of claims being made in its name. Ockham recognized that the expansion of the domain of demonstrative knowledge was intimately connected to a growing papal concern with the secular world. A novel application of scholastic arguments led to the unprec-

---

[26] Nicholas of Cusa, *On Learned Ignorance: A Translation and an Appraisal of De Docta Ignorantia*, trans. Jasper Hopkins (Minneapolis: A. J. Benning Press, 1981). For one of the most thorough accounts of the development of church doctrine in late antiquity see Adolf von Harnack, *Grundriss der Dogmengeschichte: Die Entstehung des Dogmas und seine Entwickelung im Rahmen der morgenländischen Kirche* (Freiburg: J.C.B. Mohr, 1889).

[27] Aquinas, *Summa*, I-IIq. 91 art. 1.

edented and expansive claims of the papal bull *Unam sanctam* (1302), in which Pope Boniface VIII asserted the church's temporal powers against the kings of France and England.[28] Ockham's rejection of *scientia* as a mode of justification was in part a rejection of its application to ecclesiopolitical controversies. His criticism of traditional epistemic categories was certainly related to his close association with the cause of Franciscan poverty, his call for the removal of a subsequent pope, and his support of that pope's political adversary, Louis IV of Bavaria.[29] Yet his attack on the traditional understanding of what knowledge or *scientia* entails would have consequences that extended far beyond his immediate political context.

According to Ockham, the use of *scientia* to explicate and defend the secular prerogative of the church relied on the assumption that universals or some similar self-subsisting common nature is essential to knowledge. The Scholastics who sought to defend the pope argued that certain knowledge is deduced from the hierarchically ordered world in which universal or real relations exist between God, man, and created things. Ockham, wielding his razor, argued that talk of such relations was meaningless and confusing. Human beings have no access to such universals; they have direct experience only of individual things. The universals that we employ are artificial constructs that have no independent existence outside of the mind. They are derived from our actual experience of particulars in the world, but they are contingent on that experience, not necessary or certain. We cannot know with certainty whether the universals we discern reflect some great chain of ontological links or whether they simply reflect a jumble of particulars. Yet it is this unmediated contact with particulars that must suffice for human understanding.[30]

Ockham's rejection of universals is closely related to his emphasis on the unknowable will of God. At the heart of his nominalism is a voluntarist vision of divine freedom. In his attack on what he saw as the presumption of scholastic thinkers who claimed to demonstrate the necessary connections between universals, Ockham rejected their metaphysical claims by accentuating the unfathomable freedom of a divine creator. As many commentators have pointed out, Ockham elevated the

---

[28] See Brian Tierney, *The Crisis of Church and State, 1050–1300* (Englewood Cliffs, N.J.: Prentice-Hall, 1976), 182–83.

[29] The political context of Ockham's intellectual development is presented in Arthur S. McGrade, *The Political Thought of William of Ockham: Personal and Institutional Principles* (Cambridge: Cambridge University Press, 1974), 1–78.

[30] For a good summary of the intricacies involved in these arguments, see Gordon Leff, *William of Ockham: The Metamorphosis of Scholastic Discourse* (Manchester: Manchester University Press, 1975), 76–77. See also Michael Gillespie, *The Theological Origins of Modernity* (Chicago: University of Chicago Press, 2008), 19–43.

notion of God's absolute power to such a height that it seemed to eclipse the traditional understanding of divine order or ordained power.[31] In Ockham's hands, the formulations that had been used to incorporate the mystery of divine freedom and divine order were turned into oppositions that had to be sorted out. While Duns Scotus might have emphasized the primacy of divine will over divine intellect before Ockham, it was Ockham who paved the way for Scotist voluntarism to move toward its extreme conclusion, that the world we experience is radically contingent on the impenetrable will of God. For example, individuals may be able to make tentative connections between their experiences today, yet Ockham would insist that God could completely rearrange their world tomorrow so that those connections would no longer hold. Since every particular is dependent on God's will, any principle that is taken to be certain is actually contingent. The demonstrative proof of syllogistic logic cannot provide the type of absolute certainty that the Scholastics claimed.[32]

With Ockham we can see the beginning of the deterioration of *scientia* as a category of rational justification. The increased appeal to demonstrative knowledge in political affairs that was taking place before Ockham encouraged the breakdown of distinctions between the sciences and halted the attempt to construct an all-encompassing or universal vision of the world by means of syllogistic logic. Ockham's rejection of universals combined with his elevation of divine freedom threatened to reduce the realm of certain knowledge to triviality. How can we sustain demonstrative knowledge of the world if we cannot deduce truths from first principles? How can we really know *anything* with certainty if God might intervene at any point and rearrange the natural order of things? For Ockham, we are utterly dependent on an unknowable God

---

[31] See Amos Funkenstein, *Theology and the Scientific Imagination from the Middle Ages to the Seventeenth Century* (Princeton: Princeton University Press, 1986); William J. Courtenay, "Nominalism and Late Medieval Religion," and Stephen Ozment, "Mysticism, Nominalism, and Dissent," in *The Pursuit of Holiness in Late Medieval and Renaissance Religion*, ed. Charles Trinkhaus and Heiko Oberman (Leiden: Brill, 1974). Francis Oakley, in contrast, argues that most nominalists are not as radical as they have been portrayed. They provide a space for limited, qualified order in their concept of ordained power, and thus strike a balance between covenant and omnipotence, or ordained and absolute power, that allows for a type of contingent orderliness. See Francis Oakley, *Omnipotence, Covenant, and Order: An Excursion in the History of Ideas from Abelard to Leibniz* (Ithaca, N.Y.: Cornell University Press, 1984).

[32] Ockham writes, "Although it is incompatible with Aristotle's claims, it is nevertheless true that no proposition formed from [terms] that signify corruptible things ... can be the premise or conclusion of a demonstration, since any such proposition is contingent." William of Ockham, *Summa Logicae*, ed. Philotheus Boehner (St. Bonaventure, N.Y.: Franciscan Institute, 1951), III, 2.5.

not only because we originate from God, but because our every thought and action depends on the continuing infusion of divine presence.

These new suspicions about the possibility of *scientia* were reinforced by a growing sense of uncertainty. The daily lives of many in the fourteenth century were becoming less and less explicable within traditional categories. It was a period of unparalleled misery and horror. Widespread famine in the early fourteenth century led to agrarian and urban unrest. A midcentury outbreak of the bubonic plague eliminated an estimated two-fifths of the European population. The Hundred Years' War between England and France introduced the weaponry of modern warfare, including gunpowder and heavy artillery. In addition, the great schism in the church produced no fewer than three competing popes and colleges of cardinals by 1409. The attempt to expand *scientia* as a mode of justification within this context stretched it to its limit and eventually contributed to its collapse.

The discovery and dissemination of ancient skeptical writings in the sixteenth and early seventeenth centuries reinforced these general tendencies and provided thinkers with an arsenal of arguments against those who might still cling to the possibility of demonstrative proof. Richard Popkin has carefully documented how the discovery of the writings of Cicero, Diogenes Laertius, and especially Sextus Empiricus led to a revival of interest in the rhetorical weapons of ancient skepticism.[33] In Cicero and Diogenes Laertius, readers learned about the Academic skeptics who in the third century B.C. formulated a series of dialectical puzzles to show that dogmatic philosophers (i.e., those who purported to know *some* truth about the real nature of things) could not know with absolute certainty what they claimed to know. They proposed a string of difficulties to show that the data we receive through our senses may be unreliable, the conclusions we reach with our reasoning may be uncertain, and the criterion or standard we use for determining which of our judgments are true and which are false cannot itself be guaranteed.

In the writings of Sextus Empiricus, readers became acquainted with the Pyrrhonists, who argued that both dogmatists and Academic skeptics asserted too much. Following the example of Pyrrho of Elis, they went beyond the Academics by refusing to make any positive claims at all, including the assertion that they knew nothing. Instead they sought to suspend judgment on all questions on which there seemed to be conflicting evidence. They advanced a set of *tropes*, or ways of opposing various kinds of knowledge in order to bring about the quietude (*ataraxia*) that comes with suspension of judgment (*epoche*). For the Pyrrhonists, skepti-

---

[33] Richard Popkin, *The History of Scepticism from Erasmus to Spinoza* (New York: Humanities Press, 1964).

cism was the cure for the disease of dogmatism. By ridding themselves of the anxieties of knowing, they could experience the tranquility of living in ignorance amidst the uncertainty of appearances.

Throughout the sixteenth and seventeenth centuries, a wide array of theologians and philosophers rehearsed these skeptical arguments in order to confound their opponents and show that they could not demonstrate the certainty of their claims. The careful syllogisms of scholastic thinkers seemed empty and perhaps even deceptive. Since all propositions rest on either sense perception or reasoning, and both of these sources are unreliable to some degree, no proposition can be certain. More importantly, these skeptics emphasized the fact that every demonstration rests on first principles or ultimate criteria that cannot be demonstrated. Any appeal to a criterion rests on reasons, and those reasons on other reasons. For skeptics, the answer to that nagging question, "How do you know that?" always leads to an infinite regress or a vicious circularity. The widespread use of skeptical arguments by a host of thinkers in the sixteenth and seventeenth centuries, including Francisco Sanches, Michel Montaigne, and Pierre Charron, helped to undermine public appeals to the scholastic notion of *scientia*.

Unsettling Belief

As doubts about the scope and possibility of *scientia* grew, late medieval and Renaissance thinkers sought refuge in the expanding domain of probabilities. They returned to what Aristotle and Aquinas had earlier recognized, that most religious, political, and moral claims could not be secured by demonstrative proof. Yet their renewed focus on the relatively neglected disciplines of grammar and rhetoric combined with an emphasis on the importance of antiquity posed a challenge to scholastic orthodoxy. This movement, which historians have called "humanism," spread through the universities in the sixteenth century, especially in northern Italy. In contrast to the scholastic emphasis on syllogistic logic, humanists championed *studia humanitatis,* the study of grammar, literature, and poetry. The study of rhetoric, which had occupied a minor place in earlier scholastic education, came to be seen as crucial for active, responsible citizenship as well. Teachers of rhetoric and grammar made increasingly confident claims about the importance of their subjects over and against the scholastic philosophy that had dominated the universities up to that point.

In fact, reformers in the sixteenth century began to blur the traditional distinction between logic and rhetoric. Rudolph Agricola and later Peter Ramus objected to what they saw as the redundancy of Aristotelian education. They argued that the same art of dialectical reasoning applies to both *scientia* and *opinio*. It was simpler to locate types of argumentation that had traditionally been part of rhetoric, such as the discovery and arrangement of probable arguments, in the realm of logic. The study of logic would then include both probabilistic and demonstrative reasoning. Rhetoric was reduced to a supplementary art aimed at persuasion by means of tropes and figures.[34] Adherents of Aristotle and Cicero resisted this move, insisting on the strict distinction between certain knowledge and probable opinion. They continued to promote the type of rigorous dialectical reasoning expounded in Aristotle's *Rhetoric*.

Yet both reformists and traditionalists insisted that the authority of ancient texts was a crucial source of credibility. They continued to appeal to what they saw as a tradition of reasonable opinions, an authoritative body of wisdom.[35] The newly discovered classical tradition provided unrivaled examples of both rhetorical style and philosophical sophistication. Assuming that eloquence was linked to wisdom, they taught students to imitate the style of ancient rhetoricians, especially Cicero, in hopes that they would acquire his sound political judgment as well. Yet the supposed consensus of eloquence and wisdom to which humanists appealed proved inadequate to sustain deliberations over matters of public importance. As Barbara Shapiro writes, "Neither the traditional models of logic and rhetoric nor the modification of these models in the hands of Rudolph Agricola, Peter Ramus, and other humanist reformers suited their needs."[36] This is because both dialectic and rhetoric were concerned with the effective deployment of authoritative testimony, testimony that could be universally "credited" because of its unimpeachable source.[37] Such appeals were falling into discredit.

Reformists and traditionalists could agree that best and often only way to establish the trustworthiness of a claim in the absence of demonstrative proof is to appeal to the authority of someone who concurred with it. They both assumed that practical rationality is dependent on a *sensus communis*, or communal sense, that is best articulated by approved authorities. Yet they also recognized that an argument based on such

---

[34] Wilber Samuel Howell, *Logic and Rhetoric in England, 1500–1700* (Princeton, N.J.: Princeton University Press, 1956), 168; and Dawson, *Locke, Language*, 64–66.

[35] As Peter Dear puts it, "If one could portray one's own work as implicit in, continuous with, or having precedent in the work of an ancient . . . that new work would immediately appear more respectable and hence more *likely*." Dear, *Revolutionizing the Sciences*, 45.

[36] Shapiro, *Probability and Certainty*, 227.

[37] R. W. Serjeantson points to the conceptual conflation of testimony and authority in this period. Melancthon understood all testimony as pertaining to the *locus* of authority, and Ramus made no distinction between the terms *testimonium* and *auctoritas*. See Serjeantson, "Testimony and Proof."

authorities could be ambiguous, deceptive, or simply false. Ramus and his followers argued that the probative force of such an argument derives solely from the authority of the person, and thus ascribed to it very limited force. They recognized that such an appeal could be dubious since the textual authorities could be used to support all sorts of contradictory claims. Yet both traditional Scholastics and humanist reformers remained committed to this standard. "This conviction," Serjeantson writes, "which was widespread if not universal in the period gives rise to an apparent paradox of Renaissance philosophy: for an age which is often taken to be highly reliant upon authorities, it held them theoretically in rather low esteem."[38] The shift of emphasis from scholastic syllogism to humanist dialectic placed increased weight on an already questionable standard of authoritative testimony. In this midst of profound religious conflict, this standard would become even more problematic.

The Reformation further undermined appeals to authoritative testimony. This period was not simply the working out of the logic of freedom, as Hegel would have it. It was a cataclysmic collapse that placed into question the textual inheritance within which Europeans had painstakingly developed a common life. Competing authorities seemed to multiply and diverge more sharply than ever before, and dialectical reasoning became less effective at resolving disputes. If the determination of medieval probability was a matter of discerning what authorities endorse, the sudden appearance of multiple authorities made it extremely difficult to attain probable opinion through dialectical reasoning. Without a stable and publicly recognizable tradition of authorized texts, the scholastic understanding of probability made little sense, and the domain of *opinio* was rendered unreliable.

It would be misleading to depict the tradition of rational appraisal in the medieval world as monolithic and unified. The medieval Christian tradition, like all traditions, was always more or less in conflict with itself. Yet even amidst these constant struggles, the notion of probable opinion derived from the approval of authoritative texts was a relatively stable epistemic category. Religious, legal, and moral discourses were infused with appeals to probability, and debates were carried out within the framework of that term. Even Luther's initial attack on the practice of selling indulgences began as a debate within this domain. By circulating the Ninety-Five Theses among the faculty in Wittenberg, he would have been following usual procedure for notifying the university community of a disputation. Luther sought to expose the evils of these practices by publicly weighing them against the accepted standards of the church. In his condemnation of the sale of indulgences he leaned heavily on the

[38] Ibid., 205.

authority of papal decrees and conciliar rulings.[39] He attempted to show that these practices were inconsistent with a proper interpretation of textual authorities and the tradition of probable opinion.

Yet at the Leipzig Disputation in 1519, Luther became more than just another medieval reformer criticizing the abuses of a corrupt bureaucracy. When his opponent Johannes Eck forced him into a corner, Luther took the critical step that initiated an intellectual revolution. He rejected the authority of church tradition as the standard for judging probable opinion. He discounted the overwhelming collection of authoritative texts that Eck presented as "super-subtle subtleties," and thereby provoked a crisis that overturned the traditional notion of *opinio* and undermined the shared vocabulary of public justification. He not only rejected the conclusions that papal legates and theology professors advanced in defense of church practices, he also rejected the very method by which valid opinions were distinguished from invalid ones. In his subsequent writings of 1520, he made it very clear that he disavowed the assumption that the authority of tradition or the church could justify belief. The "oceans of books, questions, opinions, human traditions" that had served as the measure of probable opinion for the Scholastics were for Luther nothing but "a tyranny."[40]

Having already rejected the role of *scientia* in matters of faith, Luther had turned to the domain of *opinio* to justify his attack on the sale of indulgences.[41] Yet the disagreements and contradictions that he found among the authorities of the church led him to view much of what he had seen in the ecclesiastical tradition as a collection of sinful pretensions and self-serving judgments. For Luther, unwavering devotion to the writings of church fathers, the decrees of popes, and the rulings of councils will not ensure wisdom, but rather inhibit true belief. Belief cannot be justified by an appeal to discordant canons because it requires a certainty that those canons simply do not provide. Those who seek to find truth in the opinions found in traditional sources will only get entangled in "super-subtle subtleties." While these texts might offer a

[39] See Martin Luther, "The Ninety-Five Theses, 1517," in *Documents of the Christian Church*, ed. Henry Bettenson and Chris Maunder (Oxford: Oxford University Press, 1999), 205–12.

[40] Luther, "The Babylonish Captivity of the Church," in Bettenson and Maunder, *Documents of the Christian Church*, 220–21.

[41] In his *Discourse Against Scholastic Theology* published less than two months before the Ninety-Five Theses, we find Luther rejecting *scientia* as a way of settling disputes over matters of faith. His infamous sneer, "The whole of Aristotle is to theology as darkness is to light" (Thesis 50), was not a rejection of rational deliberation or even Aristotle per se. It was a plea to keep syllogistic logic and demonstrative proof out of discussions of faith. See Ozment, *Age of Reform*, 231–39.

whole range of opinions, they cannot justify acceptance of one and rejection of another. By insisting that authoritative texts cannot obligate us to believe anything, Luther throws out the scholastic notion of justified or probable opinion:

> the Thomist opinions, whether they be approved by pope or by council, remain opinions and do not become articles of faith, even if an angel from heaven should decide otherwise. For that which is asserted without the authority of Scripture or of proven revelation may be held as an opinion, but there is no obligation to believe it.[42]

For Luther justification cannot emerge out of the dialectical investigation of authoritative sources. Regardless of what can be found in the tradition, we have no obligation to adhere to its teachings.

Instead, justification rests solely on the word of God found in Scripture. By replacing the multiple authorities of tradition with the singular authority of Scripture, Luther was not simply narrowing down the number of authorities he had to consult. He was arguing that the obligation or compulsion to believe does not arise when we sift through texts on our own. This compulsion arises only when we encounter God speaking to us through Scripture. Following the medieval voluntarists, Luther insisted that we cannot arrive at correct beliefs concerning our proper place in the world and our proper relations with others by investigating the order of creation or sorting through the authoritative opinions of tradition. Our only hope of grasping truth in a world created by an unknowable and all-powerful God is to wait for God to illuminate our minds. And this illumination takes place through an encounter with Scripture. Luther was convinced that the infinite distance between the creator and creation cannot be bridged in any other way. Justification can only be achieved through faith rising out of an encounter with the singular revelation of God to man.

It is in this sense that Luther declares that "we are all priests ... and have all one faith, one Gospel, one Sacrament," that we all "have the power of discerning and judging what is right or wrong in matters of faith."[43] He believed that if individual Christians actually encounter the word of God through Scripture, they will be compelled to believe the singular and unified truth of Christianity. Infused with this one faith, they will be able to discern truth from falsehood correctly. The individual conscience is the only legitimate standard for right belief, not because it

---

[42] Luther, "Babylonish Captivity," 219.

[43] Luther, "The Appeal to the German Nobility," in Bettenson and Maunder, *Documents of the Christian Church*, 217.

is the locus of subjective desire but because it is the vehicle for divine will to express itself to humanity. This new criterion takes dramatic form in his famous (albeit historically contested) refusal to recant at the Diet of Worms in 1521:

> Unless I am convinced by the testimony of the Holy Scriptures or by evident reason—for I can believe neither pope nor councils alone, as it is clear that they have erred repeatedly and contradicted themselves—I consider myself convicted by the testimony of Holy Scripture, which is my basis; my conscience is captive to the Word of God. Thus I cannot and will not recant, because acting against one's conscience is neither safe nor sound. God help me. Amen.[44]

Here we see Luther rejecting the traditional measure of probable opinion at the same time that he points to a new standard for justifying belief. Since church traditions, papal decrees, and conciliar rulings often contradict each other, they must at least partially be in error, and this makes them unreliable in matters as important as faith. If we are to distinguish justified beliefs from unjustified ones, we should not consult authoritative texts. We should listen instead to our "conscience taken captive by God's word."

Luther's alternative to the scholastic notion of probable opinion raised new and difficult questions: Can the appeal to Scripture, however conscientious, really adjudicate between rival opinions? Can the individual interaction with Scripture serve as a public standard? Luther's critics, most notably Erasmus of Rotterdam, had their doubts. Although Erasmus shared Luther's general distrust of scholastic modes of justification, he did not agree that *sola scriptura* was an adequate solution. After attempting to avoid a confrontation for several years, he was finally persuaded to point out his differences with Luther in a work entitled *A Diatribe on Free Will* published in 1524. He began by expressing skepticism about the possibility of arriving at an unequivocal interpretation of Scripture. Theologians since Augustine, he argued, have conceded that Scripture is silent on many topics. Even when it does address particular themes, its exact meaning is anything but certain. The problem of free will is a case in point. If Scripture is so clear, Erasmus asks, "why have such eminent men groped so blindly and for so many centuries in such an important matter?"[45] The answer is that the Scriptures are obscure

---

[44] This is how Reformation scholar Heiko Oberman renders Luther's speech. Oberman, *Luther: Man between God and the Devil* (New Haven: Yale University Press, 1989), 39. Scholars continue to debate whether Luther actually said the famous last line, "Here I stand, I can do no other." It is generally believed that this line was added by enthusiastic supporters shortly after the event.

[45] Desiderius Erasmus, "On Free Will," in *The Portable Renaissance Reader*, ed. James Bruce Ross and Mary Martin McLaughlin (New York: Viking Press, 1953), 681.

at many points and are by no means easy to interpret. Faced with the problems of interpretation, we should accept the traditional way of settling disputes between differing opinions. While this might not provide us with certainty, it is better than judging "in bold and wicked fashion those counsels of God which are inscrutable to men."[46] Since living a life of humility and piety is far more important than achieving certainty in religious doctrine, we should abandon such vain quests and concern ourselves instead with the virtues of simple faith and the advice of tradition.

Luther responded in a torrent of fury. He declared that Erasmus's book was like "dung carried in vessels of gold and silver."[47] It was nothing but blasphemous skepticism wrapped in the ornate costume of eloquence and erudition. In a blistering response, entitled *The Bondage of the Will,* Luther reiterates his claim that only certainty suffices in matters as crucial as religious belief. Although he concedes that there are passages in Scripture that are hard to understand, he insists that we can discover the basic truths of Christianity by simply consulting the text. If those truths remain unintelligible, it is not the fault of Scripture. It is the result of sinful and obstinate blindness in the face of obvious truth. For Luther, Erasmus's skeptical stance was a way of mocking God. To claim that Scripture is obscure is to reject the clear import of God's word. "The Holy Spirit is not a Skeptic," he roared. If we consult our consciences we will not find doubts but affirmations "more certain than sense and life itself."[48] If we encounter Scripture with pious and contrite hearts, truth is forced upon us, and it is a truth with neither ambiguity nor contradiction.

Luther's successor, the brilliant humanist Phillip Melanchthon, was less hostile to ambiguity and to the ancient rhetorical tradition. He sought to revise the standards of probability in light of Luther's break with Rome. Yet the traditional authorities that he appealed to could no longer carry the same weight.

As Luther's revolt against church authority spread throughout Europe, John Calvin sought to clarify and defend Luther's appeal to Scripture as the standard for true belief. With less vehemence but more precision, Calvin laid out his argument in the *Institutes.*[49] The defense of Scripture

---

[46] Ibid., 688.

[47] Luther, "Bondage of the Will," in Ross and McLaughlin, *Portable Renaissance Reader,* 695.

[48] Luther, *Selections,* ed. John Dillenberger (New York: Anchor Books, 1961), 171.

[49] John Calvin, *The Institutes of Christian Religion,* ed. Tony Lance and Hilary Osborne (Grand Rapids: Baker Book House, 1987), I.7. In the ninth chapter, Calvin explicitly addresses the problem of enthusiasm or fanaticism, which he believes to be one of the most dangerous threats to orthodoxy. He defines the enthusiast as one who claims to follow the Holy Spirit while rejecting Scripture and argues that by refusing to conform to the limits of Scripture, the enthusiast rejects the true faith and ultimately rejects God. For Calvin, then,

as the measure of religious truth must begin with the conviction that the Bible is the word of God. How can we be sure of this? Calvin admitted that there was no way to provide sufficient grounds for this claim outside of Scripture itself. There are no reasons that believers can offer unbelievers that will "establish in their hearts the conviction which faith demands."[50]

When believers are illuminated through the Holy Spirit, however, they experience an inner persuasion so compelling that it becomes the guarantee of their beliefs. "As God alone can truly bear witness to his own words," Calvin writes, "so these words will not be given complete acknowledgment in the hearts of men, until they are sealed by the inner witness of the Spirit."[51] This inner witness not only assures them that the Bible is the word of God, it also provides the believers with the means for discerning and believing its message. Without this illumination one would not be able to recognize Scripture as Scripture or decipher what it means. Yet for the elect, the inner persuasion of faith is self-validating. Inner persuasion originating from God is authenticated by Scripture, which is in turn understood in the light of inner persuasion. It is this understanding of *sola scriptura* that would serve as the shared language of judgment in Calvin's Geneva and later in Calvinist communities in Holland, Scotland, England, and the American colonies.

Yet the difficulties of establishing public authority by means of this doctrine came into view early on during the controversy of Miguel Servetus. Convinced that there was no scriptural basis for the doctrine of the Trinity, Servetus refused to recant when he came before magistrates in Geneva. Calvin and his followers were so sure of the truth of their own beliefs that they condemned him to death. How could this condemnation and punishment accord with Christian charity? To tolerate those who would poison the faithful with faulty doctrines, Calvin later argued, would be the far more heartless.[52] One reformer, Sebastian Castellio of Basel, responded to Calvin by asking whether anyone could claim the type of assurance in religious affairs that would justify killing another as

---

the appeal to written revelation is the ultimate criterion of right belief and the only bulwark against fanaticism.

[50] Ibid., I.7.4, 43.

[51] Ibid., I.7.4, 43.

[52] Defending what he took to be right belief, or orthodoxy, against Servetus, Calvin writes: "That clemency which they praise is cruel: it exposes sheep to being taken as prey, in order to be merciful to the wolves. [Is it reasonable that the heretics] should murder souls with the poison of their faulty doctrines and that their bodies should be protected from the legitimate power of the sword? Shall the whole body of Christ be torn apart, that the stench of one rotten member may be preserved intact?" Quoted by Edwin Curley, "From Locke's Letter to Montesquieu's Lettres," *Renaissance and Early Modern Philosophy* (Malden, Mass.: Blackwell, 2002), 285.

a heretic. In an argument that is reminiscent of Erasmus, Castellio pointed out that many aspects of religious doctrine, including some crucial scriptural passages, are too obscure to be interpreted with absolute certainty. No interpretation is so obvious that everyone would accept it, for "who is so demented that he would die for the denial of the obvious?"[53] The Calvinist assertion that the truths set up by God and revealed through Scripture are obvious to all true believers could only be sustained among those who had already accepted the Calvinist position as it had been laid out in the *Institutes*.

From this moment on, rational deliberation between reformers and church apologists became increasingly difficult, not to mention the growing numbers of radical dissenting groups critical of both Luther and Calvin. Those in the Protestant camp tended to interpret any opposition to their views as evidence that God had not chosen to illuminate their opponents. They attacked appeals to tradition in religious matters as ultimately unfounded. The scholastic method of justifying opinions by sorting through authoritative texts simply could not guarantee the absolute certainty required to support the church's position. The defenders of the church could not provide proof that its authoritative sources were in fact authoritative. Without an unquestionable standard with which to distinguish true claims from false ones, the Church of Rome could not prove that it was the true church or that its doctrines were correct. Some reformers went so far as to argue that the appeal to papal infallibility was an incoherent standard since the rest of the members of the church who are fallible would have no way to be certain that whoever claims to be the pope actually is the pope. Fallible believers would have no way of determining which authority to obey or which doctrine to believe.[54]

The defenders of the Catholic Church responded by attacking the reformers' claim that Scripture alone is the only legitimate criterion in religious matters. They pointed out that continuing controversies between Catholics and Protestants as well as within the Protestant camp undermine the claim that Scripture is an unambiguous standard of true belief. The Protestant appeal to individual conscience or inner persua-

[53] Quoted in Popkin, *History of Scepticism*, 10.

[54] Locke reproduces this argument in an essay entitled "Catholic Infallibility," written in 1675. See Locke, *Political Essays*, 226–30. He also shows his awareness of the gravity of what came to be known as the rule-of-faith controversy in the *Letter Concerning Toleration*: "The *Papists* and the *Lutherans*, tho' both of them profess Faith in Christ and are therefore called Christians, yet are not both of the same Religion: because These acknowledge nothing but the Holy Scriptures to be the Rule and Foundation of their Religion; Those take in also Traditions and Decrees of Popes and of these together make the Rule of their Religion" *A Letter Concerning Toleration*, ed. James Tully (Indianapolis: Hackett, 1983), 56. Locke's *Letter* will be cited throughout as LCT followed by page number.

sion does not solve these controversies, but exacerbates them. Instead of replacing conflicting texts of the authoritative tradition with the single authority of Scripture, they were introducing more authorities than ever before. For Catholic apologists, it seemed that reformers were arguing that every conscience constituted a separate, sovereign authority. The reformers' standard was inadequate because it left individuals without a public standard of judgment, and without such a standard they would have no means of settling disputes rationally.

One of the most able apologists for the church was François Veron of La Flèche. Veron was apparently so successful at devastating Protestant arguments that the king of France released him from his duties as a teacher and gave him free reign to attend Calvinist meetings and services in order to debate with reformers whenever they would rise to the challenge. His strategy was to draw attention to the logical incoherence of the claim that Scripture alone is the foundation of religious truth. He began by arguing that Scripture by itself cannot provide the means for distinguishing Scripture from the many other books in existence. We cannot know with certainty, unless we appeal to some extra-scriptural authority, what constitutes canonical Scripture and what does not. But even if we could be sure, on solely scriptural grounds, that Scripture is Scripture, the words would still have to be interpreted. Veron pointed out that training in a particular language or trust in a particular translator is necessary to understand the Bible. That training takes place prior to or outside of our encounter with Scripture. Finally, our ability to derive consequences from the words of Scripture or apply them to contemporary problems rests on insight that goes beyond Scripture itself.[55]

While Veron had no trouble demolishing the assertion that Scripture alone is an adequate standard for justifying our beliefs, he had difficulty showing why the traditional authority of the Catholic Church should then be privileged over rival authorities. He could not simply appeal to the scholastic notion of probable opinion construed in terms of the approval of tradition, since his opponents rejected the traditional sources as a legitimate justification for belief. Yet he could not provide them with irrefutable proof that his standard of justification was valid without appealing to some other standard that would also have to be justified. With his brilliant arguments, Veron could devastate his opponents, but he could not provide a vindication of traditional modes of discourse.

---

[55] Popkin (*History of Scepticism*, 70–80) provides a thorough discussion of what came to be known as Veron's "machine of war." Paul Feyerabend, who has applied strikingly similar tactics in his more contemporary battles with empiricism and modern science, explicitly treats Veron in "Classical Empiricism," in *The Methodological Heritage of Newton*, ed. Robert E. Butts and John W. Davis (Toronto: University of Toronto Press, 1970), 152–53.

The scholastic notion of *opinio* based on a dialectical investigation of authoritative sources became less and less useful in debating matters of public importance. It simply could not sustain rational deliberation in the wake of the Reformation. Protestant and Catholic writers not only challenged the content of their opponents' beliefs, they also attacked the way in which they justified those beliefs. As traditional modes of judgment became increasingly controversial, the practice of publicly justifying religious and political claims could no longer be sustained. In the absence of a shared vocabulary of justification, the rival camps broke off into distinct and incompatible linguistic factions.

Calvinists began to consolidate around the interpretative framework found in the *Institutes*. They used the work, which was published in pocketbook format in 1536, as a guide for assuring correct interpretations of Scripture and maintaining right belief. Calvin's book came to serve as a standard for the elect in discerning who was illuminated by God and who was not. In this way it became a substitute for the authoritative tradition that they rejected.[56] Followers of Calvin argued that the theology of the *Institutes* could not only help the faithful conform their beliefs and actions to the will of God, but could also be used to correct and discipline those who sought to resist such conformity. For radical Calvinists such as John Knox, this was a call to arms to "depose and punish" those "unworthy of regiment above the people of God."[57]

The Catholic Church responded to the Reformation challenge at the Council of Trent, which took place in three sessions between 1545 and 1563. It did not produce a reply to the arguments of the reformers, but a reassertion of church doctrine and church authority. Differences between Catholics and Protestants were emphasized, and the dogmas of the church were defined. The reformers' denial of church authority was answered by conciliar pronouncement. This is evident in the "Tridentine Profession of Faith," which was issued in 1564 to be recited publicly by

[56] In the preface to *Of the Laws of Ecclesiastical Polity*, Richard Hooker offers an insightful and not entirely unsympathetic account of Calvin's need to provide a new type of authority for his followers, who were barraged by challenges from Catholics on one side and Anabaptists and other radical dissenting groups on the other. *Of the Laws of Ecclesiastical Polity*, ed. Arthur Stephen McGrade (Cambridge: Harvard University Press, 1989). We know that Locke, who was raised in a Calvinist household, took extensive notes on Hooker's interpretation of Calvin. See Marshall, *John Locke*, 6–7. For a similar view of Calvin's assertion of authority, see Jean-Jacques Rousseau, *On the Social Contract*, III.vii, note 7. See also Eric Voegelin, *The New Science of Politics* (Chicago: University of Chicago Press, 1987), 138–39.

[57] Quoted in Quentin Skinner, *The Foundations of Modern Political Thought*, 2 vols. (Cambridge: Cambridge University Press, 1978), 2:230. For an insightful account of the political import of radical Calvinism in sixteenth-century England, see Michael Walzer, *Revolution of the Saints* (New York: Atheneum, 1968).

all bishops and beneficed clergy. It includes these lines: "I accept and profess, without doubting, the traditions, definitions and declarations of the sacred Canons and Oecumenical Councils and especially those of the holy Council of Trent and at the same time I condemn, reject and anathematize all things contrary thereto, and all heresies condemned, rejected and anathematized by the Church."[58]

After the Council of Trent, rational debate between Catholics and Protestants became almost impossible. The traditional modes of discourse could no longer serve as channels for dispute because those modes themselves had become the subject of controversy. Those who continued to wrestle with theological, political, and ethical questions were faced with a new and complex problem: How could they engage in responsible deliberation and effective persuasion when the central categories of rational justification were in such disarray? How could they arrive at authoritative judgments in matters of public importance if the very possibility of good judgment was the subject of debate?

Without a shared vocabulary, Catholics and Protestants had difficulty sustaining debate. They had no common means of defending or criticizing religious, legal, and moral claims. The Calvinist appeal to Scripture was simply irreconcilable with the Catholic appeal to the authority of church tradition. Once the inherited language that had framed debate fell apart, conflict moved quickly from the realm of words to the realm of violence. This is not to suggest that any one of these thinkers or events caused the collapse of the medieval synthesis, but rather that the widespread inability to find a common language of justification was emblematic of a larger crisis. Ingrid Creppell has pointed out that the religious violence that erupted at this time was not simply the result of conflict over doctrines; it was brought about by clashes over identity.[59] Catholics, Calvinists, and various other dissenting groups identified themselves wholly with their particular religious communities and insulated themselves within the logic and language of those communities. The struggles that ensued were struggles between unitary identities. Unable to deliberate rationally, members of contending faiths sought either to *purify* each other through conversion or to *dominate* each other through force. No other solution was possible without a shared mode of public justification. For the next hundred years, Europe would undergo the brutality and misery of religious wars.

[58] *Documents of the Christian Church*, 282.

[59] Ingrid Creppell, *Toleration and Identity: Foundations in Early Modern Thought* (New York: Routledge, 2003), 43–47.

II

Abandoning Judgment

MONTAIGNIAN SKEPTICS AND CARTESIAN FANATICS

THE INSTABILITY AND VIOLENCE of the sixteenth and seventeenth centuries signaled the difficulty of rational public deliberation within the framework of a scholastic language of justification. The traditional vocabulary had lost its meaning. Although the epistemic categories of *scientia* and *opinio* continued to be employed, they took on a hollow ring for listeners who were experiencing firsthand the irreconcilability of rival truth claims. The possibility that serious disputes could be resolved by appealing to scholastic notions of demonstrative knowledge or probable belief seemed painfully unlikely. In the midst of the incoherence of the religious wars, the line between rational justification and self-serving calculation became extremely difficult to discern. Logic, dialectic, and rhetoric all relied on appeals to textual authorities that were now themselves subject of debate and disagreement. Of course writers continued to use the inherited modes of discourse. What other language did they have? Yet the traditional practice of explicating and defending propositions by means of syllogistic proof on one hand and dialectical reasoning on the other could no longer sustain debate over matters of public importance. The available vocabularies of justification simply failed to lend coherence to political experience and action.[1]

One of the political implications of this collapse was an increased reliance on the state to ensure order and stability. Faced with the irreconcilable conflicts that accompanied the problem of multiple authorities, many thoughtful observers, from Machiavelli to Bodin to Hobbes, concluded that the only viable solution to this crisis was the centralization of the coercive power of government. The sovereign state was to be the highest earthly embodiment of moral and political authority. It is at this time that the term "reason of state" or *raison d'état* begins to emerge in the European vernacular. As we will see, the profound anxieties of the

---

[1] For extensive discussions of the way in which the existing ideological constructs in the late medieval world fail to provide a shared basis of political understanding and discourse, see Elizabeth Skerpen, *The Rhetoric of Politics in the English Revolution: 1642–1660* (Columbia: University of Missouri Press, 1992); and J.G.A. Pocock, *The Machiavellian Moment* (Princeton: Princeton University Press, 1975), chaps. 9, 10, and 12.

sixteenth and seventeenth centuries created fertile ground for the growth of a politics of power that would eventually lead to the doctrines of absolutism. Abandoning the possibility of public judgment, skeptics such as Montaigne took solace in the delights of private inquiry, and rationalists such as Descartes attempted to uncover unassailable foundations for a new science of certainty. Yet both Montaigne and Descartes ultimately acquiesced to the public supremacy of governmental and religious authorities. Their shared skepticism about the possibility of demonstrating the truth of particular religious beliefs does not lead to a defense of toleration, but public authority and imposition. It is in this context that we can best understand the young Locke at Oxford who shows himself to be both a skeptic and an absolutist.

Montaigne and the Politics of Skepticism

As we have seen, a growing number of writers in the sixteenth and seventeenth centuries came to view all attempts at rational judgment as suspect. Instead of attempting to resolve conflicts between contending claims, many retreated into smaller circles of like-minded individuals. In the context of enduring intellectual disagreement and political uncertainty, they began to accept the impossibility of arriving at any publicly accessible and uncontroversial truths. This skepticism found its most articulate voice in Michel Montaigne.[2] Throughout his essays, he ridicules both the logic of scholasticism and the probability of rhetoric, challenging the cognitive categories of *scientia* and *opinio*. Scholastics pursuing *scientia* promise far more than they can deliver, and rhetoricians weighing *opinio* practice the "art of lying and deception." They make a

---

[2] J. B. Schneewind writes that Montaigne's "moral skepticism was the starting point of modern moral philosophy. We have been concerned with Montaigne's questions ever since he asked them." J. B. Schneewind, *The Invention of Autonomy* (Cambridge: Cambridge University Press, 1998). Yet contemporary scholars have only recently begun to recognize the importance of Montaigne for the development of the modern political thought. One of Montaigne's most meticulous and provocative contemporary readers is David Lewis Schaefer, *The Political Philosophy of Montaigne* (Ithaca, N.Y.: Cornell University Press, 1990). Schaefer views Montaigne as a radical thinker who seeks to replace traditional morality with worldly utility and thus usher in the "bourgeois" morality that characterizes liberal regimes. Alan Levine offers another view, agreeing with Schaefer that Montaigne is a vital modern thinker, yet disagreeing that he represents a significant break from ancient thought. For Levine, Montaigne's skepticism is genuinely Socratic and is crucially linked to liberal toleration. Alan Levine, *Sensual Philosophy: Toleration, Skepticism, and Montaigne's Politics of the Self* (Lanham, Md.: Lexington Books, 2001). See also Richard Tuck, *Philosophy and Government, 1572–1651* (Cambridge: Cambridge University Press, 1993), 45–64.

"profession of deceiving not our eyes but our judgment, and of adulterat-
ing and corrupting the essence of things."[3]

Montaigne refrains from employing traditional categories of knowledge and opinion within the framework of rigorously structured tracts.
Instead he explores a variety of topics in loosely organized essays. In
his incomparable, rambling style, he leads his readers through a strange
and bewildering landscape of humanity. He was, in Kant's phrase, "a
sort of nomad who abhors building permanently on land,"[4] refusing to
commit to one particular argument or claim. He wanders from topic to
topic, searching for anything that might shed light on what it means to
be human. He seeks insight in the newly discovered texts of the ancient
world as well as the travel literature of the New World. In his intellectual
wanderings he finds a bewildering diversity of customs and beliefs. Setting
out to explore his own humanity, he discovers a "labyrinth."[5] He carefully
and methodically undermines the possibility of public reason that could
serve as the basis for stable, political agreement between individuals.

By refusing to lay down a definitive argument or explanation of his
subject matter in his essays, Montaigne turns his attention to the flux
and flow of human existence within the contingent temporal world. If his
reflections seem disjointed or contradictory, it is not because he is a care-
less writer, but because he wishes to convey to his readers that life itself
unfolds in disjointed and inconsistent ways. In one of his most candid
discussions of the structure of his writings, he explains: "I cannot keep
my subject still. It goes along befuddled and staggering, with a natural
drunkenness. . . . If my mind could gain a firm footing, I would not make
essays, I would make decisions; but it is always in apprenticeship and on
trial."[6] Montaigne writes essays instead of tracts or discourses, because
he believes that his subject matter—the human being—is too "various
and changeable" to portray in any definitive way. He can only attempt
(*essayer*) to record his shifting thoughts and feelings as they occur to him
from moment to moment. In a world of contingency and possibility, there
is no way to provide a final and incontrovertible justification for any
claim that he makes. He can find no "firm footing" from which he can
"make decisions." For Montaigne, human rationality, like human history,
is unstable and unpredictable.[7] Neither the rigors of *scientia* or accumulated wisdom of *opinio* can contain it.

[3] Michel de Montaigne, *Complete Essays*, trans. Donald M. Frame (Stanford: Stanford
University Press, 1958), II.51, 222.

[4] Immanuel Kant, "Preface," *Critique of Pure Reason*, trans. Paul Guyer and Allen W.
Wood (Cambridge: Cambridge University Press, 1998).

[5] Montaigne, *Complete Essays*, II.17, 481.

[6] Ibid., III.2, 610–11.

[7] Ibid.

In his longest and most philosophical essay, "The Apology of Raymond Sebond," we find Montaigne's most damning critique of rational justification. The title of the piece and the first few paragraphs lead the reader to believe that the author is intent on defending Sebond's work on natural theology. Yet it quickly becomes evident that a straightforward defense is not what Montaigne has in mind. If readers of Sebond encounter problems with his argument, Montaigne tells us, perhaps it is because they are asking too much of him. The expectation that any man could somehow use reason to decipher the divine order of creation and reveal the contents of true belief is simply unrealistic. If we look closely at ourselves we will see that our religious beliefs are not the result of such a quest. Our religious behavior and our capacity for religious insight are determined by our habits and environment. "We are Christians by the same title that we are Perigordians or Germans," Montaigne asserts.[8] Our commitments are not the result of a systematic investigation of the truths of the cosmos, but simply the manifestation of our particular life and our particular allegiances. For Montaigne our experience of divine revelation is confined by the limits of our ability to receive it. Our religious insight is always burdened by our local context, our inherited customs, and our own willfulness.

Montaigne continues his critique of natural theology by arguing that although human beings think they can comprehend creation, they are vain, puny creatures and their so-called rationality is no different than the deliberation of animals. In fact, in many ways animals are far more admirable than men. Montaigne then takes a lengthy detour, comparing almost every aspect of human behavior to the behavior of beasts in order to emphasize the vanity, stupidity, and immorality of men. Our lofty rationality does not make our lives better, but worse. It is a trap that only makes us believe that we are worthy of praise, when in actuality we are just puffed up with our own presumption.

By this point, Montaigne expands his critique beyond the confines of theology. His subject becomes the whole of human rationality. He marshals a wide array of sources in order to undermine our confidence that we can be certain of anything. He presents a long list of the conflicting and incompatible opinions of ancient thinkers to show that philosophy is the "clatter of so many philosophical brains."[9] He offers evidence from travel accounts about the natives of the Americas, from ancient literature about the peoples of the ancient world, and from his own experiences with the varying mores of contemporary Europe to reveal that human beings embrace a dizzying variety of legal, moral, and religious

[8] Ibid., II.12, 325 B.
[9] Ibid., II.12, 383 A.

practices.[10] He also deploys the arguments of the ancient skeptic Sextus Empiricus to discredit our sense perception and the certainty of our reasoning.[11] And finally he utilizes religious notions about the inscrutability of divine power to argue that any claim that we can make about the world is uncertain because it is contingent on the will of God.[12] By repeatedly pointing to the fact that human beings cannot be certain of anything on their own, Montaigne hopes to convince his readers of their limitations. He mocks those writers who would presume that we could completely understand and control the dynamic circumstances of fortune simply by applying reason. Reason itself follows "the lead of chance" and is pushed in one direction or another by "accidental impulsions that change from day to day."[13]

Montaigne suggests that if we learn to recognize the limitations of our reason we will be less likely to bicker over matters that we only partially comprehend. Instead of attempting to impose our own prejudiced views on others, we will learn to accept traditional authority in the realms of religion, politics and morality. It is for this reason that Montaigne, after undermining the possibility of natural theology, vows outward obedience to the established church. With the ambiguous statement, "I cannot reach this height with my powers," Montaigne sidesteps deeply controversial tenets of Christianity such as the Trinity, original sin, or the nature of Christ. His faith is less an affirmation of particular religious propositions than a commitment to authority. "We must either submit completely to the authority of our ecclesiastical government," he writes, "or do without it completely. It is not for us to decide what portion of obedience we owe it."[14] Hugo Friedrich explains that Montaigne's fideist rejection of rational theology "does not intend to harm faith. To the contrary, faith remains possible; but its content, like any sort of transcendence, is shifted into absolute darkness."[15] Montaigne disparages those who sort through

---

[10] Ibid., II.12, 431–33 B/C.

[11] Ibid., II.12, 370–71.

[12] Ibid., II.12, 389–90 A and 400 A.

[13] Ibid., I.34, 163–65; I.47, 205–9; III.8, 713.

[14] Ibid., I.27, 134.

[15] Hugo Friedrich, *Montaigne*, trans. Dawn Eng (Berkeley: University of California Press, 1991), 104. Some of Montaigne's most careful readers view the *Essays* as a direct challenge to Christianity. See Levine, *Sensual Philosophy*; Schaefer, *Political Philosophy of Montaigne*; Judith Shklar, *Ordinary Vices* (Cambridge: Harvard University Press, 1984). However, the question of Montaigne's orthodoxy is a controversial one. Others point to Montaigne's repeated declarations of obedience to church authority as evidence of his faith. They argue that even though the *Essays* were placed on the Index of Prohibited Books a century after publication, they do not necessarily constitute an attack on all forms of Christian devotion. Thus Ann Hartle argues that Montaigne is a sincere Christian who demonstrates "the harmony of reason and faith." Ann Hartle, *Michel de Montaigne: Accidental Philosopher*

"certain points in the observance of our Church which seem more vain or strange than others." They are deluded insofar as they believe that they can "establish the limits of truth and falsehood" by using their own judgment. Such behavior is "dangerous and fateful presumption." To avoid this impudence, we ought to "submit completely to the authority of our ecclesiastical government."[16] Unable to define the content of his faith, Montaigne asks his readers to return to the teachings of the church even though he can neither fully comprehend nor defend them.

In a similar way, Montaigne's skepticism leads him to advocate acquiescence to established political and social arrangements. The notion that legal axioms or social systems should be torn down so that new ones can be erected by human reason is as absurd to Montaigne as the idea that God's nature could be comprehended and defined. Rationalists, "these people who weigh everything and refer to reason," fail to recognize that law did not originate from reason and cannot be established by it. Hobbes's dictum that authority and not truth makes law (*auctoritas non veritas fecit legem*) is much closer to Montaigne's attitude. He writes that "the laws take their authority from possession and usage; it is dangerous to trace them back to their birth. They swell and are ennobled as they roll like our rivers."[17] Those who claim that there is a uniform, natural law are "funny" considering the manifest diversity we find in the world.[18] Montaigne mocks those who would claim that their parochial laws and moral commitments are universally applicable: "What am I to make of a virtue that I saw in credit yesterday, that will be discredited tomorrow, and that becomes a crime on the other side of the river? What of a truth that is bounded by these mountains and is falsehood to the world that lives beyond?"[19] Faced with these uncertainties, our best alternative is to follow the laws and customs that we have inherited. Montaigne writes, "The most plausible advice that our reason gives us in the matter is gen-

---

(Cambridge: Cambridge University Press, 2003), 148. Jacob Zeitlin claims that Montaigne is a loyal Catholic. Jacob Zeitlin, ed., *The Essays of Michel de Montaigne*, 3 vols. (New York: Knopf, 1934). And Donald Frame and Hugo Friedrich consider him a fideist, that is, someone who believes that truth is only available through the revealed word of God accepted by faith. Donald Frame, *Montaigne: A Biography* (San Francisco: North Point Press, 1984); Friedrich, *Montaigne*.

[16] Montaigne, *Complete Essays*, I.27, 134.

[17] Ibid., II.12, 440 A.

[18] Ibid., II.12 437 A. Montaigne's statement in its entirety runs: "They are funny when, to give some certainty to the laws, they say that there are some that are firm, perpetual, and immutable, which they call natural, which are imprinted on the human race by the condition of their being."

[19] Ibid., II.12, 437. This sentiment is powerfully restated by Pascal: "A strange justice that is bounded by a river! Truth on this side of the Pyrenees, error on the other side." Blaise Pascal, *Thoughts*, trans. William Finlayson Trotter (New York: P. F. Collier & Son, 1910), 105.

erally for each man to obey the laws of his country. . . . And what does reason mean by that, unless that our duty has no rule but an accidental one?"[20] He need not commit to the moral superiority of his regime in order to adhere to it. In fact, he points out that every regime is defective in that it is tainted by mortal hands.

Montaigne scorns those who attempt to make universal claims concerning moral and political obligations without first examining each case in its particularity. Since every situation must be dealt with on its own terms, there is no way to know what is just or honorable in advance. Although Montaigne mentions the name of Machiavelli only twice in his essays, it is clear that Machiavellian language is the political idiom of Montaigne's skepticism. Just as Machiavelli rejects abstract discussion of imagined republics and principalities in favor of the study of "life as it is," Montaigne urges his readers to open their eyes to the ways in which human beings can act both honorably and wickedly. The maintenance of order requires that we not blind ourselves to the demands of political life. Montaigne writes, "In every government there are necessary offices that are not only abject but also vicious. Vices find their place in it and are employed for sewing our society together, as are poisons for the preservation of our health . . . the public welfare requires that a man betray and lie and massacre."[21] This kinder and gentler Machiavelli recognizes that in political matters, "where the lion's skin will not suffice, we must sew on a bit of the fox's."[22] Recourse to extraordinary means of force and fraud is a politically acceptable response to the stream of contingent and unstable events in which human actors find themselves immersed. For Montaigne the recognition of the uncertainty of human reason leads to an acceptance of Machiavellian political expediency.[23]

[20] Montaigne, *Complete Essays*, II.12, 436 A.

[21] Ibid., III.1, 600 B/C.

[22] Ibid., I.5, 17 A. This imagery is almost certainly from Machiavelli, who might have found it in Cicero's *De Officiis* I.11.34, 13.4. In the *Prince*, Machiavelli writes, "Since a ruler, then, must know how to act like a beast, he should imitate both the fox and the lion. . . . Those who rely merely upon a lion's strength do not understand matters." Niccolò Machiavelli, *The Prince*, ed. Quentin Skinner and Russell Price (Cambridge: Cambridge University Press, 1988), xviii. As Schaefer puts it, "To understand Montaigne may require an openness to the possible truths contained in Machiavellianism." Schaefer, *Political Philosophy of Montaigne*, 24.

[23] In *The Machiavellian Moment*, J.G.A. Pocock argues that Machiavelli represents a paradigmatic response to the humanist emphasis on the contingency and flux of temporal affairs: "The Machiavellian moment is a name for the moment in conceptualized time in which the republic was seen as confronting its own temporal finitude, as attempting to remain morally and politically stable in a stream of irrational events conceived as essentially destructive of all systems of secular stability" (viii). Pocock has been criticized, however, for emphasizing the republican themes while downplaying the despotic elements of this Machiavellian moment. Thus Victoria Kahn writes, "For if Machiavellianism is a rhetoric for con-

Both Montaigne and Machiavelli also emphasize the play of fortune
in our political lives. In the endless stream of human events, it is foolish
to appeal to fixed and immutable laws of good and bad. Yet whereas
Machiavelli seems to imply that the study of history could help us, Montaigne is less sanguine than Machiavelli about the prospect of taming
fortune.[24] In one of his last essays, "Of Physiognomy," Montaigne revises
Machiavelli's estimate of the relative powers of fortune and prudence
over human affairs.[25] In what surely is a direct response to Machiavelli's
claim that fortune dictates one-half of our actions, Montaigne declares
that she controls "richly" two-thirds of them. Even the attempt to find
continuities and patterns in history will fail to provide us with adequate
guidance to direct events toward our desired ends. For the most part,
our lives are the dictated by the whims of fortune. While there might be
an order in the cosmos, that order is largely incomprehensible to human
beings.[26]

In the essay "By Diverse Means We Arrive at the Same End," Montaigne treats the Machiavellian question of what individuals should do
when they fall into the enemy's hands. He begins by recounting various
acts of courage and defiance that had won over conquering princes; then,
contradicting himself, he notes that many princes react better to pleas of
mercy. As Montaigne lists the various strategies of captured individuals
and their success and failure, it becomes clear that it is nearly impossible
to identify general rules or precepts of action from history. The diversity
and contingency of human affairs render the means by which we arrive
at the same ends so diverse as to defy rational elucidation: "Truly man
is a marvelously vain, diverse, and undulating object. It is hard to found
any constant and uniform judgment on him."[27] Whereas Machiavelli usually tries to account for historical differences by identifying mitigating
circumstances in order to draw general conclusions, Montaigne insists
that the only general rule we can draw from the diversity of fortunes is
the dominance of fortune over all human affairs: "So vain and frivolous
a thing is human prudence, and athwart all our plans, counsels, and pre-

---

ceptualizing and responding to the realm of contingency, it includes not only republicanism
but also tyranny; it involves the use of force and fraud not only to advance one's self interest
but also to serve the commonwealth" Victoria Ann Kahn, *Machiavellian Rhetoric: From
the Counter-Reformation to Milton* (Princeton: Princeton University Press, 1994), 10. For
Montaigne's similar response to contingency, see Victoria Ann Kahn, *Rhetoric, Prudence,
and Skepticism in the Renaissance* (Ithaca, N.Y.: Cornell University Press, 1985), 115–51.

[24] See Machiavelli, *The Prince*, II.xxix. For an insightful account of some of the implications of this difference between Machiavelli and Montaigne, see Shklar, *Ordinary Vices*,
30–35.

[25] Montaigne, *Complete Essays*, III.12, 812.

[26] Ibid., I.26,116; I.32, 59–61; II.12, 343; II.30, 538–39.

[27] Ibid., I.1, 3–5.

cautions. Fortune still maintains her grasp on the results."[28] Montaigne is anything but optimistic about the possibility of divining patterns from history or acting in ways that could significantly affect the course of fortune. Whereas Machiavelli can still valorize the man of *virtú*, Montaigne's skepticism leads to a type of political withdrawal and acquiescence.[29]

Montaigne maintains his loyalty to positive legal axioms and inherited social structures for the same reason that he expresses his allegiance to the church. In fact, one of the principle advantages of religion is that it leads us to the acceptance of those worldly powers that are already in place. "The Christian religion has all the marks of the utmost justice and utility," he writes, "but none more apparent than the precise recommendation of obedience to the magistrate and maintenance of the government."[30] The inadequacy of our theoretical investigations necessitates acquiescence to

---

[28] Ibid., II.24, 92. For other similar inversions of the classical humanist rhetoric of activist politics, see "Fortune is Often Met in the Path of Reason," I.34, and "Of the Uncertainty of Our Judgment" I.47, 205–9.

[29] The way in which Montaigne's skepticism manifests itself politically has been the subject of considerable scholarly controversy. The diversity of interpretations would surely have delighted Montaigne. Many commentators have pointed out the "deeply conservative" nature of his thought. See Nannerl Keohane, *Philosophy and the State in France: The Renaissance to the Enlightenment* (Princeton: Princeton University Press, 1980), 108; Popkin, *History of Scepticism*, 49; Skinner, *Foundations*, 2:283. One of the founders of the Frankfurt School, Horkheimer, went so far as to draw a connection between Montaigne's skepticism and the skeptical acquiescence of his contemporaries to National Socialism. Horkheimer, "Montaigne und die Funktion der Skepsis," in *Anfänger der Burgerlichen Geschichtsphilosophie* (Frankfurt am Main: Fischer Verlag, 1971). In contrast, others have followed Emerson in finding roots of liberalism in various aspects of Montaigne's liberality. Ralph Waldo Emerson, "Representative Men," in *Collected Works*, ed. W. Williams and D. Wilson (Cambridge: Cambridge University Press, 1987), 97. Thus Alan Levine finds the roots of toleration in his notion of self, Michael Allen Gillespie highlights his role in promoting the ideal of civic friendship in the modern world, Donald Frame emphasizes the humanistic potential of Montaigne's "discovery of man," and Judith Shklar focuses on the liberal impulse of Montaigne's deep aversion to cruelty. Donald Murdoch Frame, *Montaigne's Discovery of Man: The Humanization of a Humanist* (Westport, Conn.: Greenwood Press, 1983); Michael Allen Gillespie, "Montaigne's Humanistic Liberalism," *Journal of Politics* 47, no. 1 (1985), 40–59; Levine, *Sensual Philosophy*; Shklar, *Ordinary Vices*. In contrast, David Lewis Schaefer portrays Montaigne as one of the first true moderns whose "putative skepticism" masked a dogmatic liberalism that should be distinguished from the genuine "skepticism of classical philosophy as a whole." Schaefer, *Political Philosophy of Montaigne*, 83; see also 83–86, 149–50, 395–96. For a particularly insightful and balanced treatment of Montaigne that highlights both conservative and liberal elements in his writings, see Jean Starobinski, *Montaigne in Motion*, trans. Arthur Goldhammer (Chicago: University of Chicago Press, 1985). Although these various interpretations range in tone from bitter indictment to open admiration, most of these commentators would agree that Montaigne's skepticism leads him to recommend obedience to the laws and acceptance of the religion of one's native land.

[30] Montaigne, *Complete Essays*, I.23, 87–88.

traditional authorities. For Montaigne, the epistemic categories of *scientia* and *opinio* cannot rationally justify our religious, legal, or moral commitments. He clings to the husk of the scholastic notion of opinion by pointing to the authority of tradition. Yet in contrast to the Scholastics, he does not enter into a dialectical examination of traditional sources in order to uncover what is most probable. While earlier, more scholastically minded humanists used the dialectical method to arrive at approximations of the truth, Montaigne uses this strategy to undermine truth claims in general. His skepticism leaves him with no other defensible position but outward acquiescence to the powers that be.

However, it should not be overlooked that for Montaigne the very process of writing was a type of political act of resistance amid the violence and absurdity of his age. His turn inward had implications beyond his own mental world; he sought to engage his readers in ways that might counteract the political absolutism and religious dogmatism that they encountered. Yet he was adamant that such engagement must take place within the private sphere. Although his skepticism has been celebrated as a precursor to liberal toleration, Montaigne himself did not conclude that all ideas should be given free reign. He supported the imposition of intellectual conformity in the public sphere, not the flourishing of a Millian marketplace of ideas. For Montaigne, political order required the establishment of a single, reliable standard of truth, especially under conditions in which that truth seems especially vulnerable. As human beings, we have the freedom to challenge these authoritative claims and question commonly held beliefs, but this process should only take place in the private realm. In public we owe our allegiance to the established customs and local magistrates. Montaigne is very clear about his position. He writes that "a wise man should withdraw from the crowd, maintaining [his] power and freedom freely to make judgments, whilst externally accepting all received forms and fashions." For Montaigne, "the government of a community has no right to our thoughts, but everything else such as our actions, efforts, wealth and life itself should be lent to it for its service or even given up when the community's opinions so require. . . . For the Rule of rules, the general Law of laws, is that each should observe those of the place wherein he lives."[31] Although he certainly cherished intellectual freedom and independence, Montaigne believed that the only way to experience these things was by withdrawing from the political realm, a realm characterized by falsehood and violence. Recognizing the inhumanity of the governmental and ecclesiastical powers of his day, he sought to insulate himself from cruelty, embracing what Judith Shklar

[31] Ibid., I.23, 133.

calls a "conservatism of universal disgust."[32] Without a reliable method to sort out the deceptive claims of the public sphere, Montaigne's response was to encourage his readers to acquiesce to the religious, political, and moral custom, and seek the delights of an intellectual life beyond the purview of the authorities.

Montaigne's mix of skepticism and conservatism spread quickly throughout Europe as his *Essays* were translated and published. Although his own writings were widely read, the ideas and attitudes that he embraced were further disseminated by various popularizers. One of his most influential popularizers, Father Pierre Charron, took it upon himself to organize Montaigne's writings into a systematic treatise, entitled *On Wisdom*. In this monumental work, Charron laid out the case for skepticism in a way that could be studied in the schools. As a theologian, he emphasized the connections between the rejection of certain knowledge and particular strains in Christian thought that spurn intellectual pride and rationalist dogmatism. Emphasizing the politically conservative elements of the *Essays*, he marshaled Montaigne's skepticism in defense of the authority of the established church and local political authorities. Through Charron, Montaigne's work came to influence generations of Christian thinkers and Catholic apologists, including François Veron, that rabid opponent of Protestant pretension. These men reacted to the collapse of the medieval language of justification by embracing a thoroughly skeptical solution—acquiescence to outward authorities and withdrawal into a private sphere of intellectual freedom. This response would have profound implications for sixteenth- and seventeenth-century moral and intellectual life. As Popkin puts it, "Montaigne's genial *Apologie* became the *coup de grace* to an entire intellectual world. It was also to be the womb of modern thought, in that it led to the attempt either to refute the new Pyrrhonism, or to find a way of living with it."[33]

Descartes and the Rationalist Dream

As a student at La Flèche, René Descartes imbibed many of these skeptical arguments directly from his teacher, François Veron. In a world besieged by religious wars and beleaguered by widespread disagreement and uncertainty, it was not hard to realize that the traditional modes of discourse simply could not sustain rational deliberation. Yet unlike his teacher, Descartes was not satisfied with the Montaignian response. He saw that the debilitating doubt unleashed by skepticism not only

[32] Shklar, *Ordinary Vices*, 32.
[33] Popkin, *History of Scepticism*, 55.

undermined the scholastic category of *scientia*, but also destabilized the notion of justified, probable belief. The deterioration of scholasticism left his contemporaries without a way to justify their claims or resolve the uncertainties that were plaguing Europe. The skeptical appeal to inherited customs and local authority was inadequate for an age in which customs and authorities were being fiercely and sometimes violently contested. The ancient art of rhetoric had been reduced to a technique of ornamenting and embellishing arguments in order to make them persuasive. Instead, Descartes' solution was to recover *scientia*. He wanted to maintain a sphere of certain knowledge by discovering an unassailable foundation upon which such knowledge could be secured and defended. In this way he hoped to salvage the medieval notion of demonstrative truth and apply it to the natural world as well as the world of ethics and politics.[34]

Although there are good reasons to describe Descartes as the first modern philosopher, his innovations took place within an essentially scholastic framework. Following a long tradition, he divided human understanding into discrete realms of certain knowledge and probable belief. Descartes' assertion that "all knowledge (*scientia*) is certain and evident cognition" would not have drawn criticism or surprise from followers of Aquinas and Aristotle.[35] His argument in the *Rules for the Direction of the Mind* that certain knowledge can only be achieved through intuition and deduction echoes the traditional understanding of *scientia*, namely that which is arrived at by means of logical demonstration from first principles. As we have seen, Aquinas himself maintained that only demonstration could yield certainty, and conclusions derived from opinion could never reach the level of knowledge. It is this traditional view of rational appraisal that shaped Descartes' understanding of the task of philosophy: "Concerning objects proposed for study, we ought to investigate what we can clearly and evidently intuit or deduce with certainty, and not what other people have thought or what we ourselves conjecture.

[34] Descartes does concede that daily life might require us to follow principles that are less than certain. *Discourse on the Method*, in *The Philosophical Writings of Descartes*, ed. J. Cottingham, R. Stoothoff, D. Murdoch, A. Kenny, 3 vols. (Cambridge: Cambridge University Press, 1984–91), 1:118–19 (AT 6:15–16). Volume and page numbers in parentheses are from *Oeuvres de Descartes*, ed. Charles Adam and Paul Tannery, 13 vols. (Paris: Vrin, 1957–68), abbreviated AT. In *Principles* he also concedes that in many areas of life we often can achieve only "moral certainty." *Principles of Philosophy*, in *Philosophical Writings*, 2:289 (AT 9B:327). Yet, as we will see, this admonition is ultimately a skeptical and provisional appeal to tradition and custom. Probable judgment might be temporarily useful, yet it is not ultimately preferable. Descartes aspires to replace traditional belief with certain knowledge in all areas of human inquiry.

[35] Descartes, *Rules for the Direction of the Mind*, in *Philosophical Writings*, 1:10 (AT 10:362).

For knowledge (*scientia*) can be attained in no other way."[36] By insisting on the separate and inviolable sphere of certain knowledge based on incontrovertible first principles, Descartes is simply reasserting a fundamentally scholastic distinction.[37]

However, Descartes parts company with his scholastic predecessors when his focus on certainty leads him to reject received opinion as a source of understanding. Both Descartes and the Scholastics agreed that knowledge is superior to opinion; yet scholastic philosophers remained committed to the idea that the dialectical examination of probable opinions could yield insight into the workings of creation and the individual's place in it. In fact, they believed that the dialectical appropriation of a textual tradition was the best preparation for the practice of *scientia*. In contrast, Descartes argues in his *Rules for the Direction of the Mind* that the best preparation for discovering truth involves closing one's books and discarding the authoritative claims of tradition. Probable opinion does not yield insight, only error. He claims that we are better off without any opinions at all than with doubtful and misleading ones. "Someone who has doubts about many things," Descartes writes, "is no wiser than one who has never given them a thought; indeed, he appears less wise if he has formed a false opinion about any of them."[38] By dwelling on things that are uncertain, we risk mistaking our doubtful opinions for knowledge, assigning a level of confidence to them that they do not warrant. Descartes is especially dismissive of those Scholastics who constantly appeal to the authority of Aristotle. The only reasonable response is "to reject all such merely probable cognition and resolve to believe only what is perfectly known and incapable of being doubted."[39] For Descartes, we can only know something as truth if we know it with absolute certainty. As Harry Frankfurt puts it, "Certainty is his fundamental epistemological concept, and he defines truth in terms of it."[40]

Descartes' revolutionary assertion—that probable opinion cannot yield reliable insight—should be seen within the context of the rise and

[36] Ibid., 1:13 (AT 10:366).

[37] Gilson and Koyre have presented substantial evidence to show that Descartes was deeply influenced by scholasticism. They portray Descartes' project as an attempt to find a new method to reinstate an essentially medieval outlook in the face of Renaissance discoveries and the scientific revolution. Etienne Gilson and Thomas Langan, *Modern Philosophy: Descartes to Kant* (New York: Random House, 1963); and Alexander Koyré, *Descartes und Die Scholastik* (Bonn: Herbert Grundmann, 1971). For a recent rearticulation of this general thesis with an emphasis on the link between Augustine and Descartes, see Zbigniew Janowski, *Cartesian Theodicy: Descartes' Quest for Certitude* (Dordrecht: Kluwer, 2002).

[38] *Rules*, 1:10 (AT 10:362).

[39] Ibid.

[40] Harry Frankfurt, *Demons, Dreamers and Madmen* (Indianapolis: Bobbs-Merrill, 1970), 23.

fall of the doctrine of probabilism. Originally formulated in 1577 by the Dominican Bartholomé de Medina, probabilism was developed and defended in the early seventeenth century by several prominent Spanish Jesuits, including Antonio Escobar y Mendoza. The doctrine emerged out of the scholastic method of dialectical inquiry into authoritative texts. It offered a process for deliberating about difficult cases of conscience. The difference, however, was that probabilists argued that in matters of dispute, it was permissible to follow the advice of *any* respected authority even if other weightier authorities counsel the opposite course of action. Medina and those who followed him understood probable to mean approvable or safe. If something is safe or approvable, regardless of other safer or more approvable actions, then it is allowable. By bypassing the lengthy and difficult task of dialectical reasoning, probabilists could pay closer attention to the social and moral effects of adopting particular doctrines over others while making use of a wider range of authoritative texts. According to critics, however, this type of probabilist justification was nothing more than a pretense for opportunism and manipulation. It seemed as though a probabilist would first decide on the most self-serving course of action and then scour church authorities in order to find some obscure text in support of their decision. Blaise Pascal became one of the most vocal and scathing opponents of this type of argumentation, satirizing it in his *Provincial Letters* as nothing more than a method of rationalization that could be employed by anyone for the most vicious purposes.[41] For Descartes, it is *this* type of probability that could not serve as a reliable vehicle for rational discussion or debate. If we are to avoid the unacceptable consequences of the doctrine of probabilism, we must establish our knowledge on firm and unyielding foundations of *scientia*.[42]

Early in his career Descartes was confident that it would be relatively easy to secure the foundations of his universal science by means of intuition and deduction.[43] Yet his encounter with skepticism around 1628–29 forced him to consider the possibility that much of what he regarded as

[41] Blaise Pascal, *The Provincial Letters*, trans. A. J. Krailsheimer (Harmondsworth: Penguin, 1967). Franklin distinguishes between a tradition of casuistry, which involves careful weighing of reasons, and probabilism, which does not. He argues that the "propaganda of *The Provincial Letters*" did more than anything else to discredit both casuistry and probabilism. Franklin, *The Science of Conjecture*, 376, 64.

[42] Popkin speculates that Descartes rejected a type of probability "somewhat like that of Bacon, Mersenne, Gassendi and Hobbes." Popkin, *History of Scepticism*, 177. Yet it seems more historically plausible that his denunciation of probable opinion resulted primarily from its association with the discredited doctrine of probabilism. Descartes' gripe, then, was not with probability as such, but with the deteriorated scholastic notion of probability that he believed could not adequately respond to the skepticism that had become so influential in Parisian intellectual society in the early seventeenth century.

[43] *Rules*, 1:14-15 (AT 10:368–69).

intuitively certain might be illusory.[44] After studying the arguments of
the skeptics, including Montaigne and Charron, Descartes came to the
conclusion that the only way to secure certain knowledge in the context
of skepticism would be to isolate a principle that could not be subject to
doubt. In order to be sure that this principle was invulnerable, he would
have to embark on the path of radical doubt himself, casting aside all
received opinions and rejecting anything that could not be known with
absolute certainty. Such a project was unprecedented. As Peter Schouls
reminds us, "neither Euclid's *Elements* nor Aristotle's *Ethics,* neither
Aquinas's *Summa Theologica* nor Galilio's *Two New Sciences* show that
it derives its conclusions from indubitable principles known per se."[45]
This quest for absolute and apodictic certainty was Descartes' alone.[46]

In the *Discourse,* Descartes offers his method as a cure for the disease
of skepticism. By purposefully undergoing a therapy of radical doubt,
he hopes to inoculate himself against uncertainty and emerge with the
strength and confidence to establish the firm foundations of a new science. He tells his readers that although it is sometimes necessary to follow
uncertain principles in everyday conduct, the search for truth requires
that we reject as false anything about which there is the least doubt. Thus
he resolves "never to accept anything as true if I did not have evident
knowledge of its truth: that is, carefully to avoid precipitate conclusions
and preconceptions, and to include nothing more in my judgments than
what presented itself to my mind so clearly and so distinctly that I had
no occasion to doubt it."[47] In his effort to reject anything for which he
could find the least ground for doubt, Descartes dismisses sense experi-

---

[44] Descartes mentions this encounter with skepticism in the *Discourse on the Method,*
1:125 (AT 6:29) and in his replies appended to the *Meditations* in *Philosophical Writings,* 2:94 (AT 7:130). On the connection between Descartes and skepticism generally, see
Popkin, *History of Scepticism,* 175–217; and E. M. Curley, *Descartes against the Skeptics*
(Cambridge: Harvard University Press, 1978), 12–20.

[45] Schouls, *Reasoned Freedom,* 18.

[46] Stephen Toulmin argues that the shift from a Montaignian acceptance of uncertainty,
ambiguity, and diversity of opinion in 1580s to the Cartesian anxiety concerning such skepticism in 1640s is probably related to the assassination of Henry of Navarre, who had been
a close and confidant of Montaigne. Henry's death signaled an end to the possibility of
compromise between religious factions in France. The civilized skepticism of Montaigne
suddenly was no longer politically viable. The political crisis that followed his assassination became the impetus for a new "quest for certainty." Toulmin, *Cosmopolis: The Hidden
Agenda of Modernity* (Chicago: University of Chicago Press, 1990), 45–56.

[47] *Discourse,* 1:120 (AT 6:18). It has been pointed out that Descartes' path of radical
doubt did not actually lead him to doubt everything. Someone who placed everything in
doubt could not begin the process that he lays out without training in languages, both
French and Latin, and an implicit understanding of what uncertainty and certainty would
entail. Of course Descartes inherits these frameworks and employs them in his writing while
concealing from his readers (and possibly himself) his indebtedness.

ence because the senses sometimes deceive us, extended proofs because we are prone to error, and any ideas or conceptions concerning the world around us because the thoughts we have while awake might be confused with the thoughts we have in our dreams. He leads the reader to the brink of epistemological despair.

In his *Meditations on First Philosophy*, written five years after the *Discourse*, Descartes presents a potentially more unsettling account of his encounter with skepticism.[48] In the beginning of the First Meditation, Descartes reiterates many of the fundamental doubts that motivated his argument in the *Discourse* and then raises an even more unsettling possibility. If a deceiving God, or more palatably, "some malicious demon of the utmost power and cunning has employed all his energies in order to deceive me," then he would have to concede "that the sky, the air, the earth, colours, shapes, clouds, and all external things are merely the delusions of dreams which he has devised to ensnare my judgment."[49] Here Descartes is willing to entertain a more devastating skeptical possibility than anything he advanced in the *Discourse*. Not only does he imply that the information we receive from our senses might be illusory and our reasoning might be mistaken, but that our faculties, even under the best conditions, could be faulty. No matter how careful we try to be in examining and evaluating a claim, we can never be certain that we are not being deceived by the very faculties that enable us to gain knowledge. In following the path of radical doubt to its most radical conclusions, Descartes considers that an evil genius could have arranged matters so that what appears to him to be clearly and distinctly true is in fact false. He therefore resolves to treat all external signs as traps set by a powerful deceiver.

Of course Descartes' goal in undergoing this process of radical doubt is not further doubt but the discovery of a firm foundations upon which he could build a new *scientia*. He makes it clear that he does not wish to imitate "the skeptics, who doubt only for the sake of doubting and pretend to be always undecided; on the contrary, my whole aim was to reach certainty—to cast aside the loose earth and sand so as to come upon rock or clay."[50] By submitting himself to the various levels of doubt of the First Meditation, he sinks into the "a deep whirlpool" of skepticism "which tumbles me around so that I can neither stand on the bottom nor swim

---

[48] It is important to note that the *Discourse* was written in French and was intended for the general public, while the *Meditations* were published in Latin apparently for a more exclusive audience. The fact that the earlier work does not contain an account of the extreme doubt described in the First Meditation might reflect a concern that less refined readers could misuse these metaphysical reflections.

[49] *Meditations*, 2:15 (AT 7:22).

[50] *Discourse*, 1:125 (AT 6:29).

to the top."[51] Yet just at the moment of desperation and terror, Descartes finds firm footing—he realizes that even if he is being deceived by some evil genius, he undoubtedly exists. As in the *Discourse,* Descartes finds certainty in the *Meditations* by looking inward. "Let him deceive me as much as he can, he will never bring it about that I am nothing so long as I think that I am something . . . this proposition, I am, I exist, is necessarily true whenever it is put forward by me or conceived in my mind."[52] At the end of the process of radical doubt, Descartes becomes aware of one thing he could be absolutely certain of—his own existence.

Descartes does not stop at this point. He believes that his fundamental principle, *cogito ergo sum,* can yield an entire system of knowledge; it can serve as the foundation to a new universal and apodictic science. In contrast to the theoretical philosophy of Aristotle and the Scholastics, he hopes to initiate a "practical philosophy" by means of which "we could know the power and action of fire, water, air, the stars, the heavens and all the other bodies in our environment, as distinctly as we know the various crafts of our artisans, and we could use this knowledge—as the artisans use theirs—for all the purposes for which it is appropriate, and thus make ourselves, as it were, the lords and masters of nature."[53] Descartes believes that a practical philosophy based on certain knowledge could yield a set of truly *useful* sciences—a science of mechanics that would aid humanity in dominating the physical world to alleviate the drudgery of labor, a science of medicine that could aid in regulating the body in order to eliminate suffering and ultimately even death, and finally a science of morals that could aid controlling the passions in order to end all hatred and strife.

To establish this universal science, however, Descartes needs to bridge the gap between the single premise, the *cogito,* and the clear and distinct ideas that could be useful in scientific inquiry. Surprisingly, he does not offer his fundamental axiom of existence as a first principle from which all other truths can be deduced. Although his search for certainty takes place within a scholastic framework of *scientia,* Descartes is not interested in constructing syllogisms on the scholastic model. Instead he describes the experience of the *cogito* as an almost revelatory moment through which he becomes aware that whatever he perceived with clarity and distinctness was in fact true. Since his own existence strikes him so forcefully that he cannot doubt it, he can also be confident that the cri-

[51] *Meditations,* 2:16 (AT 7:24).

[52] Ibid., 2:17 (AT 7:25). Although this crucial Cartesian claim has been interpreted to be uniquely modern, Gilson points to six distinct passages in which Augustine invokes a very similar formulation. Etienne Gilson, *The Christian Philosophy of Saint Augustine,* trans. L.E.M. Lynch (New York: Octagon Books, 1983), 41–42.

[53] *Discourse,* 1:142–43 (AT 6:62).

terion of clarity and distinctness can serve as the foundation of an entire system of certain knowledge.[54] It is this role that an inner, natural light plays in his argument that led many of his critics to accuse him of fanaticism or enthusiasm.[55] For Descartes, this dramatic reversal of doubt rests on the claim that a subjective awareness of the absolute certainty of the *cogito* provides him with a standard that can be used to attain knowledge of the world beyond his own ideas.

Once he linked the certainty of his own existence to the validity of his criteria of clear and distinct ideas, Descartes could then present his defense of the existence of God. He argues that he finds within himself a clear and distinct idea of perfection, although he recognizes that he himself does not embody that perfection. The idea of perfection must come from some being outside of himself, and this being is God.[56] He can therefore be certain that God exists and that God is perfect. Once this is established, Descartes can rest assured that God "cannot be a deceiver since it is manifest by the natural light that all fraud and deception depend on some defect."[57] Descartes employs the idea of a divine perfection in order to guarantee his subjective claims to absolute knowledge. After the illumination that came through the discovery of the *cogito*, Descartes experiences an inner assurance about the truth of his own ideas. Those ideas, in turn, lead him to the notion of a God who serves as the guarantee that what is perceived as clear and distinct is objectively certain.[58]

[54] *Meditations*, 2:24 (AT 7:35).

[55] Michael Heyd has recently shown that Descartes and his followers were regularly accused of madness and fanaticism for claiming a certainty for their ideas that did not seem to be accessible to others. For many observers, Cartesians appeal to an apodictic science guaranteed by the *cogito* bore a certain resemblance to the religious enthusiast's appeal to divine illumination. Both appeals presuppose an access to absolute certainty that seems to be at odds with the continued existence of genuine controversy in the world. This link might have been more than just a passing similarity. Heyd goes so far as to suggest that the Cartesian notion of "natural light" may have influenced the Quaker Robert Barclay's conception of "inner light." Heyd, *Be Sober and Reasonable*, 122–32, 37–39. Jonathan Swift would later draw comparisons between Cartesians and religious fanatics in his scathing satire "A Tale of a Tub" (1704). See Jonathan Swift, *Gulliver's Travels and Other Writings* (Oxford: Clarendon Press, 1958), 279–394.

[56] Michael Gillespie points out that although Descartes' ontological proof has a form similar to the one Anselm originally articulated and Aquinas repeated in the beginning of the *Summa*, Descartes' proof aims at providing a clear and comprehensive understanding of God, whereas the scholastic proof was employed to demonstrate how the world participates in a divine perfection that cannot possibly be comprehended. Michael Allen Gillespie, "Descartes and the Question of Toleration," in *Early Modern Skepticism and the Origins of Toleration*, ed. Alan Levine (Lanham, Md.: Lexington Books, 1999), 111.

[57] *Meditations*, 2:35 (AT 7:52).

[58] One implication of this argument is that the atheist is not able to have this same security about the objective truth of clear and distinct ideas. See *Replies*, AT 7:139; and Frankfurt, *Demons, Dreamers and Madmen*, 172.

Thus Descartes responds to an epidemic of skepticism by portraying himself as undergoing a therapy of doubt that far surpassed the relatively mild suspicion introduced by thinkers such as Montaigne and Charron. He emerges with a criterion of truth that he believes to be indubitable and certified by a God of goodness and perfection. Once he connects the standard of clear and distinct ideas with divine honesty, the initial doubts about his ability to distinguish truth from falsehood vanish. He overcomes skepticism by supplying an unshakeable foundation upon which he can secure knowledge that is not merely probable but certain. He can now turn to the construction of a new *scientia* that will lead to the mastery of nature and alleviation of human suffering.

Yet Descartes' monumental effort to provide a solution to the crisis of skepticism was not greeted with universal approval. Critics throughout Europe denounced him either as a radical skeptic or a misguided dogmatist. Either he was claiming to search for certain knowledge while cleverly undermining that possibility, or he was simply asserting a set of ungrounded propositions. His many detractors believed that if Descartes truly accepted the argument expounded in the First Meditation, he would not be able recover from the skeptical despair that he had introduced. By accepting the possibility that an evil genius could cause that which he experienced as self-evident to be in actuality false, he had forever closed off the path to certain knowledge.[59]

The first edition of the *Meditations* was published with an extensive appendix that included objections from an impressive array of scholars, including Marin Mersenne, Thomas Hobbes, Antoine Arnauld, and Pierre Gassendi. One of the most devastating criticisms centered around the question of whether Descartes' claim to be certain of his clear and distinct perceptions actually established their certainty. Gassendi pointed out that a feeling of assurance is not the same as objective knowledge. We often think we are certain only to find out later that we are mistaken. The criterion of clear and distinct ideas, therefore, can only reflect the *appearance* of clarity and distinctness, not the objective reality. "Everyone thinks that he clearly and distinctly perceives the truth which he champions."[60] The standard of clarity and distinctness simply cannot help us distinguish that which is really clear and distinct from that which appears to be so. Descartes responded to this charge of radical subjectivity by arguing that the experience of clear perception itself leads individuals to overcome

---

[59] Descartes tells us that he was shocked when he discovered that he was being accused of skepticism, since he considers himself the skeptic's ablest opponent. He had "more accurately than any other who has written on the subject, successfully refuted that doubt." To charge him with skepticism, he contended, is like blaming doctors for the disease that they describe in order to teach the cure. (*Replies*, AT 7:573–74)

[60] *Replies* 2:194(AT 7:278–79).

any doubts they might have concerning the difference between appearance and reality: "For the very fact that they had perceived something clearly would mean that they had ceased to doubt it, and so ceased to be sceptics."[61]

Yet this argument in itself was unconvincing because, either intentionally or unintentionally, Descartes had driven a wedge between the truths he experienced subjectively and the objectively known truths of God. The only way to bridge that gap was to reassert that a benevolent God would not allow his creatures to experience something with clarity and distinctness if it were not also objectively true. "Once we have become aware that God exists," Descartes argues, "it is necessary for us to imagine he is a deceiver if we wish to cast doubt on what we clearly and distinctly perceive. And since it is impossible to imagine that he is a deceiver, whatever we clearly and distinctly perceive must be completely accepted as true and certain."[62] The possibility of attaining certain knowledge with Descartes' method hinges on the assumption of an honest and well-behaved God.

Yet Descartes' appeal to the power and goodness of a deity also came under fire. In his famous objection, Arnauld pointed out the apparent circularity in Descartes' argument. It seemed that Descartes sought to establish the criterion of clear and distinct ideas from the existence of a nondeceiving God while deriving the existence of that deity from his clear and distinct ideas. As Arnauld puts it, "we are sure that what we clearly and distinctly perceive is true only because God exists. But we can be sure that God exists only because we clearly and distinctly perceive this. Hence, before we can be sure that God exists, we ought to be able to be sure that whatever we perceive clearly and evidently is true."[63] The proof of God's existence requires the employment of faculties that can only be wholly trusted after God's existence is established.[64]

Here we see that Descartes' obsession with certainty entangles him in difficulties from which he is unable to escape. At the beginning of his argument, he resolved to reject as false any proposition that was in the least bit doubtful. By raising the possibility that in spite of his best efforts, all that he knows or experiences may be untrue, he throws doubt on any claim that he could subsequently make. The very self-awareness that leads to the *cogito* would seem to come under suspicion. Yet even if he

[61] Ibid. 2:321 (AT 7:477).

[62] Ibid. 2:103 (AT 7:144).

[63] Ibid. 2:150 (AT 7:214).

[64] This difficulty, which is known as Arnauld's Circle or the Cartesian Circle, was elaborated in Bayle's *Dictionary* ("Cartes" Rem. AA) and remains a central difficulty in contemporary scholarship.

can be certain about the *cogito*, the most Descartes can claim is that there are propositions that he, in his current state, is not capable of doubting. This does not rule out the possibility that those propositions might still be objectively false. An incurable doubt haunts his method, preventing him from establishing a universal science based on genuine, that is, certain knowledge. In the end he is unable to prove that the clear and distinct ideas that he possesses have any relation to objective reality. He can only maintain that it seems to be the case that his ideas reflect the world he inhabits. This, however, is an inadequate result for someone who had banished probable judgment from the realm of rational justification.

Faced with this difficulty, some scholars have argued that Descartes did not present a sincere argument in the *Meditations*. This interpretation, defended most forcefully by Hiram Caton, rests on the claim that the problematic justification of certainty and the circular defense of the existence of God were part of an elaborate deception. According to this view, Descartes was far more interested in physics and mathematics and turned to metaphysics in order to conceal his true intentions from the church authorities who had condemned Galileo. His goal was to overturn scholasticism and theology from within in order to clear a space for his new science.[65] By charging Descartes with impiety, Caton is in distinguished company—Henry More, Leibniz, and d'Holbach all doubted Descartes' sincerity. Yet Caton's description of Descartes as an impious defender of scientific investigation and an opponent of metaphysics and traditional scholasticism fails to account for his oft-repeated claim that his universal and apodictic science requires a metaphysical foundation. Descartes' project was framed within the context of the traditional idea of *scientia*; the scientific and mathematical conclusions that he arrived at meant nothing if they could not be placed on the firm and unshakeable basis of certain knowledge. His metaphysical speculations thus arose out of a sincere desire to respond to what he saw as a genuine theological and philosophical crisis. His solution required an indubitable foundation that could serve as the guarantor of truly scientific understanding.[66]

Descartes' attempt to uncover that foundation, however, led him into metaphysical difficulties that continue to haunt contemporary rationalists. By categorically rejecting probable opinion along with anything that could be doubted, Descartes hoped to defeat skepticism and secure

---

[65] Hiram Caton, *The Origin of Subjectivity* (New Haven: Yale University Press, 1973).

[66] Alexandre Koyré and Richard Popkin, among others, describe Descartes' project in this way. See Alexandre Koyré, *From the Closed World to the Infinite Universe* (Baltimore: Johns Hopkins Press, 1957); Popkin, *History of Scepticism*; Richard Popkin, "The Role of Scepticism in Modern Philosophy Reconsidered," *Journal of the History of Ideas* 31 (1993), 501–17.

a realm of certain knowledge isolated from historical contingency or human unpredictability. Yet his method was bedeviled by serious difficulties. The intuitive certainty that was to be the core of his science seemed to secure only those claims that were already uncontroversial. In the *Discourse*, he proclaims that his answer to skepticism will provide a foundation for all science, including ethics. Yet even if his attempt to provide an epistemological grounding for clear and distinct ideas established that there is a material world that more or less corresponds to the general perception of it, he did not help to provide the type of *useful* knowledge that could shed light on religious, political, and moral debates of his day. As we have seen, these debates were characterized by a generally perceived absence of consensus. And in the context of disagreement, the Cartesian appeal to an inner, natural light or even clear and distinct ideas contributes very little. As with any fanatical assertion, it offers no indubitable standard for distinguishing between genuinely objective certainty and mistaken conviction. The skeptical challenge that provoked his extraordinary philosophical labors remains unresolved.

Although Descartes' expectation of an apodictic, universal science propelled him to try to uncover the foundations of an unassailable morality, his practical position on religion, politics, and morality turned out to be very similar to Montaigne's. Although he did take note of the role that "moral certainty" plays in the "conduct of life," he insisted that such certainty, "in relation to the absolute power of God," is profoundly uncertain.[67] Unable to achieve apodictic certainty concerning moral obligation and responsibility, the only prudent response is to obey the established authorities. In the *Discourse,* Descartes famously sets up a "temporary house" to inhabit until such intellectual difficulties can be resolved scientifically. The cornerstone of this "temporary house" is obedience to the "laws and customs of my country."[68] Descartes' refusal to rely on his own opinions leaves him with no other choice but to follow the reigning opinions of the day. In the end, Descartes can do no better than the skeptics in providing a language of justification that can be used to assess matters of public disagreement and debate. The *cogito* simply cannot secure a cognitive realm in which religious, political, and moral propositions can be evaluated. This became evident in Descartes' more explicitly worldly writings. When he did venture to offer his opinions on ethical and political matters in his correspondence with Princess Elizabeth in the 1640s, he expressed himself in a mix of conservative Machiavellianism and political quietism that could have just as easily come from the pen of that radical skeptic, Montaigne. "For the Rule of rules, the general Law

[67] *Principles*, 2:289–90 (AT 9B:327). *Discourse*, 80–81 (AT 6:15–16).
[68] *Discourse*, 1:122 (AT 6:23).

of laws," Montaigne had written, "is that each should observe those of the place where he lives."[69]

In spite of these limitations, Descartes' vision of a new science based on mathematical certainty was enormously influential. Although his work was at first denounced and placed on the Index, by the end of the seventeenth century it overtook scholasticism in many of the major universities on the continent. Most thinkers who came after him, even those who opposed him, were indebted to his clear thinking and sharp mind. Descartes' writings, especially as they were presented in the *Port Royal Logic*, left their mark on the thought of John Locke. Yet Descartes' dream that his metaphysical speculations would somehow yield an unassailable foundation for scientific inquiry into the natural and ethical world would prove illusory. Instead it generated a rigorous and radical rearticulation of the skeptical crisis. As we have seen, it was clear for most observers in the seventeenth century that the traditional modes of discourse could no longer bind individuals together into a unified community in which public deliberation could take place, yet it was uncertain how either skeptical acquiescence or fanatical rationalism could fill this void.[70]

Young Locke as Skeptic and Absolutist

Faced with a scholasticism that was crumbling under the weight of intellectual pressures formed by Montaignian skepticism and Cartesian fanaticism, the young John Locke experienced a profound anxiety concerning the justification of moral and political claims. His first response was a familiar appeal to the established authority of the state. Locke did not start out a defender of individual rights, limited government, toleration,

[69] Montaigne, *Complete Essays*, I.23, 133.

[70] In the first chapter of his book on Locke, Peter Schouls asserts that "Locke and many later thinkers were revolutionary primarily insofar as they adopted and implemented the precepts of Descartes' method." *Reasoned Freedom*, 9. While Locke's emphasis on disciplined inquiry has certain similarities with Descartes' *Rules*, Schouls can only maintain that there is an "intimate relationship" between the two thinkers by exaggerating Locke's notion of certain knowledge and de-emphasizing the importance he places on probable belief (14–15). As we will see, what makes Locke revolutionary is not his appeal to Cartesian certainty. The possibility of genuine regime-altering revolution ultimately rests on the probable judgment of a people. Voltaire, as well as other French philosophes, recognized this difference and for this reason drew a crucial distinction between Descartes and Locke. Yet this distinction wasn't simply what later intellectual historians would characterize as the difference between empiricism and rationalism. Locke's philosophy did not simply offer a particular answer to the question of knowledge, but a broad political and philosophical teaching concerning how we should conduct our intellectual lives. See Voltaire, *Philosophical Letters: Letters Concerning the English Nation*, ed. Ernest Dilworth (Mineola, N.Y.: Dover Publications, 2003).

or revolution. In his earliest letters and tracts, he expressed the opinion of many of his contemporaries that political life is characterized by conflict rather than contract and the primary goal of political power is the establishment and maintenance of order. Scholars have described Locke's earliest writings as conventional examples of conservative Anglicanism or Neoplatonic natural law theory.[71] Locke seems to write within the form and tradition of scholastic philosophy, offering several arguments in favor of the claim that human beings can attain adequate knowledge of moral law. Yet, as David Wootton has argued, Locke also forcefully articulates skeptical arguments.[72] Echoing Montaigne and Charron, he emphasizes the power of custom, the pervasiveness of self-interest, and the limits of reason. Locke embraced the belief that political and moral disagreement can only be adequately resolved by the exercise of coercive force. Without a common mode of discourse that can sustain public deliberation, the exercise of governmental power is the only way to achieve political order. Locke either explicitly rejected or simply disregarded the liberal possibility of establishing a regime aimed primarily at preserving individual freedoms. It is telling that his first published work in 1655 is a poem praising Oliver Cromwell for delivering peace and order out of chaos. A few years later he composed a remarkably similar poem celebrating the Restoration of Charles II.[73] Although it cannot be denied that these eulogies were conveniently timed, it would be misleading to discount them as nothing but pandering opportunism. These poems are important because they reveal that the young Locke was willing to support different types of political authority as long as they could secure order and maintain conditions of peace. In practice, if not always in word, the young Locke was a political and religious skeptic. Having lived through violent conflict and political turmoil, he was convinced that questions of legitimacy should give way to questions of stability. Both Cromwell *and* Charles II served England well; they both overcame the chaos of violent conflict and successfully imposed a relatively peaceful coexistence on a war-weary land.

In his first extended manuscript, published in the twentieth century as *Two Tracts on Government*, the young Locke emphasizes the instability of political order and warns his countrymen of the danger of giving religious dissidents too much freedom. If they hope to avoid the bloodshed that grows out of the "tyranny of a religious rage," he argues, they must support the "absolute and arbitrary power" of the magistrate. Locke

[71] See Philip Abrams's introduction to *Two Tracts on Government* (TT 71–72) and W. von Leyden's introduction to *Essays on the Law of Nature* (LN 39–43).

[72] David Wootton, introduction to John Locke, *Political Writings* (London: Penguin, 1993), 27–29.

[73] Compare "Verses on Oliver Cromwell" with "Verses on King Charles II's Restoration," in Locke, *Political Essays*, 201–3.

begins his career as an ardent defender of unlimited sovereign authority: "No one can have a greater respect and veneration for authority than I" (TT 120, 121, 119).[74] Without a language in which legitimacy can be sustained, members of a community must submit to the authoritative powers that are already in place. In an untitled work on the law of nature written a few years later, he reiterates this sentiment. He asks, "For is there anything so abominable, so wicked, so contrary to all right and law, which the general consent, or rather the conspiracy, of a senseless crowd would not at some time advocate?" (LN 161).[75] Locke is adamant that each subject has the obligation "to pay dutiful obedience ... to do nor not to do at the command of a superior power" (LN 183).

In his letters and manuscripts written during his years at Christ Church College at Oxford, Locke gives forceful expression to a skepticism similar to that of Montaigne and Charron.[76] Although we know that Locke owned editions of their work, we cannot know for sure whether he was directly influenced by their writing at this point in his life. Yet we can see in Locke's early writings a profound concern with the pervasive skepticism of his age. As David Wootton has pointed out, Locke "is engaged in an intimate dialogue with sceptical themes, sceptical arguments, and, we must presume, sceptical authors."[77] This should not come as a surprise to us, since the writings of Montaigne and Charron had gained a

[74] Locke, *Two Tracts on Government*, ed. Philip Abrams (London: Cambridge University Press, 1967). Cited throughout by TT followed by page number. Although two of Locke's nineteenth-century biographers, H. R. Fox Bourne and Lord Peter King, mention these manuscripts, they were not discovered until 1947, when the Bodleian Library acquired the Lovelace Collection of Locke's papers.

[75] Locke, *Essays on the Law of Nature*, ed. W. von Leyden (Oxford: Clarendon Press, 1954). This work will be cited as LN followed by page number. Locke's untitled notes on natural law were first published as "essays." More recently a new translation has offered a different ordering of Locke's short responses, calling them "questions" to emphasize the scholastic structure of this inquiry. See *Questions Concerning the Law of Nature*, ed. Robert H. Horwitz, Jenny Strauss Clay, and Diskin Clay (Ithaca, N.Y.: Cornell University Press, 1990).

[76] The first important listing of Locke's books, in 1681, includes several works by Montaigne and by his most famous disciple, Pierre Charron. Locke owned copies of Montaigne's *Essays* in the original French and in Florio's 1603 English translation. He also possessed the complete works of Charron, individual copies of his theological reflections, *Les trois veritez*, and his Montaigne-inspired philosophical opus, *La sagesse*, in French as well as a translation of *La sagesse* in English. John Harrison and Peter Laslett, *The Library of John Locke* (Oxford: Oxford University Press, 1965), 105–6, 91. Both Paul Rahe and Peter Myers trace an even more direct connection between Montaigne and Locke. Paul Rahe, *Republics Ancient and Modern* (Chapel Hill, N.C.: University of North Carolina Press, 1992), 272–73; Myers, *Our Only Star*, 24–25, 161–64.

[77] Wootton, introduction to Locke, *Political Writings*, 29. R. S. Woolhouse places Locke in a "tradition of constructive skepticism." R. S. Woolhouse, *John Locke* (Brighton: Harvester Press, 1983), 14. See also Marshall, *John Locke*, 31.

wide audience in England in the seventeenth century. To a certain extent, their brand of skepticism is an understandable response to intellectual upheaval and widespread conflict. And Locke and his contemporaries certainly experienced upheaval and conflict.

"I had no sooner found myself in the world," Locke writes in 1660, "than I perceived myself in a storm which hath lasted hitherto" (TT 119). In this intellectual whirlwind, Locke came to view appeals to the certainty of *scientia* or even the traditional authority of *opinio* as suspect. He was suspicious of all those who sought to justify their views by wrapping them in the language of rationality. In a letter to a friend written in 1659 he asserts, "Everyone's *recta ratio* is but the traverses of his own steps." We cannot justify our actions to others by rational argument since we cannot even agree "where or what reason is." Instead "'tis fancy that rules us all under the title of reason." According to the young Locke, men think and act the way they do because they are driven by fancy; they live according to their arbitrary opinions and parochial prejudices. "Men live upon trust, and their knowledge is nothing but opinion moulded up between custom and interest, the two great luminaries of the world, the only light they walk by."[78] Here we see Locke at his most skeptical. He collapses the ancient distinction between knowledge and opinion and insists that neither term has much to do with a common or universal faculty of reason. Knowledge is nothing but opinion, and opinion is irrational, arbitrary, and thoroughly subjective.

The skepticism that runs through much of his early correspondence is also evident in his early full-length manuscripts. In the *Two Tracts on Government*, Locke employs skeptical tropes to argue against the practicality of general toleration and in the *Essays on the Law of Nature*, he employs them to undermine the claim that we can know the content of the law of nature by inscription, tradition, or the general consent of mankind. Since both of these manuscripts are unfinished drafts containing certain tensions and ambiguities, they lend themselves to a whole range of interpretations. Yet it is undeniable that Locke gives voice to skeptical arguments in these texts and, like many skeptics before him, is driven to endorse existing religious and political institutions as the best means of staving off the destabilizing consequences of uncertainty.[79]

---

[78] Locke, *Correspondence*, 1:81.

[79] In her otherwise insightful study, Kirstie McClure comes to a very different conclusion about these early texts. By focusing on the more conventional aspects of these writings, she argues that assumptions concerning "an architecture of order" not unlike the older notion of the "great chain of being" lead Locke to make a series of confident assertions concerning humanity's place in God's design. McClure, *Judging Rights: Lockean Politics and the Limits of Consent* (Ithaca, N.Y.: Cornell University Press, 1996), 27–52. Although it is reasonable to believe that Locke remains committed to the notion of an ordered creation throughout

The immediate context of the *Tracts* is a rather technical question concerning the nature of *adiaphora* or "indifferent things" and the role of government in regulating them. "Indifferent things" were those things not expressly commanded by God as revealed by Scripture. They included such practices as the wearing of surplices, bowing at the name of Jesus, making the sign of the cross in baptism, and kneeling at communion. A fellow at Christ Church, Edward Bagshaw, had published an essay arguing that "indifferent things" should not be regulated by the magistrate; they should be left to the discretion of individuals and congregations. In two separate pieces, one written in 1660 in English and another in 1661 in Latin, Locke bitterly attacked Bagshaw's proposal for toleration and argued that order can only be maintained when the magistrate has "absolute and arbitrary" power concerning all aspects of religious doctrine and practice, including indifferent things.[80]

Locke's early work on natural law is not as cohesive or as polemical as the *Two Tracts*. His aim is not to delineate the content of morality, but rather to enquire into the way in which we come to know moral truths. Locke's unpublished notes were given the title *Essays on the Law of Nature* when they were first published in 1954, yet they read more like a series of dialectical disputations than separate essays or treatises.[81] The most plausible explanation of these writings is that they are the lecture notes that Locke prepared when he was the Censor of Moral Philosophy at Christ Church in 1664.[82] The fact that Locke never sought to publish his notes even when he was urged to do so by his friends points to the possibility that he believed they did not make up a single, unified, and conclusive argument. As Robert Horwitz has rightly pointed out, the notes are organized around scholastic puzzles or questions and, as is typi-

---

his life, McClure's account obscures Locke's anxiety concerning exactly how human beings access that order, an anxiety that pervades both these early texts and his mature work.

[80] Abrams notes in his introduction to the *Tracts* that Locke combines his defense of an almost limitless reach of political power with a conspicuous neglect of the proper ends of such power (TT 103).

[81] The title of the more recent publication of these notes, *Questions Concerning the Law of Nature*, perhaps better captures their scholastic character. Yet one could certainly argue that Locke is here engaged in a Montaigne-inspired "essay" or "attempt" to explore the origins and implications of natural law. Like Montaigne, he offers tentative and perhaps even aporetic conclusions.

[82] In his Censorial Address delivered in 1664, Locke leaves little doubt that he guided his students in disputations on the law of nature during that year: "The law about which was all our strife had often eluded my fruitless quest, had not your way of life restored that very same law which your tongue had wrestled from me. . . . Hence it can be doubted whether your disputations assaulted the law of nature or your behaviour defended it, more keenly." Locke, "Censor's Valedictory Speech" (LN 237–39). Since this speech is contained in the same notebook as his notes on the law of nature, it is reasonable to assume that they are most likely the notes that he prepared for use with his students and later transcribed.

cal for scholastic disputation, they address a variety of sometimes conflicting arguments.[83] Although Locke answers each question with either an affirmation or negation, he supplies arguments in some sections that seem to undermine conclusions that he reaches in others. Most importantly he insists that our reason can and should lead us to identify our moral obligations, yet he goes out of his way to illustrate the limits and pitfalls of human rationality.[84]

Although the *Two Tracts* and the *Essays on the Law of Nature* were composed for very different purposes, they contain similar skeptical elements. In both texts Locke imitates Montaigne and Charron in drawing on ancient sources as well as contemporary travel literature to emphasize the bewildering variety of human customs and practices and to discredit simplistic appeals to universally recognized moral standards.[85] He insists that neither inscription, nor custom, nor general consent can serve as the basis for universal agreement concerning moral norms. Those who argue that all human beings have principles of morality inscribed onto their souls are unable to articulate those principles substantively without inspiring disagreement.[86] Those who insist that tradition or the general agreement of humanity can provide us with a clear set of ethical imperatives are fooling themselves. If we survey the diversity of human behavior, Locke argues, we will see that there is simply no such thing as a universally accepted principle of morality.

Although Locke forcefully articulates skeptical arguments in these early texts, he does not present himself as a thoroughgoing skeptic. In his notes on the law of nature, he insists that human beings have access to moral truths through reason. He argues that we can derive our moral obligations from the "matter, motion, and the visible structure and arrangement

[83] Horwitz, introduction to Locke, *Questions Concerning the Law of Nature*, 50–53.

[84] Richard Ashcraft, among others, has read this work as an unambiguous defense of traditional natural law teachings. Richard Ashcraft, *Locke's Two Treatises of Government* (London: Allen & Unwin, 1987), 36–44. It is true that Locke affirms that there is such a law and that it is binding. He also frets about the consequences of denying such a law. Yet at the same time, he turns his listeners' attention to the difficulties of gaining knowledge of this law. In fact, the majority of the work turns out to be a careful attack on traditional defenses of the law.

[85] John Harrison and Peter Laslett report that Locke had at least 195 books on travel, exploration, and geography. There are more indications, such as bookmarks or notations, that Locke actually read these works than those of any other category in his collection. Harrison and Laslett, *Library of John Locke*, 27–29.

[86] Locke originally included an argument in the first section of his notes based on a long quotation from Hugo Grotius that morality is rooted in our "common nature" rather than convention. Yet he later deleted this entire passage, perhaps because it directly conflicts with other arguments that he employs. The deleted passage is included as an appendix to von Leyden's collection of *Essays* (LN 282–83).

of this world" (LN 133; see also folio 147). Here we can see intimations of a line of reasoning that he will later develop in *An Essay Concerning Human Understanding* and *Of the Conduct of the Understanding*—that truth is accessible to the disciplined human mind and that disagreement is the result of individuals not making proper use of their rational faculties. The most obvious point of Locke's lectures on natural law is that there is indeed such a law and it is knowable by human beings. Yet in order to see that Locke's arguments actually subvert that law as it had been understood by many of his predecessors, we should compare it to a defense of natural law advanced by the Anglican divine Richard Hooker (whom Locke would later quote often and favorably).

In his main work, *Of the Laws of Ecclesiastical Polity*, Hooker sets out to navigate between the dogmatic appeals to infallibility made by many of his Catholic contemporaries and the subversive appeals to individual encounter with Scripture made by Calvinists. The middle way that Hooker offers rests on the possibility of an uncontroversial standard, the law of nature. We find the best treatment of this approach in the eighth chapter of book 1, entitled "Of the Natural Way of Finding Out Laws by Reason to Guide the Will unto That Which Is Good." The claim of this chapter is that there is a "law of nature, meaning thereby the law which human nature knoweth itself in reason universally bound unto, which also for that cause may be termed most fitly the law of reason."[87] In order to answer the thorny question of how human beings acquire knowledge of this law, Hooker says that we can understand this process in two ways: we can see what people actually believe, what judgments they actually come to about the law of nature, or we can investigate the process of reasoning to those judgments itself. He says that "the most certain token of evident goodness is if the general persuasion of all men do so account it."[88] For Hooker, general or universal agreement characterizes natural law. When we find the things that the varying peoples of the world agree on, we will find a universal law that is true for all times and all places. Given the universality of that law, we will be able to say that it is also God's will: "the general and perpetual voice of men is as the sentence of God himself."[89] This is because "that which all men have at all times learned, Nature herself must needs have taught; and God being the author of Nature, her voice is but his instrument."[90] This *a posteriori*

---

[87] Richard Hooker, *Of the Laws of Ecclesiastical Polity*, ed. Arthur Stephen McGrade (Cambridge: Cambridge University Press, 1989), I.viii.9.

[88] Ibid., I.viii.3.

[89] Ibid.

[90] Ibid.

proof is the first and most obvious way for us to reach the law of nature, according to Hooker.

The second way to understand the law of nature is to investigate the way we reason to this law. Here Hooker provides us with a type of *a priori* method. Since Hooker thinks that there cannot be an infinite regress of reasons, there must be some reason or set of reasons upon which we base our arguments. There must be what he calls "axioms" that are "so manifest that they need no further proof."[91] Such axioms are immediately apparent or self-evident, such as "the greater good is to be chose before the less." The problem with this appeal is that there is no way to argue whether these axioms are right or not. We are just expected to know. Some other axioms that Hooker lists, for example, "God is to be worshipped" or "Parents to be honored," are much less obvious or self-evident. In fact they begin to sound very culturally specific.[92] With Locke, this cultural specificity becomes increasingly evident when he discovers peoples who manage to get by without worshipping a god and parents and children who relate to one another in ways that clearly diverge from Hooker's supposedly universal axioms.

Of course it is possible that Hooker could have made the argument that there is a natural law even though individuals rarely recognize it as such. To put it in theological language more appropriate for Hooker, he could have claimed that there is a natural law but it is not promulgated as such by God to human beings. In fact, Thomas Aquinas considered this very possibility in the *Summa*.[93] Perhaps natural law could reflect the natural order of things without being readily accessible to the human mind. Yet both Aquinas and Hooker categorically reject this possibility. They argue that a law "in the fullest sense of the word" can only be effectual if it is set down as law by some intentional being and known as such. That is, a law has to be applied to have force, and promulgation is the application of law. Aquinas and Hooker could here have concluded that natural law is thus not a law "in the fullest sense." Instead they insist that natural law has been promulgated. How does this take place? As Aquinas puts it, "the natural law is promulgated by the very fact that God instilled it into man's mind so as to be known by him naturally."[94] Both Aquinas and Hooker embrace the argument that natural law is somehow engraved on the minds or hearts of all people. What at first seems to be the unwritten law of nature, in contrast to the written laws of societies, is actually written in its own way in the minds of men. For Hooker an appeal to the law

[91] Ibid., I.viii.5.
[92] Ibid.
[93] Aquinas, *Summa* I-II q.90 art. 4.
[94] Ibid.

of nature seems to be the best solution to the conflicting authorities of Catholicism and Calvinism because it offers a shared standard that was reflected in the universal agreement of humankind and could be traced to innate axioms that are inscribed in each human heart.

Yet the young Locke was already uncomfortable with this solution. In his notes on the natural law he cannot accept that natural law reflects a universal consensus or that it is written in our hearts. While he continues to insist that there is such thing as natural law, he does not, or cannot, provide a complete and convincing explanation of how our limited faculties can gain access to universally valid standard. In fact, he goes so far as to refer to the laws of nature as "hidden and unperceived" (LN 115). A flood of skeptical arguments and themes seems to overwhelm any intimations he makes concerning the possibility of rational justification. It is true that in the final section of the manuscript, Locke explicitly criticizes a position of self-interest that he associates with the Academic skeptic Carneades.[95] Yet this criticism is hardly a rebuttal of skepticism generally, since the majority of the arguments and evidence that he presents throughout the text seems to support the skeptical point of view. Wootton points out that although the young Locke seems to seek solutions to the problems posed by radical skeptics, he "accepts fully the sceptical account of what the world is actually like."[96]

And that world, according to Locke and his skeptical predecessors, is one of seemingly infinite diversity and endless disagreement. "Our deformity is others' beauty," Locke writes in the first *Tract*, "our rudeness others' civility, and there is nothing so uncouth and unhandsome to us which doth not somewhere or other find applause and approbation" (TT 146). In the second *Tract* he reiterates this sentiment: "For in different places different customs prevail, and a constant rule and standard could not possibly have been laid down in the divine law which would make clear what was proper for the several nations and what was not" (TT 216). He goes even further in his notes on the law of nature, declaring that

> there is almost no vice, no infringement of natural law, no moral wrong, which anyone who consults the history of the world and observes the affairs of men will not readily perceive to have been not only privately committed somewhere on earth, but also approved by public authority and custom. Nor has there been anything so shameful in its nature that it has not been either sanctified

[95] Richard Tuck argues that Grotius, Pufendorf, and others use the figure of Carneades as a stand-in for the type of skepticism exhibited by Montaigne and Charron. Richard Tuck, "Grotius, Carneades and Hobbes," *Grotiana* 4 (1983), 43–62. See also Zuckert, *Natural Rights and the New Republicanism* (Princeton: Princeton University Press, 1994), 134–36, 146–48.

[96] Wootton, introduction to Locke, *Political Writings*, 29.

somewhere by religion, or put in the place of virtue and abundantly rewarded with praise. (LN 167)[97]

Locke argues that it is impossible to infer a universal standard of behavior or a criterion of rationality by observing the practices of human beings for the simple reason that they are so emphatically diverse.

To drive his point home, Locke provides us with a list of specific exceptions to any moral principle that we might consider a universally recognized standard of behavior or belief. In passages that could just as easily have been written by Montaigne or Charron, Locke sets out to show that moral responsibility, sexual purity, familial obligation, and religious belief can mean many different things to peoples situated in various historical periods and geographical locations. Throughout his life, Locke was a tireless reader of ancient and contemporary histories, travel books, and journals. He spent a good deal of his energy collecting ethnographic references to the sheer diversity of human practices. In his early lecture notes, he summarizes some of his findings. According to his sources, piracy and theft was lawful and reputable for ancient Egyptians and Spartans. Debauchery was permitted and even encouraged for unwed women in some places of the world. Among particular tribes of Ethiopia, the institution of marriage had no place at all, and in other nations, the bridal bed was consecrated by all the wedding guests. In Sardinia sons killed their fathers when they reached a certain age, and in other lands, parents left their female infants to die. And finally, for some tribes in Brazil as well as inhabitants of Soldania Bay in South Africa, the very idea of God was foreign (LN 177–79).[98] Although neither Montaigne nor Charron is among those Locke makes explicit reference to, his list is almost identical in tone and in detail to inventories in Montaigne's *Essays* and Charron's *Of Wisdom*.[99] Just as Montaigne took pains to show that "custom is the

---

[97] According to Wootton, this is almost a paraphrase of a passage from one of the most famous skeptics of the century, Pierre Charron. In his influential text *Of Wisdom,* Charron writes: "witness the fact that whatever is held to be impious, unjust, disgraceful in one place, is pious, just and honourable in another; one cannot name a single law, custom, belief which is universally either approved or condemned." *Of Wisdom*, trans. Samson Lennard (London: Edward Blount & Will, 1630), I.16.

[98] Locke uses some of this same material in the first book of his *Essay Concerning Human Understanding* in order to show that there is no such thing as innate principles. Locke insists that it is simply impossible to establish a universal consent on moral truths. Any who "have been but moderately conversant in the History of Mankind, and look'd abroad beyond the Smoak of their own Chimneys" must admit that no single set of moral truths is held by all peoples at all times. Even such horrific practices as eating one's own children have been accepted by some (E I.iii.2).

[99] For strikingly similar lists of diverse ethical imperatives, sexual mores, familial duties, and religious beliefs, see Montaigne, *Essays*, I.12, I.30, II.12, III.5; and Charron, *Of Wisdom*, I.8, I.41–47. Although Locke does not cite these texts directly, he does make reference

queen and empress of the world,"[100] Locke points to the shocking diversity of human practices in order to undermine our confidence in any illusory appeals to universally recognized standards of virtue and rationality.

The young Locke recognized, just as skeptics before him did, that the multiplicity of practices and beliefs can be extremely destabilizing politically, religiously, and morally. A clash of customs can often lead to violent conflict, since men and women do not give up their most cherished ancestral habits and religious practices easily. In the *Tracts* Locke writes, "He that will open his eyes upon any country or age but his own will presently see that they are ready to fight and venture their lives for that in some places which we should laugh at here" (TT 146). Locke recounts a story about the inhabitants of a city in China who were forced to surrender to an enemy and had agreed to give up their wives, families, liberty, and wealth. Yet when their captors demanded that they cut the plait of hair that they wore in keeping with national custom, they took up arms again and fought until every last one of them was killed (TT 217). Locke presents this story in order to illustrate the power of tradition and custom to make men act in ways that are destructive to themselves and their communities. He recognizes that traditional practices can be so entrenched that people are more apt to give up their lives than renounce their traditions: "But in fact the power of custom and of opinion based on traditional ways of life is such as to arm men even against their own selves, so that they lay violent hands upon themselves and seek death as eagerly as others shun it" (LN 173).

Yet Locke and his contemporaries did not need to consult accounts of ancient civilizations or faraway lands to see that differences in practice and belief can disrupt political order and lead to violent conflict. A bewildering assortment of dissenting religious groups had emerged before their eyes, and debates between these groups over what constitutes true doctrine and authentic practice had become the focal point of public attention. "He must confess himself a stranger to England," Locke writes, "that thinks that *meats* and *habits*, that *places* and *times* of worship, etc., would not be sufficient occasion of hatred and quarrels amongst us" (TT 121). Calvinist Puritans had long denounced Anglican ceremonies and hierarchies as popish pomp, and quarrels over these matters had contributed to the Civil War. Yet other groups such as the Adamites, Ranters, Seekers, and early Quakers went even further, rejecting the authority of church tradition, Scripture, and even conventional morality. Some prac-

---

to the same collections of ancient sources, such as Aulus Gellius's *Attic Nights* and Gaius Julius Solinus's *Collectanea rerum memorabilium*, sources that were often used by Montaigne's followers.

[100] Montaigne, *Essays*, I.23.83.

ticed "holy nudity," renouncing the "carnal" institutions of chastity and marriage. Others threatened economic and social order by refusing to pay tithes, to recognize social superiors, or to take oaths of loyalty. And still others called for open revolt against the government.

Locke experienced these contending religious factions firsthand. In 1656 he attended the trial of one of the most prominent religious radicals in his day and a leading figure in the early Quaker movement, James Nayler. Nayler is reported to have born a striking resemblance to paintings of Jesus Christ of the period. After traveling and preaching with George Fox for several years, he proclaimed himself the Son of God and was led into Bristol on a donkey by women shouting "Hosanna." Parliament, fearing the dangerous consequences of allowing such a man to gather supporters in an uncertain political climate, had Nayler and his entourage arrested. Nayler was tried, convicted, and punished for blasphemy and fraud. In his account of the trial, Locke seems to be both fascinated and perplexed by Nayler's "uncouth and unusual expression" and threatening exhortations.[101] A few years later, Locke and his contemporaries encountered an even more menacing group of dissenters, the Fifth Monarchy Men. Members of this group believed that the execution of Charles I had ushered in a new "Golden Age" in which England would be ruled by a "church-parliament." When their hopes seemed to be dashed with the Restoration of Charles II, a group of Fifth Monarchists attempted to overthrow the new government in London. After four days of fierce fighting in the beginning of January 1661, the rebels were captured and executed. One hundred and fifty Fifth Monarchy Men and some 4,000 Quaker supporters were imprisoned.[102]

For Locke, these events confirmed his skeptical suspicion that the limits of human reason combined with the power of custom create conditions of political instability and religious violence. Conscience, he argues in the *Tracts*, is "nothing but an opinion of the truth" (TT 138), and when subjects are allowed to act as their conscience leads them, chaos is sure to ensue. Locke insists that "if private men's judgments were to be the moulds wherein laws were to be cast, it is a question whether we should have any at all" (TT 137). Such judgments are nothing more than "our own wills or fancies" (TT 148). The upshot of Locke's argu-

---

[101] Locke, *Correspondence*, 1:30. For an account of James Nayler in the context of the rise of the Quaker movement, see William Charles Braithwaite and Henry Joel Cadbury, *The Beginnings of Quakerism* (Cambridge: Cambridge University Press, 1961).

[102] The revolt of the Fifth Monarchy Men was named "Venner's Rising" after their leader Thomas Venner. For an informative account, see B. S. Capp, "The Fifth Monarchists and the Popular Millenarianism," in *Radical Religion in the English Revolution*, ed. J. F. McGregor and Barry Reay (Oxford: Oxford University Press, 1986). The collection includes several articles on other important dissident groups as well.

ment, then, is that any expression of dissent from the magistrate's will is indistinguishable from rebellion (TT 136). In times of uncertainty and doubt, "hot-headed" sectarians can manipulate religious practices and misuse doctrine for their own self-serving purposes. Under the pretense of instituting a reformation of "the errors of religion," "crafty men" and "zealous partisans" seek to "arm the rash folly of the ignorant and passionate multitude" and thus subvert the political order (TT 120, 160–62, 170, 211). The exploitation of religious differences can open the door to bloody conflict. For Locke, "Almost all those tragical revolutions which have exercised Christendom these many years have turned upon this hinge, that there hath been no design so wicked which hath not worn the visor of religion, nor rebellion which hath not been so kind to itself as to assume the specious name of reformation" (TT 160). Locke argues that cherished customs and practices, especially religious ones, are especially vulnerable to misuse and manipulation by those who seek political power. There is "no cause that can so rationally draw [people] to hazard this life, or compound the dangers of war" as can devotion to religious practices combined with the promise of eternal reward (TT 160).

For the young Locke, a society that contains a diversity of customs and forms of worship is inherently unstable. While it would be wonderful if men "would suffer one another to go to heaven every one his own way," his study of history and his observations of his fellow human beings convinced him that this is not the nature of religious devotion.[103] Any group that holds particular doctrines and practices as sacred will naturally seek to dominate others. "Grant the people once free and unlimited in the exercise of their religion and where will they stop?" Locke asks (TT 158). His answer is clear: they will not stop until they "destroy all that are not of their profession" (TT 159). For, "the multitude . . . are as impatient of restraint as the sea . . . always craving, never satisfied," and nothing can be "set over them which they will not always be reaching out and endeavoring to pull down" (TT 159). Since most men lack a sense of discipline, order, and authority, liberty would lead to anarchy. The "ignorant multitude" is but an "untamed beast" composed of individuals who "know not how to set bounds to their restless spirits if persecution hang not over their heads" (TT 169). For this reason, religious liberty "would prove a liberty for contention, censure, and persecution. And turn us loose to the tyranny of a religious rage." A "general freedom" Locke insists, "is but a general bondage" (TT 120).

---

[103] In a letter written in 1659 to Hobbes's associate, Henry Stubbe, Locke implies that he might be sympathetic to the idea of toleration theoretically. *Correspondence*, 1:75. Yet his experience of the contentious battles over religious practice during the Restoration must have convinced him that such a policy would be impracticable. By 1660 he was persuaded that any sensible magistrate would seek to impose uniformity.

Dubious about the possibility of rational public deliberation that could help individuals "set bounds to their restless spirits," and fearful of the disorder and anarchy that could result from widespread disagreement, Locke follows a well-trodden skeptical path. He recommends obedience to established religious and political institutions. In fact, in these early writings, dissent in any form is seen as illegitimate. There is simply no condition of tyranny so abhorrent and oppressive that would invalidate Locke's insistence on absolute obedience.[104] In the uncertain atmosphere of the Restoration, the established authorities were moving toward the implementation of an extremely strict policy of uniformity and repression that would come to be known as the Clarendon Code. Faced with revolt and rumors of revolt, Locke echoes many of his contemporaries in emphasizing the need for an unlimited governmental power to impose religious orthodoxy and political unity. In spite of occasional rationalist statements in his writings on natural law, the young Locke approached public disagreement in ways that are strikingly similar to skeptics like Montaigne and Charron. This skepticism went hand in hand with a certain type of political conservatism that values stability and authority above all else.

It is within this context that we should understand Locke's support of the Anglican Church in his early writings. Although he describes the prewar Church of England as the "purest church in the latter age" and conforms to it during the Restoration, his devotion has much more to do with a general tendency toward obedience than with the particulars of theology or ecclesiology (TT 127).[105] The actual content of church doctrine and practice does not seem to interest Locke at all. The polarizing theological arguments of the day concerning church ceremony are brushed aside with a condescending quip. Wearing a surplice might "add but little heat to the body," Locke writes, "but I know not why it should chill our devotions" (TT 127). In another piece that he wrote in 1661 or

[104] Locke goes so far as to insist that even if the magistrate is "indulging his own cruelty or greed or vanity" by introducing "a law only to enrich himself, to abuse his subjects," the subject is still bound "even to an active obedience" to the ruler's command (TT 220). Ashcraft points out that in the context of the toleration debates in Locke's day, "there simply is no position to the right or more conservative than this one." Ashcraft, *Revolutionary Politics & Locke's Two Treatises of Government* (Princeton: Princeton University Press, 1986), 92.

[105] Abrams emphasizes the Anglican character of Locke's discussion by pointing out that many arguments that Locke rehearses in the *Two Tracts* were gleaned from revered Anglican authorities such as Richard Hooker and Robert Sanderson (TT 71–72). Yet in contrast to Hooker and Sanderson, Locke has no vision of a particularly Anglican polity in these pages. In fact, he reveals a deep suspicion of priestly power that he maintains throughout his life. It is important to note that Locke never endorses the authority of the church, only the authority of the magistrate over religious affairs.

early 1662, Locke concedes that there are many Christian mysteries "the truth of which is certain and is to be believed, but the way in which they are true cannot be expressed in discourse nor grasped by the mind."[106] Faced with the limits of rational discourse and the difficulties of religious doctrine, Locke follows Montaigne and Charron in recommending compliance to existing institutions. The "path of obedience is safe and secure."[107]

Political stability, Locke contends, can only be ensured by the forceful imposition of order meted out by a coercive authority. The "tyranny of religious rage" can only be restrained by the "absolute and arbitrary power" of the magistrate (TT 121). In the same way that young Locke is indifferent to the actual content of religious doctrine and practice that should be enforced, he is also indifferent to the structure of government that should enforce conformity. In the *Tracts*, he tells his readers that it does not matter whether the political authority is a single monarch crowned by divine dispensation or a king-in-Parliament chosen by general consent. Regardless of its form, it is essential that the political authority enjoy unlimited and absolute power. "Society, government and order" depend on it (TT 125).

Locke recognizes that the existence of an absolute and unlimited state power might be inconvenient and perhaps even oppressive for subjects. Yet he takes a position familiar to us from Hobbes but articulated by Charron as well—regardless of the disadvantages of an absolute state authority, the alternative is worse.[108] Of course, there are certain inconveniences to a sovereign that forces a man "to hold his life as a tenant at will and to be ready to part with his head when it shall be demanded" (TT 156). Yet Locke insists that such disadvantages are insignificant compared to the "stinging swarms of miseries that attend anarchy and rebellion" (TT 156). Even the prospect that a ruler might be an Egyptian taskmaster does not deter him from his position. The duty of the subject is not to "intrude into the council chamber" but "cheerfully to obey the commands of the magistrate" (TT 159). Resistance is never legitimate,

---

[106] Locke, "Infallibility," in *Political Essays*, 208–9.

[107] Ibid., 209.

[108] Locke's absolutist statements are often cited as evidence of Hobbes's early influence on him. It is undeniable that Hobbes expresses these sentiments in strikingly similar language. See Thomas Hobbes, *Leviathan*, ed. Richard Tuck (Cambridge: Cambridge University Press, 1991), II.19 and II.26. Yet Charron also makes this type of case for absolute state authority in *Of Wisdom*, and it is possible that Charron could have been the one to influence Locke. In any case, it is almost certain that Charron's writings had an influence on Hobbes. See Richard Tuck, "Optics and Sceptics: The Philosophical Foundations of Hobbes's Political Thought," in *Conscience and Casuistry in Early Modern Europe*, ed. Edmund Leites (Cambridge: Cambridge University Press, 1988), 235–63; and Paul Grendler, "Pierre Charron: Precursor to Hobbes," *Review of Politics* 25 (1963), 212–24.

whatever the structure or origin of the ruler's authority may be. In these early texts, the skepticism that Locke articulates goes hand in hand with political absolutism. In the absence of a language of justification in which matters of public importance can be weighed and considered, the only way to ensure order is through coercive governmental power.

In December 1664, Locke completed his term as Censor of Moral Philosophy at Christ Church and delivered his valedictory speech, as was the custom, in the form of a mock funeral oration. With a morbid light-heartedness not unlike that of Montaigne, he begins by asserting that he is happy to step down from his position. He is happy to die. His life as Censor had been an unhappy and futile search for the firm foundations of moral truths in a vast ocean of uncertainty. "Many things are found there," he explains, "delightful in variety, stupendous in depth, with which you may divert the mind, but wherever you betake yourself so as to rest there with certainty, you will find nothing stable, nothing firmly fixed, and the endless waves, abounding on all sides and overwhelming, toss the uneasy and anxious mind."[109] Locke contends that the philosophical odyssey that he had undertaken with his students did not uncover indubitable foundations or generate agreement. It revealed only that such foundations are beyond our grasp: "philosophy holds out many riches, but they all are mere words rather than the property of men. Those pointed and shrewd discourses concerning the highest good do not heal human misfortunes any more than fist and sword cure wounds. . . . Philosophers in their search for happiness have not accomplished more than to tell us that it cannot be found" (TT 221–23). Unable to attain certainty by means of our own intellectual power, it is our sad fate to be "torn asunder and set in arms against one another" (TT 229). The message of this speech is very clear: the uncertainty of philosophy leads to discord. The best earthly response to this discord is the establishment of a stable and powerful political authority, yet death is the only sure way to escape the disorder and disagreement of this world. And so after many words of gratitude to his various pallbearers, Locke accepts his fate and breathes out his last cares as a teacher of moral philosophy.

Although the tone of Locke's speech is clearly ironic, perhaps there is a certain gravity to his playfulness. The pessimism that he articulates here echoes the skeptical arguments and themes that are so prevalent in his early writings. Locke emphasizes the difficulty, if not impossibility, of rational inquiry given the seemingly endless variety of beliefs and prac-

---

[109] "Locke's Valedictory Speech" (LN 223). Surprisingly, scholars rarely attend to the claims made in this important speech. Perhaps the ironic tone has discouraged Locke's often sober commentators from taking it seriously. Yet the view that he conveys here parallels the anxious skepticism found throughout his early writings and correspondences.

tices in the world. Indisputably certain knowledge of moral and political truths seems to be beyond our grasp. Without a common understanding of reason to appeal to, the only way to ensure order in this life is through the coercive power of the state. The only release from that coercion is death. The young Locke shows a keen awareness of the moral and religious incommensurability that characterized the collapse of the scholastic vocabulary of justification. His response is a typically skeptical one. In order to ensure a provisional order in this world, he appeals to the absolute and unlimited authority of existing political and religious institutions.

III

Reworking Reasonableness

THE AUTHORITATIVE TESTIMONY OF NATURE

IN HIS EARLIEST WRITINGS, we find Locke responding to the collapse of moral and intellectual authority by appealing to the ordering power of the state. He insists that external coercion is the only way to achieve security and stability in the context of radical disagreement. Although he does not reject the possibility that human beings can discover moral obligations through reason, he is pessimistic about the possibility. Without a common vocabulary of public reason, a shared source of intellectual authority, sovereign power is needed to fill the void. Only the imposition of force can create unity where no rational consensus can be achieved.[1] Yet for the mature Locke and for the liberal tradition that followed in his wake, those who are governed are expected to make the type of reasonable judgments that sustain a political community in the context of disagreement or uncertainty. In fact the legitimacy of the state rests on the considered judgment of its subjects. Neither the skeptical abandonment of rational justification nor the rationalist quest for absolute certainty captures how we should assess political and legal affairs. Reasonable people, the mature Locke assures us, avoid the extremes of radical skepticism and fanatical rationalism. They know that skepticism demands too much, rationalism attempts to supply it, and in its failure, rationalism makes skepticism look misleadingly appealing. Reasonable judgment need not rest on apodictic certainty. Locke's public reason sidesteps abstract debate over ultimate causes and concerns itself instead with determining whether something is more or less probable.

Of course the mature Locke does not reject the notion that there is an authoritative source that stands behind our moral and political principles. He insists that government is only legitimate insofar as it conforms with the law of nature, which he also refers to as the voice of God. Legitimate government does not simply rest on the presence of consent; it rests on reasonable consent. For Locke this means that public judgment must

---

[1] Richard Tuck explores the ways in which "excessive ideological repression" could be justified by moral and religious skepticism. Richard Tuck, "Scepticism and Toleration in the Seventeenth Century," in *Justifying Toleration: Conceptual and Historical Perspectives,* ed. Susan Mendus (Cambridge: Cambridge University Press 1988), 21–35.

be educated. Political justification is intimately tied to intellectual cultivation. As Locke puts it, legitimate government requires a public capable of setting "the mind right, that on all occasions it may be disposed to consent to nothing but what may be suitable to the dignity and excellency of a rational creature" (CU 31).

Yet for Locke the process of "setting the mind right" does not consist of constructing demonstrative proofs. It involves training the faculty of judgment to assess matters of public importance in the context of uncertainty and to assent only to that which conforms to their characters as free and rational individuals. In this way Lockean agents can come to understand themselves as public judges, capable of deliberating over political and moral affairs in the absence of metaphysical agreement. They can be expected to arrive at reasonable conclusions concerning political power, moral duty, and legitimate consent based on their probable judgment of the contingent world around them. For Locke, as we will see, reasonable citizens proportion their assent to the available evidence, recognizing that such evidence might render a proposition probable, but never absolutely certain. They accept particular claims concerning public affairs while granting that they may someday have good reason to change their minds. When faced with difficult political or ethical choices, they are responsible for making sound judgments based on what they can see and hear and what they can deduce from credible witnesses. The type of "reasonableness" that sustains the Lockean project involves attaining probable assurance based on the authoritative testimony of nature. In *An Essay Concerning Human Understanding* as well as *Of the Conduct of the Understanding*, we find a language of rational appraisal emerging, one that makes probability a crucial, if not primary, criterion of judgment.

What made this change possible? What made probable claims "reasonable" again? The renewed confidence in probable judgment that we find in Locke and his contemporaries is the result of a changing conception of authority in respect to testimony and evidence that began to emerge in the seventeenth century.[2] This new type of probability emerges out of the

---

[2] Until recently, the literature on the history of probability has been dominated by Ian Hacking, who argued in a brilliant but flawed book that modern probability first took form in the second half of the seventeenth century. Ian Hacking, *The Emergence of Probability: A Philosophical Study of Early Ideas about Probability, Induction and Statistical Inference* (Cambridge: Cambridge University Press, 1975). Many critics have pointed out Hacking's failure to account for similar types of probable reasoning already at work in the medieval world, especially in the legal realm. Hacking is surely mistaken to insist on the radical discontinuity of seventeenth-century notions of probability, yet he is right to point out a crucial shift at the time that affected thinkers in many fields of inquiry. Several subsequent works have provided a more balanced account of the spread of probable argument in the seventeenth century, especially in England. See Shapiro, *Probability and Certainty*; Lorraine Daston, "Probability and Evidence," in *The Cambridge History of Seventeenth-Century*

discredited vocabulary of *scientia* and *opinio*, yet provides an alternative to the scholastic dichotomy. Whereas earlier views of probable reasoning relied on common experience or belief articulated through the approved opinions of textual authorities, later thinkers refer to evidence and testimony that is distinct from the reputation of ancient textual sources. This testimony, what Robert Boyle calls "the testimony of nature," is preferable because it seems less entangled in the problem of multiple and contending authorities. In the midst of debate over traditional sources, the authority of ancient authors could be supplanted by the authority of the Supreme Author, deciphered by carefully studying the "divine book of nature." In this way, the new probability retains the structure of the scholastic category of *opinio* while distancing itself from the contested claims of authoritative texts. By emphasizing the probable evidence of nature's testimony, natural historians and experimentalists preceding Locke began to shift natural philosophy out of its traditional place as scholastic *scientia* and toward the realm of probability. This shift toward probability resonated in England throughout the fields of theology, history, and law.[3] By the late seventeenth century, it was philosophically respectable to endorse truth claims that were neither mathematically nor metaphysically certain.

The transformation of testimony and evidence was closely linked to a growing emphasis on "facts" and "matters of fact." The language of "fact" spread from the legal realm into history, theology, and natural science at the same time that it underwent a substantial shift in meaning. Originally the Latin word, *factum*, meant deed or action. In most European vernaculars, the term was derived from verbs meaning "to do" or "to make."[4] Prior to the seventeenth century, a "fact" was what someone did or was alleged to have done. Throughout the medieval period, the term was employed in the Roman and canonical legal tradition in which "matters of fact" were distinguished from "matters of law."[5] This

---

Philosophy, ed. Daniel Garber and Michael Ayers, 2 vols. (Cambridge: Cambridge University Press, 1998), 2:1108–44; Lorraine Daston, *Classical Probability and the Enlightenment* (Princeton: Princeton University Press, 1988); Serjeantson, "Testimony and Proof"; and Franklin, *The Science of Conjecture*.

[3] The is the general argument of Barbara Shapiro's work, *Probability and Certainty in Seventeenth-Century England*. For an opposing view, see W. A. Wallace, "The Certitude of Science in Late Medieval and Renaissance Thought," *History of Philosophy Quarterly* 3 (1986), 281–91.

[4] The original link between fact and doing or making—between fact and artifact—is evident in Latin as well as other major European vernaculars, for example, *facere/factum, faire/fait, fare/fatto, tun/Tatsache*. English also bears traces of this usage in terms such as "feat" and the legal term "after the fact."

[5] See Barbara J. Shapiro, *A Culture of Fact: England, 1550–1720* (Ithaca, N.Y.: Cornell University Press, 2000), 8–33. Shapiro argues that the concept of "fact" first took shape in the courts and then migrated into other intellectual spheres such as history, natural phi-

distinction was subsequently institutionalized in English law as well. For medieval and early modern courts, a "matter of fact," such as a robbery or murder, was an alleged act that might or might not be established by testimony and evidence. The testimony and evidence offered by credible witnesses provided grounds for judging the plausibility of a fact, yet could not demonstrate a fact with certainty. The courts, as always, were forced to make judgments in the context of uncertainty.

From the beginning, the language of "facts" was intimately tied to the weighing of testimony. Following guidelines derived from classical rhetoric, legal practitioners sought to determine the probable weight of particular testimony by referring to signs or *indicia* surrounding a fact in question. These signs, such as the age, gender, education, occupation, social status, or reputation of the witness, were used to determine the reliability of testimony or evidence. Just as Scholastics and humanists appealed to the reputation of approved textual authorities to justify probable arguments, practitioners of law appealed to the testimony of trustworthy witnesses based on signs. The practice of using signs to substantiate the testimony of facts was widespread in courts throughout Europe. On the continent, where "irrational proofs," such as the trial by ordeal, were replaced by an inquisition process in the twelfth century, professional judges sought "full proof" by adding up the number of credible witnesses to a fact based on *indicia*.[6] In England, where facts were adjudicated by jury trials, jurors were considered "judges of the fact" and expected to determine for themselves whether the "fact" in a case warranted belief, that is, whether it was supported by sufficient testimony and evidence.

Over the course of the seventeenth century, the language of "fact" spread into many other intellectual realms.[7] Theologians and historians established facts by assessing the character and credibility of witnesses. Following a long tradition of legal practice, they marshaled trustworthy testimony in order to provide substantiating evidence for probable judgment. Eventually the term came to refer to natural or physical events as well. Practitioners of medicine, chemistry, and biology begin to use

---

losophy, and theology in the seventeenth century. Alternatively, R. W. Serjeantson, in "Testimony and Proof," emphasizes the role of rhetoric in the growing appeal to both testimony and fact in contrast to law. Yet this seems to be a distinction without a difference since the spheres of law and rhetoric were intertwined in the ancient world, and guidelines used to evaluate testimony were used both in the practice of the courts and in the writings of rhetoricians.

[6] Since self-testimony, or confession, carried a particularly high evidentiary value, torture was often employed to attain "full proof." The English system, which relied on the probable judgment of juries, was less likely to result in the torture of the accused.

[7] Shapiro argues that "the absorption and spread of 'fact' in England was facilitated by widespread familiarity with and esteem for lay fact finding by juries." Historians, theologians, and experimentalists, as well as their readers, were comfortable with judging testimony in order to assess facts. Shapiro, *A Culture of Fact*, 209.

the term to describe what they observe in the natural world. The notion of fact was especially appealing to those who sought to defend a claim without providing the type of comprehensive explanation characterized by scholastic science. Facts fit well with this new type of probable judgment. Implicit in seventeenth-century appeals to "matters of fact" was the assumption that it is possible to gain adequate, albeit less than certain, insight into the workings of the world. It was a way to sidestep contentious arguments about the underlying causes of an action or event, and refer simply to the event itself, the "fact."

Yet the use of the word "fact" for both a natural event and a human action is striking. It seems to blur the distinction between nature and artifice. How could a term that was so closely linked to human endeavor come to represent natural events that lie beyond our manipulative power? How could a word that referred to human deeds or actions be applied to nonhuman physical events? The blurring of natural fact and human artifact was due, at least in part, to a pervasive view of God as the unknowable and unpredictable Artificer of the natural world. For seventeenth-century writers such as Bacon, Vico, and Hobbes, that which is natural was not necessarily opposed to that which is artificial. What is called natural depends on divine creativity, but sometimes also human artifice, to come into being. The facts of nature are the artifacts of both God and humanity. One of the clearest examples of the complexity and ambiguity of this relationship can be found in the first lines of Hobbes's *Leviathan*: "Nature (the art whereby God has made and governs the world) is by the *art* of man, as in many other things, so in this also imitated, that it can make an artificial animal."[8] If divine creation is parallel to human creativity, divine actions can be inferred and assessed in the same way as human actions in the courts. The natural "facts" that seventeenth-century thinkers sought to uncover were the acts of a Divine Artificer. Understanding the world involved deciphering the alleged deeds of an ultimately inexplicable Actor. It could also involve observing "experimental facts," natural events created by artificial means. Historians, theologians, and natural historians had no trouble applying the legal vocabulary surrounding "facts" to their particular fields. Practitioners of this new type of probable judgment interrogated the natural world, examined evidence, and weighed the testimony of witnesses in order to arrive at adequate, although always imperfect, knowledge of facts.[9]

---

[8] Hobbes, *Leviathan*, 9.

[9] Peter Dear argues that the contrast of nature and artifice rests on an Aristotelian view of nature's purposes as opposed to human ones. Once the teleological explanation of nature began to falter, the art/nature distinction gave way to the integration of artificial experience into natural philosophy. Dear, *Disicipline and Experience*, 151–61. See also Margaret Osler, "From Immanent Nature to Nature as Artifice: The Interpretation of Final Causes in

By employing the language of facts, seventeenth-century theologians and natural historians could make probable claims while at the same time rejecting the discredited standard of textual authorities. They could appeal to a type of public "reasonableness." The difference between Locke's reasonableness and the skepticism and dogmatism of his early years lies in his use of this new version of probability. By offering his readers a way of describing judgment and assessing truth claims through the investigation of nondemonstrative evidence, Locke could replace or at least modify scholastic categories and sidestep the extremes of radical skepticism and Cartesian rationalism. He could provide an authoritative framework through which disputes could be mediated and judgments publicly legitimized. By employing the new language of probability, he could sustain a mode of discourse through which religious, political, and moral claims could be publicly evaluated.

In his earliest writings, Locke reveals a deep anxiety concerning the moral and religious incommensurability that characterized the collapse of traditional languages of justification. It was only after leaving the confines of the university curriculum and entering into public life that Locke began to see things differently. Although he continued to worry about the capacity of his contemporaries to regulate their judgment adequately, he became increasingly interested in new ideas revolving around the evidentiary status of nondemonstrative evidence. As he worked out his thoughts concerning the limits and possibilities of human understanding, he was led to place increasing emphasis on the importance of probable belief. Although he never rejected the possibility of certain knowledge, he carefully shifted his readers' attention from the absolute certainty that was so significant for radical skeptics and Cartesian rationalists toward a standard of rational appraisal based on a new conception, "facts." The authoritative testimony of nature as expressed through facts could serve as a new type nondemonstrative evidence.

The Transformation of a Skeptic

Since the rediscovery of Locke's first writings on civil government and the law of nature more than fifty years ago, scholars have been perplexed about how these early texts relate to his mature philosophy. As we have

Seventeenth-Century Natural Philosophy," *The Monist* 79 (1996), 388–407. For a fascinating exploration of how this shift in the conceptualization of nature paralleled a particularly modern conflation of "knowing" and "making," see Hans Blumenberg, *The Genesis of the Copernican World*, trans. R. M. Wallace (Cambridge: MIT Press, 1987); and Antonio Perez-Ramos, *Francis Bacon's Idea of Science and the Maker's Knowledge Tradition* (Oxford: Oxford University Press 1988).

seen, the Locke of the early 1660s does not subscribe to a theory of natural rights; he is opposed to the toleration of religious dissenters; he does not believe in parliamentary supremacy as the embodiment of the legislative power; he has no theory of property or its importance to the formation of civil society; and he opposes the view that people have the right to resist their rulers. The radical shift that seems to have taken place between 1660 and 1680 raises important questions about the development and meaning of Locke's thought as well as liberalism in general. How can Locke, the great champion of individual liberties, religious toleration, and the right of revolution have been such an unabashed defender of the arbitrary and absolute governmental power? How and why did Locke the absolutist transform into Locke the liberal? What happened to the overriding concerns that animated and informed his earlier position?

Faced with these difficult questions, some of Locke's most able commentators have thrown up their hands. John Dunn simply declares that there "can never be a sufficient explanation ... of why the older Locke adopted his 'liberal' incoherence in place of his earlier 'conservative' incoherence."[10] Others have nonetheless ventured to offer such explanations. One response has been to depict the development of his thought as a natural process of clarification and correction. Advocates of this line of reasoning argue that Locke advanced a clearly inconsistent position at the beginning of his career. Yet after recognizing the practical and theoretical errors of his position, he modified it and moved toward an increasingly profound understanding of the requirements of a just political regime.[11] A second response has been to attribute any difference between Locke's earlier and his later position to the rhetorical stances he used to achieve particular policies within different political contexts. Thus it is suggested that the defense of absolutism in the *Tracts* stems from Locke's support of Charles II during the Restoration and his hope that the new king would grant indulgence to dissenters. In contrast, his fear of the crypto-Catholic policies of James II in the 1680s led him to oppose the unlimited authority of the magistrate in his *Two Treatises on Government* and *Letter Concerning Toleration.*[12] A third response has been to deny that there

[10] Dunn, *Political Thought of Locke*, 29.

[11] Many well-respected scholars, such as W. von Leyden, Phillip Abrams, and most recently Ian Harris, appear to advocate this position, characterizing Locke's intellectual life as a unidirectional advance from error to profundity. Von Leyden, "Introduction" (LN 60–82); Abrams, introduction to *Two Tracts on Government* (TT 84–107); Harris, *The Mind of John Locke: A Study of Political Theory in Its Intellectual Setting* (Cambridge: Cambridge University Press, 1994), 253–54.

[12] Although James Tully and Richard Ashcraft certainly do not attempt to explain everything about Locke with this approach, at times they overemphasize the pragmatic considerations involved in the development of Locke's thought. Tully writes, "Locke's analysis in the *Two Tracts* underwrites Charles' declaration of indulgence from Breda in April on

is any disparity at all. Thus J. W. Gough portrays the young Locke as a proto-liberal, insisting that his early writings are much more liberal than they might appear. He contends that Locke's "basic principles, on political power, the nature of the church, and toleration, were substantially unchanged throughout his life."[13] A fourth response has been to point to the ambiguities and apparent inconsistencies of Locke's early notes and tracts as intimations of a teaching that is never explicitly articulated in Locke's mature writings but nevertheless lies at the core of his thought.[14] Proponents of this interpretation argue that the more authoritarian impulses that motivate Locke in his early life continued to play a concealed yet decisive role in his subsequent writings.

   None of these alternatives is entirely satisfying. Proponents of the first approach, who view Locke's development as a straightforward trajectory from mistaken assumptions to obvious truths, fail to take sufficient notice of the genuine worries that animate his early writings. Advocates of the second approach, insofar as they emphasize the pragmatic considerations that might have influenced Locke at particular moments in his career, give short shrift to the overriding theoretical questions that play an undeniable role in both his early and his mature work. These first two approaches seem to disregard the possibility that there could be any theoretical continuities of interest and purpose between the *Two Tracts*

---

purely pragmatic grounds." Tully, introduction to *A Letter Concerning Toleration* (LCT 5). Richard Ashcraft makes a similar argument that Locke, as a political activist, did not see a "need" for toleration until actual political conflict pushed the issue into prominence. *Revolutionary Politics*, 88, 90. Yet both Tully and Ashcraft recognize that explanations based solely on Locke's immediate context overlook Locke's conscious attempt to make claims that transcend the political contestation in which he found himself.

[13] J. W. Gough, introduction to John Locke, *Epistola de tolerantia*, ed. Raymond Klibansky, trans. J. W. Gough (Oxford: Clarendon, 1968), 12. See also Gough, *John Locke's Political Philosophy*. This consistency thesis was first advanced by King and Fox-Bourne in order to preserve Locke's status as a liberal from his first to his last writings. Phillip Abrams also leans toward this position. Although he correctly notes that the *Two Tracts* are "in every sense profoundly conservative works," he finds only a "short distance" between Locke's early and late writings on toleration. Abrams, introduction to *Two Tracts on Government* (TT 7, 105).

[14] Many careful readers of Locke have argued that his early writings provide further evidence in favor of Leo Strauss's interpretation presented in *Natural Right and History*. Thus Robert Kraynak incorporates his reading of the *Tracts* into an argument that Locke viewed religious sectarian warfare (and perhaps religion in general) as the fundamental problem of politics. His move from absolutism to toleration was simply a "change in political strategy for managing religion." Kraynak, "John Locke: From Absolutism to Toleration," *American Political Science Review* 74, no. 1 (1980), 53. With a similar purpose, Robert Horwitz focuses on the ambiguities in Locke's early notes on natural law and finds evidence that Locke was either less confident in his later theological assertions than many interpreters recognize or knowingly misled his readers. Horwitz, introduction to Locke, *Questions Concerning the Law of Nature*.

and the *Two Treatises*. Yet the last two seem to neglect, or at least down-play, the important differences. Thus supporters of the third approach, such as Gough, discount Locke's defense of absolutism by simply deny-ing that the Locke they know could ever have advocated such a thing. And defenders of the fourth approach, such as Kraynak, minimize the significance of Locke's support of toleration by declaring that "absolut-ism and toleration are the same in principle despite their great differences in practice."[15]

By reading Locke in the context of a recovery and transformation of probable judgment, we can attend to both the similarities and the differences between Locke's earlier and later writings. We can account for Locke's continued interest in the establishment and maintenance of political order throughout his life, while also recognizing that the author-ity Locke endorses in his mature, published work is of a kind very dif-ferent from the authority of absolute and arbitrary governmental power that he supports in his early years. In Locke's earliest writings, we find a skeptic without access to a stable language of justification. Left with nothing but the eroded vocabulary of scholasticism, Locke emphasizes the difficulty, if not impossibility, of rational public deliberation. With-out a common understanding of reason to appeal to, he concludes that the only way to ensure order is through the coercive power of the state. As we will see, Locke is only able to modify his skeptical position and its absolutist political consequences several years later when he comes to embrace a new conception of probable judgment. By emphasizing the emergence of probability in Locke's mature political thought, I do not want to minimize the important biographical events that helped him embrace toleration and the right of revolution. In fact, Locke's travels on the continent (where he experienced people of different faiths liv-ing side by side) and his close association with Shaftesbury (where he

---

[15] Kraynak, "John Locke," 53. Kraynak's primary argument—that even regimes charac-terized by toleration rest on a vision of order that excludes some religious positions, such as actively intolerant ones, and therefore cannot claim to embrace all manifestations of religion—is parallel to the argument presented here. In subsequent chapters, I will expand on this important insight, showing that Locke ushers in a type of authoritative language of justification that aims at excluding certain types of intellectual conduct, or misconduct. Yet Kraynak seems to go too far in collapsing the distinction between absolutism and tol-eration, and thus ignoring or denying that there is a significant difference between the coercive force exercised by a single magistrate and the persuasion and agreement that takes place between citizens. Most importantly, he neglects the role that a common language of judgment plays in legitimating regimes among diverse groups of people. Wootton has also pointed out that Kraynak misdates a key text, tears quotations out of context, and sees Hobbes's influence where that of other, less suspect authors is equally plausible. See Woot-ton, introduction to Locke, *Political Writings*, 31.

experienced politics firsthand) reinforced what he was learning in his work with experimentalists such as Sydenham and Boyle. Whether it was through his travels in Europe, his practical experience in politics and law, his engagement with medicine, or his encounter with the new experimental science, Locke began to consider the importance of shared notions of reasonableness. The renewed emphasis on probable judgment that he witnessed led him to imagine the possibility of stable regime consisting of individuals who discipline their judgments according to a shared notion of reasonableness. For Locke the new probability could serve as a common language of justification within which both conflict and consent could take place.

The new language of probability continued to carry with it vestiges of the standard of probability that preceded it. In spite of widespread attacks on the criterion of traditional authority, the probable judgment that Locke and his contemporaries embraced did not jettison appeals to authoritative sources. It remained dependent on a new type of authoritative testimony.[16] This testimony consisted of the facts of nature as well as the reports of trustworthy observers. Steven Shapin has shown that a new form of writing emerged at this time, the scientific narrative, offering a vivid account of phenomena so that readers could become "virtual witnesses." Writers such as Boyle describe events or objects in excruciating detail in order to gain credibility with a readership that will probably neither replicate nor directly witness the event described. "The modern enterprise *in no way* dispensed with reliance on human testimony," Shapin writes, "nor is it possible to imagine what a natural scientific enterprise that wholly rejected testimony would look like. Modern practitioners were supposed to acquire a stock of factual knowledge, but most of that knowledge was necessarily acquired second hand."[17] The renewal of probable judgment did not do away with the need for authoritative testimony, but it did redefine what that testimony entailed. It transformed the notion of what constitutes a publicly persuasive claim. By emphasizing the probable deliverances of experience and testimony, the renewal of probable judgment offered a new language within which claims could be assessed by a community of reasonable inquirers. It offered a standard of public reasonableness that could be embraced by individuals who might not share underlying commitments.

By placing Locke within the context of a reemerging language of probability, I am not arguing that he is the first or even the most outspo-

[16] Serjeantson, "Testimony and Proof," 206.

[17] Steven Shapin, *The Scientific Revolution* (Chicago: University of Chicago Press, 1996), 87. See also Serjeantson, "Testimony and Proof."

ken proponent of modern probable judgment.[18] Nor am I defending the claim that Locke somehow broke free from all previous linguistic practices that had informed the arguments of his predecessors by embracing this conception. The transformation of language took place from within inherited vocabularies. Instead, I turn to Locke because he provides us with an important example of how the new notion of probability was used to advance a common political language of justification in the context of seemingly incommensurable frameworks of interpretation. Locke carefully introduced a new way of conducting one's intellectual life in the hope that he could change the way people regulated their thoughts and actions in the context of moral and political disagreement. He sought to make the language of probable judgment serve as a type of public reason.

In Locke's mature work, the criterion of certainty that bedeviled radical skeptics as well as Cartesian rationalists plays only a minor role. For those who followed in his wake, it became less and less common to see the term "knowledge" employed in ways that had anything to do with the ancient ideal of *scientia*. Knowledge became that which could be held with the highest degree of probability, and science became the painstaking investigation of probability. This new understanding became enshrined in the linguistic practices of ordinary life. Locke's emphasis on probable belief played a crucial role in the way those who came after him would understand public judgment. In the fields of natural science, law, politics, and even theology, propositions were to be deemed true or false insofar as they accorded with or diverged from the provisional evaluation of relevant evidence. This new vocabulary came to pervade public assessments of institutional organization and individual speech and behavior. By reading Locke within the context of the transformation of probability,

[18] In fact, most historians and philosophers of science who write on probability focus on the pivotal work of other thinkers and make only passing reference to Locke. Several extraordinary thinkers, including Pierre Gassendi, Thomas Hobbes, and Blaise Pascal, shift away from to the criterion of certainty by pointing to the importance of less than certain realm of probable belief long before Locke came onto the scene. Lynn Joy and Thomas Lennon single out the skeptical Epicurean Pierre Gassendi for his attack on *scientia* and defense of probable signs. Richard Tuck points to the importance of Hobbes in the development a nondemonstrative science of optics. And Ian Hacking is one of many who have emphasized the significance of Pascal's famous wager as an alternative to Descartes' rationalism, which Pascal derided as "useless and uncertain." See Richard Tuck, "Hobbes and Descartes," in *Perspectives on Thomas Hobbes*, ed. G.A.J. Rogers and Alan Ryan (Oxford: Clarendon Press, 1988) and Tuck, "Optics and Sceptics"; Lynn Sumida Joy, *Gassendi the Atomist: Advocate of History in an Age of Science* (Cambridge: Cambridge University Press, 1987); Thomas M. Lennon, *The Battle of the Gods and Giants: The Legacies of Descartes and Gassendi, 1655–1715* (Princeton: Princeton University Press, 1993); and Hacking, *The Emergence of Probability*, 63–72.

we can gain new insight into aspects of his thought that have perplexed many of his most attentive readers. But more importantly we can move toward a better understanding of some of the continuing difficulties that this mode of discourse has passed down to us.

Precursors to Lockean Reasonableness

The claim that Locke encountered a new type of probable judgment that influenced his move away from the skepticism and absolutism leaves us with several nagging questions: What made the new probability so persuasive to Locke and his contemporaries? Why did this language of justification seem reasonable to Royal Society virtuosi surrounding Locke and not to radical skeptics and Cartesian rationalists? How could this new vocabulary fill the cognitive space left by earlier epistemological categories? An answer to these questions involves the changing evidentiary status of experience. As several scholars have recently made clear, "experiential fact" could serve as a criterion of judgment for those surrounding Locke in a way that it could not for earlier skeptics and rationalists. The following account of this transformation is meant not as a rehearsal of direct influences on Locke or an argument for Locke's originality, but rather as a description of the changing language of rational appraisal that provided a rich and varied soil from which the Locke's version of probable judgment grew. The notion of nature's testimony and the new type of probability that it made possible did not emerge out of thin air one day in Boyle's laboratory. A new language of justification, like any language, is not conjured up out of a void.[19] It is the result of a series of subtle modifications and sometimes imperceptible changes in the meaning and use of words over time.

The notions of experience and testimony that the members of the Royal Society employed can be traced back to the ancients. Yet they emerged as primary criteria for the new probability only after a series of conceptual shifts had taken place. First, the "experiential fact" had to be seen as a type of authoritative testimony that could secure truth claims. Second, the testimony of facts had to be seen as yielding *degrees* of assurance that rose above mere opinion yet fell short of absolute certainty. Once these modifications were in place, the testimony of experience could be seen to

---

[19] At times Ian Hacking seems to lose sight of this. In his attempt to emphasize the discontinuities between this new probability and the conceptions that had preceded it he often overlooks the continuities. For thoughtful and cautious criticism of Hacking on this point see Daston, *Classical Probability*, 11–15; and Douglas Lane Patey, *Probability and Literary Form: Philosophic Theory and Literary Practice in the Augustan Age* (Cambridge: Cambridge University Press, 1984), 27–34.

authorize rational deliberation and justify public judgments in the context of fractured and competing traditions.

Locke and his contemporaries were not the first to appeal to experience as the basis of cognitive assessment. In fact Aristotle was as adamant as Locke that all knowledge begins with sensory experience. Yet Aristotle and Locke meant very different things by this. For Locke experience is the authoritative testimony of nature that helps observers reach probable conclusions. For Aristotle experience is the foundation of demonstrative science. As Peter Dear has shown, Aristotelian invocations of experience are appeals to "what most people know."[20] They are universal statements about how things are or how they behave. Experience for a scholastic Aristotelian is not observation of a particular event or action as it would be for seventeenth-century experimentalists. This is because a particular observation could never yield the type of universal principle that could serve as the basis of a demonstrative syllogism. Perception produces this type of universal experience though memory. According to Aristotle, "from perception there comes memory, and from memory (when it occurs often in connection with the same thing), experience; for memories that are many in number form a single experience."[21] Taken together with common opinions and the assertions of philosophers, this type of experience revealed a common and largely unproblematic understanding of how things generally happen in the world. For the Scholastic, this type of experience does not need to be carefully obtained or rigorously tested; it is familiar and accessible to all. It provides *data,* literally "givens," that would serve as the major premise in a universally applicable demonstration. Testimony concerning discrete and particular events simply could not serve this purpose, since it would be too uncertain and too anomalous to be the principle on which a demonstrative syllogism could be based.[22]

In contrast, experience in the seventeenth century increasingly took the form of detailed statements describing a particular historical event or experiment. Instead of general statements about how things habitually behave, seventeenth-century observers offered a specific descriptions of what they took to be the facts. The best example of these descriptions can be found in the countless reports of singular events in the *Philosophical Transactions* by the Fellows of the Royal Society. Yet as evidential weight came to be attached to the singular testimony of natural facts, individuals could no longer rely on the kind of universal consensus that estab-

---

[20] Dear, *Discipline and Experience,* 21–25. See also Dear, *Revolutionizing the Sciences,* 3–7.

[21] Aristotle, *Posterior Analytics,* I.31.

[22] Dear, *Discipline and Experience,* 22.

lished the certainty of scholastic experience. A single observance could not establish a universal truth. As Dear puts it, "The singular experience could not be *evident*, but it could provide *evidence*."[23] As the experience of natural facts came to replace the communally embedded experience of scholasticism, the testimony of nature came to serve as a helpful yet sometimes problematic source of judgment. Evidence derived from natural facts carried the evidentiary status of testimony. It might lead to probable assurance, yet it could no longer serve as the basis for demonstrative certainty.[24]

One of the most colorful examples of the move from a scholastic notion of experience as a universal axiom toward the view of experience as probable testimony appears in the work of Paracelsus.[25] Originally named Philippus Aureolus Theophrastus Bombastus von Hohenheim, this sixteenth-century physician and mystic chose the more concise "Paracelsus" probably to claim that he had gone beyond all ancient physicians including the celebrated first-century Roman physician Celsus. Paracelsus refused to accept the superiority of traditional medical authorities. He was impatient with the scholastic emphasis on contemplation, and argued that scholars have a moral responsibility to uncover practical knowledge, especially in the case of medicine. Known as "the Luther of the Physicians," he derided the authority of Galen and Avicenna in medicine. At the same time that religious reformers across Europe were challenging the doctrines and hierarchies of the Catholic Church, Paracelsus threw out the medical texts that were revered by his contemporaries.[26] It was not Galen but nature that would provide him with the most useful text to read. The firmament, he writes, "is like a letter that has been sent to us from a hundred miles off, and in which the writer's mind speaks to

[23] Ibid., 25.

[24] It is in this context that we can understand an increasing reliance on "facts" at the same time that they become a source of anxiety. Hume's criticism of induction in the eighteenth century makes sense only as a response to the transformation of what "experience" entails and increased emphasis on the authoritative testimony of natural facts. The "problem of induction" did not exist for scholastic Aristotelians because they did not believe that universal propositions of experience could be derived from specifiable propositions regarding specific events.

[25] For more on the work and influence of Paracelsus, see Charles Webster, *From Paracelsus to Newton: Magic and the Making of Modern Science* (Cambridge: Cambridge University Press, 1982); Walter Pagel, *Paracelsus: An Introduction to Philosophical Medicine in the Era of the Renaissance* (New York: Karger, 1982); and Andrew Weeks, *Paracelsus: Speculative Theory and the Crisis of the Early Reformation* (Albany: State University of New York Press, 1997).

[26] In fact, a widely circulated story that Paracelsus publicly burned the *Canon* of Avicenna in Basel in 1527 in the same way that Luther had burned the papal bull a few years earlier earned him his title as "the Luther of the Physicians."

us."[27] By carefully deciphering the testimony of the creator, Paracelsus thinks he can attain novel insight into the natural world and develop unprecedented medical treatments.

For Paracelsus the letter of the firmament, the testimony of nature, is legible to those who understand the true properties of things and their correspondences.[28] Writing in the context of what has been called "the emblematic world view," in which nature is seen as rife with signs and resemblances, Paracelsus insists that each object in the world has a signature that connects it to other objects.[29] These signatures might include shapes, numbers, similarities, or even names. The shapes of plants or the names of stars can guide the observant physician in finding appropriate substances to heal diseases. Thus he reasons that liverwort can cure diseases of the liver. The walnut, since it is shaped like a brain with a hard outer shell, can cure maladies of the head. Paracelsus came upon his most influential finding—that the metal mercury, in the correct dosage, would cure syphilis—in a similar way. Although his colleagues were routinely killing their patients by prescribing mercury, he reasoned that syphilis is signified by the marketplace where it is contracted; the marketplace is signified by the planet Mercury; and since the metal mercury bears the same name, it is must be the cure for syphilis. Paracelsus reads the world around him by searching for God's signatures in the relationships between things and names. He does not distinguish between natural signs of things and conventional signs of names.[30] For him they all are a part

[27] Paracelsus, *Sämtliche Werke*, ed. K. Sudhoff, 14 vols. (Munich: R. Oldenbourg, 1922–23), 11:171–76, quoted by Hacking, *The Emergence of Probability*, 41. As an anti-Galenist physician, Locke was certainly familiar with Paracelsus. He even owned one of his books. According to Romanell, however, Locke was more directly influenced by the writings of a moderate Paracelsan named J. B. van Helmont. See Romanell, *John Locke and Medicine: A New Key to Locke* (Buffalo, N.Y: Prometheus Books, 1984), 53–65.

[28] Peter Dear points out that Paracelsus's approach "reflects a long-standing, if somewhat unorthodox, position that had been represented in the thirteeth century by the English friar Roger Bacom, who had advocated something called *scientia experimentalis*." Dear, *Revolutionizing the Sciences,* 49. For more on Roger Bacon, see Jeremiah Hackett, "Roger Bacon on 'scientia experimentalis,'" in *Roger Bacon and the Sciences*, ed. Jeremiah Hackett (Leiden: Brill, 1997).

[29] William Ashworth, "Natural History and the Emblematic World View," in *Reappraisals of the Scientific Revolution*, ed. David Lindberg and Robert Westman (Cambridge: Cambridge University Press, 1990), 303–32; and Michel Foucault, *The Order of Things* (New York: Random House, 1970), 26–30.

[30] The search for a natural language in which words and things correspond continued to fuel imaginations well into the seventeenth century. In the tradition of Paracelsus, Jacob Boehme sought a "language of nature" in which he could read the "essences and forms" of things. See Allison Coudert, "Forgotten Ways of Knowing: The Kabbalah, Language and Science in the Seventeenth Century," in *Shapes of Knowledge from the Renaissance to the Enlightenment*, ed. Donald Kelley and Richard Popkin (Dordrecht: Kluwer, 1991), 83–99.

of the testimony of a distant and often elusive God. The reasoning that guides Paracelsus to his conclusions strikes us as bizarre and irrational. Yet it is here that we see the scholastic notions of probability and authoritative testimony begin to generate new frameworks of evidence. The signs that Paracelsus observes in the world are given authority by the author of those signs, God. Natural events can now speak for themselves. They need not await the approval of a book or person to become probable. If nature is God's book, that is, if nature is the visible manifestation of an invisible divine will, than it is indeed authoritative testimony.[31] Although much of what Paracelsus defends is obscure, his importance in the development of probable judgment lies in his emphatic rejection of traditional authorities, his belief that knowledge should be practical instead of merely contemplative, and his emphasis on nature as divine testimony. Although he did not refer to experiential facts, Paracelsus speaks about the testimony of nature in a way that opens the door to the new probability.

It is Francis Bacon who first appeals to the "facts of nature" as a type of authoritative testimony to secure truth claims. As an English statesman and philosopher who presided over the Chancery, Bacon inhabited a world very different from that of the mystic and occultist Paracelsus. Yet he spoke of nature in very similar terms.[32] For Bacon, investigating the natural world involves reading "the ideas of the divine mind . . . the genuine signatures impressed on created things, as they are discovered to be."[33] Instead of appealing to the type of textual authorities that characterize the scholastic and rhetorical tradition, Bacon urges his readers to look to the testimony of nature itself. The shift from specious authorities to the direct investigation of nature is what Bacon saw as the distinguishing mark of his *New Organon*, which he hoped would replace the corpus of Aristotle's writings on logic, traditionally known as the *Organon*. The *New Organon*, published in 1620, proclaims that the Aristote-

---

[31] Recent historical scholarship on the origins of modern science has shown that the boundary between empirical inquiry and occult practice was surprisingly permeable during this period. The clear distinction between science and magic only emerges much later in retrospective accounts. See Keith Thomas, *Religion and the Decline of Magic: Studies in Popular Beliefs in Sixteenth and Seventeenth Century England* (New York: Oxford University Press, 1997); and Brian Vickers, *Occult and Scientific Mentalities in the Renaissance* (Cambridge: Cambridge University Press, 1984).

[32] For an investigation of the connections between Bacon and the work of mystics, alchemists, and Paracelsians, see Paolo Rossi, "Hermeticism, Rationality, and the Scientific Revolution," in *Reason, Experiment, and Mysticism in the Scientific Revolution*, ed. M. L. Bonelli and William R. Shea (New York: Science History Publications, 1975), 255–74. See also Julian Martin, *Francis Bacon, the State, and the Reform of Natural Philosophy* (Cambridge: Cambridge University Press, 1992).

[33] Francis Bacon, *Novum Organum*, ed. Lisa Jardine and Michael Silverthorne (Cambridge: Cambridge University Press, 2000), I.23.

lian approach to logic, with its commitment to demonstrative science on
the one hand and dialectical opinion on the other, is inadequate. Bacon
denounces a traditional view of experience that relies on "the reputation
of ancient authors" and the approbation of traditional authorities.[34] He
scorns a science in which nothing is "duly investigated, nothing verified,
nothing counted, weighed or measured."[35] It is important to note that
Bacon's critique is not simply an appeal to reform the way his contemporaries pursued *scientia* and *opinio*. It is a radical call to reconceive these
categories entirely. "For the discovery of things is to be taken from the
light of nature, not recovered from the shadows of antiquity."[36]

As Barbara Shapiro has recently shown, Bacon's approach involves
uncovering the "facts of nature."[37] Bacon was a crucial figure in trans-
porting the language of "fact" from the courts to the laboratories. As
both a legal practitioner and a natural philosopher, he was ideally situated to show that an attentiveness to "matters of fact" could aide in making judgments in both civil and natural realms. Just as judges must assess
the alleged deeds of the accused, natural historians should attempt to
uncover the "deeds and works of nature" by compiling facts and carefully weighing testimony. By applying the legal language of "facts" to
the natural world, Bacon invited his readers to apply familiar legal techniques of interrogation and verification to natural phenomena. The facts
that are discovered and substantiated do not in themselves reveal the type
of underlying causes that scholastic science attempts to explain. Facts
supply evidence for subsequent conclusions.

Yet if they are properly verified and recorded, experts could use them to
arrive at certain and apodictic knowledge of the natural world. Although
the approach has changed, the goal of the *New Organon* was the same
as scholastic science, the discovery of real essences and ultimate causes.
Bacon harbored the hope that an abstract model of the world could be
constructed from which absolutely certain truths could be deduced. His
interest in a new method of induction was tied to his larger project of
discovering true axioms. He sought the "forms" that existed behind the
fluctuating world of experience and could lead to certain knowledge and
not merely opinion. His enumeration of the idols of the mind and his
procedure for compensating for those idols was part of an attempt to
provide a steadier path to universal, apodictic knowledge.[38]

---

[34] Ibid., I.32.

[35] Ibid., I.98.

[36] Ibid., I.122.

[37] Shapiro, *A Culture of Fact*, 107–12. Bacon refers to "facts of nature" at several points
in his writings, including *Novum Organum*, I.112 and 124.

[38] Although the Royal Society deemed Bacon the patron saint of experimental method
and inductive science, they were able to do so only by refashioning this extraordinary figure

Whereas Bacon sought to achieve the goals of *scientia* by attending to facts, Pierre Gassendi challenged the aspiration to demonstrative certainty itself.[39] Gassendi did not want to revise or transform traditional epistemological categories; he wanted to discredit them completely. Gassendi's animosity toward the scholastic language of justification was reinforced by years of studying the skeptical writings of Sextus Empiricus. He concluded that the scholastic aspiration for universal and apodictic knowledge, even in its modern Cartesian or Baconian guises, was absurd. A section heading in one of his works makes this point crystal clear: "*Quod nulla sit Scientia, et maxime Aristotelea* [There is no demonstrative science, especially of the Aristotelian kind!]"[40] If there is no *scientia* in the sense of universal and demonstrative knowledge, then the distinction between knowledge and opinion that was so fundamental to Aquinas and so crucial to Descartes loses its importance. Gassendi explains, "We use the expressions 'to have an opinion' and 'to know' interchangeably, as the practice of everyday speech shows, and if you look at the matter carefully, knowledge and opinion can be considered synonyms."[41] This discovery did not lead Gassendi to abandon all knowledge claims or accept all opinions as equally valid. Instead he proposed a method of for-

---

after their own image. Bacon came to stand for much more than the specifics of his scientific method. The Royal Society constantly appealed to the Lord Chancellor because of his rigorous critique of scholasticism, his emphasis on the utility of learning, his study of nature as a means to glorify God, his dream of dominating and controlling nature for the benefit of mankind, his theory of the sources of human error, and his procedure of natural history based on observation, experience, and collection of data. As Barbara Shapiro explains, "The post-Baconian generation thus took to heart Bacon's Idols but no longer believed that his New Organon or any other method would result in certain natural knowledge. The essentialist search for real essences and ultimate causes or the reality behind appearances was largely abandoned." Shapiro, *Probability and Certainty*, 63.

[39] Thomas Lennon, in a sweeping account of the emergence of modern philosophy, posits a Gassendist tradition of probable belief over and against a Cartesian tradition of rationalism. Lennon sees the rivalry between the two as an example of what Plato in the *Sophist* calls the battle of gods and giants. Descartes and later Spinoza represent "gods" insisting that everything that can exist does exist and that the mind, if properly regulated, will be able to comprehend that existence. They also believe that certainty is the final and proper aim of philosophy. In contrast, Gassendi and later Boyle and Locke represent "giants" believing that it is possible that some things that can exist do not (yet) exist and that the mind can only grasp the world in a limited, probabilistic way. Lennon explicitly describes Locke as a "Gassendist anti-Cartesian" and reads the *Essay* as "an anti-Cartesian polemic from beginning to end." Lennon, *Battle*, x. For a thorough account of Gassendi that emphasizes his use of historical (rather than syllogistic) reasoning in constructing philosophical arguments, see Joy, *Gassendi the Atomist*. Lisa T. Sarasohn has recently explored the ethical implications of Gassendi's thought in *Gassendi's Ethics: Freedom in a Mechanistic Universe* (Ithaca, N.Y.: Cornell University Press, 1996).

[40] Pierre Gassendi, *Opera Omnia* (Stuttgart: Friedrich Frommann Verlag, 1964), II.vi.

[41] Ibid., II.vi.6.

mulating and regulating judgment that relied on neither demonstrative syllogism nor the dialectical investigation of traditional authorities. He did this by adapting the notion of a sign that he traced back to debates between Epicureans and the skeptics but was also being employed by physicians and alchemists in his own day.[42] While Gassendi's doctrine of signs might strike the modern mind as more acceptable than the odd ruminations of Paracelsus, it is important to remember that they both appealed to the same concept of sign as evidence, with its implications of testimony, reading, and probability. Although Gassendi does not use the language of facts, he treats natural signs in a very similar way.

For Gassendi, observations or sense perceptions are signs of natural events and objects. They are not the same as the event or object, nor do they perfectly correspond to the actual event or object as a picture might correspond to an actual landscape. Signs have a much more tenuous connection to reality. As a nominalist, Gassendi believed that we cannot gain access to the underlying structure of the world. We have no way of getting at the "substances" and "essences" that are indispensable to scholastic thought. Yet we do experience signs that seem to be brought about or caused by something other than themselves. They are a testimony of something beyond themselves. These signs cannot give us absolutely certain knowledge, but by investigating and analyzing them, we pursue the most reliable method we have to expand our understanding. Gassendi goes so far as to claim that by examining the probable signs of nature, "we can preserve a science which can be called the science of experience or appearance."[43] Here Gassendi purposely blurs the traditional terminology or *scientia* and *opinio* in order to emphasize that some probable insights, especially the insights derived from signs, might rightfully be placed in the realm of science. Here the division between knowledge that is demonstrative and opinion that is probable begins to collapse into itself.

With Gassendi we can imagine something that would have been impossible before him—probable *knowledge*. Having thrown out the demonstrative knowledge of the Scholastics, Gassendi opens up the possibility of a science of appearance, in which a new type of partial knowledge can be gleaned from the evidence of signs. By employing the sign as evidence or testimony, Gassendi is able to avoid the abstractions of traditional philosophy and concentrate instead on the history of events in the world. Just as Bacon called his readers to look to the "facts," Gassendi appealed to probable signs in order to make judgments about the world. By attend-

---

[42] See Ralph Walker, "Gassendi and Skepticism," in *The Skeptical Tradition*, ed. Myles Burnyeat (Berkeley: University of California Press, 1983), 319–36.
[43] Gassendi, *Opera Omnia*, III.260.

ing to the testimony of both written texts and natural signs, Gassendi reminds his readers of the limits of human cognition while urging them to seek probable knowledge.[44]

Thomas Hobbes, a onetime amanuensis to Francis Bacon, echoes both Bacon and Gassendi in emphasizing the limits of human certainty and the impossibility of *scientia* as practiced by the Scholastics. In fact, Richard Tuck has pointed out that the "burgeoning friendship" between Gassendi and Hobbes may have played an important role in Hobbes's intellectual development.[45] After reading Gassendi's massive *magnum opus*, Hobbes wrote that "it is as big as Aristotle's philosophy, but much truer and excellent Latin."[46] Years before, when they were both recruited by Mersenne to respond to Descartes' *Meditations*, Hobbes joined Gassendi in rejecting the Cartesian solution to the problem of skepticism. They agreed that the type of apodictic and universal science that Descartes sought to establish was simply beyond the grasp of human beings. For both Gassendi and Hobbes, the actual or real causes of our particular perceptions cannot be known with certainty. Our senses do not provide us with clear and distinct access to the underlying workings or the ultimate causes of the external world. The only access we have is through the testimony of signs, what Hobbes also referred to as facts. This type of testimony is not demonstrative; it is only more or less probable. Hobbes explains, "This taking of signs by *experience*, is ... but *conjectural*; and according as they have often or seldom failed, so their *assurance* is more or less; but *never full* and *evident ... experience concludeth nothing universally*."[47] By observing signs or facts, we can develop prudence, which plays an

[44] Leibniz was one of the first to note the similarities between Gassendi and Locke. In his *New Essays on Human Understanding*, he writes of Locke that "this author is pretty much in agreement with M. Gassendi's system, which is fundamentally that of Democritus: he supports vacuum and atoms, he believes that matter could think, that there are no innate ideas, that our mind is a *tabula rasa*, and that we do not think all the time; and he seems inclined to agree with most of M. Gassendi's objections against M. Descartes." *New Essays on Human Understanding*, trans. and ed. Peter Remnant and Jonathan Bennett (Cambridge: Cambridge University Press, 1982), I.i.70. Many contemporary scholars have agreed with Leibniz that Gassendi and Locke have many commonalities, yet the question of whether Locke was directly influenced by Gassendi's work remains unanswered. For recent reviews of the possible connections and available evidence, see Lennon, *Battle*, 149–63; and J. R. Milton, "Locke and Gassendi: A Reappraisal," in *English Philosophy in the Age of Locke*, ed. M. A. Stewart (Oxford: Clarendon Press, 2000), 87–110.

[45] Tuck, "Hobbes and Descartes," 23. On the relationship between Hobbes and Gassendi, see Robert Hugh Kargon, *Atomism in England from Hariot to Newton* (Oxford: Clarendon Press, 1966), 68–69.

[46] Mersenne, *Correspondence*, 23:250, quoted by Tuck, "Hobbes and Descartes," 31.

[47] Hobbes, *The Elements of Law, Natural and Politic: Part I, Human Nature, Part II, De Corpore Politico; with Three Lives*, ed. J. C. A. Gaskin (New York: Oxford University Press, 1994), I.4.10. See also Hobbes, *Leviathan*, I.3.10.

important role in conduct, yet falls short of demonstrative certainty. Any insight that stems from observation alone cannot yield universal and apodictic conclusions.

Hobbes followed Gassendi in arguing that there could be no science of natural facts. Demonstrative science must rest on reason alone, not observation or experiment. For this reason Hobbes vehemently opposed Boyle's experimental program later in his life, especially Boyle's claims concerning the possibility of the void.[48] For Hobbes, genuine philosophical inquiry involves demonstrating necessary truths from universal principles. Boyle was merely dabbling, pointing to correlations of natural signs. He was not *demonstrating* anything. While Boyle believed that a type of limited knowledge could be gained by carefully consulting the nondemonstrative signs of nature, Hobbes insisted that "scientific" truths could only be secured within the closed system of philosophical argument. In this way he clung to the traditional scholastic distinction between *scientia* and *opinio* and rejected Boyle's program of "experiential philosophy" as merely conjectural. Observed phenomena are untrustworthy; they cannot provide universal justification for the claims they make. The only way to be absolutely certain about a claim is to show that it follows necessarily from universally acceptable definitions. This is a position that many contemporaries, including Locke, will reiterate. Yet the conclusions they draw from this insight differ dramatically. Hobbes argues that the only way that certain demonstrations can be recognized and embraced publicly is through the imposition of universal definitions by an absolute Sovereign. It is for this reason that the leviathan must be armed with both the sword and the dictionary. Demonstrative certainty is made possible only through a Sovereign who can guarantee epistemic unity. Most of Hobbes's contemporaries, however, shied away from this extreme position. Instead they focused increasingly on the importance of nondemonstrative facts. As the goal of demonstrative certainty became more questionable, the nondemonstrative evidence of "experiential facts" seemed to gain in epistemic status.

This emphasis on the testimony of experience not only played a role in experimental philosophy, but also influenced the development of theology in the seventeenth century. As Barbara Shapiro has shown us, several influential theologians responded to the demand for religious certainty that had emerged after the Reformation. They suggested that there are

---

[48] For a captivating and provocative account of the conflict between Hobbes and Boyle, see Steven Shapin and Simon Schaffer, *Leviathan and the Air-Pump: Hobbes, Boyle, and the Experimental Life* (Princeton: Princeton University Press, 1985). Although he is in general agreement with Shapin and Schaffer, Richard Kroll offers an alternative view of Hobbes in *The Material World: Literate Culture in the Restoration and Early Eighteenth Century* (Baltimore: Johns Hopkins University Press, 1991).

multiple levels or degrees of assurance, from absolute or infallible knowledge available only to God, through the limited assurances of sound
human judgment, down to the conjecture or guesswork of mere opinion.[49] By appealing to the nondemonstrative facts of history, individuals
might establish the "moral certainty" or "probability" of a religious truth,
yet they cannot attain the certainty of mathematical demonstration. This
is the argument of Hugo Grotius, who wrote in *The Truth of the Christian Religion* (1624) that Christianity is a historical religion that rests
on "matter of fact." The events reported in Scripture cannot be directly
witnessed or mathematically demonstrated and thus must be assessed by
the same means as secular histories. At best they can be established as
probable because they have been "attested by credible witnesses . . . men
whose judgment and integrity has never been called into question."[50] By
careful evaluation of the available testimony, individuals can arrive at the
most reasonable interpretation of scriptural events.

In England a group of tolerant and broad-minded thinkers known as
the Great Tew Circle echoed Grotius by advocating intellectual modesty
in the face of religious disagreement. These men, including John Hales,
Viscount Falkland, and William Chillingworth, sought to achieve religious unity and charity by shifting religious debate toward standards of
probability. They insisted that there was always a possibility of error in
the realm of faith. Viscount Falkland not only argued that popes and
church councils were fallible, he rejected the idea that any religious principles were capable of demonstration.

However it was William Chillingworth who articulated the position of
this group in the most complete and influential way. In his *Religion of the
Protestants* (1638), Chillingworth insists that God did not provide any
person or institution an infallible guide. Emphasizing that any religious
commitment should accord with the available evidence, he argues that
the beliefs that many of his contemporaries considered certain should
actually be placed within the realm of judgment. The conclusions that
we reach in matters that are less than certain should be tentative, provisional, and revisable. Chillingworth warns his readers that they entangle
themselves in unnecessary conflicts when they take the deliverances of
their judgment for undeniably certain and infallible knowledge.[51]

---

[49] Shapiro, *Probability and Certainty*, 74–82; and Shapiro, *A Culture of Fact*, 168–88.

[50] Grotius, *The Truth of the Christian Religion*, trans. John Clarke (Cambridge: J. Hall &
Son, 1860), book I, sec. xiii, 18.

[51] In a typical statement Chillingworth writes, "For, as he is an unreasonable Master, who
requires a stronger assent to his Conclusions than his Arguments deserve; so I conceive him
a forward and undisciplin'd Scholar, who desires stronger arguments for a conclusion than
the Matter will bear." William Chillingworth, *The Religion of Protestants, a Safe Way to
Salvation* (Oxford: Printed by Leonard Lichfield, 1638), Preface, ii. Locke thought so well

While Chillingworth's theory was initially formulated as an appeal for moderation in the midst of the rule-of-faith controversies raging between Catholics and Protestants, defenders of the new experimental philosophy were quick to embrace it as well. Seeking to develop a method that could resolve controversies in both religious *and* scientific spheres, many members of the Royal Society took up Chillingworth's project of carefully delineating various gradations or degrees of human understanding.[52] By marking out these boundaries, they sought to create a space in which they might be able to rationally deliberate about matters in which certainty cannot be attained; they sought "the satisfaction of breathing a freer air, and of conversing in quiet one with another, without being engaged in the passions and madness of that dismal Age."[53]

In the last half of the seventeenth century, a new type of probable reasoning emerged. Proponents of this new standard of cognitive assessment, Lorraine Daston tells us, "simultaneously insisted upon the incorrigible uncertainty of almost all human knowledge and on our ability to nonetheless attain to inferior degrees of 'physical' or 'moral' certainty." They appealed to the testimony of facts in order to arrive at probable judgments. "A proof for a hypothesis in natural philosophy or the precepts of Christianity need not achieve mathematical rigor, but only that threshold of certainty sufficient to persuade a reasonable man to act in daily life."[54] As we will see, this new standard would have revolutionary consequences for religious, moral, and political modes of justification.

From Lecture Halls to Laboratories

While still at Oxford, Locke came into contact with a diverse group of thinkers who were seeking an alternative to the deteriorating scholastic curriculum and the skepticism and dogmatism that it seemed to engender.

---

of Chillingworth that he recommended his work to every young gentleman who aspired to be reasonable. In *Some Thoughts Concerning Education*, he writes, "if you would have your son *reason well*, let him read Chillingworth" (STCE 188).

[52] John Wilkins, *Of the Principles and Duties of Natural Religion: Two Books*, ed. John Tillotson (London: Chiswall, Battersby and Brome, 1699), 9; and Robert Boyle, "Some Considerations about the Reconcileableness of Reason and Religion (1675)," in *Works of the Honourable Robert Boyle*, ed. Thomas Birch (London: J. and R. Rivington, 1772), 4:182. For a thorough account of the way in which Wilkins, Boyle, John Tillotson, Joseph Glanvill, and others employ and adapt Chillingworth's divisions, see Henry G. Van Leeuwen, *The Problem of Certainty in English Thought, 1630–1690*, vol. 1 (The Hague: Martinus Nijhoff, 1963), 32–120. For a general discussion of the emergence of degrees of certainty, see Shapiro, *Probability and Certainty*, 28–37.

[53] Thomas Sprat, *History of the Royal Society*, ed. J. Cope and H. W. Jones (St. Louis: Washington University Press, 1958), 53.

[54] Daston, *Classical Probability*, 56–57.

It was through his interaction with these men outside of the university that Locke began to move away from his early views. As Richard Ashcraft explains, "Locke's rethinking of his position on certain religious and political questions . . . did not take place within the context of academic discussions, nor were they an outgrowth of the fulfillment of his tutorial obligations at Oxford."[55] Instead, Locke's change of mind occurred in the context of public affairs, in his struggle to find political and social solutions to difficulties he encountered outside of the sterile atmosphere of academic life at Oxford.

A group of men had gravitated around Robert Boyle, a man of noble birth and considerable means who transformed his home on High Street into a laboratory and meeting place for like-minded clergymen, lay theologians, philosophers, and experimentalists. As he entered into this circle, Locke met several leading practitioners of the "new experimental philosophy." He forged a lifelong friendship with Boyle, through whom he met many others, including Boyle's assistant Robert Hooke, the experimentalist John Wilkins, and physicians such as Thomas Willis, Richard Lower, David Thomas, and Thomas Sydenham. A few years later they would welcome Locke into the newly formed Royal Society of London. These men shared many intellectual commitments. They all recognized that the language of scholasticism was battered and discredited. Many of them also believed that Descartes' categorical rejection of probable claims combined with his attempt to overhaul *scientia* was ultimately unsuccessful in refuting the arguments of the radical skeptics. However, they were unwilling to join the skeptics in rejecting the possibility of rational deliberation. These thinkers were, in Popkin's phrase, "mitigated skeptics."[56] Joseph Glanvill changed the title of *The Vanity of Dogmatizing* in his second edition to *Scepsis Scientifica*, suggesting that a type of skepticism was the antidote to dogmatism, and Robert Boyle described himself as the Sceptical Chymist. In his *History of the Royal Society*, Thomas Sprat reports that members might "perhaps be suspected" of being "a little too much inclined" to the "fault of skeptical doubting" because they were reluctant to embrace settled principles of fixed doctrine. Yet he points out that this charge is not justified, because they actually sought to steer a middle course between dogmatism and skepticism by not rushing to hold opinions without evidence, but after due consideration "to give the advantage of probability to one opinion, or cause, above another."[57]

---

[55] Ashcraft, *Revolutionary Politics*, 78.

[56] Popkin uses the term (which he derives from Hume) to describe Mersenne and Gassendi, but it is equally fitting for the Royal Society virtuosi. Popkin, *History of Scepticism*, 132–54. See also G.A.L. Rogers's chapter, "Locke and the Sceptical Challenge," in *Locke's Enlightenment: Aspects of the Origin, Nature and Impact of His Philosophy* (Hildesheim: Georg Olms Verlag, 1998).

[57] Sprat, *History of the Royal Society*, 101, 107.

These thinkers were skeptics insofar as they abandoned the hope that a universal, apodictic science could establish every justifiable claim. Yet they were mitigated skeptics because they refused to conclude that rational judgment was therefore impossible.[58]

Instead, they sought more practical standards of assessment. They sought a way to defend their experimental methods and secure their findings concerning the natural world. Yet they also sought to sustain rational deliberation over matters of religion, politics, and morality, in which absolute certainty seemed to be beyond the grasp of human beings. In the spirit of Francis Bacon, they believed that practical inquiry into the book of nature could yield not only insight, but also unprecedented social and political benefits. They attempted to achieve these aims by employing a language of justification that differed from the epistemological framework of the radical skeptics and dogmatic rationalists in two important ways: They appealed to a modified criterion of probability, the testimony of experiential fact, to determine the relative validity of less than certain claims without becoming entangled with the problem of multiple and conflicting authorities. And they adopted a schema that would allow for *degrees* of assurance in which these less than certain claims could be rationally justified, instead of accepting the stark dichotomy between absolute certainty and mere opinion. These two elements are interrelated. The view that most of the propositions that we encounter can only be justified to a degree of assurance that lies somewhere between apodictic certainty and unfounded opinion went hand in hand with the emergence of a new criterion that could be used to judge claims that are less than certain. Instead of appealing to the traditional criterion of textual approval, the Royal Society group appealed to the nondemonstrative evidence of natural facts. For these thinkers, a natural fact was any type of discrete, observable deliverance emanating from the external world. These facts were understood to reveal only imperfectly the order and structure of creation. A natural fact was seen as a partial reflection of an unobserved whole that itself depended on an inscrutable divine will. Yet these facts carried a probability that rose above authoritative texts because they were viewed as the direct testimony of the author of creation.

It was this new mode of discourse that Locke encountered when he entered into the circle of theologians, experimentalists, and medical men surrounding Robert Boyle. And this encounter had a profound effect on his subsequent intellectual development. Although Locke might have hinted at the deliverances of empirical testimony in his early writings, he did not work out the implications of this new type of evidence in any

---

[58] Lisa Jardine, *Ingenious Pursuits: Building the Scientific Revolution* (London: Little, Brown, 1999), 280–83, 325–27.

detail until after he left his official position at the university and plunged into the world of experiment and observation. It was only after engaging in the new experimental philosophy and working within the framework of the new probability that he began to consider how the priority of natural signs might shape a new, more useful mode of discourse that would have implications for religious, political, and moral debate. The new probability could serve as an authoritative language within which rational deliberation could take place and public judgments could be sanctioned. It is telling that the men Locke would later praise as the "master builders" of his age—Robert Boyle, Thomas Sydenham, Christian Huygens, and Isaac Newton—were all committed in some way to the testimony of facts as a basis for justifying their claims.[59] They rejected the possibility that we could have direct and perfect access to the underlying structure of creation, and turned instead to the probable deliverances of natural signs. This shift was made possible by the underlying assumption that there existed a fundamental order of nature that held together the buzzing and bubbling plentitude of appearance and experience. The seemingly chaotic movements of all created things were assumed to be part of a divine design that was still partially concealed. As Locke imbibed the mitigated skepticism of Boyle and his associates, he began to develop the outlines of a theory of knowledge that would retain certain aspects of the skepticism that he exhibited at the beginning of his career while shifting away from the epistemological despair and political absolutism that he articulated so forcefully in his early writings. In short, he embraced a new type of reasonableness. As Richard Kroll has pointed out, this new notion served "at once as an epistemology, a method, and a rhetoric."[60]

The Royal Society thinkers that Locke encountered sought to avoid the extremes of radical skepticism and Cartesian radicalism by arguing that various propositions attain various gradations of certainty and probability. Boyle, Wilkins, and a great many others in this circle vehemently rejected the stark dichotomy between absolute certainty and complete ignorance. They insisted that the demonstrative reasoning that characterizes the scholastic syllogism or geometric proof is not the sole or even

---

[59] See Locke's "The Epistle to the Reader" (E 9). Boyle and Sydenham were numbered among the first members of the Royal Society, and were clearly committed to this new thinking. Christiaan Huygens was a Dutch mathematician and avid experimentalist who became a founding member of the Academie des Sciences in Paris and a foreign member of the Royal Society. He wrote the first published work in mathematical probability, *Ratiocinii in aleae ludo*, in 1657. Although the "incomparable Mr. Newton" seems to have diverged at times from the tentative language of other Royal Society members (see his debate with Robert Hooke over optics), he shared the belief that the underlying structure of creation remains mysteriously dependent on divine will and that the best we can do is to investigate and describe the constant and regular conjunction of observed phenomena.

[60] Kroll, *The Material World*, 52.

most appropriate mode of establishing the validity of every proposition. Adapting the Aristotelian dictum that different fields of inquiry demand different kinds of proof, they argued that the process of establishing a claim in a field such as mathematics is simply different from establishing a claim in theology, history, or experimental philosophy.[61] If we look at the range of claims that we make, we will recognize that there are various types of assurance that are appropriate for various types of claims. They do not all rise to the same level of certainty. In Wilkins words, "Things of several kinds may admit and require several sorts of proofs, all which may be good in their kind."[62]

Although they differ in detail and terminology, the various schemas that they developed exhibit certain similarities. They all place the majority of our intellectual endeavors, especially those that concern matters of public importance, at a level above mere conjecture but below absolute certainty. In cases involving religion, history, or the physical world, demonstrable knowledge is unattainable; the best we can hope for is a high level of probability. The authors of these schemas maintain that a proposition can be justifiably accepted if the *appropriate* level of certainty is reached. Although we cannot be absolutely certain in many cases, we can attain a level of assurance that warrants our belief in the validity of a claim.[63] For example, Boyle argued that in some cases a "concurrence

[61] Almost all of these writers appealed either obliquely or explicitly to Aristotle: "Our discussion will be adequate if its degree of clarity fits the subject matter: We should not seek the same degree of exactness in all sorts of arguments alike, any more than in the products of different crafts . . . for it is the mark of an educated mind to expect that amount of exactness in each area which the nature of the particular subject admits. It is equally unreasonable to accept merely probable conclusions from a mathematicians as to demand strict demonstration from a rhetorician." *Nicomachean Ethics* I.3, 1094b.

[62] Wilkins, *Principles and Duties*, 23.

[63] M. Jamie Ferriera makes a similar observation, pointing out that the emergence of a bridge concept lying between certain knowledge and opinion was crucial for overcoming radical skepticism. He traces its emergence to John Wilkin's use of "moral certainty." Prompted by a comment in Hume's *Inquiry Concerning Human Understanding*, he calls this middle term "proof." However, Ferriera follows Hume too closely when he insists that Locke rigidly maintains the old dichotomy and does not contribute to the development of a type of bridge concept that emphasizes disciplined probable belief. The issue at stake is whether Locke insists on a qualitative distinction between knowledge and belief that precludes a continuum. Ferriera argues that this is the case, yet Locke's presentation is hardly unambiguous. I will argue that Locke makes a crucial shift in emphasis toward the type of spectrum characterized by degrees that Wilkin's presents. Although Locke never completely rejects the division between certain knowledge and belief or opinion, he certainly agrees with Wilkins on the importance of justifying beliefs that do not reach the level of absolute certainty according to a type of evidence that is neither demonstrative nor based on textual approval. In this way Locke joins Wilkins, Boyle, and Tillotson in ushering in a new standard for warranted belief. M. Jamie Ferreira, *Scepticism and Reasonable Doubt: The British Naturalist Tradition in Wilkins, Hume, Reid and Newman* (Oxford: Clarendon

of probabilities" suffices to warrant or justify a judgment.[64] By moving away from the stark dichotomy between absolute certainty and blind faith, these mitigated skeptics increased the range of epistemological categories in which justification or warrant could be achieved without demonstrative knowledge.[65]

In order for this new schema to be persuasive, however, the Royal Society group also had to employ a new criterion to judge the relative validity of claims in these less than certain realms. The traditional method of dialectically investigating authoritative texts simply would not work. The authoritative testimony of texts had been shaken by the Reformation and brought to ruins by subsequent battles between Catholics and Protestants over the rule of faith. The traditional criterion of probability was inextricably tied to the problem of multiple authorities that fueled the epistemological crisis of Locke's day. The theologians and experimentalists surrounding Boyle could not employ this beleaguered standard in the same way that it had been employed by the Scholastics. Instead, they salvaged a modified version of probability by appealing to the nondemonstrative testimony of natural signs.

This new testimony was to be *read* in the same way that Scholastics *read* the testimony of authoritative texts to determine the probability of *opinio*. For Locke's colleagues, the world was a somewhat perplexing book that could provide nondemonstrative guidance for those who took the time to learn from it. Natural signs were written in the "Book of Nature" that had been composed and made available to us by the "Author of Nature." Signs were the authoritative testimony of God, and as such they retained the dual meaning of the Latin term for authority, *auctoritas*, signifying both authorship and sanction. Since God is the author of natural signs, when we read them we are interpreting a text that is marked with divine authority. Wilkins, Boyle, and other members of the Royal Society often described their work in terms of consulting the hidden signs of nature.[66] Boyle writes, "There be hid in the bosom

---

Press, 1986), 13–27. Ferriera makes his case again in "Locke's 'Constructive Skepticism'—a Reappraisal," *Journal of the History of Philosophy* 24 (1986), 211–22.

[64] Boyle, *The Christian Virtuoso*, in *The Works of the Honorable Robert Boyle*, ed. Thomas Birch (London: Printed for A. Millar, 1744), 5:526.

[65] The fact that the Royal Society's experimental pursuits would later be called "science" although no one at the time claimed that they reached the level of *scientia* shows that the introduction of degrees of certainty brought about the blurring of the traditional categories. For a recent account of this development see Shapiro, *A Culture of Fact*.

[66] References to reading "God's Book of Nature" are endemic at this time; they abound in John Wilkins, *A Discourse Concerning a New Planet* (1640) and Robert Boyle, "Of the Study of the Book of Nature" (1649). A statement by William Harvey is typical in both its skepticism toward the books of men and its optimism about the book of Nature: "How unsafe, and degenerate a thing it is, to be tutored by other mens commentaries, without

of all human actions, certain secret axioms and principles of wisdom ... and there are certain hints ... which to discerning eyes (as plants do to physicians by their signatures reveal their properties;) disclose much of what they conceal."[67] This view of natural signs or facts conformed to a voluntarist view of God's absolute and ordained power. These signs were direct communication from an ultimately unknowable God, what Locke would later call "natural Revelation" (E IV.xix.4).

Natural facts make up an authoritative text that can be read and interpreted. In order to read this text more closely and decipher its meaning, Robert Hooke invented his "interpreter's glass," an instrument that would later be known as the microscope. In these early years of modern science, experimentation was understood within the context of a type of quasi-textual hermeneutics. For the experimentalists surrounding Boyle, the testimony of nature carried with it authority, and just like the older authorities that sustained medieval *opinio*, it had to be read and interpreted. The testimony of nature signifies something to which we cannot have direct access. The author of the book of nature is beyond our grasp. But that should not deter us from appealing to natural signs as authoritative testimony. Boyle explains, "If there be an effect, that we discern must proceed from such a cause or agent, we may conclude, that such a cause there is, though we do not particularly conceive how, or by what operation it is able to produce the acknowledged effect."[68] A natural sign is an effect that comes about as a result of some cause, but that underlying cause remains hidden from us. But if we carefully and methodically attend to these signs, we will find that they provide us with hints concerning those things we cannot know with certainty. Here we can see that this new standard of judgment not only takes on the function but also the form of the old standard. Natural signs provide the observer with authoritative, yet nondemonstrative, evidence in the same way that the written words of traditional texts supply the dialectician with clues to the probability of a claim that cannot be shown to be demonstratively certain.

Even though the Royal Society virtuosi were committed to the notion that natural signs provide us with authoritative testimony, they were not prepared simply to throw out traditional textual authorities, especially the Scripture. They were certainly hostile to what they perceived as the manipulation of the textual tradition by self-interested clergymen, yet

---

making trial of the things themselves: especially, since Natures Book is so open, and legible." *Anatomical Exercitations* (London: James Young, 1653), 23.

[67] Robert Boyle, quoted by J. R. Jacob, *Robert Boyle and the English Revolution* (New York: Bert Franklin, 1978), 101. I have modernized Boyle's spelling, while preserving his original punctuation.

[68] Boyle, "Discourse of Things above Reason," in *Works* (1772), 4:455.

most of these men remained committed to the authority of revelation. However, years of bloody conflict over the interpretation of that authoritative text led them to seek less ambiguous standards for public deliberation. Faced with marked disagreement over how Scripture should be read and understood, they came to believe that consulting the signs of nature was preferable to debating over ambiguous phrases found in authoritative texts, even the Bible. Natural signs provided a more reliable, albeit still imperfect, access to God's will. The book of nature, which had long been cited alongside the book of Scripture as a source of divine testimony, began to eclipse the authority of the written word. For the experimentalists, theologians, and philosophers around Boyle, the signs that they read in nature began to take precedence over the signs that they read in traditional texts. More accurately, the signs of nature came to be used to reinterpret and explain all other signs, including revelation. The motto of the Royal Society was *nullius in verba* ("on no one else's word")—they refused to accept the testimony of ancient texts or solitary individuals as sufficient justification to establish truth claims. The shift away from scholastic authorities and toward experience and experimentation was made possible by the assumption that God's great design was most clearly (although still imperfectly) revealed through creation. By attending to the signs of nature instead of the controversial signs of authoritative texts, Boyle and his like-minded collaborators could sidestep the arguments of radical skepticism and establish probable truths based on a new type of nondemonstrative evidence.

How do we know that this new probability had any influence on Locke? Although he never distinguished himself as an experimentalist in his own right, Locke took part in a number of investigations. He surrounded himself with practitioners of the new experimental philosophy and devotedly collected their written work.[69] He remained in constant contact with Boyle, collaborated with the chemist Peter Stahl, set up a small laboratory with the physician David Thomas, and probably assisted Richard Lower in his revolutionary blood transfusion in 1667.[70] Boyle dedicated his *Memoirs for the Natural History of Human Blood* (1683)

[69] Harrison and Laslett have found that Locke owned some sixty distinct books authored by Boyle and as well as works by Hooke, Lower, Sydenham, Wilkins, Willis and a host of other virtuosi. Harrison and Laslett, *Library of John Locke*, 91–93, 157, 79, 242, 64, 65.

[70] For evidence of Locke's experimental pursuits at this time, see Woolhouse, *Locke: A Biography*, 32–37, 66–69; Cranston, *John Locke*, 40, 76, 90; Kenneth Dewhurst, *John Locke (1632–1704), Physician and Philosopher: A Medical Biography* (London: Wellcome Historical Medical Library, 1963), 13–14, and "Locke's Contribution to Boyle's Researches on the Air and on Human Blood," *Notes of the Royal Society of London* 17 (1962), 198–206; M. A. Stewart, "Locke's Professional Contacts with Robert Boyle," *Locke Newsletter* 12 (1982), 19–44. For a fascinating and lively account of the culture of experiment that animated this circle, see Jardine, *Ingenious Pursuits*.

"to the very ingenious and learned Dr. J.L." and allowed Locke to edit and revise for publication his *History of Air* (1692). Boyle also appointed Locke to be one of his literary executives.[71] Yet Locke's most significant professional partnership of this period was the one he formed with one of the most famous physicians of his day, Thomas Sydenham. Sydenham "was as distinguished in the fields of medical research and therapy as Boyle was in the fields of chemistry and general science."[72] As Peter Gay points out, Locke "was a physician before he was a philosopher, and a philosopher largely because he was a physician."[73]

Locke shared with Sydenham an abiding interest in medicine and an intense dissatisfaction with the traditional ways it was being taught and practiced.[74] The university curriculum was organized around ancient, authoritative texts. Just as Aristotle's writings served as the benchmark in matters of philosophy, Galen's work remained the ruling orthodoxy in the study of medicine. Instead of devoting himself to these ancient sources, Locke accompanied Sydenham on his visits with patients and served as his secretary and assistant. During this time Locke not only honed practical skills that would lead to his employment as Shaftesbury's personal physician, he also began to internalize a framework of investigation that centered on the importance of interpreting natural signs. According to Sydenham, the abstract speculation of *scientia* and traditional authorities of *opinio* were of little use to the practicing physician. "The function of a physician," he explains, is the "industrious investigation of the history of diseases, and of the effect of remedies, as shown by the only true teacher, experience." This is because "true practice consists in the observations of nature: these are finer than any speculations. Hence the medicine of nature is more refined than the medicine of philosophy."[75]

A fragment that Locke wrote at the time of his friendship with Sydenham reveals that he was thinking along very similar lines. "True knowledge grew first in the world by experience and rational observations," Locke writes, "but proud man, not content with the knowledge he was capable of, and which was useful to him, would needs penetrate into

[71] Neal Wood, *The Politics of Locke's Philosophy: A Social Study of "An Essay Concerning Human Understanding"* (Berkeley: University of California Press, 1983), 65–66.

[72] Cranston, *John Locke*, 91.

[73] Peter Gay, *The Enlightenment: An Interpretation* (New York: Random House, 1969), 14.

[74] Locke sought several times to obtain a doctorate in medicine without having to suffer through the traditional requirements. Yet even his attempt to use political connections failed. He eventually secured a degree of bachelor of medicine and a license to practice as a physician in 1675, but he never attained a doctorate. See Cranston, *John Locke*, 96–97, 138–39. For a discussion of the importance of Locke's medical work in the development of his philosophical ideas, see Dewhurst, *John Locke*; and Romanell, *John Locke and Medicine*.

[75] Quoted by Cranston, *John Locke*, 92.

the hidden causes of things, lay down principles, and establish maxims to himself about the operations of nature, and thus vainly expect that nature, or in truth God, should proceed according to those laws which his maxims had prescribed to him.[76] For Locke and Sydenham, a physician need not know the real essence or ultimate cause of a disease when treating a patient in order to diagnose it or counteract its effects. In fact even if "knowledge" of such essences could be achieved, it would be useless if a cure could not be found. "All speculations in this subject however curious or refined or seeming profound and solid, if they teach not their followers to do something either better or in a shorter and easier way than otherwise they could, or else lead them to the discovery of some new and useful invention, deserve not the name of knowledge, or so much of the vast time of our idle hours to be thrown away upon such empty idle philosophy."[77] In a fragment on smallpox written in 1670, Locke writes that it is but "ostentation" to "make a show to enquire into the essences of things" when "we cannot know beyond the information of our senses."[78] As a physician Locke recognizes that he must make judgments under conditions of uncertainty by attending to nondemonstrative, natural signs. Thus medicine provides Locke with an example of the new probability at work. Although he is constantly reminded of the limits of human knowledge, he is forced to consider possible solutions and act on them according to the deliverances of nondemonstrative observation. If his judgments correspond to the available evidence, they can be seen as highly probable, but they can never be demonstratively certain.[79]

For Locke and many of his contemporaries, there was something commonsensical, something eminently reasonable, about this new notion of probability. Moderate theologians, physicians, and experimentalists

---

[76] John Locke, "De Arte Medica" (1669), in Fox Bourne, *The Life of John Locke*, 2 vols. (London: Harry S. King, 1876), 1:224. The authorship of this fragment is disputed. Fox Bourne, Cranston, and many others attribute it to Locke since it is in his handwriting. Dewhurst argues that Locke was simply transcribing a work that was originally written by Sydenham. Dewhurst, *John Locke*, 73.

[77] Locke, "De Arte Medica," 1:226.

[78] Romanell, *John Locke and Medicine*, 71. This fragment, like "De Arte Medica," could have been simply transcribed by Locke for Sydenham. Yet whether the true author of these lines is Sydenham or Locke, it is clear that they express one of the principal themes of the *Essay*, the first draft of which Locke completed the following year.

[79] In his later work, *The Conduct of the Understanding*, Locke contrasts his preferred method of tentative observation with the method of those who choose a school of thought and then attempt to defend the certainty of its principles: "For example, were it my business to understand physic [medicine], would not the safer and readier way be to consult nature herself, and inform myself in the history of diseases and their cures, than espousing the principles of the dogmatists, Methodists, or chemists, engage in all the disputes concerning either of those systems, and suppose it true, until I have tried what they can say to beat me out of it" (CU 35).

turned away from the demanding standard of demonstrative knowledge and instead embraced the notion that most of human understanding should be viewed in terms of degrees or gradations of certainty. They were convinced that we make our best judgments when we take pains to consult the book of nature. This conviction was sustained by a shared assumption concerning the underlying purpose and order of God's natural design. The conflict and chaos that we encounter is not inherent in the world, but rather due to the difficulty we have in accessing the order of creation. Although we all live under conditions of uncertainty, many of the disagreements that emerge are simply unnecessary and could be resolved if we would only make the testimony of nature the public standard for warranted belief. This new notion of probability supplied Locke with a language with which he could mitigate his philosophical skepticism and moderate his political absolutism. As he experimented with the possibilities of this new framework, he began to work out a way in which he and his contemporaries could engage in responsible deliberation and effective persuasion in a world in which the central categories of rational justification had collapsed. He began to articulate a new type of reasonableness.

Locke's changing views of knowing and believing went hand in hand with his increased interest in the practicality of toleration. At the same time that he was engaging in medicine and other experimental inquiries, Locke was reevaluating his views on toleration. In 1667 he wrote *An Essay on Toleration* moving away from the type of theoretical consideration that dominated the *Two Tracts*, and focusing instead on the practical conditions of England.[80] In this work, he argues that coercion is ineffective and that toleration is the most prudent policy, given the way in which his contemporaries have embraced their religious identities. Locke ends the essay by pointing out that it is a mistake to think that "severity and force are the only arts of government."[81] What other "arts of government" might lead to peaceful and tolerant societies? Locke tells us here that such "particulars" must wait. Yet perhaps one such art of government involves the intellectual and ethical transformation of his countrymen.

As Locke followed the growing debate concerning toleration at the end of the 1660s, he also continued to attack the uselessness of idle speculation, and defend the importance of probable reasoning.[82] In the midst of his inquiries into toleration and reasonableness, he began work on his

[80] Locke, "An Essay on Toleration," in *Political Essays*, 134–59.

[81] Ibid., 159.

[82] In this period Locke took extensive notes on Samuel Parker's book on nonconformists and dissenters and continued to wrestle with the problem of toleration. See "On Samuel Parker," in *Political Essays*, 211–15.

Essay. Locke set out to write a "true *History of the first beginnings of Humane Knowledge;* whence the Mind has its first Objects" (E II.xi.15). To do this he would have to avoid any outside textual authorities and rely wholly on the authority of natural signs or "facts."[83] This is what Locke means when he says that he is simply "following Nature in its ordinary method" (E II.xi.14). The *Essay Concerning Understanding* is itself a work of natural history, written in a "Historical, plain Method" (E I.i.2). Although this work was not published until 1690, the first draft was finished in 1671. As we will see, the ideas that Locke articulated in this text shaped his mature political and religious writings. If we wish to understand how Locke's use of the new notion of probability informs his political understanding, we must first turn to the *Essay.* It is here that Locke emphasizes the importance of probable judgment and develops a mode of justification that seeks to navigate between the desolation of radical skepticism and the dogmatism of Cartesian rationalism. In the *Essay* Locke shows his readers how to govern their judgments in ways that are conducive to self-government in the context of religious disagreement.

---

[83] Locke reported to Edward Clark that while thinking through the ideas of his *Essay,* he had studiously avoided reading books on the subject or consulting the opinions of others. *Correspondence,* 3:89.

IV

Forming Judgment

THE TRANSFORMATION OF KNOWLEDGE AND BELIEF

WHEN LOCKE SAT DOWN to write the *Essay Concerning Human Understanding*, he was not simply trying to explicate philosophical difficulties or construct an integrated system of abstract speculations. He turned his attention to epistemology in order to provide practical guidance for readers who found themselves confounded by the profound disagreements and sometimes violent controversies of his day. Instead of offering them a set of answers to their questions, however, he set out to change their intellectual conduct, to transform the way they governed their thoughts and behavior. He sought to convince them to embrace a new practice of rational appraisal. By teaching his readers to discipline themselves according to the deliverances of probable judgment, he could help them take up the arduous journey of intellectual self-discipline through which they could constitute themselves as naturally free, equal, and rational individuals. It is worth noting that human nature, from this point of view, is not something that human beings possess, but something they enact. It is something that they achieve by adopting appropriate rules of thinking and acting.[1]

The goal of the *Essay*, then, is to persuade readers to pursue natural liberty and rationality by taking up the intellectual practices that would make possible institutions of self-government. If Locke is best understood as proposing a Great Recoinage of public reason, it is in the *Essay* that he begins to show his readers just what this new political reasonableness entails. The arguments that Locke will make in his explicitly political texts are thus embedded in a much larger and more extensive engagement with the psychological and cognitive conditions within which lib-

---

[1] Locke's perplexing use of the term "natural" to describe something that is acquired through hard work and constant vigilance is not unique to him. It parallels the approach of many writers in the early modern era who employ the language of nature and artifice in ways that highlight their interconnectedness. As we have seen in chapter 3, the language of fact that pervades the seventeenth century rests on the analogy between man as the artificer of the civil realm and God as the artificer of the natural world. In addition, much of what is deemed natural requires both divine and human creativity to come into being. For a discussion of the ways in which Locke tries to navigate between nature and convention, see Myers, *Our Only Star*.

eral institutions could flourish. Locke recognized the difficulties inherent in government by consent and sought to respond to (if never entirely to resolve) these philosophical and practical challenges by setting out to transform the individual judgment of his contemporaries.[2] As Mark Button puts it, he sought to shape consensual government "from the inside out" by teaching his readers to govern their judgment in particular ways.[3]

Seen in this light, Locke's epistemological writings take on a decidedly political character. Locke himself draws this connection in the "Epistle to the Reader" at the beginning of the *Essay*. He tells us that the idea to write the *Essay* emerged out of a discussion that he had with five or six friends in his apartment at Exeter House in London. When their conversation turned to the controversial matters of revealed religion and morality, the discussants "found themselves quickly at a stand by the difficulties that rose on every side" (E I.i.7). Locke and his associates were perplexed by their inability to provide satisfying answers to questions that were not only of "great concernment" to them personally, but were also extremely important politically.

The difficulties that puzzled this group of thinkers were the same difficulties that were unsettling people throughout Europe. The collapse of traditional modes of justification left individuals wondering how they could publicly distinguish warranted beliefs from unwarranted ones, how they could tell the dangerous fanatic from the reasonable believer. Uncertain about the deliverances of scholastic demonstration and cut off from a tradition of shared authoritative texts, a once unified Christendom had split into a multiplicity of warring factions. How Locke and his contemporaries answered controversial questions of morality and revealed religion not only meant the difference between eternal salvation and damnation, but also the difference between peaceful coexistence and chaotic and bloody conflict. It is in the context of these questions that Locke's circle of friends "found themselves quickly at a stand," and it was the attempt to provide a resolution to these very palpable difficulties that "gave the first rise to this Essay concerning the understanding" (E I.i.7).

Yet it is significant that Locke does not offer a conclusive solution to the moral and political debates that circled around him. In fact, he does not even spell out the specific questions that he and his friends were discussing. He simply asserts that their doubts and disagreements were the result of taking the "wrong course." They had rushed headlong into controversial moral and theological debates without first examining their

[2] Nathan Tarcov puts it exactly right when he states, "The *Essay* argues on behalf of toleration or liberalism not as a set of political institutions or doctrines, but as a set of moral dispositions supportive of such institutions or doctrines." Nathan Tarcov, "John Locke and the Foundations of Toleration," in Levine, *Early Modern Skepticism*, 191.

[3] Button, *Contract, Culture, and Citizenship*, 132.

intellectual abilities to determine the limits of their own understanding. In response Locke offers an example of how to conduct oneself when faced with disagreement and uncertainty. He rejects the disputational style of the Scholastics because it reflects the arrogance and hollowness of a type of thinking that assumes an expansive, perhaps unlimited, scope of knowledge. Following the narrative style of the Royal Society experimentalists, he provides tentative explanations of the workings of the mind only insofar as they might be conducive to recognizing appropriate mental behavior. "Our business here is not to know all things," he writes, "but those which concern our conduct" (E I.i.6).

Locke's epistemology is not so much *explanatory* as *performative* or *regulative*. He is more interested in recommending a set of intellectual practices than constructing a philosophical system.[4] The traditional classification of the *Essay* as the founding document of the empiricist tradition has been successfully challenged in recent years.[5] Yet Locke should not be classified as wholly rationalist either. In fact academic quarrels over empiricist and rationalist labels distract from the central concern of the *Essay*. Locke wants to show his readers how they should govern their thoughts because he believes that their thoughts have a direct effect on their behavior. "The ideas and images in men's minds are the invisible powers that constantly govern them," Locke tells us. It is therefore "of the highest concernment" that "care should be taken of the understanding" (CU 1). Greg Forster calls Locke's project "an epistemology of limits."[6] Although different individuals might possess varying intellectual and physical skills, Locke insists that we are all able (and even obligated) to constrain our sometimes busy minds and discipline our judgment.[7]

If we are to understand this political-epistemological project, we must take a closer look at how Locke works in the *Essay* to convince his readers to accept a particular type of rationality based on intellectual self-discipline. It is important to note just how much Locke's attitude of quiet contentment and intellectual modesty in the *Essay* contrasts with the audacity of his earlier writings. In the first three books, Locke clears away unreliable epistemologies that might tempt readers to think that

---

[4] As we will see in greater detail below, Locke associates those philosophers who attempt to construct "systems" with partisanship and fanaticism (e.g., E IV.iii.6).

[5] Schouls, *Reasoned Freedom*; Wolterstorff, *Ethics of Belief*; and Nicholas Jolley, *Locke: His Philosophical Thought* (New York: Oxford University Press, 1999).

[6] Greg Forster, *John Locke's Politics of Moral Consensus* (Cambridge: Cambridge University Press, 2005), 40–83.

[7] Nicholas Wolterstorff challenges traditional readings of the *Essay* by arguing persuasively that Locke's epistemology is primarily aimed at "belief regulation" and not demonstrative knowledge. Wolterstorff, *Ethics of Belief*.

they can have easy access to divine certainty and knowledge. He ridicules the notion that God places innate ideas in minds and casts doubt on the idea that God reveals anything directly to individuals that would conflict with reason. Any communication with God is mediated through the world around us. After clearing away dangerous fallacies that lead to intellectual overconfidence, he turns in book 4 to limit the scope of what we can call "knowledge" in the strict sense. Here he blurs the rigid distinction between "knowledge" and "belief" (or *scientia* and *opinio*) in order to show the crucial importance of belief in our daily lives.[8] Locke places the messy and often uncertain process of making probable judgments about the world at the center of his political project. By learning to adjust their intellectual aspirations to their powers, Locke's readers can learn how to govern their own thoughts and actions. It is the widespread acceptance of a new approach to probable judgment that will provide a common vocabulary of justification through which matters of public importance can be discussed and debated.

Locke's Political Pedagogy

For Locke the coherence and stability of self-government rest on a capacity to foster a particular understanding of the individual as properly bounded. For this reason, he was not simply concerned with establishing boundaries *between* persons; he wanted to establish them *within* persons as well. Yet proper intellectual conduct involves the recognition of these boundaries as well as the recognition that the urge to exceed these boundaries can never be fully eliminated and must always be vigilantly monitored and carefully controlled. This pedagogical project is most apparent in *Some Thoughts Concerning Education*, where Locke presents a curriculum for raising children in order to curb their brute desires as well as their intellectual passions. Yet this project also pervades Locke's mature writings and is explicitly taken up in the *Essay*.

As we will see, the intellectual self-governance that Locke recommends involves stepping back from the commitments and assumptions that make up our individual identity and determining the relative validity of those beliefs according to empirically accessible standards of reasonableness. Of course, Locke doesn't expect us to evaluate the validity of every belief that we might act upon. Such continuous monitoring would be mentally paralyzing. Yet he does think that we should be prepared to evaluate our

---

[8] See ibid., 180–226; and G.A.J. Rogers, "John Locke: Conservative Radical," in *Margins of Orthodoxy*, ed. Roger Lund (Cambridge: Cambridge University Press, 1995), 103–8.

commitments whenever they become subject to public disagreement or debate. And it is here that the focus on a new notion of probability plays such an important role. Locke wants to restrict claims to certainty to a very narrow compass and place all other claims within the realm of probability. In matters of conduct, we can only rarely, if ever, attain absolute certainty, but we can strive to achieve the highest level of probability. This readiness to evaluate our commitments and assumptions in accordance with probability is what Locke recommends when he tells his readers, "*Reason* must be our last judge and guide in every thing" (E IV.xix.14).

For some readers there is something gloomy and apprehensive about Locke's call for cognitive self-governance. By anxiously demarcating boundaries between what it can and cannot seek to know and by constantly evaluating its thoughts and actions, the Lockean agent seems to cut itself off from the infinite and immeasurable possibilities of human existence. By rigidly sequestering its private, native impulses from the contestation of the public realm, the properly governed self seems to stifle its deepest and most powerful longings. It is not, nor can it ever be, fully autonomous or spontaneous. Proper intellectual conduct involves limiting oneself. Some scholars have wondered about the legitimacy of such a directive. John Dunn has worried about the "boundless repression" in Locke's conception of the self-regulating individual.[9] Uday Singh Mehta has joined an imposing group of critics—including Rousseau, Nietzsche, and Freud—in hinting that Locke's call for self-restraint is nothing more than a veneer that conceals the systematic suppression of intense disorderliness and yearning.[10]

Yet it is important to remember that Locke has good reason to be wary of disruptive intellectual yearnings. It is his anxious recognition of the unpredictable, anarchic potential of the individual judgment that leads him to emphasize the political importance of self-control and self-mastery. By teaching his readers to regulate their own thoughts and actions, he can shift the primary locus of constraint from external coercion to internal discipline. In this way he can facilitate the establishment of a regime in which individuals are not simply governed, but govern themselves as well. In order to judge whether Locke's project is ultimately tenable, however, we must turn to his attempt to convince his readers to take on the burdens of intellectual self-discipline and self-limitation. We must examine how he helps form judgment.

In order to reach the broadest audience possible, Locke takes pains to write in a seemingly painless way, avoiding jargon and allowing himself

---

[9] Dunn, *Political Thought of Locke*, 259–65.

[10] Mehta, *The Anxiety of Freedom*. See also Pangle, *Spirit of Modern Republicanism*, 178–79, 207–8.

to be chattier than would commonly be expected in a philosophical treatise.[11] By titling his book an essay rather than a treatise, he signals that it is meant to be an accessible work written for a general audience rather than a narrow philosophical tract written for fellow philosophers. He explains that the *Essay* is not primarily for "men of large thoughts and quick apprehensions," but for "men of my own size, to whom, perhaps, it will not be unacceptable, that I have taken some pains, to make plain and familiar to their thoughts some truths, which established prejudice, or the abstractness of the ideas themselves, might render difficult" (E, "Epistle to the Reader" 8). In order to make his argument "easy and intelligible to all sorts of readers," he carefully details each of his arguments and repeatedly clarifies them with so many examples that he risks appearing long-winded and pedantic (E 9).

Yet his goal is not to dazzle, but to instruct: "I had much rather the speculative and quick-sighted should complain of my being in some parts tedious, than that any one, not accustomed to abstract speculations or prepossessed with different notions, should mistake or not comprehend my meaning" (E 9). Locke was determined to make his work simple and clear because he wanted to reach as many of his contemporaries as possible. Neal Wood explains that the *Essay* "was not meant to be an arcane manual for a restricted audience of academicians and experts." Locke wrote "for ordinary educated readers of common sense: peers, landed gentry, merchants, manufacturers, administrators, physicians, lawyers, clerics, men of letters. The *Essay* was conceived primarily to aid them in their everyday lives, to guide them in the great practical concerns of religion, morality, politics, and law, and in normal intercourse."[12] Just as Francis Bacon had planned to initiate a program of intellectual regeneration through his *Instauratio Magna*, Locke sought to disseminate a notion of moral agency and cognitive responsibility by means of a careful inquiry into the workings of the understanding.

[11] Steven Shapin and Simon Schaffer are right to point out that scientific writing in the seventeenth century was shaped by the need to develop trust between individuals and thus emphasized "gentlemanly" manners and self-discipline. Yet they are mistaken, especially in the case of Locke, that this emphasis on conduct reinscribed aristocratic social hierarchies. See Shapin and Schaffer, *Leviathan and the Air-Pump*; and Steven Shapin, *The Social History of Truth: Civility and Science in Seventeenth-Century England* (Chicago: University of Chicago Press, 1994).

[12] Wood, *Politics of Locke's Philosophy*, 2. In addition to Wood's excellent chapter "Intentions and Audience" in *The Politics of Locke's Philosophy*, see Rosalie Colie, "The Essayist in the *Essay*," in *John Locke: Problems and Perspectives*, ed. John W. Yolton (Cambridge: Cambridge University Press, 1969). For a more recent treatment of the rhetorical strategies behind Locke's "plain style," see Peter Walmsley, *Locke's Essay and the Rhetoric of Science* (Lewisburg, Pa.: Bucknell University Press, 2003).

Locke's project of reform begins with the recognition that human beings have an entrenched and dangerous tendency to reach beyond their own capacities. "The busy mind of man," he writes, tends to meddle "with things exceeding its comprehension" (E I.i.4). It is our thirst for "universal knowledge" that leads us to "raise questions, and perplex ourselves and others with disputes about things, to which our understandings are not suited" (E I.i.4). "There is nothing more restive and ungovernable than our thoughts" (CU 45). Locke observes a profound yearning in human beings that drives them to know more and more about their world and that which lies beyond their world. While some of the intellectual quests that we are driven to undertake will prove useful to us, this yearning can also be profoundly harmful. It can lead us out into "the vast ocean of being" where we either cling to shreds of ungrounded opinion as if they were indubitable truths or we "despair of knowing anything" (E I.i.6).

The proper response to this dangerous longing, Locke tell us, is to learn to monitor our thoughts and regulate our judgments. He writes, "The eagerness and strong bent of the mind after knowledge, if not warily regulated, is often a hindrance to it" (CU 25). The natural proclivity of the mind is not toward the moderate reasonableness that Locke associates with the well-governed intellect. The individual conscience is characterized by a disquieting yearning that threatens to undermine its goal of achieving a settled understanding of matters of "great concernment" in politics, religion, and morality. The picture that emerges in the *Essay* and the *Conduct* is one in which the mind finds itself cut off from the static, ordered cosmos of the medievals and is thrown into the ebb and flow of a sea of particulars of an "almost infinite variety" (CU 45). The swirling waves of ideas and experiences wash over the unwary intellect and push and pull it in all sorts of directions until it finds itself unable to stay afloat and submits to the tyranny of the tides. Those who are willing to submit to "tyranny of the understanding," Locke argues, will eventually participate in more public and overtly political tyrannies (CU 45; E IV.xvi.4, IV.xix.2).

The first step in gaining control of our understanding, then, is to learn to recognize the limits or boundaries of our capacities. Locke tells us that we should not venture out into this unpredictable ocean without first being familiar with the length of our plumb line (E I.i.5). Throughout his epistemological writings, he is constantly setting methodological limits to his own inquiry as an example of what it means to discipline one's mind. He focuses on the proper boundaries, borders, and limitations of our intellect. For example, at the very beginning of the *Essay* he writes, "I shall not at present meddle with the physical consideration of the mind; or trouble my self to examine, wherein its essence consists." For Locke, such speculations might be "curious and entertaining," yet extend far beyond the more modest aims of his work (E I.i.2). Locke's inquiry into the "extent of human knowledge" is carefully limited to the immediate objects of observation. Writing in the "historical, plain style" used by the practitioners of a new, modest natural philosophy, Locke refuses to "meddle with the physical consideration of the mind" or attempt to explicate "essences." As Peter Walmsley points out, Locke's description of ideas "is treated as a phenomenon rather than a conception; it remains unproven. . . . The way of ideas is never theorized or analyzed, just simply and insistently practiced."[13] In this way he declines to delve into the perplexing questions about the relationship between the "ideas" that play such a crucial role in his discussion and whatever physical motions or sources may be involved in their production. Locke begins his inquiry by refusing to go beyond the "appearances" of simple and mixed ideas.[14]

Locke is surely aware that such epistemic caution differs from the approach of many of his contemporaries, yet he insists that we should not venture into waters that are too deep. Consider Hobbes's explicit discussion of the workings of the mind in the first chapter of his *Leviathan*: "The cause of sense, is the external body or object, which presses the organ proper to each sense, . . . which pressure, by the mediation of nerves, and other strings, and membranes of the body, continued inwards to the brain, the heart, causes there a resistance, or counterpressure."[15] Whereas Hobbes tries to move beyond appearance to arrive at a starting point from which a demonstrative argument based on matter and motion can be made, Locke limits himself to surface observation.

This process of epistemological limitation is repeated in his discussion of passions as "modes of pleasures and pains" (E II.xx.5). Instead of speculating on the source of such modes or simple ideas, he announces that it is not "my business here, to enquire any farther, than into the bare *ideas* of our passions" (E II.xx.5). In contrast, Hobbes identifies pleasure as "the appearance or sense of good" and then goes beyond the appearance to inquire into the "motion of endeavor which consists in appetite," and "appetite" is described as "a corroboration of vital motion, and a help

[13] Walmsley, *Locke's Essay*, 95.

[14] Locke found an intellectual ally in Pierre Nicole, whose *Essais de Morale* he was translating at the time he was working on the *Essay*. Nicole reminds his readers that "the sight of our minds and of our bodies are much alike: both superficial, both bounded. Our eyes pierce not to the inside of things: they stick at the surface. . . . Just after this manner is the view of things in our minds: we know nothing of most of them, beyond the shell and surface." In a later passage, Locke translates Nicole to assert, "The discovery of truth, in most cases, depends upon our comparing probabilities together." From "On the Weakness of Man," in *John Locke as Translator: Three of the Essais of Pierre Nicole in French and English*, ed. Jean S. Yolton (Oxford: Voltaire Foundation, 2000), 60, 63.

[15] Hobbes, *Leviathan*, I.i. I have modernized the spelling, while retaining the original punctuation.

thereunto."[16] Thus Locke, in the very performance of the *Essay,* signals that by limiting himself to that which is observable he can avoid cognitive overextension. Inquiring deeper into the underlying sources of that which is observed is to submit to a longing for "universal knowledge" that would at best be a waste of time and at worst a groundless provocation for disagreement and possibly even violent conflict.[17]

Instead of trying to comprehend the mysteries of creation, Locke narrows his inquiry to those things that might prove beneficial to human beings. This is what he means when he says that he aims "at truth and usefulness" (E, "Epistle," 9). An inquiry into the "extent of human knowledge" is useful only insofar as it aids us in regulating our mental activities and governing our conduct. In the spirit of Bacon, Locke rejects "bare contemplation" and "inactive speculation" in favor of insight that can benefit us in our daily affairs. The most useful insight, he insists, involves discerning the proper way to govern our thoughts and actions (E II.xxi.34, 37). Thus Locke's philosophical investigations are nothing more (but nothing less) than an inquiry into proper behavior. "Our business here, is not to know all things, but those which concern our conduct" (E I.i.6).[18]

By repeatedly setting limits to his own inquiry, Locke echoes the admonitions of many of his contemporaries. It is the recognition that the human mind must be actively restrained from its own overextension that leads him to instruct the "busy minds" of his readers to "be more cautious in meddling with things exceeding its comprehension; to stop, when it is at the utmost extent of its tether; and to sit down in a quiet ignorance of those things, which, upon examination, are found to be beyond the reach of our capacities" (E I.i.4). It is significant that the *Essay,* which has been both celebrated and derided as the archetypical Enlightenment defense of the unlimited powers of human reason, begins with an admonition to sit down in quiet ignorance of those things that are beyond our reach. In stark contrast to the almost limitless confidence of many of his eighteenth-century adherents, Locke exhibits a deep concern for the dangers and pitfalls of thinking and presents his readers with an extended defense of epistemic temperance and self-restraint.

[16] Ibid., I.6.

[17] For comparable explorations of the *Essay* as an application of a new natural philosophy based on signs of nature, see Wood, *Politics of Locke's Philosophy*; and Myers, *Our Only Star.*

[18] Locke's focus on mental governance and right conduct instead of constructing philosophical systems continues to have a powerful rhetorical appeal. As Harold Laski commented a generation ago, it is "one of the primary characteristics of the British mind to be interested in problems of conduct rather than of thought." Harold Laski, *Political Thought in England: From Locke to Bentham* (London: Oxford University Press, 1950), 11.

Locke tells us that we inhabit a "state of mediocrity" and should "learn to content our selves with what is attainable by us in this state" (E IV.xiv.2, I.i.4). The ignorance that we experience is not simply a temporary handicap to be overcome by method or sheer will power, but a permanent and ineluctable part of the human condition. As creatures in a universe that we have not created, some things are simply beyond our grasp. Our capacities fall short "of an universal or perfect comprehension of whatsoever is" (E I.i.5). They are not "fitted to penetrate into the internal fabric and real essences of bodies" (E IV.xii.11).

Although our capacities to know the world around us are limited, our capacity to overstep the proper boundaries of our understanding is almost boundless. For Locke, the mind is in constant danger of launching out into waters that are too deep, and it must be carefully monitored if it is going to "be of use to us" (E I.i.5). The proper governance of our intellectual faculties, however, will yield "advantages of ease and health, and thereby increase our stock of conveniences for this life" (E IV.xii.10). If properly trimmed, "the candle, that is set up in us, shines bright enough for all our purposes" (E I.i.5). Yet if we wish to achieve the "truth and usefulness" that Locke sees as the aim of rational inquiry, we must learn to recognize the "bounds between opinion and knowledge" and learn to "regulate our assent, and moderate our persuasions" (E I.i.3). Locke's emphasis on securing the limits and boundaries of our intellect is the guiding theme of the *Essay* and the *Conduct of the Understanding*. It is for this reason that Locke chose a Latin quotation from Cicero's dialogue *De Natura Deorum* for the title page of the *Essay*. It reads, "How delightful it would be ... if when you did not know a thing you would admit your ignorance, instead of uttering this drivel which must even disgust yourself."[19] In the original context, this statement is a derisive gibe directed at a defender of dogmatic theology by the skeptic Cotta. The title page of the *Conduct* offers a similar skeptical admonition from *De Natura Deorum*: "What is so rash and so unworthy of the dignity and firmness of the wise as to believe falsely or to maintain without any doubt what is perceived and conceived without enough investigation?"[20] Although it is difficult to determine

---

[19] The quotation is from Marcus Tullius Cicero, *The Nature of the Gods*, ed. P. G. Walsh (New York: Clarendon Press, 1997), I.i. Subsequent controversy over the *Essay* might have been the reason Locke added a second quotation to the fourth and fifth editions. The quotation was a similar admonition, this time translated into English, from a more canonical text—the Bible: "As thou knowest not what is the way of the Spirit, not how the bones do grow in the Womb of her that is with Child: even so thou knowest not the works of God, who maketh all things." Ecclesiastes 11:5. For a discussion of Cicero's influence on Locke's thought, see Marshall, *John Locke*, 299–315; Wood, *Politics of Locke's Philosophy*, 29–30.

[20] Cicero, *Nature of the Gods*, I.i.

to what extent Locke is allying himself with Academic skepticism here, it is unmistakable that he is at pains to remind his readers that human beings too often fail to hold their judgments in a way that is fitting to their capacities.

Fanatics and Philosophizers

Locke was well aware that not everyone shared his view of properly governed judgment. He was especially worried about two groups of people who had little interest in determining the limits of human understanding: religious enthusiasts and philosophical dogmatists. The urgency and resolve in his writing comes from almost palpable anxiety concerning those who let their thoughts race out into "the vast ocean of being, as if all that boundless extent, were the natural, and undoubted possession of our understanding" (E I.i.7). Locke is convinced that when individuals stretch beyond their capacity in search of a certainty that is unobtainable, they are likely to become either dogmatically zealous or despondently skeptical. In either case, intellectual overextension leads to a type of intellectual enslavement. Some insist that "they have wings to fly, and can soar on high when they please," while others "sit still, because they think they have not legs to go" (CU 39). Both alternatives have dangerous political consequences for Locke. As zealots grow accustomed to imposing on their own minds, they will be more apt to impose on others through violence and domination (E IV.xix.2). As the skeptics acquiesce to their own despair, they are left without resources for resisting either the continued domination of those in power or the manipulation of zealots who seek power (E I.i.7). Locke repeatedly reminds his readers that the failure to discipline one's judgment correctly leads to either skepticism or bigotry (CU 33, 34).

The more urgent danger, however, is not posed by those who "despair of knowing anything" but by those who claim certainty in controversial matters in which certainty cannot be confirmed. The philosophical or academic skeptic plays less of a role in the *Essay*. For Locke there is something absurd about those who doubt everything that cannot be affirmed by absolute and certain knowledge. "He that in the ordinary affairs of life, would admit of nothing but direct plain demonstration," Locke writes, "would be sure of nothing in this world, but of perishing quickly." This is because there is precious little the skeptic could conclude that would be invulnerable to doubt or objection: "The wholesomeness of his meat or drink would not give him reason to venture on it" (E IV.xi.10). For Locke, philosophical eccentrics such as the radical skeptic pose little threat to civil order or rule of law. The real danger of skepticism is that it seems to pave the way for Locke's far dodgier adversaries, the philosophical and the religious fanatics.

These individuals assume falsely that there is an unproblematic correspondence between their own thoughts and the "boundless Extent" that exists outside of them. They convince themselves that they are somehow predisposed or attuned to a deeper order of things and that their private judgments reflect that order. This type of fanatic believes that the principles he embraces are "standards set up by God in his mind to be the rule and touchstone of all other opinions" (E I.iii.25). Locke does not deny that there is some deeper order that exists outside of us; in fact his defense of regulated judgment relies on such an assumption. Yet he opposes the claim that this purposive structure of creation easily and naturally corresponds to our private judgments. By presupposing such a connection, philosophical and religious fanatics can avoid the pains and the labor of setting boundaries and constraints on their thoughts and rest assured that the claims they make and the actions that they take will be the right ones. They are a law unto themselves.[21]

It is this notion of the unregulated self that is common to the religious zealot, the scholastic divine, the Cartesian innatist, and the madman. They all fail to recognize the limits of the understanding; they claim a level of certainty that is simply inaccessible to them. They all fail to govern themselves according to a criterion that lies outside of their beliefs and desires. Locke links these various figures to a single set of characteristics in order to make room for an alternative understanding of properly self-governed judgment. As we have seen, Locke was especially disturbed by the unswerving confidence of a particular type of religious believer. In the wake of the Reformation, many English dissenters, from moderate Puritans to more radical Quakers and Ranters, had grown increasingly adamant in their rejection not only of traditional Roman Catholic authority but also of the authority of the established Church of England. Taking the Protestant insistence on the priesthood of all believers a step further, they insisted that each individual should look to his or her inner light as the final and ultimate adjudicator in matters of religion, politics,

---

[21] Locke certainly was aware of a connection between philosophical and religious enthusiasm. When Locke told Molyneux of his intention to add a critique of the "enthusiasm" of the Cartesian thinker Malebranche to the *Essay*, Molyneux welcomed the idea. He responded, "I should very much approve of your Adding a Chapter in your Essay concerning Malbranches Hypothesis. As there are Enthusiasmes in Divinity, so there are in Philosophy; and as one proceeds from not Consulting, or misapprehending the Book of God; so the other from not reading and Considering the Book of Nature. I look upon Malbranches Notions, or rather Platos, in this particular perfectly unintelligible; And if you will ingage in a Philosophick Controversy, you cannot do it with more advantage than in this matter." Locke, *Correspondence*, 4:668.

and morality. The sincere believer, they argued, is transformed by the grace of God and experiences a regenerate conscience, so that the private judgments prompted by it are such that God would condone them. Thus the believer who has a regenerate conscience can assert claims with utter confidence in their certainty and authority. How can believers know that their consciences are regenerate? They experience an inner assurance of their own regeneracy or election. Thus the conscience becomes the sovereign guarantor of its own authority.[22] As Catholic opponents were quick to point out, these radical dissenters set up their own consciences as new infallible popes. The conscience could not rightfully be subordinated to any external authority.

Whether in its Puritan form or adapted by other religious and philosophical movements, the appeal to an inner light struck many in Locke's day as dangerously subversive. This type of belief, disparaged as "enthusiasm" because of its implied appeal to a God within, became the subject of increasingly anxious polemics in the late seventeenth century.[23] Like many of his contemporaries, Locke was preoccupied with the radical and unsettling subjectivity of this doctrine from the very beginning of his career. He added a chapter specifically addressing it in the fourth edition of the *Essay*, yet the entire work could be seen as a response to those for whom the "firmness of persuasion is made the cause of believing, and confidence of being in the right, is made an argument of truth" (E IV.xix.12). Instead of submitting themselves to the "tedious and not always successful labor of strict reasoning," enthusiasts claim to have direct access to divine truth and to act under the guidance of heaven (E IV.xix.5). Locke argues that such men undermine both reason and revelation rightly understood, substituting "the conceits of a warmed or overweening brain" for verifiable beliefs authorized by some common source of justification (E IV.xix.7).

By asserting that their own conscience is the ultimate arbiter of truth and falsehood, enthusiasts unleash a subjectivity that threatens public order and subverts the possibility of public deliberation. "For if the light, which every one thinks he has in his mind, which in this case is nothing

---

[22] For moderate Puritan examples of this teaching, see William Ames, *Conscience with the Power and Cases Thereof* (Norwood, N.J.: W. J. Johnson, 1975); William Perkins, *William Perkins, 1558–1602, English Puritanist; His Pioneer Works on Casuistry: "A Discourse of Conscience" and "The Whole Treatise of Cases of Conscience,"* ed. Thomas F. Merrill (Nieuwkoop: B. De Graaf, 1966).

[23] For two excellent treatments of enthusiasm, see Heyd, *Be Sober and Reasonable*; and J.G.A. Pocock, "Enthusiasm: The Antiself of Enlightenment," in *Enthusiasm and Enlightenment in Europe, 1650–1850*, ed. Lawrence E. Klein and Anthony J. La Vopa (San Marino, Calif.: Huntington Library, 1998).

but the strength of his own persuasion, be an evidence that it is from God, contrary opinions may have the same title to be inspirations," he writes. "God will be not only the father of lights, but of opposite and contradictory lights, leading men contrary ways; and contradictory propositions will be divine truths" (E IV.xix.11). If individuals with opposite and contradictory views on politics, religion, or morality are convinced that God has spoken to them directly, they will be motivated to fight and die for their beliefs. Locke recognizes that when appeals to individual conscience are seen to be as certain as demonstrable proofs, there will be a clash of certainties. Violence and coercion will be the inevitable result. Once the enthusiast "does violence to his own faculties" and "tyrannizes over his own mind" by imposing groundless beliefs on himself, he will inevitably tyrannize others as well. Those who exhibit "this bias and corruption" of judgment will almost always assume "an authority of dictating to others, and a forwardness to prescribe to their opinions" (E IV.xix.2). For how can it be otherwise, Locke asks, "but that he should be ready to impose on others' belief, who has already imposed on his own?" (E IV.xix.2; see also IV.xvi.4).

The tendency toward enthusiasm is a constant danger in matters of religion, Locke tells us. Even good people fall prey to the appeal to immediate (and erroneous) inspiration. Locke counsels supposed recipients of direct or indirect revelation to disengage from the experience and ask themselves: "How do I know that God is the revealer of this to me; that this impression is made upon my mind by his holy spirit, and that therefore I ought to obey it?" (E IV.xix.10). Locke insists that mere subjective assurance is inadequate. In order to conduct our thoughts and actions properly, we must be able to compare the ideas and inspirations of our minds with some set of publicly accessible reasons. The zealot's attempt to justify the imposition of a sectarian belief based on his own sense of conviction or the cleric's attempt to justify the rule of a king based on an inaccessible claim to divine certainty represents epistemological misconduct. The enthusiast is simply failing to regulate his judgment properly by refusing to subject his beliefs to evidence or argument.

Thus Locke's rejoinder to the enthusiast is not that religious zealots are too religious, but that they are religious in the wrong way and in the wrong setting. They are religious in roles and institutions where unbridled religious devotion is inappropriate. Here Locke echoes moderate theologians from Grotius to Chillingworth to Boyle. He confronts zealots by pointing out that their unregulated assertion of certainty is prideful and impious, yet he also wants to teach them to speak, think, and act within a new language of probability. He wants to encourage them to embrace religious beliefs that are conducive to reasonable self-

discipline and a peaceful commonwealth. Of course this leaves a genuine
and undeniable clash between some strands of religious commitment and
the Lockean teaching. He seeks to supplant the unregulated faith of the
religious enthusiast with a bounded and self-governing judgment. It is
important to note, however, that Locke is transforming, not dissolving,
religious devotion. He does not completely rule out religious sensibilities
in all areas of human life—in fact, as we will see, he relies on them.

For Locke, there is a parallel between the ecstatic claims of various marginal religious sectarians and the doctrine of innate ideas, held by almost
all of the prominent thinkers in his day. Neither the religious enthusiast
nor the defender of innate ideas respects the limits of the understanding.
Instead, both insist that there is some type of easy connection between
their moral claims and the world outside their minds. This leads them to
insist improperly on their own certainty, and, as if to convince themselves
of the incontestability of their contestable claims, they force them upon
others. Locke's well-known attack on innate ideas in book 1 of the *Essay*
was of a piece with this larger political project.[24] Innatists, including Descartes, insisted that God had implanted ideas or principles in the human
mind. Most moralists and theologians during Locke's lifetime maintained
that innate knowledge, particularly innate practical knowledge (knowledge of moral principles), was essential to the stability of the established
moral and religious order. As John Yolton has shown, some variant of
the theory "can be found in almost any pamphlet of the early part of the
century dealing with morality, conscience, the existence of God, or natural law."[25] The assumed universality of a particular set of beliefs served
as the foundation of moral justification and responsibility for many in
power. Theologians were eager to establish that every generation naturally accepted certain basic moral axioms regardless of cultural differences: murder is wrong, covenants should be honored, honesty should
be upheld. By denying that we are predisposed in some way to assent to

---

[24] Nicholas Jolley has shown that the passages on enthusiasm added to the *Essay* in later
editions were not an afterthought but an extension of the theme of the work as expressed
in the first chapter on innate ideas. Nicholas Jolley, "Reason's Dim Candle: Locke's Critique
of Enthusiasm," in *The Philosophy of John Locke: New Perspectives*, ed. Peter R. Anstey
(New York: Routledge, 2003).

[25] John W. Yolton, *John Locke and the Way of Ideas* (London: Oxford University Press,
1956), 31. For a thorough overview of the many defenders of innate ideas in Locke's day,
see Yolton, 30–71. The "Cambridge Platonists," such as Ralph Cudworth and John Smith,
were among those who explicitly linked innate ideas to morality, yet this line of argument
was commonplace. See Richard Ashcraft, "Faith and Knowledge in Locke's Philosophy," in
Yolton, *John Locke: Problems and Perspectives*, 199; Shapiro, *Probability and Certainty*,
89–92; Marshall, *John Locke*, 292. In his attack on the *Essay*, Edward Stillingfleet, the
bishop of Worcester, saw Locke's claim about innate ideas as the most dangerous aspect
of the work.

what is good and dissent from what is evil, it seemed to many critics that Locke was opening the door to a radical strain of moral relativism.

Yet in the *Essay* Locke treats appeals to innate ideas or innate dispositions as nothing more than a façade, concealing intellectual laziness and ungrounded suppression of dissent.[26] He sets out to convince his readers of the absurdity of both the naïve view of innatism—that we all share a set of moral principles that are immediately accessible to us—as well as the more sophisticated dispositional innatism—that innate principles are inert and must be activated by some external stimulus. The naïve view is implausible since it would mean that we would already be in some type of agreement on those principles. Locke responds to this position by referring to some of the same anthropological evidence that he employed in his early writings to show that large portions of humanity have never even conceived of the principles that proponents insist are innate (E I.ii.24, I.iii.2). There are places in the world were people abandon their children to the elements without scruple, or bury them with their mothers if their mothers die in childbirth, or simply fatten and eat them. Or, most shocking of all, there are whole tribes that do not even recognize the existence of God (E I.iii.9, I.iv.7–17). The point here is not whether Locke actually believes all of the stories that he has read in the travel literature. At times he seems to delight in them while hinting that he is not convinced of their veracity. The point is that he employs this literature, like Montaigne and Charron before him, to show his readers that there is such a diversity of moral practices in the world that a simple appeal to universal consensus in defense of a naïve view of innate practical principles is untenable.

Yet Locke also rejects the dispositional innatism that insists that there are inborn principles that remain passive and unrecognized until they are activated by external teaching or experience. Although he grants that there are certain tendencies that seem to be held in common, such as "a desire of happiness and an aversion to misery," he insists that these tendencies are "inclinations of the appetite to good, not impressions of truth on the understanding" (E I.iii.3). In fact, the principles of action that are "lodged in man's appetites" are "so far from being innate moral principles, that if they were left to their full swing, they would carry men to the overturning of all morality" (E I.iii.13). The dispositional innatist view, that the individual conscience contains the basic moral principles

---

[26] Locke was not the first to criticize the theory of innate ideas. Hobbes rejected innatism more than thirty years earlier in *Leviathan*, I.1–6. The argument that Locke makes in the *Essay*, however, more closely parallels the famous attack launched by Pierre Gassendi, including the choice of opponent, Lord Herbert of Cherbury. Here again we see Locke aligning himself with proponents of the new probability against the defenders of innate knowledge and *scientia*. See Gassendi, *Syntagma philosophicum*, in *Opera Omnia*, I.90–93.

even if it does not recognize them, is just as mistaken as the naïve view. Locke states it bluntly, "No Proposition can be said to be in the mind which it never yet knew, which it was never yet conscious of" (E I.ii.5).

In this way Locke comes to the unequivocal conclusion that there is no moral law that can be shown to be innate. Human beings have never recognized any moral rule as good in and of itself and for its own sake. The reason for this is simple: "there cannot any moral rule be proposed, whereof a man may not justly demand a reason" (E I.iii.4). This is the key to both Locke's rejection of the Scholastics' and Cartesians' appeal to innate ideas and the enthusiast's appeal to inner light. Fanatics and philosophizers refuse to give reasons for the claims they are making. They are unable to show the constraining motives or inducements that led them to choose their principles. Of course, from the perspective of innatists and enthusiasts, this expectation makes no sense. They assent to certain propositions because they are inherently and innately moved to do so. Yet Locke seeks to supplant such thinking with an alternative understanding of reasoned and disciplined judgment. For Locke there are no preexisting moral certainties—no shared moral knowledge prior to inquiry and debate. Since we can always ask for reasons for moral rules, it must be the case that "the truth of all these moral rules, plainly depends upon some other antecedent to them, and from which they must be deduced, which could not be, if either they were innate, or so much as self-evident" (E I.iii.4). If we are to discipline our thoughts and actions correctly, we must limit them to those claims we can make by appealing to verifiable reasons or motives that lie beyond the actual claim that we are making. Here Locke is preparing us to accept a new process of judgment as providing the types of reasons that we need to govern ourselves properly.

Locke's critics, however, howled that his rejection of innate ideas and dispositional moral insight constituted wholesale denial of religion and morality. And it is undeniable that Locke undermines a particular type of religion that gains its adherents by insisting that particular innate commitments provide certain knowledge of God's will or the external moral world. To those who would look to the individual conscience as a repository of the principles of moral law, Locke replies that "conscience . . . is nothing else but our own opinion" (E I.iii.2). Any who "have been but moderately conversant in the history of mankind, and looked abroad beyond the smoke of their own chimneys" must admit that "some men, with the same best of conscience, prosecute what others avoid" (E I.iii.2, 9). "View but an army at the sacking of a town," Locke warns his readers, "and see . . . what touch of conscience, for all the outrages they do" (E I.iii.9).

Locke is at pains to convince his readers that the type of certainty that the ungoverned intellect seeks is erroneous and deceptive. When people act on beliefs that they claim to be innate or directly revealed by God, they are actually submitting to education, custom, or passion. For Locke, the claim that one's private conscience is somehow attuned to the "boundless extent" of the external world is absurd. It is based on the dangerous illusion that spontaneous, unregulated judgment will naturally reflect the morally marked world we inhabit. In the midst of a political realm characterized by contingency and disagreement, the religious enthusiast and the philosophical dogmatist are not only absurd; they are despotic. Their failure to constrain their yearning for certainty leads them to embrace a type of mental tyranny.[27]

Defining and Redefining Knowledge and Belief

For this reason Locke carefully steers his readers away from yearning for absolute certainty and turns them toward a search for the probable. At first glance, however, Locke seems to present a traditional dichotomy between *scientia* and *opinio*. In the beginning of the fourth book of the *Essay*, he divides all of human understanding into the two realms of knowledge and belief (E IV.i.3). Knowledge is that which is directly perceived with certainty. In contrast, opinion, judgment or faith (he seems to use these terms almost interchangeably) is that which is taken to be true or assented to without the immediate perception of certainty. Knowledge involves the *passive reception* of relations; it is a type of inactive awareness. Belief involves the *active judgment* of relations; it is a type of intentional investigation of alternative possibilities. Locke spends a great deal of time reiterating this Platonic understanding of knowledge as a different kind of thing from opinion or assent. There is a *qualitative* difference between the two: "the highest probability, amounts not to certainty, without which, there can be no true knowledge" (E IV.iii.14). In fact in the opening chapter of the *Essay*, Locke presents this distinction as one of the work's primary concerns: "it is therefore worth while, to search out the bounds between opinion and knowledge; and examine by what measures, in things, whereof we have no certain knowledge, we ought to regulate our assent, and moderate our persuasions" (E I.i.3). In cases of

---

[27] As we will see in chapter 6, this unregulated yearning for divine insight is exactly what Locke sees as so dangerous about Robert Filmer's patriarchal politics. Locke's response to such cognitive impropriety, both in the *Essay* and in the *First Treatise*, is to drive a wedge between the infallible mind of God and the fallible minds of men.

knowledge, the mind is compelled to accept a proposition and is certain of its truth. In cases of opinion, the mind is called to assess the probability of a proposition and grant to it a proportionate degree of assent or belief. Thus the mind passively receives knowledge and actively regulates belief. As we will see, however, Locke does not consistently maintain this position. Although he presents his readers with an elegant framework that clearly distinguishes between knowledge and belief, he strays from that framework as soon as he begins to work out the details. His quiet retreat from this sharp distinction is crucial in his move away from the traditional language of scholasticism and toward the new probability and judgment.

Locke begins by defining knowledge by what he calls "perception" (E IV.i.2). Like many before him, he uses the metaphor of sight to describe the experience of being directly aware of the truth of a particular proposition. "What I see I know to be so, by the evidence of the thing itself," he tells us (E IV.xv.3). Locke not only asserts that perception is an element of knowing, but that the two can be equated. In later writings this claim becomes a slogan: "knowledge is vision" or "knowing is seeing."[28] By emphasizing the metaphor of sight, Locke can underscore that the process of knowing is immediate and passive. That which is known with certainty is perceived "without any pains, labor, or deduction" (E IV.i.4). Truths are simply recognized as self-evident by a passive perceiving mind (E II.ix.1, IV.vii.1–4). Without attempting to account in any detail for the faculty of perception, Locke insists that when we experience something directly, we "just know" it; we are immediately aware of it. Perception is our best and only access to certain knowledge.

Although Locke repeatedly describes the immediate perception of certain knowledge in terms of sight and vision, the metaphor can be misleading. When he writes of the eyes that perceive knowledge, he is referring to "a perceptive faculty of the mind" (E IV.xvii.4; see also I.i.1, I.iv.23, II.ix.1, IV.xii.2, IV.xiii.2, IV.xvii.15).[29] For Locke, perception takes place within the mind, not outside of it. When we perceive the truth or falsity of something, we actually perceive the correlation of two ideas that have somehow appeared and now reside in the mind. The perception that is so central to Locke's understanding of certain knowledge is an internal faculty. Knowledge is the perception of agreement or disagreement of ideas in the mind's eye (E IV.i.1). Thus it is mental knowledge or, as he

[28] Locke, *Fourth Letter of Toleration*, in *The Works of John Locke*, 12th ed., vol. 5 (Oxford: Oxford University Press, 1823), 558. Locke also uses this slogan in *Conduct of the Understanding*, 24.

[29] It is for this reason that the characterization of the *Essay* as "empiricist" can be misleading. For Locke, the "perception" that yields knowledge is internal, not external. See Jolley, *Locke*; and Wolterstorff, *Ethics of Belief*.

calls it at one point, "mental truth" (E IV.v.2). For "all general knowledge lies only in our own thoughts, and consists barely in the contemplation of our own abstract ideas" (E IV.vi.3; see also IV.vi.16, IV.vii.8). This type of seeing is indubitable; nothing else is needed to determine the truth or falsity of a proposition. Perception itself is its own justification. Locke makes the surprising claim that even reason is unnecessary in gaining certain knowledge. "In the discovery of, and assent to these truths, there is no use of the discursive faculty, *no need of reasoning*, but they are known by a superior, and higher degree of evidence" (E IV.vii.14; the italics are Locke's). The agreement or disagreement of our ideas is perceived immediately. Reason, as the faculty that investigates and regulates those things that are not immediately perceived, plays no role in perception. In contrast to probable belief, Locke tells us, certain knowledge is internal, instantaneous, and passive. He goes so far as to speak of two distinct faculties of the mind: knowledge involves the immediate perception of the agreement or disagreement of ideas, while judgment involves all other ways of thinking when certain agreement or disagreement is not immediately perceived (E IV.xiv.4).

Yet Locke begins to modify these strict dichotomies almost as soon as he presents them. There are other types of knowledge, he concedes, that cannot strictly be defined as the immediate perception of the agreement or disagreement of ideas. Sometimes we know things not because we perceive them immediately but because we remember having perceived them. Locke calls this kind of knowledge *habitual* knowledge, distinguishing it from the *intuitive* knowledge gained through immediate perception. Habitual knowledge is not as certain as intuitive knowledge, but it is almost as certain. Next Locke presents us with another type of knowledge that is less certain than the first two. This knowledge, called *demonstrative* knowledge, is arrived at through demonstration. It is "the perception of the certain agreement, or disagreement of two ideas, by the intervention of one or more other ideas" (E IV.xvii.15). By applying other ideas to our initial perceptions, we can tie a series of perceptions together to produce a proof. But Locke cautions that even the best demonstration is not as certain as direct perception. He likens a proof to a series of mirrors in which an object can be reflected but becomes increasingly hazy and obscure with each subsequent reflection. Since demonstrative knowledge is mediated, it is not as certain as perception. It "is not altogether so clear and bright as in intuitive knowledge" (E IV.ii.4). Locke then presents his readers with yet another category of knowledge that is even less certain than intuitive, habitual, or demonstrative knowledge. Here he completely departs from his original definition of knowledge as immediate and internal perception. Although we cannot perceive it in our minds or demonstrate it by proofs, Locke argues that we still have a *sen-*

sitive knowledge of the existence of particular external objects. Sensitive knowledge does not provide the same degree of certainty that intuitive and demonstrative knowledge do since there is always doubt whether one's ideas exactly reflect objects in the world. Yet Locke still classifies it as a type of knowledge. It goes "beyond bare probability," Locke writes, but it does not reach "perfectly to either of the foregoing degrees of certainty"(E IV.ii.14).

By introducing the categories of habitual, demonstrative, and sensitive knowledge into his original definition, Locke begins to blur the line between certain knowledge that is involuntary and probable belief that is voluntary. Locke specifies various degrees of knowledge that entail various degrees of certainty and warrant various degrees of acceptance. No longer is knowledge a discrete faculty based on perception of a passive mind distinct from belief based on a different faculty of withholding or conferring assent to propositions. According to the initial distinction between knowledge and belief, awareness of certain knowledge is the inevitable and immediate result of perceiving the agreement of ideas. The acceptance of perceived knowledge is automatic: "what a man sees, he cannot but see; and what he perceives, he cannot but know that he perceives" (E IV.xiii.2). By introducing degrees of knowledge, Locke admits that some types of knowledge cannot be equated with immediate perception. The *passive* awareness of perception, which distinguishes knowledge from belief, is here replaced with the *active* capacity to judge propositions. In this way aspects of habitual, demonstrative, and sensitive knowledge fit more closely to Locke's initial definition of belief and judgment than they do to his definition of knowledge. They are not directly perceived with certainty, but rather assented to or rejected without immediate and certain perception. Our acceptance of them is not passive and automatic, but active and voluntary. Although Locke never openly disavows his distinction between certain, compelling knowledge and uncertain, voluntary belief, by admitting degrees of knowledge into his original definition, Locke pushes the greater part of our knowledge in the direction of voluntary belief.[30]

---

[30] In fact, in his debates with Stillingfleet, Locke repeatedly appeals to this formulation, insisting on the distinction between certain knowledge, as that which is immediately perceived, and belief, as that which is not immediately perceived but taken to be true on probable evidence. Thus he seems to simultaneously maintain and undermine this distinction, not only throughout the *Essay*, but in other writings as well. This confusion is most evident when Locke speaks of "experiential knowledge," which according to his definitions is an oxymoron (E IV.iii.29, IV.vi.7). Michael Ayers notes Locke's slippage as well, but he insists that in spite of it, Locke held to his initial, rigid distinction between knowledge and belief. Ayers goes to great lengths to reconcile the two positions; however, in this case I believe his efforts are ultimately unpersuasive. Michael Ayers, *Locke: Epistemology and Ontology*, 2 vols. (New York: Routledge, 1993), 1:88–95.

So what is Locke's aim in discussing knowledge and belief in this way? Ultimately, it seems that he wants to draw attention away from claims of absolute and universal certainty and focus instead on the types of truth claims that would be located in the realm of probability or belief.[31] Although Locke retains the Cartesian categories of intuitive and demonstrative knowledge, he narrows the realm of knowledge in which insight is certain and automatic and expands the realm in which active judgment is required. The task of describing the passive processes of knowledge formation seems to slip into a very different type of task involving the justification of mental practices that are in our power to control and regulate. Locke seems to set out to explain the mechanics of our understanding, yet he ends up consigning absolute certainty to a very narrow compass within the workings of the individual mind and emphasizing instead that the vast majority of our reasoning about the world concerns various degrees of probability. As William Walker has put it, "By representing the difference between believing and knowing and between probable propositions and knowledge as differences of amount, quantity and degree, Locke's dynamic terminology contests his explicit identification of these differences as differences in kind."[32] In other words, Locke's own account of the degrees of knowing undercuts his hard-and-fast distinction between the traditional categories of knowing and believing.

In fact, Locke repeatedly qualifies his distinction between the supposedly distinct faculties of knowledge and judgment, eventually merging them into a single faculty of reason (E IV.xvii.2). Locke transforms the difference between knowledge and belief (or certainty and probability) into a difference between levels of reliability that can be perceived by a single agent or faculty. The *qualitative* distinction that Locke begins with becomes a *quantitative* difference. The picture that emerges is that of a continuum on which the highest point is the certainty of intuitive knowledge, and below that, the lesser certainty of other types of knowledge, and below that, various degrees of probability and improbability. Locke writes of "there being degrees herein, from the very neighbourhood of certainty and demonstration, quite down to improbability and unlikeliness, even to the confines of impossibility" (E IV.xv.2). By placing all types of understanding on one scale, Locke obscures the categorical

---

[31] On a similar note, Peter Myers argues that "Locke's insistence throughout much of the *Essay* upon a strict methodological separation of moral from natural science represents a deliberate rhetorical exaggeration, as does the closely related distinction between the abstract, normative-theoretical principles of political science and the historically grounded prudential art of governing." Myers, *Our Only Star*, 60. See also Forster, *John Locke's Moral Consensus*, 42–46.

[32] William Walker, *Locke, Literary Criticism, and Philosophy* (Cambridge: Cambridge University Press, 1994), 110.

distinction between knowledge and belief. Knowledge can now be seen as something with extremely high probability. In this way knowledge is a species of belief. This also means, as Barbara Shapiro has shown, that "probability thus effectively becomes knowledge. For, if assent is as much compelled to the highest degree of probability as it is to demonstration, then the distinction between compelled and voluntary consent, which was crucial to the old boundary between knowledge and probable opinion, has been obliterated."[33] The emphatic distinction that Locke presents in the beginning of the fourth book seems to recede as a new standard for justification advances. What is most important for Locke is that we pay careful attention to the gradations of certainty and probability so that we do not assent to any claim with greater or lesser firmness than the evidence warrants.

We can also see this subtle shift in the way in Locke's portrayal of human understanding in his description of our perception of ideas. Locke describes the process of acquiring knowledge as internal perception. We are directly aware only of that which takes place in the mind, since the mind can only know its own modifications. These modifications, Locke tells us, consist of ideas: "Whatsoever the mind perceives in itself, or is the immediate object of perception, thought, or understanding, that I call *idea*" (E II.viii.8). It is this emphatic claim—that knowledge is only conversant about ideas and nothing else—that led Thomas Reid to characterize Locke's thinking as the "way of ideas." In contrast to Descartes, from whom Locke takes the term, Locke insists that no idea is inherent or innate to the human mind. As we have seen, the entire first book of the *Essay* is a polemic against the dangerous consequences of such a doctrine. Instead Locke argues that all ideas originate from either experience of the outer world or experience of our own thinking—either through sensation or reflection.

Locke's broad use of the term "idea" has led many readers both in his own day and in our own to scratch their heads. For Locke the mind houses a blank tablet upon which ideas appear and then fade away. These

[33] Shapiro, *Probability and Certainty*, 42. Shapiro (267) points to "the erosion of the traditional dichotomy between 'science' and 'probability' as the crucial development" in epistemology in general from 1550 to 1700. Richard Ashcraft and Henry van Leeuwen also point out the dissolving distinction between knowledge and probability in the *Essay*. Richard Ashcraft, "Faith and Knowledge," 209–10; van Leeuwen, *Problem of Certainty*, 141. Douglas Patey and Richard Kroll point out the effacement of the distinction between knowledge and probability as well, yet they do not call attention to the tension between this effacement and Locke's explicit statements. Kroll, *The Material World*, 49–79; Patey, *Probability and Literary Form*, 27–34. Daston, on the other hand, fails to see that Locke's "refusal to join probability with certainty at the extreme point of the continuum" is undermined by a host of conflicting claims. Daston, *Classical Probability*, 201.

ideas originate in either sensation or reflection. That means ideas appear in our mind either because an external object acts on our sensory mechanisms or our own mind acts on itself.[34] The result of either one of these events is the appearance of a type of sign that comes before our mind's eye and signifies something other than itself, or more precisely, points to the existence of its cause. Ideas are present in the mind but signify a cause that is not present. As Michael Ayers puts it, ideas are "present signs of absent significata."[35] Locke summarizes it this way: "For since the things the mind contemplates are none of them, besides it self, present to the understanding, 'tis necessary that something else, as a sign or representation of the thing it considers should be present to it: And these are *ideas*" (E IV.xxi.4; see also IV.v.2).[36]

Locke divides all ideas (or signs) into two types, simple and complex. A *simple idea* "contains in it nothing but one uniform appearance" (E II.ii.1). It cannot be broken down into constituent parts. A *complex idea* results from combining and comparing simple ideas. Locke goes on to distinguish two kinds of complex ideas, ideas of substance and modes. *Ideas of substance* are combinations of simple ideas that "are taken to represent distinct particular things subsisting by themselves" (E II.xii.6). *Modes* are combinations that are not taken to represent things subsisting by themselves. Modes may be either simple or mixed. A simple mode is a

---

[34] For a thorough introduction to the complexities of Locke's theory of ideas and the many debates that it has engendered, see Vere Chappell, "Locke's Theory of Ideas," in *The Cambridge Companion to Locke*, ed. Vere Chappell (Cambridge: Cambridge University Press, 1994). Also see Ayers, *Locke: Epistemology and Ontology*, 1:13–77.

[35] Ayers, *Locke: Epistemology and Ontology*, 1:62.

[36] Although Locke uses the term "representation" to describe ideas, he does not seem to think that *all* ideas are representations. He explicitly states that "archetypes"—complex ideas of nonsubstances such as the triangle—are "not intended to be copies of anything, nor referred to the existence of anything" (E IV.iv.5). In reply to an objection by Stillingfleet, Locke distinguishes between primary qualities that are images or representations and secondary qualities that are not representations "but only effects of certain powers in bodies to produce them in us." John Locke, *The Works of John Locke* (Oxford: Oxford University Press, 1823), 3:75–76. Whether all ideas are representational or not, however, it seems clear that Locke wishes to insist that our thinking about extramental entities requires ideas that are signs present in the mind and signify or point to external objects that are not present. Yet even this claim has been challenged. John Yolton has argued that ideas are not mental objects present in the mind but mental acts, that is, acts of perceiving. For Yolton, ideas are somehow achieved through will and action. However, both Vere Chappell and Michael Ayers have argued persuasively that Locke holds that ideas are indeed mental objects. By emphasizing Locke's description of ideas as *signs* of things not immediately present in the mind, I am presenting an interpretation that is in general agreement with Chappell and Ayers. See John Yolton, "Locke and Malebranche: Two Concepts of Ideas," in *John Locke: Symposium Wolfenbüttel, 1979*, ed. Reinhard Brandt (New York: Walter de Gruyter, 1981).

combination of the same simple idea (e.g. a dozen or a score) and a mixed mode combines several different simple ideas.[37]

Whenever we interact with the world or reflect on our own thoughts, we employ complex ideas. Complex ideas come before the mind's eye as signs signifying absent causes. Ideas of substances point to their cause in external objects that lie beyond the mind. Since we do not have access to the ultimate causes of substances, our ideas of substances are imperfect and ultimately uncertain. We can never be sure that the signifier that we are contemplating (the idea of a substance) is exactly the same as what it signifies (the actual substance). Modes, in contrast, point to nothing but their own constituent parts, which originate in the mind. Since modes exist as independent entities only in our minds, there is no mysterious gap between the idea and what the idea signifies. In Locke's jargon, the nominal essence is identical to the real essence. Our mind constructs mixed modes out of simple ideas, and can break them back down into their component parts. In this way the properties of a given mixed mode can be deduced from its definition.

When we reason with mixed modes, Locke tells us, we can arrive at conclusions that are more certain than when we reason with ideas of substances. We can move from definitions to necessary and certain conclusions. Pure mathematics is the model for this type of reasoning. Given certain terms, the mathematician or geometer can demonstrate the necessary relations between their parts. From the definition of a triangle it can be demonstrated that the sum of its angles is equal to two right angles. Demonstrative reasoning of this sort qualifies as *scientia* since the conclusions that we draw necessarily follow from our definitions. The results are indubitable and secure. Thus even though a natural science based on natural substances seems to be always out of our reach, a deductive science of mathematics is possible for us (E II.xxv.8).

It is in this limited way that I think Locke can claim that "morality is capable of demonstration, as well as mathematics" (E III.xi.16 see also IV.iii.18, IV.xii.8). Locke means that pure (and not applied) morality is capable of abstract certainty in the same way that pure (and not applied) mathematics is capable of abstract demonstration. We can arrive at abstract moral truths by demonstrating necessary relationships between mixed modes. Locke gives us a few examples of this type of reasoning. If we define the terms "gratitude" and "justice" is a particular way, we can be certain that the proposition "Gratitude is justice" is absolutely certain. Yet Locke himself admits that such conclusions are "trifling" (E IV.viii.12). More significant are the two examples he gives in the context

---

[37] For a clear and concise explanation of Locke's many categories of ideas, see Grant, *John Locke's Liberalism*, 14–21.

of claiming that moral propositions can be "as certain as any demonstration in Euclid" (E IV.iii.18). The first is that "no government allows absolute liberty." At first glance this seems to be a substantial and useful political truth. Yet upon further reflection, it turns out to be merely definitional, or trifling. The proposition is sustained by a particular understanding of liberty as doing "whatever one pleases," a definition that is actually at odds with Locke's own definition presented elsewhere. His second example is "where there is no property, there is no injustice." Again this proposition at first appears to be significant, but is actually either false or trivial. As Leibniz pointed out, this proposition is false if we use a conventional understanding of property as "private ownership of material goods."[38] Under conditions in which material goods are held in common, a person's rights could still be unjustly infringed. On the other hand, if we define property as any right at all, that is, if we define property in the expansive sense of propriety, then the proposition is nothing more than the trifling claim that "where there is no right, there is no violation of a right." It is true that mixed modes can yield certain conclusions, but such reasoning can only establish the truths that are already entailed in definitions. Mixed modes can secure demonstrative certainty only in the abstract.[39]

It is crucial that Locke does not offer readers of the *Essay* or any other work the type of philosophical demonstration of which he speaks.[40] One reason for this is that he is far more interested in practical conduct than he is abstract speculation. In order to arrive at a more tangible or practical account of natural law, he must be able to show how it applies to our

[38] Leibniz, *New Essays on Human Understanding*, IV.iii.18.

[39] Locke himself seems to recognize this difficulty: "But it will here be said, that if moral knowledge be placed in the contemplation of our own moral Ideas, and those, as other modes, be of our own making, what strange notions will there be of justice and temperance? What confusion of virtues and vices, if every one may make what ideas of them he pleases?" (E IV.iv.9). His solution is to focus on the constituent parts of the terms and not the terms themselves. He insists that "If we but separate the idea under consideration from the sign that stands for it, our knowledge goes equally on in the discovery of real truth and certainty, whatever sounds we make use of" (E IV.iv.9). Yet, as Bishop Berkeley recognized, this does not solve the difficulty. "To demonstrate morality," Berkeley commented, "it seems one need only make a discovery of words and see which included which.... Locke's instances of demonstration in morality are, according to his own rule, trifling propositions." Quoted by Leslie Stephen, *The History of English Thought in the Eighteenth Century* (New York: G. P. Putnam's Sons, 1876), 86.

[40] Locke, *Correspondence*, 4:110–13, 767–68, 786–87. See also Robert Horwitz, introduction to John Locke, *Questions Concerning the Law of Nature*, trans. by Robert Horwitz, Jenny Strauss Clay, and Diskin Clay (Ithaca, N.Y.: Cornell University Press,1990), 22–28; Pangle, *Spirit of Modern Republicanism*, 197–98; Grant, *John Locke's Liberalism*, 26n; John Dunn, *Locke: Past Masters* (Oxford: Oxford University Press, 1984), 65. For further discussion of Locke's failure to provide a demonstration for morality, see chapter 5.

lives. As Peter Josephson reminds us, "In the end it is not enough that our moral constructs be coherent; they must also correspond in some way to empirical examples or to our experience."[41] Yet as soon as we attempt to apply this knowledge to the world outside our minds, we encounter the contingencies and uncertainties of nature. We find that our definitions and thus our conclusions might not match any actual state of affairs. For Locke, even the seemingly straightforward term "man" does not easily map onto our experience of nature. We form a complex idea of a "man" by combining ideas such as rationality, physicality, and shape that we distinguish from the definition of "beast." Yet when we encounter a child born with severe defects (what Locke calls a "changeling") or a seemingly rational parrot, our artificial definitions are subverted (E IV.iv.13–14, II.xxvii.8). In passages that bring to mind Montaigne's delight in the anomalous, Locke dwells at length on the oddity of the changeling and the parrot, creatures that simply do not fit into our abstract categories. The difficulty of coming to terms with the complexity of the external world as it appears to us is central to Locke's view of the limitations of human knowledge.[42]

While mixed modes are complex ideas that signify nothing but their own constituent parts, ideas of substances are signs of an ultimately inaccessible external world. Locke often refers to these ideas as "the testimony of the senses," since they provide us with nondemonstrative evidence of something that lies beyond the mind (E IV.xi.8, IV.xi.9). If we attempt to trace these complex ideas of substances to their source, we will find that we are unable to grasp their underlying causes. Locke states it bluntly: "we know not the manner wherein they are produced" (E IV.xi.2). If we analyze these ideas by breaking them down into the simple ideas that form them, we will be left with an inexplicable remainder. We assume there is a causal link between the appearances that we encounter in the mind and some real object in the world. Yet we have no direct access to that cause. "Not imagining how these simple ideas can subsist by themselves," Locke writes, "we accustom ourselves to suppose some substratum wherein they do subsist and from which they do result,

---

[41] Josephson, *Great Art of Government*, 5.

[42] It is for this reason that Locke writes in an early draft of the *Essay* that "we must not expect a certain knowledge of any universal proposition." Or even more emphatically: "all universal propositions are either certain and then they are only verbal but are not instructive. Or else are instructive and then are not certain." John Locke, *Drafts for the Essay Concerning Human Understanding, and Other Philosophical Writings*, ed. P. H Nidditch and G.A.J. Rogers (Oxford: Clarendon Press, 1990), sections 31, 29. Here Locke is committed to the nominalist principle that our access to the world is limited to particulars of sense experience and that experience cannot yield absolutely certain, universal conclusions.

which therefore we call substance" (E II.xxiii.1). Locke recognizes that the term is inadequate because it is without clear signification. Giving the unknown cause of our ideas, the name "substance" is no better "than the Indian before mentioned, who, saying that the world was supported by a great elephant, was asked what the elephant rested on; to which his answer was—a great tortoise: but being again pressed to know what gave support to the broad-backed tortoise, replied—something, he knew not what" (E II.xxiii.2). Substance—the very basis of our understanding—remains essentially unintelligible. It is something, but we know not what.

In spite of the groundlessness of this position, Locke insists that we have no other alternative. As human beings, our connection to the world outside our minds is a tenuous and ultimately mysterious one. That which lies at the very source of our ideas of the external world is inexplicable. Substance "has something in it, which manifestly baffles our understandings" (E IV.iii.6). By refusing to pursue his inquiry further, Locke seeks to avoid the metaphysical and theological firestorm over "substance" sparked by Spinoza and consuming many of his contemporaries.[43] Locke simply passes over the difficulty by conceding that the source of our ideas of the world around us is ultimately mysterious. He goes on to point out that any findings that we base on our ideas of substances, therefore, simply cannot reach the level of certain knowledge or *scientia*. It is in this sense that Locke argues that "natural philosophy is not capable of being made a science" (E IV.xii.10). Any inquiry into nature can never attain the certainty of mathematics, and in Locke's rigorous use of the term "science," any such inquiry cannot yield scientific knowledge. However, this does not mean we should discount the "testimony of the senses." In fact, it is this testimony that turns out to be our most promising "guide and compass" as we navigate through an uncertain world.

For Locke, only mixed modes can yield certain and universal conclusions. Those conclusions follow necessarily from certain causes; that is, they are contained within the arbitrary and conventional terms we posit. Locke shares with Hobbes the belief that we can only genuinely know those things that we construct ourselves. By arranging mixed modes we can construct absolutely certain and universal demonstrations. Yet our interaction with the world outside our minds requires that we make observations about substances. And ideas of substances can only yield conclusions that are less than certain and universal. They are signs or representations emanating from an ultimately uncertain cause, the substance of an external world. Universal and apodictic knowledge, or *scientia*, is

[43] Jonathan Israel, *Radical Enlightenment: Philosophy and the Making of Modernity, 1650–1750* (Oxford: Oxford University Press, 2001), 438–41, 468.

limited to the "contemplation of our own abstract ideas" (E IV.vi.13), while the experience of "the nature of things themselves" yields something less than *scientia* (E IV.xvi.6).

When we act or think about the world, we rely on the "testimony of our senses," which attests to the existence of some type of causality at the core of nature that cannot be known. There is "no visible necessary connection" between the signs that come before our mind's eye and the external world (E IV.iii.10). By arguing that our ideas of substances are produced by an underlying structure that is inaccessible to us, Locke is claiming that whatever generates these appearances is not a *certain cause* but a *probable cause*, that is, a cause that can only be grasped in degrees of probability. Although there is something at the source of our ideas that "manifestly baffles the understanding," we should trust in the authoritative testimony of our senses to provide us with truths that are highly probable.

It is important to note here that Locke's understanding of the probability of natural signs is not simply dependent on empirical regularities or patterns in the world, but on an assumption that those regularities are a manifestation of a divine design. Natural signs are authoritative because they are authorized by the author of creation, and they are trustworthy aids in navigating through the world because they reflect, however dimly, an orderly and morally structured world.[44] God has decided that particular objects will produce particular ideas, and this arrangement enables us to distinguish things in the world by their contrasting effects on us: "God in his wisdom . . . set . . . marks of distinction in things, whereby we may be able to discern one thing from another; and so choose any of them for our uses as we have occasion" (E II.xxxii.14). The signs of nature are "legible characters of his works and providence," and God has "given all mankind so sufficient a light of reason" to read and interpret these signs (E III.ix.23).

Reassured by this belief, Locke is unbothered by what will later become the great modern philosophical problem of induction. Unlike Descartes, he simply assumes that there is a connection between our ideas of the world and the actual world outside our minds. As Nicholas Jolley puts it, "Locke's worry is not the Cartesian one . . . that the human intellect

[44] This Lockean assumption helps to hold together the tension between divine will and divine order that had been so troublesome to early modern thinkers since Ockham. Yet as a nominalist and voluntarist, Locke does not resolve this tension in either direction. He insists that God is the unfathomable and unpredictable source of the moral structure of creation, but also claims that that structure is revealed through nature to be orderly and rational. For discussions of this problematic, see Otto von Gierke, *Natural Law and the Theory of Society, 1500–1800*, trans. Ernest Barker (Boston: Beacon Press, 1960); Oakley, *Omnipotence, Covenant and Order*.

is systematically unreliable; he is not haunted by the fear of a malicious demon who endows us with only false beliefs."[45] Instead Locke inclines to the view that there is some type of mechanism that leads to the appearances in our minds. That connection, he concedes, cannot be known with absolute certainty: "The certainty of things existing *in rerum natura*, when we have the testimony of our senses for it, is not only as great as our frame can attain to, but as our condition needs" (E IV.xi.8). The signs of nature, certified by the wisdom and benevolence of God, are "sufficient for our purposes" if we carefully regulate our judgments according to the appearances that emerge from their source. Here we can see how the medieval authority of *probabilitas* is reassigned to a world of natural signs and appearances authorized by an ultimately inaccessible and incomprehensible God.

Locke's transformation of how we should understand our intellectual faculties has obvious implications for the new experimental philosophy, yet it also has important consequences for the status of moral and political judgment. Locke seems to redefine knowledge and belief in a way that reinforces his recommendations concerning intellectual self-discipline and restraint. Whenever we attempt to apply abstract principles to the world of human affairs, we must judge whether and how our principles fit the circumstances. We must weigh and balance the probable consequences of those principles, making judgments that may be reasonable or unreasonable, but never absolutely clear and certain. Locke points out that most of the propositions that we think and act upon "are such, as we cannot have undoubted knowledge of their truth" (E IV.xv.2). Yet it would be foolish to discount the deliverances of our senses just because of the uncertainty that lurks at their source. If we did that, we would not survive. "He that in the ordinary affairs of life would admit nothing but direct demonstration," Locke tells us, "would be sure of nothing in this world, but of perishing quickly" (E IV.xi.10). And again: "Man would be at a great loss, if he had nothing to direct him, but what has certainty of true knowledge. For that being very short and scanty, as we have seen, he would be often utterly in the dark, and in most of the actions of his life, perfectly at a stand, had he nothing to guide him in the absence of clear and certain knowledge" (E IV.xiv.1).

One of the central teachings of the *Essay Concerning Human Understanding*, then, is that responsible human agents must conduct their lives according to impressions they have of a world that they cannot completely comprehend. Reasonableness under these conditions involves making careful judgments about things to which we do not have access according to those things that we do. By employing a type of analogical

[45] Jolley, *Locke*, 21.

reasoning, we can use the book of nature to shed light on some of the most puzzling and contentious issues that we face as human beings living in communities. Our experience of natural signs can help us decipher an underlying structure to our moral world that can aid us in forming judgments about the specific composition of our moral and political obligations to one another. The resulting conclusions will not be absolutely certain, but they will carry a type of authority; that is, they will carry sufficient authorizing power to justify decisions concerning our intellectual and physical conduct in the world.[46]

What is vastly more important than the narrow province of certainty is the expansive realm of uncertainty. Locke turns our attention to the vast expanse of contingency and doubt in which we carry out our daily lives, an expanse that Descartes, and in a certain sense Hobbes, had consigned to a dark corner of our intellectual world. Richard Ashcraft writes, "For Locke, the practical dimensions of our lives are almost wholly shaped by the probable information we derive from empirical generalizations, or from the testimony and experience of others."[47] What we are most in need of, therefore, is a way to distinguish between trustworthy and untrustworthy claims "in the absence of clear and certain knowledge." While at times Locke presents his *Essay* as a straightforward explanation of human cognition, here we see that it is actually a justification of a new type of probable belief. If carefully attended to, the new probability is "sufficient to govern all our concernments" (E I.i.5).[48] Locke is not simply explaining how the mechanisms of the brain function, he is telling us how to conduct our inquiries properly in an uncertain world. As Gilbert Ryle puts it, "Locke's *Essay* is, in intention and in effect, much less a theory of knowledge than it is a theory of opinion. He is not, as Descartes had been, primarily pointing out the strait and very narrow path to certainties. He is teaching us how we can in some matters, and why we cannot

---

[46] David Soles describes Locke's embrace of Boyle's corpuscular hypothesis in very similar terms. Both in regard to "insensible" corpuscular objects and the underlying structure of creation, Locke's "rule of analogy" provides a probabilistic justification for inferring from sensation and experience to the existence of "unobservables." However, Soles is wrong when he suggests that Locke viewed the inability of seventeenth-century science "to discover the atomic real essences of objects" as a "contingent limitation to be overcome." Locke believed that the limits of our faculties could not simply be overcome; they were part of being human and existing in a "state of mediocrity." David E. Soles, "Locke's Empiricism and the Postulation of Unobservables," *Journal of the History of Philosophy* 23, no. 3 (1985), 368. Peter Myers makes a similar connection between Locke's acceptance of Boyle's hypothesis and Locke's method of moral reasoning. Myers, *Our Only Star*, 85–96.

[47] Ashcraft, *Revolutionary Politics*, 54.

[48] This is further evidence that Locke did not mean to argue that a demonstrative ethics is necessary to the construction of a sufficient moral theory, or the success of his larger political project.

in other matters, make reasonably sure."[49] In order "to make reasonably sure," we must learn to govern our judgment according to natural signs. Thus Locke steers his readers between the dangers of radical skepticism and dogmatic rationalism by introducing a new way of regulating their assent in matters of uncertainty. This is the best way to make use of "our dim candle, reason" (E IV.xix.8).

In the end, Locke does not deny that human beings can attain a demonstrative knowledge of certain principles. In fact, he adamantly defends this possibility in the *Essay* as well as in his subsequent exchanges with Stillingfleet. Yet the certainty of abstract and arbitrary demonstrations remains useless if it cannot guide our conduct in the world. And the application of those principles in a world of substances (of which we have only uncertain and imperfect understanding), necessarily involves judgment. Locke, who has little patience for the useless speculations of the Scholastics, insists that the measure of any principle is its usefulness or application in the world.[50]

One of the crucial purposes of the *Essay*, then, is to provide us with a new way to deliberate rationally and make judgments when *scientia* cannot be attained. And if the *Essay* teaches us anything, it is that *scientia* is limited to a very narrow realm of the understanding. It is for this reason that Locke points to the importance of a new type of knowledge that rises above *mere* opinion but does not reach to the level of certainty. And here again we see the blurring of Locke's initial dichotomy between certain knowledge and probable belief. Although he is adamant that ideas of substance cannot be traced back to certain causes but only probable ones, he includes the deliverances of these complex ideas in the realm of knowledge, speaking of a less than certain "experiential knowledge" (E IV.iii.29, IV.vi.7). Just as Gassendi had subverted the scholastic terminology by defending a "science of appearances," Locke seeks to usher in a new way of speaking about truth claims. He retains the scholastic distinction between knowledge and belief, yet it seems to fade in importance. Knowledge of the world outside our minds, including external objects

---

[49] Gilbert Ryle, "John Locke," in *Collected Papers* (New York: Barnes & Noble, 1971), 1:153.

[50] Margaret Osler argues that Locke both reiterates the traditional view and paves the way for radical change: "By insisting that knowledge and certainty are equivalent, he remained at one with Aristotelian and Cartesian traditions which maintained the ideal of certainty as the standard of science and for all knowledge. By recognizing, however, that a large proportion of the assertions we make—particularly about the external world—can never yield certainty or knowledge of real essences, he recognized the inadequacy of the old idea as it was challenged by Boyle and Newton. In this light, Locke can be seen as having taken a major step toward providing new epistemological underpinnings for empirical science." Osler, "John Locke and the Changing Ideal of Scientific Knowledge," *Journal of the History of Ideas* 31, no. 1 (1970), 16.

and, we presume, external minds, is not apodictically certain. The direct, passive awareness that Locke had offered as the hallmark of knowledge is confined to the internal workings of the individual mind and turns out to characterize only a narrow region of the realm of knowledge. There are other degrees of knowledge that are less certain.[51]

One of Locke's most ardent critics, Henry Lee, charged him with attempting to introduce a new language.[52] And Lee was right. Locke presents his readers with a new mode of discourse in which the realm of *scientia* is consigned to a very limited sphere and the realm of *opinio* is no longer tied to the authority of traditional texts. By emphasizing the inescapable uncertainties that haunt our interactions with the world outside our minds, Locke can subtly move toward replacing the categorical distinction of knowledge and belief with a continuous spectrum of degrees of assurance. Instead of arguing that we should distinguish between more and less probable claims by appealing to the written word, Locke insists that we have access to a more authoritative testimony—the nondemonstrative evidence of natural signs. These signs cannot establish claims concerning the outside world with absolute and universal certainty, but they can point to a probable cause. If we carefully form our judgments in the way Locke suggests, we can be reasonably sure.

---

[51] Peter Myers has aptly described this Lockean effort to transform premodern notions of knowledge while avoiding the dangerous extremes of dogmatism and skepticism: "Locke's natural-historical inquiry represents a delicate attempt to preserve a commonsense understanding of the nonarbitrariness of our ideas, while yet promoting a spirit of openness to scientific progress grounded in an awareness of the incompleteness of those ideas." Myers, *Our Only Star*, 68.

[52] Confused by Locke's use of the term "idea," Lee insists that he was not always able to understand the *Essay* because it was "writ in a kind of new Language." Later he ridicules Locke for "introducing a new way of talking." Henry Lee, *Anti-Scepticism: Or, Notes upon each Chapter of Mr. Lock's Essay concerning Humane Understanding. With an Explication of all the Particulars of which he Treats, and in the same Order* (London: R. Clavel & C. Harper, 1702), 1, 260; see also 48. John Dunn offers a remarkably similar judgment, arguing that the *Essay* is not concerned "with the exposition of effective obligation but with the possibility of constructing a coherent moral language." *Political Thought of Locke*, 191.

V

Liberating Judgment

FREEDOM, HAPPINESS, AND THE REASONABLE SELF

LOCKE PLACES A NEW NOTION of probable judgment at the center of his political-epistemological project in order to sidestep divisive and seemingly irreconcilable metaphysical debates without becoming embroiled in the thorny problem of multiple authorities. By appealing to the probable signs of nature, he offers his contemporaries an authoritative framework through which disputes can be mediated and judgments legitimized. Locke wants to enable self-government in the context of deep disagreement by cultivating a capacity to govern judgment according to public reasonableness. He urges his readers to combat their yearnings for absolute certainty as well as skeptical withdrawal by turning their attention away from demonstrative proof and toward the probabilities of daily conduct. As Neal Wood explains, Locke's "aim in treating probability was apparently not so much concerned with its implications for science, although he did not ignore the question, as it was with this interest in promoting the principles of a free and tolerant civic order, of a peaceful, law-abiding, and economically prosperous political society."[1]

Locke asserts that it is this very capacity to make probable judgments that is the source of our freedom. We are genuinely free insofar as we are able to constrain our thoughts and actions according to the deliverances of our considered judgment. At first glance, however, Locke seems to follow Hobbes in arguing that there is a type of liberty that can be understood as the absence of restraint, as self-expression through action. Yet he argues that there is another—more genuine—type of liberty that requires cognitive self-discipline and self-restraint. This type of freedom is the result of hard work; it is an achievement, not an original condition. In the *Second Treatise,* Locke writes, "We are born free, as we are born rational; not that we have actually the exercise of either" (2T 61). The natural freedom that we claim as human beings is not something we possess, but something we enact. We exercise this freedom not simply by expressing our will, but by transcending it and adjusting it to conform to our long-term happiness. We experience ourselves as naturally free and

[1] Wood, *Politics of Locke's Philosophy*, 171.

reasonable insofar as we are able to step away from our own process of willing and determine whether our desires are shaped by what is most important and most valuable. It is through this type of cognitive self-evaluation that we hope to harmonize our volitions and our actions with the good. For Locke it is through the hard work of self-scrutiny that we attain our natural liberty. It is through cognitive self-discipline that we gain ownership of ourselves and our actions. This means that neither our natural reason nor our natural liberty is naturally spontaneous; both depend on our capacity to cultivate them.

One of the purposes of the *Essay*, then, is to persuade readers to embrace the intellectual practices that will lead them constitute themselves as persons capable of liberty and happiness. This rests on the wide-spread acceptance of a new type of probable judgment. Here we see that Locke's explicit political project is embedded in a much larger and more extensive engagement with the psychological and cognitive conditions within which a liberal polity can flourish. Although Locke understands his project as defending and expanding individual liberty, he is at pains to convince his readers that they are not self-created or self-constructed beings; they are not completely autonomous, sovereign agents. They are dependent in important ways on what lies outside of them, on the contingencies of a morally marked world. Yet they are also able to respond to those dependencies and cultivate their liberty by restraining themselves according to their probable judgments of what constitutes their "true and solid happiness." For Locke, it is only by disciplining our understanding according to the probable signs of nature that we can become free and reasonable selves. It is only as genuinely free and reasonable selves that we can sustain constitutional self-government.

Unrestrained and Restrained Freedoms

However, the claim that Lockean freedom requires intellectual self-regulation seems at first glance to conflict with Locke's explicit statements on the matter. The definition of freedom that he presents in the *Essay* does not mention any type of intellectual self-restraint. In fact, his view of freedom seems to follow that of Hobbes. In his famous exchange with Bishop Bramhall, Hobbes stakes out an unambiguous position: "For he is free to do a thing, that may do it if he have the will to do it, and may forbear if he have the will to forbear."[2] Locke furnishes us with several strikingly similar formulations throughout the *Essay*. At one point, for example, he

[2] Thomas Hobbes, "Of Liberty and Necessity," in *Hobbes and Bramhall on Liberty and Necessity*, ed. Vere Chappell (Cambridge: Cambridge University Press, 1999), sections 3, 16.

writes, "Liberty 'tis plain consists in a power to do, or not to do; to do, or forbear doing as we will" (E II.xxi.56; see also II.xxi.8, 15, 21).

Here Locke echoes Hobbes in defining freedom as nothing more than the absence of external restraints to the performance of the will. A free agent is someone who has the capacity to act (or refrain from acting) according to his or her volitions. Both Locke and Hobbes assert that we are free if our actions are "up to us," and our actions are "up to us" if they are determined by our will and not thwarted by external impediments. Liberty, then, is simply the ability to express ourselves through action. A free agent is one who wills and is able to act in accord with his or her will.

This type of self-expressive freedom involves a capacity to make choices, a capacity to will one thing and not another. We must have some volition to express if we are to qualify as free. For this reason we would not consider a tennis ball a free agent, Locke tells us, because "we conceive not a tennis ball to think, and consequently not to have any volition" (E II.xxi.9). The type of liberty that Locke is discussing here is a freedom of those who are able to make choices, of those who have a will.

It is important to note, however, that neither Hobbes nor Locke would say that we must always be free to choose between one action and its incompatible alternative in order to be free agents. Our freedom relates to the action or nonaction that we take, not to alternative actions that we *might* have taken. If we are able to act (or forbear acting) according to our will—that is, if we are able to act on our choices without being impeded from acting by external obstacles—we are free. It is irrelevant whether there happen to be impediments in place that would keep us from taking alternative actions based on alternative choices that we did not make. To illustrate this, Locke explains that a man who willingly sits in a room that is locked, sits there voluntarily. He is free agent in relation to his action even though he is not free to leave the room if he were to desire to do so. The freedom that Locke expounds here involves the relation between action and volition. If we can perform an action (or restrain from performing an action) in accordance with our will, then we are said to be free. Freedom in this sense is simply the ability to express oneself through action without external restraint.

Locke is certainly attracted to the clarity and simplicity of this view. Throughout the multiple revisions of the *Essay*, he remains committed, in part, to this fundamentally Hobbesian definition of liberty. Yet he also implies that there is something more to thoroughgoing free agency than this account provides. The Hobbesian view of freedom does not seem to capture everything he wants to include within the category of liberty. There are instances in which agents act according to their will yet still seem to lack some important aspect of free agency. Having the capacity to act on every whim is not the same as having the capacity to act with genuine freedom. This is because compulsive longings, destructive habits, or sheer ignorance seem at times to deform the will. One might even say that they enslave the will. An agent who acts under such harmful influences seems to lack a crucial element of true liberty. Such an agent is, in a certain sense, less than free.

In his response to Hobbes, Bishop Bramhall voices this same concern. Bramhall argues that the Hobbesian notion of liberty is inadequate because it rules out instances in which agents act in conformity with the will yet suffer under a type of compulsion that seems inconsistent with genuine freedom. There are moments, Bramhall writes, when an individual's "will do[es] not come upon him according to his will." Such an individual cannot be said to possess thoroughgoing free agency when his immediate volition is, as it were, imposed upon him. "If the will have no power over itself," Bramhall writes, "the agent is no more free than a staff in a man's hand."[3] In order to possess true or proper liberty, an agent must be determined by a will that has control over itself.

In a scathing response, Hobbes ridicules Bramhall's enigmatic formulations. These mystifying perplexities are simply the result of the bishop's inability to settle on circumscribed definitions of freedom and will. Reiterating his claim that freedom is nothing more than the ability to act (or forbear from acting) according to the will, Hobbes unequivocally denies that the source of a volition has any bearing on whether an agent is free or not. The whole notion of determining the will is unintelligible, "For the will is appetite; nor can a man more determine his will than any other appetite, that is, more than he can determine when he shall be hungry and when not. When a man is hungry, it is in his choice to eat or not eat; this is the liberty of man."[4] For Hobbes, it is irrelevant whether the will is the result of harmful compulsions or careful deliberations. We are free regardless of what determines the will if we are able to act upon our volitions without external impediment. Liberty in the Hobbesian sense is a type of unrestricted self-expression through action.

To an extent Locke accepts this Hobbesian account of freedom. Yet, as Gideon Yaffe notes, he seems to share Bramhall's worry that there is something missing here.[5] While it is true that we experience *a type* of freedom when we are able to act according to our will without impediment, thoroughgoing free agency seems to require *another*, more robust, type of freedom. What type of freedom could this be? Locke implies that true

---

[3] John Bramhall, "A Defence of True Liberty," in Chappell, *Hobbes and Bramhall*, sections 3(d), 44.

[4] Hobbes, "Of Liberty and Necessity," section 1(c), 72.

[5] Gideon Yaffe, *Liberty Worth the Name: Locke on Free Agency* (Princeton: Princeton University Press, 2000), 19–20. See also Myers, *Our Only Star*, 137–45.

liberty requires the capacity to break away from the pernicious influence of immediate volitions. An agent must be able to transcend the will and adjust it to what is most conducive to long-term happiness. Anything less than this type of self-mastery falls short of genuine free agency. Locke asks,

> Is it worth the name of freedom to be at liberty to play the fool, and draw shame and misery upon a man's self? If to break loose from the conduct of reason, and to want that restraint of examination and judgment, which keeps us from choosing or doing the worse, be liberty, true liberty, mad men and fools are the only freemen. (E II.xxi.50)

Locke's point is hard to miss. True freedom—that is, freedom worth the name—requires something more than unrestrained self-expression through action. It requires the capacity to stop oneself from "choosing or doing the worse." If we are thoroughgoing free agents, we are not simply determined by immediate volitions. We are able to step away from our volitions and ascertain whether they will bring about misery or happiness. If we judge our volitions to be deficient, we are somehow able to adjust them appropriately. To experience true liberty, then, is to be able to stand apart from ourselves and somehow accord our will with what is best for us.

Bramhall refers to this capacity to control one's volitions as "freedom of the will." Locke, however, rejects this way of speaking. He points out that it conflicts with his precise definitions of will and freedom. Displaying a fastidious attachment to his terms, he dismisses the entire theological and philosophical debate over free will as a verbal confusion. For Locke, it simply makes no sense to use the phrase "freedom of the will" because the will cannot possess freedom. This is because the will is not an entity within us; it is a power or ability that we exercise. Likewise, freedom is a power or ability and not an entity.[6] It is absurd to say that one power has another power because powers belong to agents. Powers cannot belong to other powers. As agents, we might or might not possess the power of freedom and the power of willing in particular instances. The will, however, is not an agent but a power of an agent. So we cannot properly say that the will possesses freedom or that there is such a thing as "free will" (E II.xxi.14–18).

So Locke technically rejects Bramhall's term "freedom of the will," yet he nonetheless accepts something like Bramhall's position. He agrees

---

[6] Powers, as Michael Ayers points out, are placeholders in our understanding. They are necessarily presupposed by our causal explanations, yet we do not know their exact nature. Whenever one state or change causes another, we presuppose an active power in the first and a passive power in the second. Both will and freedom are powers that seem to cause change. Ayers, *Locke: Epistemology and Ontology*, 1:163, 2:104.

that thoroughgoing free agency involves more than self-expression in action. The Hobbesian view of liberty is incomplete because it does not account for the requirement, in our notion of freedom, of some type of control over the process of willing itself. It is also politically dangerous because it erases the distinction between tyrannical self-assertion that is unable to restrain disorderly desires and ordered freedom that recognizes the importance of self-restraint. Locke wants to salvage this latter type of freedom—a more complete and thoroughgoing freedom—that involves transcending one's own immediate desires and governing one's self-expression. At times Locke even equates this second kind of freedom with what is "improperly called free will" (E II.xxi.47). For Locke (as for Bramhall) thoroughgoing free agency is more than acting according to our will. It involves the ability to distance ourselves from our will in order to judge whether our volitions are, in fact, good for us.

It is because our liberty involves judging and ultimately transforming our will that Locke spends so much time exploring how our volitions are formed and how we can go about reforming them. In the first edition of the *Essay*, he assumes that our will is shaped by our immediate perception of the greater good. We perceive the greater good and it determines our volitions. However, many of Locke's readers were dissatisfied with this simple determinism. It could not explain why individuals so often fail to act in ways that enhance their happiness. If we are really determined by the greater good, why do we so often willfully choose to do things that are good only for us? With encouragement and criticism from his friend, William Molyneux, Locke reworked his argument.[7] In his revised and final account, Locke takes a position that retains the mechanism of his original view, yet opens up a space for human agency and responsibility. He argues that the will is not determined by the greatest good, but by the most proximate one. The most proximate stimulus is not our future good, but the immediate pain we feel because of the presence or absence of something we desire. Locke calls this pain "uneasiness." This uneasiness is a type of dissatisfaction, an inarticulate ache that cries out to be relieved (E II.xxi.31). It is this uneasiness that in turn determines our will.

The most powerful uneasiness that we feel arises from our immediate surroundings. The greatest and most pressing pains, Locke tells us, are often the most proximate. This is why we will things that are often at odds with our long-term happiness. Our will is frequently determined by the closest, most powerful uneasiness that we feel and not by a careful evaluation of absent pleasures and pains. Often our uneasiness stems from unconsidered habits, opinions, passions, and aversions (E II.xxi.38–39). In these instances, we are not determined by our judgment of the greater

[7] Locke, *Correspondence*, 6:1544.

good, but by immediate and misleading desires. The actions that result from this type of determination are not completely or fully free. When we are governed by the pleasures and pains of our immediate surroundings, we lack a crucial aspect of genuine liberty.

Yet Locke insists that the uneasiness that determines our will need not always be the uneasiness that arises from our immediate experience. We are not just machines reacting to external pleasures and pains, but rational agents able to make judgments about those experiences that can transform our uneasiness and thus determine our will. The mind has "a power to *suspend* the execution and satisfaction of any of its desires, and . . . is at liberty to consider the objects of them; examine them on all sides, and weigh them with others" (E II.xxi.47). After assessing the probable consequences of various desires and the actions that might flow from them, we are able to judge which desires are most conducive to our long-term happiness. Then we can place those desires in the central, governing position of our minds. We do this by raising the appropriate uneasiness so that it will in turn determine our will. By "due, and repeated contemplation" we can bring a temporarily absent uneasiness "nearer to our mind, give some relish of it, and raise in us some desire" so that it will come "to determine the will" (E II.xxi.45).

This ability—to suspend our desires, deliberate over them, and then allow our will to be adjusted appropriately—is the source of genuine, thoroughgoing liberty. The "hinge on which turns the liberty of intellectual beings" is their capacity to "suspend their desires, and stop them from determining their wills to any action, till they have duly and fairly examined the good and evil of it" (E II.xxi.52). As free agents, Locke teaches, we have the power to step away from our immediate desires and judge whether our will is conducive to our long-term happiness. If our will is inconsistent with what is good for us, we have the power to reform our volitions appropriately by raising an alternative uneasiness in our minds.

This capacity to suspend and examine our desires is a crucial aspect of our freedom. Locke is careful to point out that it does not, by itself, constitute us as free agents. He does not praise deliberation for the sake of deliberation. The point of examining alternative desires and raising uneasiness in our minds is to adjust our will *appropriately*. We do not simply seek to conform our particular volitions to our particular judgments, but to conform our volitions to what is good. If Locke were simply interested in having us conform our volitions to our judgments, then he would not have been so insistent about pointing out the ways in which custom, habit, and fashion mislead us into making false choices. Indeed he would have no basis for criticizing us for failing to free ourselves from our own parochial interests and biases. If we need only conform our desires to our judgments to be free, it should be sufficient to make sure that our misguided volitions are in line with our misguided judgments. Yet Locke insists that we *can* be criticized for such failures, and we have a duty to struggle against our native propensities toward error.

Our capacity for judgment is important for Locke as the *means* by which our will is made to accord with what is best for us. Our liberty lies not simply in our ability to make judgments, but also in our ability to distinguish what is truly good for us from what is counterfeit.

> The highest perfection of intellectual nature lies in a careful and constant pursuit of true and solid happiness; so that care of ourselves, that we mistake not imaginary for real happiness, is the necessary foundation of our *liberty*. (E II.xxi.51; see also 52, 29, 60 and IV.xxi.3)

I take Locke to be saying that the necessary foundation of our liberty is our ability to care for ourselves by choosing correctly, that is, by choosing in ways that conform to a real rather than imaginary happiness. We pursue a "true and solid happiness" by learning to attune our choices to what is best for us.[8]

This process is not easy because our untutored appetite pushes us to "mistake imaginary for real happiness." Far from leading us to what is good, our immediate desires are the greatest obstacle to it (see E I.iii.13, II.xxi.52–56; STCE 33, 38, 107). We are only able to attune our will to our true and solid happiness because we have the ability to modify the causal determinates of the will. That is, we can generate a more pressing uneasiness in our mind that surpasses our current uneasiness. In this way, Locke tells us, we can bring it about that our will conforms to what is truly best. This capacity for assessing and reforming our will is the source of liberty for Locke not simply because it allows us to modify our volitions, but because it allows us to accord our will to our "true and solid happiness." That is, it allows us to accord our will to what is truly good for us.

Some critics have wondered whether Locke's introduction of this power to suspend and judge really adds much to his account of volitional free-

---

[8] For Uday Singh Mehta, however, the Lockean agent is not "authentically free" because it is cut off from its "willful eccentricity." From Mehta's Nietzschean perspective, such individuals "must live in a condition of permanent tutelage." They "surrender" to a set of intellectual practices that shape them into the "complaisant inmates of a Lockean panopticon." *The Anxiety of Freedom*, 124–33, 38–41, 61–63, 71–72. While Mehta is right in pointing out the centrality of intellectual restraint in Locke's political project, he does not address Locke's own argument that these contraints are constitutive of freedom and importantly linked to the maintenance of a peaceful and tolerant regime. Mehta also seems to overlook the ways in which the internal constraints that Locke advocates facilitate the establishment of a regime in which external constraints are less necessary.

dom. The entire process of will formation could be seen as a result of a preceding uneasiness and thus simply a more sophisticated version of his earlier determinism. Locke's determinism would appear to be no different than Hobbes's determinism. Yet this is mistaken. For Locke, freedom does not rest on indeterminacy, but determination by reasonable judgment. To distinguish himself from Hobbes, Locke need not prove that the will is undetermined, but rather determined by reason rather than by brute desire.[9] Locke does not make reasonable judgment the servant of the passions. Our reason, as Peter Schouls puts it, is "a master passion," a desire for careful judgment that is able to govern and control all our other desires.[10] To be free is not to be undetermined, but to be determined by what is reasonable.

For Locke, allowing reason to govern or restrain the will does not limit freedom. Such determination is "not a restraint or diminution of freedom" but rather "the very improvement and benefit of it" (E II.xxi.48). Locke implies that the more our choices are determined by what is truly good for us, the closer we approach genuine happiness and true freedom. The less our choices are determined by the good, the closer we draw to "misery and slavery" (E II.xxi.48). We need only consider God and angels, Locke tells us, to recognize that determination by the good is compatible with true liberty.

> If we look upon those superiour beings above us, who enjoy perfect happiness, we shall have reason to judge that they are more steadily determined in their choice of good than we; and yet we have no reason to think they are less happy, or less free, than we are. (E II.xxi.49)

Although it might be so that the choices of these higher beings are more "steadily determined" by the moral structure of the world than ours are, the fact that they are determined does not constitute a lack of freedom. These heavenly agents are free even though their choices are determined by, and dependent on, a good external to themselves. As John Colman points out, this is an adaptation rather than a rejection of the view "that properly free actions are those which are grounded in rational decisions."[11]

We can see that this type of free agency is very different from the Hobbesian liberty that Locke embraces at other points in the *Essay*. Here thoroughgoing free agency involves much more than the expression of our will through action; it involves an almost divine capacity to transcend our immediate desires and then adjust them so that they conform to what is good for us. In fact it seems that divine agency serves as ideal

---

[9] Myers, *Our Only Star*, 143.
[10] Schouls, *Reasoned Freedom*, 40.
[11] Colman, *John Locke's Moral Philosophy*, 215.

or model for Locke's notion of thoroughgoing free agency.[12] "God himself cannot choose what is not good," Locke writes; "the freedom of the almighty hinders not his being determined by what is best" (E II.xxi.49). Similarly, our true freedom is not limited but perfected through our capacity to align our will with what is good. We might not be as "steadily determined" by the good as are divine beings, yet we do have a extraordinary capacity to turn our will away from what is not good and align it with that which is most conducive to our long-term happiness. Locke's teaching is clear: as thoroughgoing free agents, we are meant to make use of our ability to suspend and examine our desires in order move closer toward divine perfection, in order to attune our will to what is truly good for us.

The Pursuit of True and Solid Happiness

Yet all of this leaves us with a set of nagging questions. How exactly are we supposed to know what is conducive to our "true and solid happiness"? How are we supposed to attune ourselves to the good if we are not exactly sure what the good is? At first glance it would seem that we need only align our will with what is pleasant to us, since for Locke happiness is reducible to pleasure. In fact, Locke goes so far as to say that the highest degree of happiness is simply "the utmost pleasure we are capable of" (E II.xxi.42; see also II.xxi.55, 62). Yet Locke's hedonism is not as straightforward as it appears. Attaining the type of happiness that is conducive to perfect freedom is a much more complicated process. In order to achieve "true and solid happiness" we must take care "that we mistake not imaginary for real happiness" (E II.xxi.51; see also II.xx.2, II.xxi.52, 56, 60). We must distinguish between those desires that are good for us and those that are not. For Locke, the unrestrained appetite does not lead to happiness but misery (E I.iii.13, II.xxi.52, 56).

At this point Locke seems to follow Aristotle in placing rational happiness at the center of the exemplary life.[13] Yet Locke distances himself

---

[12] One could further speculate that the differences between the Hobbesian account of free agency and Locke's second account are tied to differing views of divine power. Hobbes follows Luther and Calvin in conceiving of divine sovereignty as unknowable, unlimited, and unrestrained and shares their general approach to the philosophical puzzles surrounding freedom and necessity. Locke, on the other hand, joins many Anglican clergy in his day in embracing the Dutch theologian Arminius, who rejected the image of God held by orthodox Calvinism. Arminius developed a theory of freedom that shares many of the same concerns that animate Bramhall and Locke. It seems that the assumptions that these thinkers make about divine agency shape how they conceive of human free agency as well. Divine agency serves as a model for what they imagine human beings capable of being.

[13] Aristotle, *Nicomachean Ethics*, 1097b22–1098a20.

from Aristotle by emphasizing the difficulty, if not impossibility, of defining happiness once and for all. Locke has too much in common with
Montaigne to ignore the fact that the origins of human happiness are
varied and unpredictable.[14] He ridicules "the philosophers of old" who
argued in vain over the *summum bonum* or greatest good: "They might
have as reasonably disputed, whether the best relish were to be found
in apples, plums, or nuts; and have divided themselves into sects upon
it." For Locke, happiness is a matter of taste, since "the greatest happiness consists in the having those things which produce the greatest pleasure.... these to different men are very different things" (E II.xxi.55).
Individuals achieve happiness through infinitely varied ways, and their
differing views of happiness lead to differing views of what is good and
bad for them (E I.iii.6; II.xxi.42, 54–55).

   Yet we should hesitate before we dub Locke a relativist. Although he
recognizes that people hold diverse views concerning happiness, he does
not conceive of happiness in purely subjective terms. As Steven Forde
points out, "Though some may prefer apples to nuts, no one seems to
relish hemlock."[15] Locke recognizes that human beings have a propensity
to avoid certain things that will impede their happiness (E I.iii.3, II.x.3).
He insists that certain tastes or relishes simply do not lead to happiness.
Habitual drunkenness and profligacy, though they might be motivated
by a certain view of happiness, prevent us from achieving it (E II.xxi.35,
II.xxii.17). While allowing for a ride range of pursuits, Locke does not
want to say that anything can make people happy. Locke's hedonism
involves making distinctions between imaginary and real happiness; it
involves an act of mental labor that goes beyond passive response to
untutored desire. Attaining true and solid happiness is not the same as
following one's whim. In fact Locke argues that humans are uniquely
capable of happiness for the very reason that happiness is *more* than the
immediate perception of pleasure (E II.xx.5, II.xxvii.17, 26). Those who
seek happiness must strive to conform their taste to "the true intrinsic
good or ill that is in things" (E II.xxi.53).

---

[14] The mature Locke retains many similarities with Montaigne, yet ultimately parts ways
with Montaigne's radical skepticism. In a diary entry written during Locke's stay in the
Netherlands, he comments on Montaigne's "gentle sort of negligence," then disparages him
because "he reasons not" and is "full of pride and vanity." Excerpted in Peter King, *The Life
and Letters of John Locke, with Extracts from His Journals and Commonplace Books* (New
York: B. Franklin, 1972), 159. Rahe cites part of this entry to link Montaigne and Locke,
but passes over Locke's emphatic disapproval of Montaigne's method. Rahe, *Republics
Ancient and Modern*, 272–73. Peter Myers also points out several ways in which Montaigne's influence can be seen in Locke's mature writings. Myers, *Our Only Star*, 162–65.

[15] Steven Forde, "What Does Locke Expect Us to Know?" *Review of Politics* 68 (2006),
236.

Yet this brings us back to the same difficulty. If we are to achieve "true and solid happiness," we need a way to uncover "the intrinsic good or ill of things." We need to know what this happiness entails. One solution that Locke offers is that happiness involves conforming our will and action to the law of nature (which is also the law of God). As we have seen in chapter 4, Locke claims at several points in the *Essay* that it is really not so difficult to discover what the law entails. Every human being should be able to uncover the law of nature because it is "knowable by the light of nature; i.e. without the help of positive revelation" (E I.iii.13). He insists that we can produce a demonstrable proof of our moral obligations if we are careful to proceed logically from abstract, moral concepts to necessary conclusions. By positing moral concepts and then demonstrating what those moral concepts necessarily entail, we can arrive at conclusions that would be acceptable to anyone who could follow the proof. This is what Locke means when he says that "morality is capable of demonstration, as well as mathematics" (E III.xi.16; see also IV.iv.7, IV.xii.8).[16]

Locke presents the most complete account of this intended demonstration in the fourth book of the *Essay*. He writes that "the idea of a supreme being, infinite in power, goodness, and wisdom, whose workmanship we are, and on whom we depend . . . would, I suppose, if duly considered and pursued, afford such foundations of our duty and rules of action as might place morality amongst the sciences capable of demonstration" (E IV.iii.18). In spite of his insistence that morality is capable of demonstration, it is worth noting just how hesitant Locke is in this passage. He offers some tentative starting points, yet he does not provide his readers with a conclusive account of how this method could help us uncover the content of natural law. The ideas that serve as the foundation of Locke's moral demonstration are ideas of substances—man and God. Ideas of substances are something that Locke insists we *cannot* perfectly know.[17] He does, however, insist on the importance of God as the promulgator of law. Throughout the *Essay*, Locke maintains that morality depends on a divine legislator and enforcer.[18] The "true ground of moral-

[16] Greg Forster is certainly mistaken when he writes, "Purely demonstrative morality is nothing more than a hypothetical idea in Locke's philosophy, a sidebar mentioned once, in passing, in the *Essay*." *John Locke's Moral Consensus*, 100. Yet, as we will see, Locke's failure to produce a demonstrative proof is far less troublesome for Locke himself than for many commentators.

[17] For an interesting exploration of Locke's argument, see Jeremy Waldron, *God, Locke, and Equality* (Cambridge: Cambridge University Press, 2002), 44–82.

[18] Steven Forde links Locke's philosophical conviction that morality can exist only by a legislating will with his devotion to the new science. For the experimentalists surrounding Locke who rejected the traditional, teleological view, nature required direction from outside. That is, if material nature is devoid of intrinsic moral content, morality must be

ity" can only be "the will and law of a God, who sees men in the dark, has in his hand rewards and punishments" (E I.iii.6). These rewards and punishments must consist of "some good and evil that is not the natural product and consequence of the action itself" (E II.28.6). Only providential enforcement with its rewards and punishments can outweigh the gains of immorality and bring the individual's pleasure and pain fully in line with moral action (E I.iii.13, II.xxi.70, II.xxviii.6, 8). It is the existence of divine rewards and punishments that makes conformity to the law of nature conducive to "true and solid happiness." Locke repeats this fundamentally theological argument many times throughout his life, both publicly and privately.[19]

However, it is hard to see how anyone could determine the content of God's laws or uncover what "true and solid happiness" entails through examination of these abstract, moral concepts. Yet even if the content of the law of nature could be demonstrated, we would still have difficulty with the enforcement mechanism. If we are to understand the law of nature as law, Locke tells us, then we must not only be able to recognize the *content* of the law but the *punishments and rewards* of the law as well. And the content and promulgation of this law has to be recognized as such by all people at all times; it cannot be something that an isolated scholar might arrive at after manipulating mixed modes in some extraordinary way. Yet Locke concedes that the divine enforcer of this law is "incomprehensibly infinite" and thus beyond "our weak and narrow thoughts" (E II.xvii.17). Since we cannot even know the real essences of simple things such as a pebble or a fly, we surely cannot know the real essence of a God who is immeasurably more inaccessible (E II.xxiii.35). At best we can form an imperfect and incomplete idea of a "most powerful, and most knowing being" (E IV.x.6). As for divine rewards and punishments, Locke concludes that they are beyond the reach of human reason (E IV.xvii.23, IV.xviii.7). These statements seem to constitute a retraction, or at least drastic qualification, of the original promise of demonstrable knowledge of a providential God. In his private correspondence, Locke acknowledged that he had never produced the type of proof that he said was readily accessible.[20]

Faced with this curiously incomplete theological demonstration, some commentators have argued that Locke's claims regarding God are simply

---

imposed from outside of it, by supernature. By insisting that natural law originates from a transcendent lawgiver, Locke was positioning himself against Cambridge Platonists, Hugo Grotius, and others who understood moral law to be intrinsic to nature. Forde, "What Does Locke Expect," 239.

[19] See Locke, LN, 109–13, 205–7; STCE 136, 139; RC, 44.

[20] Locke, *Correspondence*, 4:110–13, 729, 786–87.

a rhetorical cover for a fundamentally antitheistic teaching.[21] Others have concluded that Locke was forced to retreat to revelation to tie up the loose ends in his thinking.[22] They view his later religious writings, starting with *The Reasonableness of Christianity*, as stemming from a recognition of the fundamental inadequacies in the *Essay*. Yet, as Steven Forde points out, both of these views fail to address Locke's continuing revisions of the *Essay* at the same time that he was writing *The Reasonableness of Christianity*. He worked to improve the arguments of the *Essay* and respond to critics at the same time that he launched into a study of the New Testament. He proceeded to develop his ideas despite the acknowledged absence of a demonstrable theological proof. "In short," Forde writes, "Locke did not behave as though the lack of this proof stymied his overall moral project."[23] He simply was not bothered by his failure produce an absolutely certain demonstration of morality.

Perhaps this is because Locke is more interested in teaching his readers to take up the labor of probable reasoning than providing them with certain knowledge of natural law. In spite of his claims about demonstrable morality, Locke is hardly sanguine about our epistemological condition. We live in a "fleeting state of action and blindness," a "state of mediocrity," in which certain knowledge is "short and scanty" (E IV.xvi.4, IV.xiv.1, 2). Yet even though we often find ourselves fumbling through the darkness of our ignorance, "the candle, that is set up in us, shines bright enough for all our purposes" (E I.i.5). Locke insists that God provides us with what we need. In our condition of intellectual neediness, individual judgment must suffice.

In this way he can resist those clergymen and theologians who claim to have special access to the content of natural law as well as those thinkers who claim that individual power and self-assertion are the only trustworthy standards of morality in the world. Locke can concede that human agents often fail to achieve absolute perspicuity concerning the existence, the content, or even the promulgation of a transcendent law, while continuing to insist that they find themselves in a morally marked world created by God and infused with purpose and law. He can acknowledge the skeptical insights of Montaigne and Charron concerning a human propensity to confound and confuse universal moral standards without rejecting the assumption that such standards exist. He can insist that virtue and convenience do ultimately complement each other without having to provide demonstrative proof of such an agreement. An assump-

[21] Strauss, *Natural Right and History*, 212–14; Pangle, *Spirit of Modern Republicanism*, 201–3; Rahe, *Republics Ancient and Modern*, 296.

[22] Dunn, *Political Thought of Locke*, 187–88; Dunn, *Locke: Past Masters*, 66–68, 84–85, 88; Waldron, *God, Locke, and Equality*, 103–5.

[23] Forde, "What Does Locke Expect," 240.

tion concerning "God's great design" seems to permeate his epistemological and political writings. Although we have probable evidence of this ordered and purposive cosmos in the deliverances of nature, certain knowledge of the source and meaning of that cosmos lies outside of human comprehension. The assumption of a divine design governed by steady and reliable laws plays a crucial role in Locke's account of the proper regulation of one's intellectual and physical conduct. It allows him to embrace the possibility of an overarching moral law while also resisting dogmatic claims concerning the specific content of that law. Thus natural law is both present and not present in Locke's account of reasonable human action.

Locke suggests that the probability that there is a providential God is sufficient for the purposes of conduct (E II.xxi.70). In fact, we should "not peremptorily, or intemperately, require demonstration and demand certainty, where probability only is to be had." For probability is "sufficient to govern all our concernments" (E I.i.5). We need only make use of our well-governed judgment to distinguish our real from our imaginary happiness. In the context of Christianity, this process of reasoning takes place in two steps: First, the grounds of probability for the belief that revelation is the word of God and that heaven and hell are real possibilities are assessed. Then the relative pleasures and pains involved with any action are weighed and compared. To help his readers, Locke offers a variant of Pascal's wager to show that the pleasures and pains of a probable heaven and hell infinitely outweigh any earthly pleasures that might be passed over: "The rewards and punishments of another life, which the Almighty has established as the enforcement of his law, are of weight enough to determine the choices, against whatever pleasure or pain this life can show, when the eternal state is considered but in its bare possibility" (E II.xxi.70).[24] In the *Reasonableness of Christianity* Locke will go on to say that the probability of an afterlife makes virtuous living "visibly the most enriching purchase, and by much the best bargain" (RC 252; see also 245). Even though we cannot attain certain knowledge of the rewards and punishments of the moral law, we can assume that such sanctions would be consonant with a divine design that we can infer

[24] For Patrick Riley, this shift from a demonstrative ethics to an argument of probability shows that Locke remained committed to the notion of a divine design in spite of his difficulty establishing his commitments with certainty. In opposition to scholars such as Leo Strauss who distrust Locke's sincerity, Riley argues that "If Locke did not believe that the immortality of the soul was demonstrable by reason unaided by revelation, he did at least think that such immortality was probable and that a Pascalian wager on that point was reasonable; but Strauss, by not even mentioning Locke's theory of probability, strives to create the impression that Locke's theory of immortality is utterly groundless." Riley, *Will and Political Legitimacy*, 89.

through the probable signs of nature. From this standpoint we are called to make the best judgments that we can: "Judging is, as it were, balancing an account, and determining on which side the odds lies" (E II.xxi.67). James Tully concludes that once Locke had discovered the ways in which probability could be used in moral reasoning, he realized that a demonstrable ethics was no longer necessary.[25] Probable judgment turns out to be sufficient for all our greatest concernments. It is for this reason that Locke's turn to Scripture at the end of his life is not a retreat from reason as he understood it, but a particular application of it.[26]

It is worth noting, however, that Locke's theological investigations actually aim at steering readers away from metaphysical speculation about the nature and purposes of God. It turns out that we need only investigate the probable signs of nature in order to learn all we need to know about the law of nature and the law of God. The mind derives all of its ideas—including its moral ideas—from an encounter with the world. This is the underlying premise of the *Essay*, yet it is explicitly applied to theology in Locke's *First Treatise of Government*. Locke states that God has placed in man "a strong desire of self-preservation, and furnished the world with things fit for food and raiment and other necessaries of life" (1T 86). Man is also furnished also with reason, which is "the voice of God in him," and helps him discern the natural law from his natural surroundings. "God, I say, having made man and world thus, spoke to him, directed him by his senses and reason . . . to the use of those things, which were serviceable for his subsistence" (1T 86). Not only our yearning for preservation, but also our desire to provide for ourselves in smaller ways through food, shelter, and clothing, is nothing less than a divine command. Our natural reason is God's voice in us. By rationally pursuing our God-given appetites, we are following God's will.

Here Locke rejects the view of many of his Calvinist-leaning contemporaries that human reason is so degraded by original sin that it requires divine renewal through the miracle of grace. In fact, Locke seems to throw out the entire notion of original sin, insisting that our natural appetites

---

[25] Tully, *Approach to Political Philosophy*, 216.

[26] By assessing Scripture according to the new grounds of probability, Locke finds that it is highly probable that it is the revelation of God and thus rational to believe as true. Given the overwhelming pleasures and pains of heaven and hell, this probability is sufficient to provide motivation for Christians to follow its dictates. In his "Discourse of Miracles," Locke argues that the appearance of "outward and visible signs" is sufficient evidence for the belief that Scripture is the word of God. Locke writes that "the marks of a superior power accompanying it, always have, and always will be, visible and sure guide to divine revelation; by which men may conduct themselves in their examining of revealed religions, and be satisfied which they ought to receive as coming from God." John Locke, "A Discourse of Miracles," in *John Locke*, ed. I. T. Ramsey (Stanford: Stanford University Press, 1958), 86. See also E IV.xiv.15, IV.xvi.13.

and desires are a window into God's design.[27] The will of God, at least insofar as it relates to humanity, is not mysterious. It can be uncovered through a very ordinary and mundane process of human reasoning. We follow God's will when we pursue our happiness according to our probable judgment. Locke's God encourages this-worldly happiness by presenting us with a moral law that is conducive to human flourishing in both this life and the next. In fact, it is Locke's God who placed our desire for happiness within us, so that it could serve as our guide.

At times, however, Locke seems to recognize that the demands of morality and the allures of personal happiness might not always reinforce one another. In cases of conflict, he insists that we should choose virtue even if "the virtuous life here had nothing but pain, and the vicious continual pleasure" (E II.xxi.70). Here we can see the importance of the possibility of an afterlife. Divine rewards and punishments must at least be possible if we are to bring happiness completely in line with morality. It is important to note, however, just how quickly Locke plays down this conclusion. In the very same sentence, he asserts that "for the most part" the virtuous and vicious receive appropriate rewards and punishments in this life. "Wicked men," Locke tells us, "have even the worse part here." Even in the midst of his discussion of the afterlife, Locke minimizes the need for heavenly rewards and punishments by insisting that virtue promotes worldly happiness, and the sober man "ventures nothing" in wagering on eternal happiness (E II.xxi.70). Following God's law is simply "the most enriching purchase, and by much the best bargain" (RC 252).

Locke's appeal to theology does not yield an austere set of moral dictates, but rather a divine endorsement of our this-worldly pursuit of happiness. Locke's exploration of natural law minimizes the ascetic, mysterious, and ethereal aspects of the divine in favor of a fundamentally liberal God who wants nothing more than to see humanity "be fruitful and multiply" (1T 33). In the course of seeking our ultimate reward, we are directed to pursue this-worldly happiness. Yet this type of flourishing will take hard work.[28] Locke's God not only allows us, but indeed commands us, to use our faculties to improve our mundane condition. It turns out that the moral law that a just God promulgates is indistinguishable from

---

[27] Marshall, *John Locke*, 127, 194; John Marshall, "Locke, Socinianism, 'Socinianism,' and Unitarianism," in Stewart, *English Philosophy*; Victor Nuovo, "Locke's Theology, 1694–1704," in Stewart, *English Philosophy*; W. M. Spellman, *John Locke and the Problem of Depravity* (Oxford: Clarendon Press, 1988).

[28] Locke's description of God providing the raw materials for human happiness in order to foster industry and thoughtfulness is similar to Robert Boyle's argument in *Some Considerations Regarding the Usefulness of Experimental Natural Philosophy*. Cited by Rahe, *Republics Ancient and Modern*, 361.

our own well-considered judgment of what is good for us. The pursuit of rational happiness is obedience to God.

Seen in this light, the type of "knowing" that Locke seems to require for thoroughgoing free agency is different from the certainty promised by moral demonstration. This type of knowing has less to do with the content of moral law than with the practices of intellectual self-governance. If we are to learn to attune our will to our long-term happiness, we need to develop certain dispositions to our own good that will allow us pursue it regardless of where it should happen to be found. To have this type of disposition is not to have demonstrable knowledge of morality or the precepts of natural law, but to have a capacity to make choices in a context of profound uncertainty. We have to be ready to make probable judgments about the possible consequences of our volitions and the actions that result from them. Our capacity to pursue "true and solid happiness" does not depend on a proof accessible only to the philosophical few, but on an ordinary state of mind available to almost everyone. What is most important to thoroughgoing free agency is the fashioning of a certain type of disposition with regard to probable goods. By suspending our immediate desires and making absent pains and pleasures come alive in our minds, we can raise uneasiness concerning what we take to be our "true and solid happiness." In this way we can incrementally adjust our will until it accords with our long-term good.

At times, Locke seems to imply that the type of intellectual discipline required for pursuing "true and solid happiness" might not be available to everyone. He writes that "the greatest part of mankind, who are given up to labour, and enslaved to the necessity of their mean condition" are unable to make out "most of the propositions, that, in societies of men, are judged of the greatest moment" (E II.xx.2). Passages such as this led C. B. Macpherson to argue that Locke believes that there are some who "cannot be left to the guidance of the law of nature or the law of reason" since "they are not capable of drawing the rules of conduct from it."[29] Shortly after Macpherson's original article, Leo Strauss published *Natural Right and History*, a work that presents a strikingly similar account of a type of differential rationality in Locke's thought from a significantly different interpretive standpoint.[30] Both Macpherson and Strauss argue that Locke maintains a fundamentally hierarchical distinction between

---

[29] C. B. Macpherson, *The Political Theory of Possessive Individualism* (Oxford: Oxford University Press, 1962), 225. Macpherson's influential thesis was first articulated in "Locke on Capitalist Appropriation," *Western Political Quarterly* 4, no. 4 (1951), and subsequently presented in his important work *The Political Theory of Possessive Individualism*. For discussions of some of the debate that continues to surround "the Macpherson thesis," see Tully, *Approach to Political Philosophy*, chaps. 2, 3, and 4.

[30] See Strauss, *Natural Right and History*, especially 248.

the few who are "in the know" and the many who are not. Yet if we understand Locke's project to involve convincing his readers to shift from arguments over certain knowledge to the regulation of probable belief, we find that he sought out a much larger audience. His project for intellectual reform and self-governance is not limited to a rational few who find themselves at the top of an ascending wave of bourgeois supremacy or exclusive philosophical insight. When Locke refers to "the lazy and inconsiderate part of men" at the beginning of the *Essay,* he is speaking of those who squandered their opportunities, not those who never had them (E I.iv.15). Instead of working to clarify their thoughts and govern their behavior appropriately, it is the well-fed philosophers who "raise questions and multiply disputes" (E I.i.6). The type of "quarrelsome and contentious" individuals whom Locke condemns in the *Second Treatise* can be found in universities, parliaments, and perhaps even in the royal residence itself. There is no reason to suppose that Locke believed that laborers by virtue of being laborers were less capable of thinking for themselves. Locke repeatedly defends a fundamentally egalitarian vision of intellectual self-governance—every individual, regardless of educational or economic background, is responsible for his or her own judgments, especially in matters of "great concernment" such as law, morality, and religion. It is the almost universal capacity to make probable judgments and attune our volitions and our actions to our long-term good that makes us genuinely free.[31]

Thus Locke presents us with two accounts of freedom in the *Essay.* In one sense we are free when we are able to act according to our volitions without external impediment. Yet in another, more important sense, we are thoroughgoing free agents insofar as we are able to suspend our immediate desires, examine them in light of our long-term happiness, and adjust our will appropriately. The first account of freedom stems from Hobbes and is limited to a type of self-expression through action. The second account is distinct from Hobbes's notion and requires a type of self-transcendence through judgment and contemplation. For Locke, the first account is an accurate description of one aspect of freedom, yet it is ultimately inadequate. We should not accept Hobbesian freedom as thoroughgoing free agency. Locke wants to show his readers that we are free not simply because we are able to act without impediment. Our freedom precludes blind obedience to any power, including the power of our own immediate desires. We are free because we are able to respond appropriately to what is good and valuable in the world. We are able to rationally pursue happiness by utilizing our capacity to make probable judgments.

---

[31] See Ashcraft, *Revolutionary Politics,* 247–48; Dunn, *Political Thought of Locke,* 233ff.; Tully, *A Discourse on Property*; Waldron, *God, Locke, and Equality,* 85–91.

If we wish to experience ourselves as thoroughgoing free agents, we must strive to conform our choices to our long-term good and govern our conduct according to something beyond our own immediate desires.

The Formation of the Reasonable Self

For Locke the capacities that enable us to conform our will to our long-term happiness—and to exercise free agency—are the same capacities that constitute us as persons. In the face of intellectual yearnings that pull us toward lazy submission to authority as well as unrestrained self-expression, Locke encourages us to constitute ourselves as *free agents*, as responsible and self-governing persons. It is our ability to govern our minds combined with an awareness of that ability that makes this possible. This is because Locke locates what he calls the "self" or the "person" not in substance, but in consciousness. We are persons not because we have the shape or the substance of persons, but because we are aware of ourselves as persons. This view, he concedes, "will look strange to some readers," and it is worth noting just how strange it is. In fact, Locke's view of personal identity is much more peculiar than is often recognized. The consequences of his view are in turn more significant.

By locating our identity in consciousness instead of corporeality, Locke rejects our tendency to link who we are as individuals with our particular, tangible substance. This is odd, since we readily think of ourselves and others as complex substances, and personal identity as analogous to substance identity. Aren't we persons for much of the same reasons that the objects around us are things? Both persons and things seem to gain their identity from the substance that gives them form. For example, I assume that my daughter is now the same person who, an hour ago, came running through the door for the same reason that the door is still the same one that she opened an hour ago. Both my daughter and the door appear to be substances that maintain material and spatial continuity with earlier substances.

Yet Locke rejects this commonsensical notion. For him there is no persisting substance, no underlying essence of our identity, that makes up who we are. We are selves insofar as we are conscious of the world around us and our actions within that world (E II.xxvii.10). We are not selves because we possess substance, but because we possess awareness. "Self is that conscious thinking thing," Locke writes, "which is sensible, or conscious of pleasure and pain, capable of happiness or misery, and so is concerned for itself, as far as the consciousness extends" (E II.xxvii.17). For Locke consciousness is *constitutive*. It is our consciousness that sets the boundaries of who we are. The unity or identity of a person is not given prior to consciousness; it exists only in and through our consciousness. We become properly selves only in the process of recognizing and responding to the world *as* selves. We become aware of the external world as distinct from us, and of the actions that we take in response to that world as belonging to us as agents.

Locke explains that it is our awareness of our actions as properly ours that bundles the various events we experience into a unified self. We are conscious of our past actions when we conceive of those actions as something that we performed. A self is properly a self, Locke writes, insofar as it "owns all the actions of that thing, as its own" (E II.xxvii.17). As selves we recognize the actions that we have taken in our lives *as our actions*. Whether admirable or embarrassing, we accept them as somehow part of who we are. In a similar way, Locke seems to hint that we are also aware of the stimulus of our actions—that is, our volitions—as properly ours. We view our volitions as ours insofar as we conceive of them as arising, at least in part, from our own capacities. Our identity as selves depends on a capacity to recognize both our conduct and our will as properly ours. The creation of the self, then, establishes itself by gathering or appropriating to itself its actions and its volitions.

It is this self-gathering or self-appropriating that makes us capable of law. Locke believes that a consciousness of voluntary action entails an acknowledgment of responsibility. A person is by definition someone who is capable of being held accountable for his or her actions. To be accountable for an action is to accept the consequences for the performance of that action. It is to recognize that the action, as well as the will that preceded it, was at least partly in our power. The punishments or rewards that our conduct merits are thus properly assigned to us as persons. This is why the term "person" can be applied only to those who are capable of recognizing that they exist within the matrix of laws and obligations. It is "a forensic term," Locke tells us, "appropriating actions and their merit, and so belongs only to intelligent agents capable of a law, and happiness and misery" (E II.xxvii.26). We are capable of law insofar as we are able recognize that there is some moral standard or ideal that connects our past actions with our present ones. Whether this standard is the elusive natural law or a more accessible measure of probable happiness is ambiguous. Yet Locke believes that the reasonable self is not only able to acknowledge an action as its own, but also to recognize the consequences of that action as its own. It is this awareness of accountability that constitutes us as selves.

The self-conscious person is aware that there is a link between his or her actions and volitions and his or her long-term happiness. Locke tells us that a concern for our future happiness is "an unavoidable concomitant" of our consciousness (E II.xxvii.26). To be a self or a person is to be concerned with the happiness and misery that result from one's actions. This concern leads the self to abstract from immediate pains and pleasures in order to construct an idea of long-term happiness. This idea can serve as a regulatory principle as the self learns to suspend the demands of immediate desires and strive to conform the will to a real instead of an illusory good. Our "great privilege" as "finite intellectual beings," Locke tells us, is our capacity to care for ourselves by attending to our "true and solid happiness" (E II.xxi.52). What makes us free agents is our ability to make absent pleasures and pains alive to ourselves in order to influence the present determination of our will. It is through this capacity that we can rationally pursue happiness; that is, we can struggle to bring about a correspondence between our will and the moral good that structures our experience in the world.[32]

Locke argues that the self is thus conscious that it is the master or the owner of itself. In a sense, the self is its own property. It claims ownership of its body, but also its volitions and actions. The volitions and actions of the self come to be owned by the self in the same way that anything else comes to be owned by the self—through labor.[33] Nature supplies the "raw materials," yet human beings as persons are largely self-made. As Ross Harrison puts it, "God may create our bodies, but it is we who make them into persons."[34] As the creator and author of nature, God owns each human being, but a human being is the author of his or her own person, and can therefore claim a type of ownership or proprietorship of that person.[35] We come to own our self by carefully gathering

---

[32] Charles Taylor argues that Locke presents a "punctual self," a "radically subjectivist view of the person," which is characterized by its capacity to "disengage" from the world of things and people. By standing apart from and "objectifying" one's surroundings as well as one's self, the Lockean agent becomes a "self-defining subject." Yet, as I have tried to argue here, the reasonable self that Locke promotes is one that is constantly at work apprehending and conforming to a good that is not self-generated but rather discovered through interaction with a morally marked world. Taylor, *Sources of the Self*, 171–72. For a recent corrective to Taylor's distorting account, see Jerrold Siegel, *The Idea of the Self: Thought and Experience in Western Europe since the Seventeenth Century* (Cambridge: Cambridge University Press, 2005).

[33] See Zuckert, *Natural Rights*, 285–86. Zuckert's description of the self as "the empty center of consciousness" ignores Locke's insistence that the self must be something other than pure potentiality; it must be properly ordered, conforming to its long-term happiness, which is necessarily limited by the natural world.

[34] Ross Harrison, *Hobbes, Locke, and Confusion's Masterpiece* (Cambridge: Cambridge University Press, 2003), 232.

[35] Some commentators, including Thomas Pangle, Michael Zuckert, and David Foster, have argued that there is a tension between Locke's argument concerning divine ownership and his insistence on human self-ownership. See Pangle, *Spirit of Modern Republicanism*, 160; Zuckert, *Natural Rights*, 220–21, 239, 276, 278–83; David Foster, "The Bible and Natural Freedom in John Locke's Political Thought," in *Piety and Humanity: Essays on*

together our ideas and our actions into a single self that persists through time. We then use our faculty of judgment to explore the probable signs of nature in order to conform our volitions and actions to our "true and solid happiness."[36]

Considering what Locke tells us about the tenacity and pervasiveness of epistemic immodesty, it is not surprising that he believes this type of intellectual self-discipline should not come easily. Locke insists that it requires strenuous mental labor. It is such demanding and difficult work that at one point Locke wonders whether grown men "settled in their course of life" will be able to undertake it. He concludes that they can, but warns that they will not succeed "without industry and application" (CU 6). In fact, throughout his philosophical writings, Locke associates the type of self-restraint required to form the reasonable self with the "industry and labor of thought" (E IV.iii.6). Those who fail to govern their actions and volitions do so out of "lazy ignorance" (E IV.xx.6). In the *Essay* Locke persistently identifies reasonable self-governance with "industry," "industriousness," "pains and assiduity," and the "steady application and pursuit" of truth (E I.iv.22, II.xiii.27, III.vi.30, IV.ii.4), and the *Conduct of the Understanding* abounds with similar labor metaphors (CU 6, 25, 26, 28, 35, 38, 45). Locke describes himself in the beginning of the *Essay* as one who refuses "to live lazily on scraps of begged opinions" and thus "sets his own thoughts on work." He is "an underlabourer in clearing ground a little, and removing of the rubbish, that lies in the way of knowledge" (E, "Epistle" 6, 10). Throughout the *Essay* Locke depicts the properly functioning mind as something that "works on" or is "employed" with the ideas it contains, and he suggests that this employment is what gives us the "quiet and secure possession of truths, that most concerned us" (E I.i.7). For Locke, thinking is not simply pleasurable; it is the hard work that we must do in order to achieve a pleasurable state.[37]

Religion and Early Modern Political Philosophy, ed. Douglas Kries (Lanham, Md.: Rowman & Littlefield, 1997), 183, 200. Yet I believe that Locke would see these arguments as interlinked: As the master and owner of creation, God commands (and reason teaches) that humans should strive toward self-ownership in this world. In Locke's account, the recognition of divine ownership actually encourages human self-ownership (2T 25–27).

[36] See also Simmons, *Lockean Theory of Rights*, chap. 5; and Jeremy Waldron, *The Right to Private Property* (Oxford: Oxford University Press, 1988), where the self-ownership is not limitless but seen in the context of duties within a morally marked world.

[37] Locke explicitly emphasizes the importance of both mental and physical labor in an essay on the topic in his commonplace book. After arguing that men of study should commit at least a third of their time to physical labor and laborers should commit at least a third of their time to study, he writes, "To conclude and this is certain, that if the labour of the world were rightly directed and distributed there would be more knowledge, peace, health, and plenty in it than now there is. And mankind be much more happy than now it is." "Labour," in Locke, *Political Essays*, 328. For the prevalence of labor imagery through-

By identifying disciplined thinking with mental labor, Locke provides us with a cognitive analogue to the labor theory of property that he presents in the fifth chapter of the *Second Treatise*. Just as physical exertion is required to warrant a claim to possess material property, mental exertion is required to warrant a claim to possess ourselves as persons capable of liberty and happiness. In the chapter "Of Property" in the *Second Treatise*, Locke explains how a world that was given to all in common was parceled into privately held units. Individual agents give the commonly held but nevertheless nearly worthless natural world value by infusing their own labor into it. They are thus entitled to the portions on which they have labored and added value. It is this process that establishes distinction among individuals and property: "And 'tis plain, if the first gathering made them not his, nothing else could. That labor put the distinction between them and common. That added something to them more than nature, the common mother of all, had done; and so they became his private right" (2T 28). For Locke a person expresses his or her individuality through the capacity for purposeful labor. Thus property is associated with the creativity, dignity, and distinctness of human beings. In fact capacity to possess property involves the capacity of self-possession and self-governance. When Locke describes his regime as one that aims solely to protect property, he is alluding to a much grander task of ensuring space for this noble self to flourish.

This applies to the acquisition of material as well as intellectual goods. In contrast, those who simply let others carry out the mental labor for them can never "own" their own opinions as truth even if they happen to be true. What a man "takes upon trust, are but shreds; which however well in the whole piece, make no considerable addition to his stock, who gathers them. Such borrowed wealth, like fairy-money, though it were gold in the hand from which he received it, will be but leaves and dust when it comes to use" (E I.iv.23). This passage, filled with the same terminology as the chapter on property in the *Second Treatise*, makes it clear that only those who employ their own mental labor instead of attempting to benefit from the labor of others have actual title to the products of intellectual inquiry.

Even more striking, however, is the parallel sense in which the world in its original state in both the *Essay* and the *Two Treatises* is of very little use to human beings. Despite Locke's initial claim that God or nature has "given us all things richly," the "plenty" that he assigns to the state of nature is potential, not actual (2T 31). It is through labor—whether intellectual or physical—that the "waste" of the natural world is expo-

---

out the *Essay* see James Gibson, *John Locke* (London: H. Milford, 1933), 36–37; Walker, *Locke, Literary Criticism*, 45–51; Wood, *Politics of Locke's Philosophy*, 121–42.

nentially improved and the "needy and wretched" inhabitants are transformed into satisfied, rational beings (2T 33, 37, 40–48). Our original
intellectual and physical condition is one of neediness. Just as we find
unimproved nature unable to support our growing desires, so also we
find an intellectual world unable to provide comfort and solace to our
"busy minds." At times, the metaphors of physical and mental labor seem
to collapse into each other. "We are born ignorant of everything," Locke
tells us, and it is through "labor, attention and industry" that we can
clear away the "darkness and chaos" that we find within ourselves and
construct a livable abode (CU 38).

Locke contrasts the hardworking few who "employ" and "use" their
faculties to "acquire" and "attain" ideas with the "lazy and inconsiderate
part of man, making far the greater number" who take up their notions
by chance (E I.iv.15). The great error of the majority is that they assume
that the external world, as we experience it in its original state, provides
us with all that we need without having to be tilled and harvested. Those
who fail to recognize that they must labor in order to gather together
useful ideas are like the man who thinks his understanding is like "For-
tunatus's purse, which is always to furnish him without ever putting anything into it beforehand; and so he sits still satisfied without endeavoring to store his understanding with knowledge" (CU 38). Those who
believe that there is an easy correspondence between their unimproved
and undisciplined minds and the external world will fail to recognize that
governing judgment correctly requires constant vigilance and hard work.
They will too easily grasp hold of their unexamined beliefs and opinions
and defend them as unquestionable certainties. Locke warns his readers
that those who refuse to keep watch over the limits of the understanding
and discipline their own thoughts accordingly will never earn the rewards
of hard work.

Thus Locke calls all of his readers to take up the difficult task of cognitive self-discipline in order to constitute themselves as rational free
agents. This type of self-discipline is appropriate for human beings who
find themselves in a middling position between a yearning for certainty
and perfection and a retreat into subjectivity and skepticism. Locke tells
us that we should engage in this process with an aim toward perfect
happiness, yet he warns us that we will always fall short. To be perfectly
happy "every uneasiness we feel" must "be perfectly removed: which in
the multitude of wants, and desires, we are beset with in this imperfect
state, we are not like to be ever freed from in this world" (E II.xxi.46).
Although we cannot hope to free ourselves from every uneasiness, this
type of limitless freedom is not what we should desire anyway. It is our
ability to modify and make use of our uneasiness that enables us to move
toward our "true and solid happiness." It is through uneasiness that we

can experience the limited type of happiness that is within reach of finite intellectual beings. Indeed for Locke, not only our happiness but also our liberty rests on our willingness to take up this endless struggle to align ourselves with what is most valuable and most important in the world. It is through this industrious striving that we constitute ourselves as genuine persons, free and reasonable agents capable of self-government. As we will see, Locke's appeal to natural liberty, consensual politics, and even revolution depends on a conception of the individual as "master of himself, and proprietor of his own person" (2T 44). Our capacity to experience freedom is tied to our capacity to restrain ourselves according to our probable judgments, to adjust our volitions and our actions to our long-term happiness.

VI

Enacting Judgment

DISMANTLING THE DIVINE CERTAINTY
OF SIR ROBERT FILMER

WHEN LOCKE FINALLY SETS OUT to convince readers that they are naturally free and equal and that the legitimacy of government depends on the
consent of the people, he begins with a confrontation. Instead of laying
down a set of first principles or explicating a set of definitions, he starts
the *Two Treatises of Government* by taking aim at the doctrines of Sir
Robert Filmer. He asserts that Filmer's justification of absolutism is not
only logically dubious—it is politically disastrous. Then he painstakingly
reproduces and refutes Filmer's defense of a patriarchal right to unlimited sovereign power passed down from the biblical figure of Adam. In
order to show that Filmer's argument is both groundless and irrespon-
sible, Locke lays before us 169 sections devoted wholly to repudiating
this position, and these sections constitute only a fraction of what he says
he had originally intended.[1]

For many readers, there is something puzzling about Locke beginning
this way. Many commentators have come to assume that the normative
core of Lockean theory resides in the *Second Treatise* and that the long-
winded diatribe in the first half of the book adds little to this argument.
The *First Treatise* reads as if Locke wants to convince his readers to put
down the book rather than take up arms. As Peter Laslett puts it, the "cum-
bersome and uninviting" nature of the first half of Locke's *Two Treatises*
makes it almost "unreadable" compared with the much more engaging
and pertinent arguments of the second half.[2] Numerous thoughtful commentators have agreed with Laslett's assessment. Dante Germino seems
to sum up the opinions of many when he writes, "The *First Treatise*,
which virtually no one reads any more, is a line-by-line refutation of Filmer's tome. Tedious would be perhaps too flattering an adjective for it."[3]

---

[1] Locke tells us in the preface that a section of the *Two Treatises* that would have constituted "more than all the rest" had been lost. Preface, 137.

[2] Peter Laslett, introduction to *Two Treatises of Government*, 61.

[3] Dante Germino, *Modern Western Political Thought* (Chicago: University of Chicago
Press, 1972), 118. The publishing history of the *Two Treatises* reveals that this view is not
unique to contemporary scholars. Starting with a French translation during Locke's life-

In a similar vein, Thomas Pangle dubs it "a masterpiece of forbidding boredom."[4]

Locke's tirade can certainly be tiresome. Page after page, he wages a seemingly endless assault on arguments that appear to be confused or patently absurd. He not only refutes Filmer's position, he reduces it to rubble. Unwilling to leave a single phrase unchallenged, he insists that there is absolutely nothing in Filmer's argument that could be persuasive to a thoughtful reader. It seems odd that he should go to such lengths, especially since he exhibits a disdain for Filmer that makes it clear that he does not consider him to be a serious adversary. If he understands his task to be nothing more than a ground-clearing exercise to make room for his own political doctrine, he could have achieved this aim with far less effort. So why does he spend so much time on a position that he declares in the preface of the *Two Treatises* to be already "thoroughly confuted"? Why does he go to so much trouble attacking in meticulous and excruciating detail a position that he refers to as "glib nonsense"?

The answer is that Filmer is much more of a threat than he first appears. Locke spends so much energy refuting him because he believes that the success of his larger project depends on it. Filmer represents an approach to political justification that Locke considers the chief obstacle to self-government. Filmer embodies both the longing for absolute certainty and the retreat into radical subjectivity that undermine the maintenance of a common mode of justification. Filmer teaches the agent to abandon individual judgment and simply obey. By challenging Filmer's appeal to divine certainty based on the indisputable authority of Scripture, Locke hopes to detach the all-knowing and infallible mind of God from the struggling and imperfect minds of human beings. He hopes to convince his readers that claims of legitimacy must take into account the contested judgment of individuals. A shared language of justification cannot rest on a set of assertions handed down from an authoritative interpreter of absolute truths. By taking up the arguments of Filmer, Locke does more than attack a political adversary. He sup-

---

time, the *Second Treatise* has been translated and published by itself dozens of times, while the *First Treatise* has languished in relative obscurity. In fact, before Peter Laslett included it in his edition, it had hardly been included in editions of Locke's political writings for almost a hundred years. For a complete publishing history, see Laslett, introduction to *Two Treatises of Government*, 13–15.

[4] Pangle, *Spirit of Modern Republicanism*, 137. It should be noted, however, that Pangle goes on to find that the *First Treatise* is far more interesting than it first appears. For other studies of the *First Treatise* as central to Locke's political project, see Robert Faulkner, "Preface to Liberalism: Locke's *First Treatise* and the Bible," *Review of Politics* 67, no. 3 (2005), 451–72; Mehta, *The Anxiety of Freedom*; Tarcov, *Locke's Education for Liberty*, 9–76; Charles D. Tarlton, "A Rope of Sand: Interpreting Locke's *First Treatise of Government*," *Historical Journal* 21, no. 1 (1978), 43–73; Zuckert, *Launching Liberalism*, 129–68.

plants Filmer's clumsy appeal to scriptural authority with a new standard of judgment.[5]

It is in this context that we can understand Locke's own view of the *First Treatise* as an indispensable part of his larger argument. In the preface he explicitly states that the two books constitute "the beginning and end" of a single discourse.[6] The argument of the *Second Treatise* grows out of the confrontation in the first half of the book. By dismantling the divine certainty of Robert Filmer, Locke attempts to circumscribe the role of Scripture in political discourse and moderate declarations of dogmatic conviction. He insists that even revelation cannot release free and equal persons from the burdens and privileges of private judgment. Although Locke does not reject the authority of Scripture, he emphasizes the difficulty of deducing politically relevant standards from biblical narratives. For Locke scriptural revelation should remain important for believers in their private lives, yet should no longer serve as an independent criterion of political justification. A ruler does not gain legitimacy by claiming biblical sanction or divine authority.

It is the failure of Filmer's approach that makes consensual politics necessary. Locke tells us at the beginning of the *First Treatise* that if the foundation of Filmer's "wonderful system" is shown to be unsustainable, then "governments must be left again to the old way of being made by contrivance, and the consent of men (ἀνθρωπίνη κτίσις) making use of their reason to unite together into society" (1T 6).[7] Locke understands Filmer to be arguing that polities can be established and sustained without having to rely on the contentious opinions of individuals. His system

[5] It is for this reason that Locke is at pains to show that Filmer does not offer a vocabulary of judgment that can sustain a stable polity. Filmer is nothing but a language abuser, akin to the scheming Schoolmen and tyrannizing enthusiasts of the *Essay*. He offers a "flourish of doubtful expressions" and "contradictions dressed up in popular style" in order to confound his readers (Preface, 138). Since "clear distinct speaking" does not serve "every where to his purpose," he presents a web of "doubtful and general terms" that results in "a medley and confusion" (1T 23, 20). By "playing with names" he can make them "say any thing" and "mislead his reader" into assenting to a position that is never clearly specified (1T 138, 63, 141).

[6] Laslett tells us that Locke's original intention was to print the two parts as a single treatise, and he only divided them into "treatises" during the printing process. Laslett, introduction to *Two Treatises of Government*, 50.

[7] The Greek term, ἀνθρωπίνη κτίσις, means "human institution" or "institution ordained by men." Locke takes the phrase from 1 Peter 2:13, which along with Romans 13 was a central verse in the New Testament used to show that Christians have a duty to obey political authority. The verse reads in full: "submit yourselves to every ordinance of men." Here we see Locke carefully turning the tables on his opponents, using their primary proof text against them. By emphasizing the human origin of polities and political authority, he can cast doubt on Filmer's putatively scriptural understanding of government as directly instituted by God.

is an attempt to replace individual judgment with abstract certainty. By demonstrating that such an attempt is foolish, Locke seeks to show his readers that they have no choice but to rely on their own reason if they are to unite together in society. The authorizing source or, in Locke's language, the "original" of government turns out to be the sober and well-regulated consent of free persons. Political authority is established and sustained by individuals making reasonable judgments based on their own limited but trustworthy experiences of nature. On this plane of terrestrial existence—what Locke calls "the state of mediocrity"—we are removed from the perfection of divine power and knowledge. Locke is at pains to show that government is a humanly instituted arrangement, for it is this finding that will allow him to argue that government is therefore subject to human alteration.

Preaching *Patriarcha* from the Pulpit

By arguing that Locke uses Filmer to discredit a particular approach to political justification, I do not want to imply that he was indifferent to the role Filmer was playing in his immediate political context. Locke was well aware that Filmer's writings were the most visible example of an absolutist position that he wanted to combat. By demolishing Filmer, Locke could embarrass those who were using Filmer's books to justify their support for royal supremacy over Parliament. Although the genesis of the *Two Treatises* remains a matter of heated (if somewhat obscure) historical debate, most scholars now agree that Locke wrote most of the text long before the Glorious Revolution in 1689 that brought William and Mary to the throne.[8] Instead of writing to justify the revolution after

[8] Peter Laslett was the first to challenge the traditional assumption (based on Locke's own preface) that the *Two Treatises* were written to justify the Glorious Revolution after the fact. Citing Locke's notes and the books that he had in his possession, Laslett made the case that most of the text was written in 1679–81 during the Exclusion Crisis. Richard Ashcraft, taking issue with some of Laslett's arguments (such as the dating of Locke's journal), responded that the actual date of composition was probably later, sometime after the king dissolved the Oxford Parliament in 1681. If Ashcraft is right and Locke was writing his defense of the right of revolution after the king had called for an end to debate, it gives the *Two Treatises* a far more radical luster. He contends that Locke probably meant to publish the *Two Treatises* at the moment insurrection commenced in order to convince both aristocrats and artisans to join the resistance and establish a new, legitimate government. David Wootton has offered a moderate rebuttal of Ashcraft, arguing that Locke was most probably writing in the middle or later half of 1681, before any actual resistance was planned. For Wootton, the text is meant less as an explicit tool of revolution than as a reflection on resistance should it eventually emerge. John Marshall has responded with a partial defense of Ashcraft, arguing that none of the evidence rules out the possibility that Locke wrote the document in 1682–83. Marshall insists, however, that this does not show Locke's radicalism

the fact, Locke was composing his discourse sometime during the struggles over monarchical power taking place in the early 1680s.

At this time, many of Locke's countrymen were terrified that there would soon be an English Louis XIV ascending the throne. Responding to what was almost a national hysteria following the rumors of a "popish plot" to assassinate Charles II and place his Catholic brother James in power, Parliament sought to pass legislation that would exclude James from succession. Since Locke's patron, Shaftesbury, was at the forefront of this battle, Locke was actively involved in these debates. Those in favor of exclusion believed that a Catholic monarch would inevitably be intolerant and absolutist. They also feared that a Catholic would bring England into closer relations with France and perhaps even compromise its sovereignty. The secret name that Locke used for the *Two Treatises*, "De Morbo Gallico," shows how closely these fears were related. The name is a double entendre referring to the two French diseases of syphilis and absolutism. David Wootton points out that at the time Locke was composing the *Two Treatises*, Charles II issued a *Declaration* so full of Gallicisms that it seemed to be translated from the French, and it was revealed that the French ambassador had received a copy of it before the king's own Council.[9] As the possibility of a Catholic king with ties to France began to appear increasingly likely, dissidents in England feared the worst. These fears were later reinforced when Louis XIV revoked the Edict of Nantes in 1685, reversing the toleration that had been granted Protestants in France. Shaftesbury articulated a common view when he wrote that "popery and slavery, like two sisters, go hand-in-hand."[10]

So when Charles II abruptly dissolved Parliament in 1681, concern began to turn into panic. A crisis of legitimacy that had already begun during the civil wars of 1642–49 and had led to the trial and execution of

---

but rather his hesitance to advocate revolution. According to Marshall, Locke probably did not compose the *Two Treatises* until it was clear that absolutism threatened his own preservation and the stability of England. As we can see, the debate over the dating of the *Two Treatise* is also a debate over the nature of the text and whether it is primarily an exclusion tract, a theoretical argument, or a radical polemic. Laslett, introduction to *Two Treatises of Government*, 47; Ashcraft, *Revolutionary Politics*, 332–37; Marshall, *John Locke*, 223, 39, 60; Wootton, introduction to Locke, *Political Writings*, 49–88.

[9] Wootton, introduction to Locke, *Political Writings*, 64.

[10] Quoted by Dunn, *Political Thought of Locke*, 44. The fear that Catholicism is linked to despotism was not only prevalent during the years prior to the Glorious Revolution, but was also central to the self-understanding of the new regime. In "An Acte for Declareing the Rights and Liberties of the Subject and Setleing the Succession of the Crowne" presented by the Parliament in 1688, the grievances against James II opened by condemning his "endeavor to subvert and extirpate the Protestant Religion, and the Lawes and Liberties of this Kingdome." Printed as Appendix I in Lois Schwoerer, *The Declaration of Rights, 1689* (Baltimore: Johns Hopkins University Press, 1981).

Charles I emerged with renewed intensity. Deceivingly simple questions of political obligation once again made their way to the forefront of public consciousness: To whom is obedience owed? Are there limits to political obedience? Dissenters began discussing how the proper boundaries of monarchical power could be enforced on a monarchy that seemed uninterested in restraining itself. As Richard Ashcraft has shown, Locke was surrounded by such men and was himself willing to risk his life to engage in seditious plots, secretly conspiring with those who sought to resist the crown. After the failure of parliamentary solutions, many began to contemplate the possibility of insurrection or assassination. Seeing their alternatives slowly vanish, these men began to whisper about the possibility of violent overthrow.[11]

Faced with this growing discontent, supporters of royal supremacy found in Filmer's writings a passionate defense of the unlimited and absolute power of the monarchy. After the dissolution of Parliament, defenders of the royalist cause became increasingly dependent on the clerical support of divine right. They came to link a *jure divino* monarchy to a *jure divino* episcopacy and associate both monarchical and ecclesiastical power with Filmer's patriarchalism. For that reason, they recovered and published several of Filmer's books that had been written decades earlier. One of those works was *Patriarcha*, published for the first time in 1680.

It was this political deployment of Filmer's writings, Locke tells us, that compelled him to attack a work "which has lain dormant for so long" (1T 2). A group of supporters including a number of powerful clergymen were using Filmer's arguments to convince their countrymen to accept the absolute and unlimited power of the monarchy, regardless of who ascended the throne. "I should not speak so plainly of a gentleman long since past answering," Locke writes, "had not the pulpit of late years, publicly owned his doctrines and made it the current divinity of the times" (Preface, 138). Locke claims that he initially considered Filmer's work to be a type of joke, an "exercise of wit . . . rather than a serious discourse meant in earnest" (1T 1). He would never have bothered to respond "were there not men amongst us" whom he found "crying up his books, and espousing his doctrines" (Preface, 138). In an attempt to answer the arguments of his political opponents, Locke turned to Sir Robert.

In this context, it makes sense that Locke should pour scorn on Filmer's defense of unlimited sovereignty. Locke had good reason to both

---

[11] Ashcraft goes so far as to argue that Shaftesbury and Locke were involved in the Rye House Conspiracy, which was an attempt to assassinate both Charles II and James as they returned from Newmarket. Ashcraft, *Revolutionary Politics*, 332–37. Although this is an intriguing possibility, John Marshall is right to point out that Ashcraft's evidence can only point to a possibility and does not prove Locke's involvement. Marshall, *John Locke*, 206.

fear and despise these arguments. Yet this historical explanation does not completely account for the character of Locke's critique. There were certainly others, including Locke's friend James Tyrrell, who had already catalogued Filmer's absurdities.[12] John Dunn points out that if the *Two Treatises* were meant to be no more than an exclusion tract, it is "a notably ham-fisted one."[13] Locke digs deeper into the convoluted details of Filmer's scriptural argument than the circumstances required if his goal was merely to lay out a simple and convincing case for the right of Parliament to exclude a monarchical heir. In any case, reference to the historical struggles of the Exclusion Crisis does not explain why Locke would want to include the *First Treatise* in the text he published in 1689, long after Filmer's arguments had become politically irrelevant.

If we treat the *First Treatise* as merely a political polemic, we misunderstand how this text fits into Locke's larger project. We risk obscuring the deeper tension between Locke and Filmer concerning political judgment. Locke is still interested in refuting Filmer in 1689 because he believes that the type of thinking that props up Filmer's system has not disappeared. He still sees a tendency among his countrymen to escape the burdens of judgment by fleeing into the arms of professed certainty. He recognizes Filmer's theory as a manifestation of the widespread propensity toward unrestrained intellectual conduct, the type of thinking that fluctuates wildly from submissiveness to subversiveness because it lacks the grounding of sober self-reflection and self-regulation. It is this type of unrestrained confidence in an indefensible and unexamined system of thought that he seeks to puncture.

Locke wants to show that Filmer's approach to justification does not help to resolve genuine conflicts of authority. It does not supply readers with a way to deliberate over contested matters of public importance. It merely lulls them into a state of passive acceptance, slowly convincing them that they should submit to that which they cannot understand. Insofar as any author insists on the divine certainty of his system, he releases his readers from the responsibility of judging for themselves. For Locke this danger is always present. The persistent belief that political authority can only be asserted, not justified, breeds slaves and masters and undermines the plausibility of the self-regulating human agent that lies at the heart of Locke's political theory. The tendency of individuals to surrender their judgment and rest in either the dogmatism of absolute certainty or the capitulation of skepticism remains a constant threat to the possibility of Lockean self-government. Thus the confrontation between Locke and

---

[12] James Tyrrell, *Patriarcha Non Monarcha. The Patriarch Unmonarch'd* (London: Printed for Richard Janeway, 1681).

[13] Dunn, *Political Thought of Locke*, 53.

Filmer is not simply a skirmish over the exclusion controversy or even a struggle over the doctrine of the divine right of kings. It is a momentous battle over the place of individual judgment in political affairs.

Probable Judgment and the Authority of Scripture

In the portion of the *First Treatise* that has come down to us, Locke's attack on Filmer is carried out almost entirely on the terrain of biblical interpretation. This is appropriate, Locke tells us, since it is "scripture-proofs" upon which Filmer "pretends wholly to build" (Preface, 138). Yet several commentators have pointed out that this depiction of Filmer's thought is not entirely correct.[14] In the very works that Locke cites, Filmer develops his position in the context of refuting Aristotle, Hobbes, Grotius, and other political thinkers. In short, his defense of the divine right of kings is not merely a collection of biblical quotations. It is possible, as John Marshall maintains, that Locke intended to provide a more comprehensive treatment of Filmer's writings in the missing sections of the *First Treatise*.[15] Yet this seems unlikely. Locke's persistent focus on Filmer's use of Scripture in the sections that Locke did publish gives the impression that he was particularly eager to draw attention to this aspect of Filmer's thought. It does not seem unreasonable to assume that it is Filmer's appeal to revelation that Locke finds most menacing and thus most important to refute.

This is because Filmer can inoculate his system from critique by identifying it with the infallible word of God. He can respond to critics by claiming that any challenge to his position is a challenge to God's explicit command. Filmer's use of Scripture forces his readers into the awkward predicament of either accepting his propositions as divinely established or rejecting Scripture as authoritative. In order to make room for human judgment, Locke sets out to decouple Filmer's position from the authority of Scripture. He does this by introducing a new way to interpret the sacred text, insisting that Filmer's claims must be judged by evidence that comes from sources outside the text itself. It is here that we see most clearly how Locke attempts to supplant Filmer's invocation of divine certainty with a new conception of probability. Locke seeks to respond to Filmer by offering a reading of divine injunctions that places them within a larger context of historical experience. He argues that God speaks not

---

[14] See Tarcov, *Locke's Education for Liberty*; as well as Dunn, *Political Thought of Locke*; and Gordon Schochet, *Patriarchalism in Political Thought* (New York: Basic Books, 1975), 115–36.

[15] Marshall, *John Locke*, 206.

only through written revelation, but also through our "senses and reason" (1T 86). To understand the text of Scripture, we should compare it with the evidence of natural signs, which Locke refers to as "the legible characters of his works and providence" (E III.ix.23). Locke's criticism of Filmer's use of the Bible need not stem from a concealed animosity toward revelation itself, as some commentators insist. Instead, it arises from the conviction that written revelation must be interpreted within the context of natural revelation.

This emphasis on the deliverances of "sense and reason" as the proper standard for deciphering the meaning of Scripture marks a shift from "precritical" to "critical" methods of interpretation. Locke is not simply looking for internal consistency; he is measuring the claims of revelation over and against evidence that he gathers from the external world. The deliverances of nature provide us with the authoritative or probable justification for interpreting the written word. It is striking how this shift in biblical hermeneutics parallels the emergence of probability that we encountered in chapter 3. According to Hans Frei, ecclesiastical writers before the seventeenth and eighteenth centuries simply did not concern themselves with the questions that animate modern, critical interpretation.[16] They viewed the Bible as an authoritative whole and the task of interpretation as a matter of synthesizing the oftentimes-perplexing claims and peculiar stories found within the text. As an oracle of God to humanity, Scripture served as its own standard of meaning and cohesiveness. Readers sought to harmonize contradictions and search for deeper truths behind confusing and ambiguous passages. They did this by employing several types of approaches simultaneously, including analogical, allegorical, moral, and figurative readings. Since the text was understood to be operating on several levels, difficulties with one path of interpretation could be seen as an invitation to explore another path.

Although there were a few exceptions—such as when Origen concluded from internal evidence that Paul could not have written the epistle to the Hebrews or Origen's disciple Dionysius inferred on linguistic grounds that the book of Revelation could not be written by John— generally questions of authorship, date, and historical context were seen as trivial and beside the point. An exclusive focus on literal or historical veracity would have appeared wrongheaded or reductionistic to precritical readers. Deliberations over the genuine meaning of a contested passage consisted of appealing to various scriptural authorities and harmonizing various literal, figurative, and typological readings of the text. The

---

[16] Hans Frei, *The Eclipse of Biblical Narrative: A Study in Eighteenth- and Nineteenth-Century Hermeneutics* (New Haven: Yale University Press, 1974).

primary task of the precritical interpreter was to gain insight into the manifold mysteries that were hidden within its many layers.

For example, Thomas Aquinas explains in the *Summa* that the systematic study of sacred doctrine begins with taking certain principles on faith, on "the authority of those men through whom the divine revelation ... has come down to us."[17] Theology is most appropriately based on "arguments from authority" in that "it rests on the authority of those to whom the revelation has been made."[18] For Aquinas any adequate approach to the meaning of the Bible rests on what I have called the old probability, the authorizing interpretations of textual authorities. When faced with perplexities, Aquinas tells his readers, they should consult the authority of probable testimony. To reason about revelation is to compare carefully considered interpretations that have been articulated within the tradition. Thus an event that would become intrinsically improbable to later generations—such as a virgin birth—can be deemed highly probable by Aquinas because it had the right type of authority speaking on its behalf. Aquinas recognizes that many harbor doubts about particular articles of faith and that they will continue to struggle with these doubts, yet such doubts arise "not because the reality is at all uncertain, but because the human understanding is feeble."[19] By carefully and methodically consulting various authorities, we can be assured that certain articles of faith are true even if we cannot see clearly *how* they can be true. We are warranted in assenting to particular claims because they are shown to be probable. When the authority in question is God's word, "probability" is too weak a term for our assurance. Divine authority is the best conceivable warrant for belief. So even if we encounter other claims that seem to be incompatible with God's word, we should disregard them because God's revelation "joins us to him as to an unknown."[20]

Before the Bible could be subjected to critical analysis, the notion of authority that characterized the precritical approach would have to erode. A language of judgment based on the synthesis of authoritative texts would have to deteriorate beyond recovery. As we have seen, this collapse began to take place in late medieval and early modern Europe. In the midst of intellectual collapse and religious struggle, the probity of textual authority could no longer be sustained, and the type of justificatory reasoning recommended by Aquinas was simply no longer viable. Readers of the Bible were faced with two uncomfortable alternatives. Either a particular interpretation remained authoritative because it was

---

[17] Aquinas, *Summa*, I q.1 art.2.
[18] Ibid., I q.1 art.8.
[19] Ibid., I q. 1 art. 5.
[20] Ibid., I q.12 art.13.

endorsed by the Catholic Church, or it was authoritative because it was embraced by the individual believer. The first of these involved an unacceptable submission to ecclesiastical dogma and the second a destabilizing emergence of radical subjectivity. Locke's turn to external standards of judgment was of a piece with a widespread cultural effort to salvage a common, authoritative approach to these crucial texts, an approach that could transcend sectarian battles and provide a stabilizing context for authorizing judgments.

By placing Locke into this larger account of hermeneutic upheaval, we can better understand the confrontation of the *First Treatise*. When he turns to revelation, he does not invoke Richard Hooker or any of the church fathers as a source of authoritative interpretation. He does not suggest that deciphering the sacred text involves a unique moment of divine assistance, a community of believers, or a tradition of textual authorities. He parts ways with medieval methods of interpretation and advocates a thoroughly modern approach. He suggests that an individual who wishes to understand should simply read the text carefully, for "scripture itself is the best interpreter" (1T 25). All revelation must ultimately accommodate itself to common sense. This is because God can be assumed to communicate with human beings in a way that they can understand. Locke explains:

> God, I believe, speaks differently from men, because he speaks with more truth, more certainty: but when he vouchsafes to speak to men, I do not think, he speaks differently from them, in crossing the rules of language in use amongst them. This would not be to condescend to their capacities, when he humbles himself to speak to them, but to lose his design in speaking, what thus spoken they could not understand. (1T 46)

Everything that God has deemed important enough to convey to humanity will be clear to any careful reader. Revelation seems inaccessible and obscure only because it has been manipulated and confused by centuries of misleading commentary. The actual message is simple and clear.

This general approach is affirmed in *The Reasonableness of Christianity*, where Locke argues that revelation is not a collection of "speculations and niceties, obscure terms and abstract notions." Instead, it is made up of a series of "plain and intelligible" stories that are designed "for the instruction of the illiterate bulk of mankind" (RC 252). It is purposely "suited to vulgar capacities, and the state of mankind in this world, destined to labor and travail" (RC 252). Here Locke is not belittling Christianity or implying that it is fit only for the poor and illiterate, but rather pointing with approval at the way Christianity can appeal to all types of understandings. We should also note that Locke is not contrasting "vulgar" capacities with the philosophical ones; he is contrasting the simple and plain truth of the Gospel with the "superfine distinctions of the schools"(RC 252). The message of the Bible is superior because it is far more accessible than other systems of morality. Not only is this part of its "reasonableness," but it also reflects the wisdom and mercy of God, who designed all human beings with capacities sufficient to recognize and follow his dictates. In order to encounter Scripture as God promulgated it, one need only clear away "the learned, artificial, and forced senses ... put upon them in most of the systems of divinity" (RC 1).

Locke's most extensive discussion of the nature of biblical interpretation, however, is found in the introductory essay to his *Paraphrase and Notes on the Epistles of St. Paul.* There he states again that the best way to approach Scripture is to put aside systems of divinity and traditional commentaries and simply read the words. At times the meaning of a passage might seem obscure, but with a bit of mental labor it can almost always be deciphered.[21] How do we go about doing this? Locke advises that we treat St. Paul, and every other figure who compiled sacred Scripture, like "any other author."[22] If we wish to understand the meaning and purposes of particularly difficult verses, we should reconstruct the personal and historical context of the text. We should try to uncover "the disposition Paul was in," keeping in mind that he was "a man of quick thought and warm temper" who "when he gave his thoughts utterance upon any point, the matter flowed like a torrent."[23] We should seek to uncover the "temper and circumstances" of the day and the "actions, expectations, or demands of those to whom he writ."[24] Once we have rid ourselves of the misleading glosses of tradition and come to terms with the context of a particular passage, then the words will interpret themselves.

In this spirit, Locke instructs his readers in the *First Treatise* to look to "the plain express words of scripture ... the plain construction of the words ... the obvious meaning" (1T 32; see also 36, 38, 39, 40, 46, 49). By attending to the text, we can easily spot Filmer's willful distortions. Although the Ten Commandments include the admonition to "honor thy father and mother," Filmer drops the reference to mothers in order to use the command to justify his assertion of paternal authority. Locke repeatedly attacks Filmer for manipulating the "express text of scripture" (1T 60; see also 61, 62, 64, 65, 66, 67). Filmer is so attached to his system

[21] John Locke, *A Paraphrase and Notes on the Epistles of St. Paul to the Galatians, 1 and 2 Corinthians, Romans, Ephesians*, ed. Arthur William Wainwright (Oxford: Clarendon Press, 1987), 4–5, 14–17.
[22] Ibid., 21.
[23] Ibid., 5, 19.
[24] Ibid., 4, 16.

that he is willing "to warp the sacred rule of God, to make it comply with his present occasion" (1T 60). He appeals to his own opinionated and biased interpretations in order to adorn his system with signs of authority. Locke responds that opinions that are not supported by the text or by experience simply cannot serve as an adequate interpretive guide. "The prejudices of our own ill grounded opinions, however by us called probable, cannot authorize us to understand scripture contrary to the direct and plain meaning of the words" (1T 36). By pointing out the great distance between Filmer's claims and the clear words of Scripture, Locke can cast doubt on Filmer's entire system.

Yet for all of his emphasis on the plain language of the text, Locke concedes that the express words are at times obscure and their true meaning can only be arrived at through careful interpretation, a process that involves more than just the written word. In an important gloss on the first chapter of Genesis, Locke asserts that God speaks through our senses and reason as well as through direct command. In order to decipher the injunctions of revelation, we must use all of our faculties. Scripture does not simply interpret itself. Thus Locke can argue that God meant for Adam to eat animals although he never explicitly states it, since God gave him "a strong desire of self-preservation, and furnished the world with things fit for food and raiment and other necessaries of Life." By examining Adam's needs and nature's bounty, we can come to an understanding of God's will for humanity. "And therefore I doubt not, but before these words were pronounced, I Gen. 28, 29. (if they must be understood so literally to have been spoken) and without any such verbal donation, man had a right to a use of the creatures" (1T 86). Our observations of human desires and natural conditions must guide us in interpreting God's commands.

Yet this finding seems to be in direct conflict with what Locke asserts in the paragraph directly preceding this one. In an effort to discredit Filmer's appeal to divine injunction, Locke argues that "positive grants give no title farther than the express words convey it" (1T 85). Earlier in the *First Treatise* he tells us that Adam "could not make bold with a lark or a rabbit to satisfy his hunger, and had the herbs but in common with the beasts" (1T 39). According to the positive grant of God and the clear and unambiguous words of Scripture, Adam did not have "full property as an owner" but only "liberty to use" that which is owned by God, "who is sole lord and proprietor of the whole world" (1T 39). He insists that it was only after the flood that Noah and his sons were explicitly granted the right to eat animals (1T 38–39).

In these passages Locke seems to argue both that Adam has a right to eat meat and that he does not have that right. While criticizing Filmer, he insists that Adam was not given a positive grant and therefore does not have unlimited dominion over animals. Yet he later insists that Adam has a right to eat meat even if God did not explicitly declare it. Many commentators point to this apparent discrepancy as proof that there is something odd going on in the *First Treatise*. This is certainly a perplexing passage, yet we should be careful not to read too much into Locke's explanation.[25] It is likely that Locke is leaning heavily on a distinction that he makes between an unlimited right of dominion that Filmer deduces from the text of Genesis and a limited liberty of use that can be inferred from the conditions human beings find themselves under. Locke insists that God simply does not grant Adam or any other person the type of dominion that Filmer attributes to him. Human beings are not given the utmost form of property in anything; they never possess boundless dominion over creation or even over themselves. Such power is reserved for God, "who is sole lord and proprietor of the whole world" (1T 39). When human agents come to possess property, it is always limited by moral and theological considerations. "The same law of nature" that gives us "property," Locke tells us, "does also bound that property too" (2T 31). Thus Locke can insist that Adam has the right to make use of animals for his own preservation, yet deny Filmer's implication that such a right has no limitations or boundaries. To solidify this argument concerning the proper rights of Adam, Locke introduces a standard that exists outside of the text and is used to deduce rights that are not explicitly present in the text.

The deliverances of "sense and reason" are not meant to erase what the "express words convey" but rather to clarify and extend the written word. For Locke the most appropriate way to interpret the Bible is not by lifting out phrases and interpreting them in isolation, but by construing the most probable meaning of God's word given what we know about the nature and conditions of human life. Scripture, it turns out, should be viewed through the lens of nature. The meaning of God's commands must ultimately be tested by our own sober judgment based on our experience in this world. The signs of the written word must be verified by the signs of nature, what Locke calls "natural revelation" (E IV.xix.4). It is important to note here that Locke is not simply teaching his readers to

[25] John Calvin, in his commentary on Genesis, concedes that this passage implies that before the flood it was unlawful to make use of animals. Yet even he doubts that such a prohibition ever existed because it would have been incompatible with the obligations that antediluvian men had to God, both to make animal sacrifices and to survive and flourish. Like Locke, Calvin reads this passage with the assumption that his God is reasonable. Yet unlike Locke, Calvin refuses to make a final determination. He concludes that "it will better for us to assert nothing concerning this matter." *Commentaries on the First Book of Moses, Called Genesis*, ed. John King (Grand Rapids: W.B. Eerdmans, 1948), Gen. 1:28–30.

assess Scripture by some universally accepted standard of reason. He is trying to model a *particular type* of reasoning that would transform the way his readers approach sacred texts.[26]

Although Scripture, insofar as it is God's word, is infallible for Locke, readers cannot "but be very fallible in the understanding of it." Nor should we be surprised when we find that the will of God, "when clothed in words, should be liable to that doubt and uncertainty, which unavoidably attends that sort of conveyance" (E III.ix.23). We experience the truth of the Bible only indirectly and imperfectly. The "volumes of interpreters and commentators on the Old and New Testaments" are "but too manifest a proof of this" (E III.ix.23). Although we are certainly justified in affirming the revealed word of God, we should be wary of mistaking the abstract theories or complex systems of divinity for actual revelation. For this reason the claims that individuals make on the authority of Scripture should be subject to reason. Locke insists that "no proposition can be received for divine revelation, or obtain the assent due to all such, if it be contradictory to our clear intuitive knowledge" (E IV.xviii.5). He concedes, however, that in cases in which the clear testimony of revelation conflicts with the probable signs of nature, revelation should prevail. Pure revelation should take precedence over other probable sources in the sense that evident revelation requires assent even when the content of that revelation runs counter to its likeliness to be true (E IV.xviii.8–9). Yet Locke is quick to point out that we have a duty to use our reason in determining whether putative revelation is indeed revelation. And this process of certification must be accomplished through probable reasoning (E IV.xix.15). Although he gives pride of place to revelation, he insists that we use our probable judgment to determine just what that revelation entails.[27]

---

[26] This careful and cautious approach to scriptural exegesis is certainly at odds with what Thomas Pangle describes as a "refutation of the biblical faith" and a "delicious . . . benevolent blasphemy." Pangle, *Spirit of Modern Republicanism*, 145, 58. We need not impute to Locke radically irreligious intentions in order to maintain that he advocates a particular approach to sacred Scripture bounded by probable reasoning. In fact, Locke insists that such disciplined interpretation is a *religious* duty. His rejection of Filmer's approach to the Bible is not an attempt to undermine sacred text, but to show that his political teaching conforms to written revelation, properly understood.

[27] This is why miracles become so important for Locke and those who sought to maintain his brand of reasonable Christianity. He argued that we can only know that alleged revelation is in fact revelation if it confirms something that we already know or if it is certified by attendant miraculous signs. Locke's appeal to the evidential power of miracles is found in "A Discourse of Miracles," published after his death. He writes that miracles are "the foundation on which believers of any divine revelation must ultimately bottom their faith." Locke, "A Discourse of Miracles," 86. Yet miracles proved to be an unreliable source of evidence for the veracity of Scripture. In the mid-eighteenth century, David Hume made short work of this type of argument in his essay "Of Miracles." See David Hume, *An Enquiry*

For Locke, individuals cannot be released from the responsibility to judge what counts as authentic Scripture and interpret what that Scripture actually means. The best way of doing this is to begin with God's "goodness, that he hath spread before all the world, with legible characters of his works and providence" (E III.ix.23). By comparing revelation with the "legible characters" of nature, we can work to uncover its proper meaning. The signs of nature, authorized by God, offer us an irreplaceable supplement to the often-ambiguous signs of Scripture. It is by reasoning about our experience in the world that we can make informed judgments about the meaning and significance of written revelation. Locke never denies that human beings can gain an understanding of God's will through positive revelation, but he insists that this understanding also can also occur through observation and experience. It is in this sense that Locke asserts, "Reason is natural revelation" (E IV.xix.4).

Throughout the *First Treatise* Locke is at pains to show that Filmer's use of Scripture is incompatible with an emerging standard of probable judgment. Filmer finds himself in an especially vulnerable position, however, because he neither embraces the precritical commitment to textual authorities nor the critical turn to natural signs. Filmer's use of the Old Testament differs from the medieval method in that he does not argue from typology or analogy. Instead he seeks to demonstrate a direct and observable connection between contemporary forms of authority and their scriptural origin.

As Locke points out, Filmer attempts to deduce a "history out of scripture," an account of how divine right is conveyed by God to contemporary monarchs through time and place (1T 128). According to Figgis, Filmer surrenders his most defensible position by "partially deserting" the "older mode of arguing from Scripture texts, as direct divine injunctions." Believing that "a natural system of politics was more likely to prove well-founded than a purely theological scheme," he thought his account of Adamic succession would be a clear and obvious solution to the problem of political justification.[28] Yet by departing from the older mode of justification based on authoritative interpretations of Scripture, he "paves the way" for Locke's critique.[29] "Nothing was easier than to meet Filmer on his own ground," Figgis writes, "and Locke did so."[30] After Filmer had already taken a wobbly step away from the precritical

Concerning Human Understanding, ed. Thomas Beauchamp (Oxford: Oxford University Press, 2001), 169–86.

[28] John Neville Figgis, *The Divine Right of Kings* (New York: Harper & Row, 1965), 154–55.

[29] Ibid.

[30] Ibid., 157.

understanding of Scripture, Locke, wielding a new standard of probable judgment, had no trouble knocking him down.

The recognition that Locke's approach to Scripture should be seen as the application of a new type of probability helps us gain a new perspective on one of the most difficult problems of Locke scholarship. Students of Leo Strauss have argued that the *First Treatise* is a crucial text because it reveals that Locke's religious commitments are not sincere.[31] Although he presents himself as a pious believer, the subtle inconsistencies of Locke's use of Scripture reveal him to be a secret deist or atheist whose primary aim is to undermine orthodox belief. These interpretations are right in pointing out the potentially revolutionary consequences of Locke's approach to Scripture. Yet they are wrong to insist that Locke's shift from a precritical to a critical approach necessarily stems from radically antitheological intentions. In fact Locke's appeal to the signs of nature as adequate criteria for judging revelation makes sense only within the context of a larger commitment to God as author of the book of nature and authorizing source of a morally marked universe. The assumption that Locke's attack on Filmer's use of Scripture is an attack on the entire Christian tradition rests on a strangely monolithic view of religious traditions. It also ignores the fact that Locke introduces his new standard of probability in and through the conceptual framework of post-Reformation theology.[32]

Yet if Locke's position rests on certain religious assumptions, what type of assumptions are they? More than thirty-five years ago, John Dunn argued that we can best understand Locke's social and political theory by viewing it as an elaboration of Calvinist social values.[33] Dunn played an important role in calling attention to the importance of Locke's religious thought. Yet, as he was certainly aware, there was something misleading about depicting Locke as a Calvinist. Although Locke grew up in a Calvinist home, he did not remain committed to anything that could be recognized as orthodox Calvinism. In fact, in *The Reasonableness of Christianity* he openly attacks what he sees as the excesses of Calvinist theology (RC 1). Although many recent scholars join Dunn in recognizing

---

[31] Pangle, *Spirit of Modern Republicanism*; Strauss, *Natural Right and History*; Michael Zuckert, "Locke and the Problem of Civil Religion," in *The Moral Foundations of the American Republic*, ed. Robert Horwitz (Charlottesville: University Press of Virginia, 1986).

[32] See Joshua Mitchell's review of Michael Zuckert's *Launching Liberalism*. Joshua Mitchell, "In the Beginning Was the Word," *First Things* 129 (January 2003). For an important corrective to the overly secular and thus anachronistic readings of Hobbes and Locke, see Joshua Mitchell, *Not by Reason Alone: Religion, History, and Identity in Early Modern Political Thought* (Chicago: University of Chicago Press, 1993). See also Forster, *John Locke's Moral Consensus*.

[33] Dunn, *Political Thought of Locke*, 259.

the importance of the relationship between Locke's theology and political philosophy, there is still substantial disagreement over the precise nature of this relationship and its implications for Locke's writings. William Spellman has presented the most thorough argument that Locke was a Latitudinarian rather than a Calvinist.[34] He has shown that by the time he moved to London in 1667, Locke was familiar with the work of early Arminians such as Henry Hammond, John Hales, and Richard Allestree and had probably rejected the Calvinist version of justification by faith alone. He quickly became allied with liberal Anglicans such as John Tillotson, Simon Patrick, and Edward Fowler, who believed that the core of Christianity was its moral teaching. They also taught that the essentials of the faith were few and simple, that human fallibility was the strongest evidence against imposing one's religious view on another, and that while some religious truths might be above reason, none are contrary to it. Spellman and others have convincingly shown that Locke shared with the Latitudinarians many of these commitments and at various times in his life he formed alliances with these influential Anglican churchmen. Yet other scholars have begun to question this view of the Latitudinarian Locke. Working from Locke's notebooks, John Marshall has found that Locke's theological speculations led him to question a range of orthodox beliefs that most of his Latitudinarian friends explicitly endorsed. Although Locke kept his personal beliefs hidden from public view, there is ample evidence that he questioned the doctrines of original sin and the Trinity. For this reason both Marshall and David Wootton have come to the conclusion that Locke is best understood as a type of Unitarian or Socinian rather than a Latitudinarian.

Regardless of where we place Locke in the shifting religious categories of post-Reformation England, it is clear that he would scorn these scholarly debates just as he scorned such labels during his lifetime. In fact, he spent a good deal of his intellectual energies trying to avoid being associated with any party at all. In spite of his rejection of labels, it is undeniable that Locke's endorsement of a particular approach to Scripture in the *First Treatise* was also a rejection of rival methods of interpretation. Locke wrote his critique of Filmer in the midst of a whirlwind of radical new ideas and knowingly aligned himself with those early advocates of historical-critical interpretation who were seeking to introduce a new way to read and understand revelation.

[34] W. M. Spellman, *John Locke: British History in Perspective* (New York: St. Martin's Press, 1997); Spellman, *Problem of Depravity*; Spellman, *The Latitudinarians and the Church of England, 1660–1700* (Athens: University of Georgia Press, 1993). See also Harris, *Mind of John Locke*; Ian Harris, "The Politics of Christianity," in *Locke's Philosophy: Content and Context*, ed. G.A.J. Rogers (Oxford: Clarendon Press, 1994); Rogers, *Locke's Enlightenment*.

Recent scholarship has shown that Locke had a voracious appetite for heterodox literature in the early 1680s.[35] In an effort to come to terms with the proper understanding of Scripture, he read and took notes on tracts written by a range of marginal figures in the English context, from radical Socinians to French Catholics. In particular, he took extensive notes on Richard Simon's *Histoire Critique du Vieux Testament* (1678) at the very time he was composing his attack on Filmer.[36] Simon, a French priest with an unrivaled understanding of ancient history and languages, is now recognized as one of the founders of modern biblical criticism. He wrote several important commentaries on the Old Testament that were translated and widely read in England. Simon approached the text as an impartial observer, using linguistic evidence to call attention to the multiple narratives and variation of style in the Pentateuch. By placing this sacred text in its historical and cultural context, he could argue that it should be read as a collection of older writings recorded by public scribes. In this way Simon could continue to maintain that the revelation itself is divinely inspired while granting that over time many errors and alterations have crept into the text. Since a perfect God would not have made such obvious mistakes, the texts must be adjusted or explained in such a way that would account for these variations.

Locke was also reading a variety of other tracts that advocated a new way of interpreting revelation. In spite of his later protestations to Stillingfleet that he had never read a word of Hobbes or Spinoza, we now know that he owned works by both, and it is likely that he was familiar with the radical views expressed in the second half of the *Leviathan* and the first twelve books of the *Theologico-Political Tract*.[37] Many of Locke's contemporaries, including Isaac Newton, suspected him of harboring Hobbesian and Spinozistic tendencies. Yet Locke seems to have spent most of his energies in engagement with works that scholars now refer to as Socinian or Unitarian.[38]

[35] Marshall, *John Locke*; Marshall, "Locke, Socinianism"; Nuovo, "Locke's Theology, 1694–1704."

[36] Marshall, *John Locke*, 337; Gerard Reedy, *The Bible and Reason: Anglicans and Scripture in Late Seventeenth-Century England* (Philadelphia: University of Pennsylvania Press, 1985), 113, 38. Locke learned of Simon's work through correspondence with thinkers on the continent. See *Correspondence*, 2:18, 129, 163, 742–43, 748–51. Part of Simon's project was to counter the Protestant appeal to *sola scriptura* and defend the authority of the church by insisting that Scripture alone could not solve the Trinitarian controversy. Locke seems to apply this lesson in a very different way. In contrast to Simon's call for a return to the authoritative hierarchy of the church, Locke argues that any theological quarrel that cannot be answered by Scripture must not be essential to the faith.

[37] Locke, *Works of John Locke*, IV.420, 77.

[38] See Marshall, "Locke, Socinianism." Yet elsewhere Marshall makes the important point that while Locke might have privately held unorthodox beliefs, his overriding public con-

In the religious polemics of the late seventeenth century, the term "Socinian" was an ill-defined slur that was hurled at a wide variety of writers from reformers within the church to outright opponents of the church. In its widest sense, Socinianism came to signify any type of religious inquiry that places too much emphasis on human reason and not enough on Scripture. John Redwood and Gerard Reedy both point out that the term was used in a variety of conflicting ways by a range of religious apologists trying to discredit the arguments of their opponents.[39] In a narrower sense, the term refers to followers of Fautus Socinus, an Italian religious thinker of the sixteenth century who moved from Siena to Krakow and eventually formed a community whose tenets are most clearly outlined in the *Racovian Cateschism* (1605). These tenets include an emphasis on the role of reason in scriptural interpretation, the rejection of the divinity of Christ (and thus the Trinity), the limiting of Jesus' role in human redemption to one of moral exemplarity, and the advocacy of tolerance for believers of all creeds.[40] Some who held all these things still denied that they were Socinian, because they believed the label to be derogatory, signifying a heterodox or heretical theological position. Toward the end of the seventeenth century, many of those who held to one or more of Socinus's teachings began to call themselves "Unitarians," in an effort to emphasize the fact that they held to uncontroversial scriptural teachings concerning the unity of God. Although some who might be called Socinians left the established church, most did not.

Whether or not Locke should be categorized as a Socinian, it is clear that he agreed with Socinians that one's observations of nature and nature's signs should shape one's reading of Scripture. This led him to be very reticent about confirming religious tenets, even orthodox ones such as the doctrine of original sin or the Trinity, without clear and unequivocal scriptural support. If there is one thing that we know about Locke's religious commitments it is that he had no interest in formulating controversial doctrines from scriptural sources, especially if they might be used to force theological uniformity. Locke strenuously attacked anyone who sought to superimpose his own doctrine on Scripture. And among these

---

cern was with toleration and antidogmatism, and he was therefore loathe to declare himself a supporter of any sect for principled as well as pragmatic reasons. Marshall, *John Locke*, 184.

[39] John Redwood, *Reason, Ridicule and Religion: The Age of Enlightenment in England, 1660–1750* (Cambridge: Harvard University Press, 1976); Reedy, *The Bible and Reason*.

[40] In many ways, the debates over Socinianism paralleled the controversies that occurred in the early church over the nature of the Trinity, the uniqueness of God, and the divinity of Christ. By returning to beliefs that had been articulated among early Christians, Newton and others saw themselves as returning to a purer and unadulterated version of their faith. See H. John McLachlan, *The Religious Opinions of Milton, Locke, and Newton* (Folcroft, Pa.: Folcroft Library Editions, 1941); Webster, *From Paracelsus to Newton*.

"systems" Locke included Socinianism. In his *Second Vindication of the Reasonableness of Christianity,* Locke explains:

> The same genius seems to influence them all, even those who pretend most to freedom, the Socinians themselves. For when it is observed, how positive and eager they are in their disputes; how forward they are to have their interpretations of scripture received for authentic, though to others, in several places, they seem very much strained; how impatient they are of contradiction; and with what disrespect and roughness they often treat their opposers; may it not be suspected, that this so visible a warmth in their present circumstances, and zeal for their orthodoxy, would (had they the power) work in them as it does in others.[41]

The interpreter who imposes a system on the text, whether he is a High Church scholastic or a Socinian dissident, is equally culpable in Locke's eyes. What Locke is offering the readers of the *First Treatise* is not a new set of doctrines or a new system, but a way of approaching sacred texts free of such systems of divinity. Ultimately he wants to convince his readers to view revelation as a species of probable testimony. Although it is the testimony of God, it comes to us through the mouths of human beings who are shaped by specific historical contexts and linguistic restraints. If we are to arrive at a clear understanding of this testimony, we must hold the text up to accessible standards of reasonableness, comparing it to the "outward or visible signs" of nature in order to determine whether it is genuine revelation or not. Scripture is authorized (and authoritative) only insofar as it can be validated by our reason. For this reason the deliverances of Scripture cannot provide us with the type of divine certainty that Filmer claims. As in all other aspects of our lives, we are called on to use our judgment to determine the relative probability of allegedly scriptural arguments. By quietly advocating this seemingly modest shift in emphasis, Locke seeks to transform the way his readers approach Scripture. Although he does not question the authority of revelation, he encourages his readers to distinguish between scriptural authority and the various systems of divinity that hide behind it. He urges his readers to use their judgment by comparing the claims they encounter with their own experiences and observations.

The Slavishness of Systems

Locke presents Filmer's scriptural argument as an attempt to erect a simple and absolute standard of political justification, a standard that is

---

[41] Quoted by Reedy, *The Bible and Reason*, 136.

indisputable and applicable to any future political situation. Filmer's is a "short system of politics" or a "short model" that purports to provide readers with a "pattern" and "perfect standard for the future" (1T 5, 2). Locke goes out of his way to emphasize that it "lies in a little compass" (1T 2). Its extreme simplicity gives the appearance of clarity and coherence. Yet readers should beware of the theoretical parsimony of such systems and models of politics. Although Filmer's system rests on a self-contained and seemingly straightforward set of principles, there is something about such an approach that is directly at odds with the Lockean view of judgment. With all of its elaborate rationalizations and meandering reasonings, Filmer's position is no more than a web of bald assertions. It reveals itself as the type of system of divinity that is a hindrance to clear and careful thinking. When Locke attempts to uncover "arguments" and "evidence" supporting it, he finds only the claim "that all government is absolute monarchy" since "no man is born free" (1T 2). All of the dizzying complexities of his "wonderful system" can be reduced to the "bare supposition of this foundation" (1T 11). It is on this basis that Filmer erects a strikingly simple defense of the absolute and unlimited political power.

Filmer contends that we are all born subject to our fathers and that this relationship is the standard of all other relationships, whether they are public or private. He traces this patriarchal authority back to God's original donation to the biblical figure of Adam. Adam was given dominion over all things and people in the world, and that dominion was confirmed through the act of begetting. The unlimited political authority of fathers and inescapable servitude of children was transmitted through the generations by the rule of male primogeniture. Thus the direct descendents of Adam rightfully rule over their children as well as their mothers, brothers, uncles, and other relatives. They deserve to be obeyed and respected as God's instruments of political authority on earth.[42]

The appeal of this theory is that it provides an account of political authority that is unchanged and uninterrupted throughout history. What is absolutely certain at the beginning of time is just as certain today. God's commands are consistent, clear, and unalterable. Filmer presents his system as timeless and universally applicable. It is in defense of the integrity of his system that Filmer rejects Grotius's suggestion that property that was once communal has now become properly private.[43] This type of historical change is incompatible with Filmer's insistence on God's irreversible commands. A God who does not change cannot sanction both communal ownership and private ownership without making self-

[42] Robert Filmer, *Patriarcha and Other Political Works*, ed. Peter Laslett (Oxford: Blackwell, 1949), 57–61, 187–89, 231, 41, 83–84, 88–89.
[43] Ibid., 262.

contradictory demands on human beings.[44] Filmer's static theory of divine providence rests on the assumption that God has always supplied human beings with a complete moral and political framework. The proper political arrangement for humanity, then, remains the same throughout history. By tracing all government to a single authorizing source, the direct grant of dominion to Adam, Filmer is able to argue that our obligations are the same today as they always were. The original state was a state of perfection, and any deviations are signs of deterioration, not improvement.

By submitting to established authorities we can come to experience the certainty and harmony of Filmer's system. Only the undiluted power of a monarch can liberate subjects from the unsettling consequences of partisan struggles and intellectual disagreement and return them to the loving embrace of providential harmony. Filmer follows the French absolutist Jean Bodin, whom he quotes at length, in order to establish that submission to an absolute sovereign is the only way to resolve the conflicts that plague political life. To reject the absolute certainty afforded by a divinely ordained monarch is to court anarchy. To think that government can emerge from the disputable judgments of individuals is to replace stability with chaos. It is for this reason that Filmer seems so shocked by his adversaries. Since the only alternatives in his mind are the certainty of his system or the misery and bloodshed of anarchy, Filmer is unable to imagine that anyone would honestly disagree with him. His opponents must therefore be ignorant, confused, or wicked.[45]

The problem, of course, is that Filmer maintains the simplicity and clarity of his system by stubbornly refusing to acknowledge the contingencies of history and the reality of political contestation in the world. Filmer seeks certainty in political life by reducing it to some axiomatic core, abstracted from the uncertainties of human interaction. Locke points out that Filmer "raises so mighty a structure" by shutting out the world as we experience it.[46] He builds his system "so high above all earthly things, that thought can scarce reach it" (1T 6). By ignoring the natural deliverances of experience and embracing his own solipsistic reasonings, he actually begins to believe "his own fancies for certain and divine truths" (1T 55). Filmer insolates himself from the unpredictable consequences of human will by wrapping his system in a tight framework of divine certainty that "leaves no room for humane prudence, or consent" (1T 126).

Locke insists that political authority must be politically feasible; that is, it must be recognized as authoritative by those who submit to it. If an

<hr/>

[44] "If there hath been a time when all things were common, and all men equal, and that it be otherwise now; we must needs conclude that the law by which things were common, and men equal, was contrary to the law by which now things are proper and men subject." Filmer, *Patriarcha*, 262.

[45] Ibid., 260–78.

[46] See also E I.iv.25.

appeal to authority is going to be anything but an empty conceit, it must elicit obedience in the actual observable world. To ignore this fact is to risk absurdity. Locke mocks Filmer for arguing that Adam "was governor in habit, and not in act: a very pretty way of being a governor without government, a father without children and a king without subjects" (1T 71). The clear meaning of such a claim, Locke insists, is that "Adam, as soon as he was created, had a title only in habit, and not in act, which in plain English is, he had actually no title at all. . . . actually no king at all" (1T 72). For Locke anyone who seeks to assert a title to rule must be able to establish that title in fact by "settling" the consciences of those who are to be ruled (1T 81). He must show subjects that a certain individual or institution is not only claiming authority, but has a legitimate and actual right to it.

Yet Filmer's system simply cannot help individuals confront the fundamental problem of contested authorities. If we accept Filmer's premise that rulers derive their authority from God's grant to Adam, Locke argues, then our ability to trace the line of succession from Adam to our current ruler would seem to be especially important. Yet Filmer simply cannot supply us with the positive evidence to prove that present-day rulers are the rightful heirs to Adam through the eldest male line. In fact, we have quite a bit of scriptural and historical evidence to the contrary. Not only do the biblical examples of Cain and Abel, Jacob and Esau, and Jacob and Judah contradict Filmer's claim, but the convoluted histories of contemporary European monarchies also run counter to his simple model of conveyance (1T 74–77). In the face of this evidence, it is clear that Filmer's "principle could not be made to agree with that constitution and order which God had settled in the world and therefore must needs often clash with common sense and experience" (1T 137).

It is at this point that we find that Filmer's ultimate goal is *not* to present a criterion of justification that conforms to common sense and experience. Instead he wants to convince his readers to suspend their judgment and obey. It is for this reason that he seems to be unconcerned with distinguishing usurpers from rightful heirs. He admits as much when he includes usurpers among those who are to be obeyed:

> It is true, all kings be not the natural parents of their subjects, yet they all are, or are to be reputed, as the next heirs of those progenitors who were at first the natural parents of the whole people, and in their right succeed to the exercise of supreme jurisdiction.[47]

Filmer's easy acceptance of usurpers as "reputed" heirs reveals his impatience with the difficult question of legitimacy. He is quick to jettison his

---

[47] Filmer, *Patriarcha*, 61.

system of rigorous paternal descent when it becomes difficult to sustain. Such determinations depend on private judgment, and private judgment is notoriously contestable.

Filmer fills the gap between his system of patriarchal succession and the problem of the usurper by attributing any discrepancies to the unfathomable judgment of God. We can rest assured that "the judgment of God, who hath power to give and take away kingdoms, is most just."[48] If God allows a usurper to take the throne, we are to treat that usurper as the rightful heir of Adam. In this view any manifestation of political authority, whether it is the result of proper succession or violent usurpation, turns out to be an expression of God's will. Locke shows his readers that Filmer's scriptural system boils down to this: obedience is always required and resistance is always forbidden. That is, God will never sanction rebellion, although he will endorse successful rebels after they have taken power.

Thus Locke can show that Filmer is most interested in convincing his readers that any existing authority—regardless of how it achieved its power or how it maintains it—is ordained by God and deserving of obedience. Subjects need only know that those in power deserve obedience; they need not bother distinguishing between legitimate rulers and tyrants. In fact the very idea of tyranny seems to be without meaning for Filmer; he insists that "there is no such form of government as tyranny."[49] And since there is no tyranny, it would seem that there is no such thing as political subjugation or slavery either. All government is divinely ordained and thus justified. Filmer thus guides his readers to surrender their capacity to judge political legitimacy and accept whatever authority is in power. Filmer seeks to convince his readers to embrace their political enslavement.

It is in this context that we can best understand Locke's persistent emphasis on the evil of slavery in the *Two Treatises*. From the first word of the first chapter of the *First Treatise* to the penultimate chapter of the *Second Treatise* in which Locke likens the tyrannous king to a ship captain steering a hostage nation toward Algiers, slavery plays a crucial rhetorical role in Locke's argument.[50] It is "so vile and miserable an estate"

[48] Ibid., 62.
[49] Ibid., 229.
[50] Locke's rhetorical emphasis on the evil of slavery throughout the *Two Treatises* should be juxtaposed with his apparent acquiescence to the practice of chattel slavery in the American colonies. Locke helped draft the Fundamental Constitutions of Carolina in 1670 that granted every free man "absolute power and authority over his negro slaves." He also helped draft a letter to Governor Nicholson of Virginia that argued that negro slaves are justifiably held because they were captives taken in a just war (an application of an argument that Locke makes in 2T 178, 182, 189). In addition, Locke invested in the Royal

that he compares it to death (1T 1). In fact, he defines slavery as death delayed, the state between the pronouncement of a death sentence and its execution (2T 23). To be enslaved is to be yoked to the absolute despotic power of another. It is "to be subject to the inconstant, uncertain, unknown, arbitrary will of another man" (2T 22). Locke repeatedly identifies slavery with absolute monarchy and tyranny (2T 17, 20, 91, 149, 222, 226–27, 232, 239). The subjects of an absolute monarch are like slaves in that they have the status of beasts; they resemble herds of cattle (1T 156; 2T 93, 163). Filmer is an especially insidious opponent, however, because he defends the political slavery of absolutism by employing a type of mental slavery or methodological absolutism that commands the reader to acquiesce to his intellectual and spiritual authority.

Although Locke is certainly aware of the whole range of dangers posed by an absolute monarchy, it is not only the capricious incarceration or the arbitrary seizure of property that inspires his greatest fear. It is the way an absolute monarch could claim authority to enforce a particular set of beliefs. For Locke the most dangerous type of subjugation emerges when individuals abandon their capacity (and their duty) to use their own judgment. As we have seen in the previous chapter, Locke understands freedom as intimately related to the human capacity to reason and to judge. This capacity can neither be taken from us nor bartered away (E II.xxviii.10).

When we employ this capacity to suspend our immediate desires and govern our thoughts and actions according to the evidence we gather, we experience liberty. When we fail to do this and instead act according to whim or passion, we experience enslavement. Locke recognizes that some might think this obligation to self-constraint is a paradoxical type of freedom, yet he is adamant that it is the only alternative to slavery: "This is

Africa Company in 1672, which had a monopoly on the slave trade, and in a company of merchant adventurers who sought to trade with the slaveholders of the Bahamas. These awkward historical facts have fueled a continuing debate over the relationship between Locke's theory and his practice. Some commentators, such as Jennifer Welchman and Jacqueline Stevens, have reintroduced the argument that the *Two Treatises* in some ways rationalize and justify the type of slavery in which Locke was involved. Jacqueline Stevens, "The Reasonableness of John Locke's Majority," *Political Theory* 24 (1996), 423–63; Jacqueline Stevens, *Reproducing the State* (Princeton: Princeton University Press, 1999), 100; Jennifer Welchman, "Locke on Slavery and Inalienable Rights," *Canadian Journal of Philosophy* 25 (1995), 67–81. See also Seymour Drescher, "On James Farr's 'So Vile and Miserable an Estate,'" *Political Theory* 16 (1988), 502–3; Harris, *Mind of John Locke*, 172. More convincing, I believe, are the commentators who acknowledge Locke's involvement in the slave trade yet insist, as Jeremy Waldron puts it, that "there is simply no possibility of reconciling Locke's very limited theory of legitimate enslavement with the reality of the institution in the Carolinas or anywhere else in the Americas" (206). Waldron, *God, Locke, and Equality*, 197–206. See also Dunn, *Political Thought of Locke*, 174n; James Farr, "'Slaves Bought with Money': A Reply to Drescher," *Political Theory* 17 (1989), 471–74.

so far from being a restraint or diminution of freedom, that it is the very improvement and benefit of it: 'tis not an abridgment, 'tis the end and use of our liberty; and the farther we are removed from such a determination, the nearer we are to misery and slavery" (E II.xxi.48). Locke characterizes genuine freedom as the liberty to engage in intellectual labor of one's own. The worst type of slavery, therefore, involves subjecting the labors of the individual mind to the arbitrary authority of another. Whether this results from the coercion of government, the manipulations of scholasticism, or the excesses of religious enthusiasm (which Locke describes as tyrannizing one's own mind), Locke insists that this type of intellectual subjection is the most vile and miserable state imaginable (see E I.iv.24, IV.iii.2, IV.xix.2, IV.xx.17).

Filmer's argument, then, exposes us "to the utmost misery of tyranny and oppression" not simply because it endorses absolute rule, but because it habituates the mind to accept its own enslavement (1T 3). It preaches cognitive surrender, a type of capitulation that is disastrous for individuals as well as for the commonwealth. The aim of Filmer's system is to raise up a class of subjects who will embrace their intellectual enslavement. Such individuals would be "degraded from the common state of rational creatures" since they would be denied "a liberty to judge of, or to defend" their rights (2T 92). As Locke puts it in the *Essay*, "he is certainly the most subjected, the most enslaved, who is so in his understanding" (E IV.xx.6).

Locke goes on to argue that this type of mental slavery perpetuates itself. There is something about the spread of submissive and obedient subjects that leads to the emergence of masters and tyrants. Those who abdicate their responsibility to judge confer that right to someone else, and it is no small power "to have the authority to be the dictator of principle and teacher of unquestionable truths" (E I.iv.24). Here Locke uncovers the link between epistemological control and political power: To allow another the power to dictate principles is literally to make that person one's dictator. Granting individuals such authority will "flatter natural vanity and ambition, too apt of it self to grow and increase with the possession of power" (1T 10). Such a state of affairs would not ensure the stability that Filmer advertises. In fact it would invite sedition and rebellion (1T 3, 72, 81, 106). If obedience is granted to anyone in power, Locke argues, it emboldens the ambitious and cunning to rise up and overthrow legitimate rulers and seize authority for themselves. Thus the unitary simplicity to which Filmer desperately clings fractures into political chaos. Filmer's "frenetic over-assimilation of differences to unity" does not achieve its desired purpose.[51] His insistence on the absolute clar-

---

[51] Dunn, *Political Thought of Locke*, 76.

ity of his particular system makes it especially vulnerable to skeptical refutation and cynical manipulation. Not only does Filmer's system lead to political and mental slavery, but it also destabilizes polities by opening the door to endless bloodshed and upheaval.[52]

For this reason Locke insists that individuals who wish to be free cannot rest in the comfortable serenity of Filmer's divine certainty. There is no paradise of intellectual repose in this world. There is no self-contained system of political justification that can relieve us of our intellectual responsibilities. By showing that Filmer's confidence is ultimately an illusion, Locke can direct our attention to the inescapable necessity of judgment. If Filmer's foundation is not as stable as he claims, we must fall back on our own cognitive faculties. It is only by refuting the type of thinking that is the basis of Filmer's divine certainty that Locke can guide us toward the politics of probable judgment that he explicates in the *Second Treatise*. Locke transforms the terms of the debate by challenging Filmer's appeal to certainty with a gentle insistence on the importance of probable judgment. By carefully calling attention to the inescapable ambiguity of our political lives, he can show that the drive to achieve certainty is not only illusory but also politically dangerous. Even Filmer's appeals to the unquestionable authority of divine revelation cannot hide the fact that his system offers nothing but slavery and chaos. An authentically scriptural response to political justification must take another shape.

Locke's attack on Filmer in the *First Treatise* should therefore not be read as an assault on revelation itself, but rather as an attempt to revise and reinterpret the role revelation should play in political affairs. For Filmer, Scripture provides the faithful reader with a type of divine certainty. It serves as a direct link between the believer's mind and the mind of God, providing the believer with direct insight into the normative structure of creation. One need only look to revelation to know that God granted Adam unlimited dominion and that this dominion has been passed down to the rulers of the contemporary world. Since Scripture assures that this patriarchal model of political governance is written into the very fabric of the universe, we can rest assured that God provides us with all that we need and has done so from the very beginning of time. Any attempt to transform or alter this structure would constitute rebellion against divine providence. For Filmer, the Bible is read as a reminder that we have already been supplied with both material and intellectual abundance. We have been granted an unalterable place in the context of

---

[52] Locke is surely aiming his vitriol at these types of philosophical "systems" when he writes in the *Essay* about the "empty speculations" that have "obscured and perplexed the material truths of law and divinity; brought confusion, disorder, and uncertainty into the affairs of mankind; and if not destroyed, yet in great measure rendered useless, those two great rules, religion and justice" (E II.x.12).

a divinely ordained totality and the only faithful response to such a grant is to accept the unfolding of providence with passive acquiescence. Revelation teaches us to embrace the world as it is and accept it as wholly adequate and complete.

Yet Locke rejects this account. His engagement with Scripture turns Filmer's position on its head. By insisting that Scripture must be interpreted within the context of human experience of natural signs, he replaces Filmer's narrative of providential design with a new understanding that makes room for transformative human agency. Again, it is important to note that Locke is not discarding religious commitment to written revelation; he is emphasizing that it can be used to combat absolutism and defend consensual politics. This is most evident when Locke discusses the passage that Filmer uses to demonstrate Adam's rightful dominion; Locke interprets it as a declaration of the fundamental incompleteness of creation. Locke reads the injunction of Genesis 1:28, "Be fruitful and multiply, and replenish the earth," not as a directive aimed at Adam alone, as Filmer does, but as an appeal to all human beings to improve their natural condition. Instead of accepting Scripture as proof that God has prearranged our political institutions and provided for our every need, Locke takes it as a reminder that we are born into a world that cannot be sustained without our active involvement.[53]

It is true that Locke cites Genesis to remind his readers of the abundance of creation. Yet the original "plenty" to which Locke refers should not be understood to mean a condition of "completeness." According to Locke the Bible's description of "the plenty of natural provision" does not refer to the "fruits" of nature but to its raw materials. Nature is "apt to produce in abundance," but it has not yet done so. Thus the abundance of our natural state is one of potentiality and not actuality.[54] It turns out that "the great and primary blessing of God Almighty" is that creation is not yet complete (1T 23). The natural condition we find ourselves in is not one of plenty, but one of material impoverishment and intellectual neediness. Locke tells us that "we are born ignorant of everything" and are only able to furnish our intellects with "labor, attention, and industry" (CU 38). Human beings are called on to transform their condition and enrich their surroundings. As Locke argues in the *Second Treatise*, "God commanded man also to labour and the penury of his condition required it of him" (2T 32). It is by actively transforming the world in which they find themselves that Lockean individuals can "promote the

---

[53] Steven Forde writes, "It is scarce an exaggeration to say that the whole theology of the *Two Treatises* (indeed, the moral teaching of the *Treatises* in general) is an extended gloss on "be fruitful and multiply." Forde, "What Does Locke Expect," 242.

[54] Myers, *Our Only Star*, 117–20; Zuckert, *Launching Liberalism*, 144–46, and *Natural Rights*, 259–72; Strauss, *Natural Right and History*, 224–26, 34, 39.

great design of God, increase and multiply" (1T 41). It is through action and labor that we can fulfill our duty to God.[55]

By insisting that this injunction is the central teaching of the Bible, Locke can sever Filmer's link between divine command and the status quo. Human beings promote "the great design of God" when they learn to flourish as human beings. This divine purpose is easy to discern in "the legible characters of his works and providence" (E III.ix.23). "The works of nature and the words of revelation display it to mankind in characters so large and visible," Locke writes, "that those who are not quite blind may in them read and see the first principles and most necessary parts of it" (CU 23). Thus for Locke our religious duty involves acting to promote the prosperity and happiness of humanity. We can come to recognize what such prosperity and happiness requires, then, by carefully studying written revelation as well as observing the "course of nature" and learning how to improve on it (1T 89).

The first implication of this focus on the "great design" is that the deep desire for self-preservation that we experience in ourselves and others should be understood as an essential component of the divine plan. This desire is "wrought into the very principles of nature" (1T 88). As he tells his readers in the beginning of the *Second Treatise,* human beings are God's "property" and "workmanship" and are "made to last during his, not one another's pleasure" (2T 6; see also E I.iv.13, IV.vi.9, IV.iii.18, IV.x.18, IV.xviii.5). This "workmanship model" plays a crucial role in shaping Locke's account of both the limits of proper human conduct and the boundaries of divine action. A benevolent and rational God would not create human beings in order to see them destroy themselves and one another. For Locke, God may be omnipotent and unfathomable, yet his actions must still be ordered by reason: "The freedom of the Almighty hinders not his being determined by what is best" (E II.xxi.49; see also 2T 195). Thus we can assume that the widespread desire for self-preservation is actually a manifestation of a divine plan to promote the general prosperity of humankind. For Locke, the strong desire of self-preservation was planted in each individual "as a principle of action by God himself"

---

[55] In an insightful study, Vivienne Brown points out that the metaphorical "figure" of God is deployed in Locke's various writings for different purposes. In the *Essay,* Locke argues that the man's notions provide no more than an incomplete understanding of God in order to unsettle theological speculation. In the *Two Treatises,* Locke appeals to God who is absolute monarch and maker of man in order to circumscribe political activity. Although Brown is right about Locke's dual use of God, the various treatments he employs cannot be so easily divided into separate texts as Brown suggests. Locke's appeal to the "figure" of God to both unsettle his opponent's claims and secure his own arguments runs through both the *Essay* and the *Two Treatises.* Vivienne Brown, "The 'Figure' of God and the Limits to Liberalism: A Rereading of Locke's *Essay* and *Two Treatises,*" *Journal of the History of Ideas* 60, no. 1 (1999), 83–100.

and thus, "reason, which was the voice of God in him, could not but teach him and assure him, that pursuing that natural inclination he had to preserve his being [and at the same time] he followed the will of his maker" (1T 86).

Yet mere preservation is not enough to further the "great design." Locke argues that it would be an impious challenge to God's goodness to believe that our natural condition of penury and neediness is God's will for our lives. Since the "great design" must ultimately conform to our understanding of the benevolence and justice of the creator, then we must conclude that our natural condition of want is something that we are expected to surpass. In this way Locke can insist that the amelioration of our estate is a scriptural command. For example, he declares that there is nothing in the Bible that obliges a woman to "bring forth her children in sorrow and pain, if there could be found a remedy for it" (1T 47). The agony of childbirth turns out to be nothing more than an inconvenience that can and should be altered.[56]

What is most important for Locke is our willingness and capacity to respond to God's charge to "increase and multiply." This requires both physical labor and intellectual labor as we struggle to make judgments concerning how we should arrange our lives and our political institutions in order to best achieve our divine purpose. Locke's response to Filmer thus ultimately takes a theological form. He insists that the type of submission to absolute authority that Filmer advocates is simply incompatible with the "great design." We can see that surrendering ourselves to the unlimited power of a monarch "is not the way to people the world" (1T 33). One way to observe this fact, Locke argues, is to consider what types of government encourage the improvement of the arts and sciences and what types of government discourage them. Countries that live under political systems that discourage progress do not grow and prosper. Since absolute monarchy fears the progress of the arts and sciences, its existence is a hindrance to the increased prosperity of humankind (1T 33). In this way Locke can reverse Filmer's argument, insisting that a careful analysis of Scripture along with evidence from our experience will lead

[56] It is important to note that many of Locke's contemporaries read Scripture to imply that the pain of childbirth is a necessary and inescapable consequence of original sin. It is a punishment that had been placed on humanity as a result of the fall. Yet Locke seems uncomfortable with the entire notion of original sin. In *The Reasonableness of Christianity*, he simply rejects the claim that we have been punished for the sins of Adam and Eve. To believe that God would punish his creatures for something that they did not do "would be hard to reconcile with the notion we have of justice, and much more with the goodness and other attributes of the supreme Being, which he has declared of himself and [which] reason, as well as revelation, must acknowledge to be in him" (RC 6). Instead we should expect that a just and good God rewards the just and punishes the wicked "for their own deeds" (RC 6).

us to recognize that submission to the absolute and unlimited power of a king is in direct disobedience to the overarching command of God, to increase and multiply.[57]

Locke also appeals to the biblical injunction to promote the "great design" as a way of circumscribing the place of revelation in our political lives. Filmer's most glaring error is to assume that Scripture can supply human beings with all that they need to live according to God's plan. Locke points out that the Bible alone simply does not provide answers to the urgent political questions that human beings pose. To search for answers where they are not to be found leads to the epistemological over-reach that characterizes Filmer's argument. One could almost say that Locke embarks on a thorough investigation of Scripture in the *First Treatise* in order to show its irrelevance to our social and political lives. "In a matter of such moment, and so great and general concernment" as the relation of husbands and wives, Scripture offers "too doubtful an expression" for one to arrive at irrefutable conclusions (1T 49). He finds other passages "doubtful and obscure" as well (1T 112, 118). At other points, the Bible is "utterly silent." It simply does not provide the reader with any information concerning "the rulers or forms of government" after the collapse of the Tower of Babel (1T 144, 145).

By pointing out these ambiguities and silences, Locke suggests that the Bible should not be used as a proof text for political questions. As Dunn puts it, "The entire *First Treatise,* which is designed to discredit Filmer's extrapolations from the Old Testament, ends up making the latter seem almost irrelevant to issues of political right."[58] It is for this reason that scriptural references seem to drop away from the main argument in the *Second Treatise.* Locke has made it very clear that Filmer's appeal to Scripture cannot help us identify who has a right to rule. "The great question which in all ages has disturbed mankind, and brought on them the greatest part of those mischiefs which have ruined cities, depopulated

[57] Michael Zuckert makes the argument that Locke's focus on increase and amelioration runs counter to a "biblical" understanding of humble acceptance of the world as it is provided. With this generalization he can equate both Hebrew and Christian traditions with the belief in the world as "provided" and Locke's recognition that men must labor to provide for their needs as a radical departure from those traditions. Zuckert, *Launching Liberalism,* 144–46. Yet both Locke and his most zealous religious opponents would certainly have been surprised by this division. They would have agreed that the fulfillment of one's religious duty necessarily involves self-discipline and labor. For more thorough accounts of the diverse religious landscape in which Locke wrote, see Christopher Hill, *Intellectual Origins of the English Revolution—Revisited* (Oxford: Clarendon Press, 2001); Nuovo, "Locke's Theology, 1694–1704"; Margo Todd, *Christian Humanism and the Puritan Social Order* (Cambridge: Cambridge University Press, 1987); Walzer, *Revolution of the Saints.*

[58] Dunn, *Political Thought of Locke,* 99.

countries, and disordered the peace of the world, has been, not whether there be power in the world, nor whence it came, but who should have it" (1T 106). Appealing to the Bible alone cannot solve this fundamental difficulty of political justification.[59]

Faced with these limitations, sober and rational individuals will turn to their God-given capacities of reason and observation in order to determine what they should do. In this way Locke is able to replace Filmer's version of Christianity with his own. Locke's version is not the type of flaccid obedience that Filmer seems to embrace (and Machiavelli denounced as fit only for slaves). Lockean religion is not characterized by acquiescence or passivity. The appeal to the "great design of God" promotes action and demands the amelioration of our estate through physical and intellectual labor. It is not a hindrance to human agency but an encouragement. By insisting on the responsibility of all individuals to utilize their judgment, Locke can deprive scheming priests and religious charlatans of the power to derive political precepts from passages of a Bible only they can interpret. In Locke's hands, written revelation becomes an instrument to encourage readers to rise up and improve their intellectual and political condition. An assumed complementarity between the book of Scripture and the book of nature allows Locke to reject the inscrutable pieties of the defenders of boundless monarchical authority while encouraging readers to strive to bring about the divine design by carefully regulating their judgment.

Having shown that Filmer's appeal to divine certainty is nothing but a foolish and dangerous fantasy and that the foundation of his "wonderful system" is unsustainable, Locke directs his readers to the "old way" of establishing government, by the "contrivance, and the consent of men" (1T 6). We find ourselves in a state in which no one has special access to the mind of God. Since we all "share in the same common nature, faculties and powers, are in nature equal," we "ought to partake in the same common rights and privileges" (1T 67). One of most important rights is the right to make use of our "reason to unite together into society"

---

[59] In the "Eighteenth Brumaire," Karl Marx notes that the language of prophetic illumination is supplanted at this time by the language of evidence and circumspection. Remarking that the seventeenth century had appropriated "the language, passions and illusions of the Old Testament," he notes that when "the bourgeois transformation of English society had been accomplished, Locke drove out Habbakkuk." Karl Marx, "Eighteenth Brumaire," in *Political Writings: Surveys from Exile*, ed. David Fernbach (New York: Random House, 1974), 148. This does not mean that the Bible ceased to be appealed to among contemporaries of Locke, only that public justification moved slowly away from the contested terrain of Scripture. For a related discussion, see Deborah Baumgold, "Pacifying Politics: Resistance, Violence and Accountability in 17th Century Contract Theory," *Political Theory* 21, no. 1 (1993), 6–27.

(1T 6). This is the natural freedom that Locke describes in the *Second Treatise*, the unsettling freedom of private judgment. It is a freedom that both necessitates government and holds it in check. Having dismantled Filmer's seductive yet ultimately illusory appeal to divine certainty, Locke can now turn to the difficult business of establishing government by the judgment and consent of fallible individuals.

VII

Authorizing Judgment

CONSENSUAL GOVERNMENT AND THE POLITICS
OF PROBABILITY

FOR MANY MODERN READERS, the language of the *Second Treatise* carries an almost instinctive familiarity. The terms that animate Locke's argument—liberty, equality, rights, and property—have become the common currency of contemporary liberal political discourse. While there have been substantial shifts in the use of these terms, the fact that we continue to employ them is evidence that they still have a hold on our collective imagination. These terms continue to shape the way we understand ourselves and our relationship to political power. However, the familiarity we have with Locke's language can sometimes obscure the profoundly revolutionary character of the *Second Treatise*. In these pages Locke is not simply explicating an abstract political theory or defending a particular institutional arrangement as so many of his commentators assume. He is inciting revolution. By declaring that legitimate government rests on the consent of the governed, Locke is informing his readers that they have a right to resist rulers they deem to be abusing their delegated powers and threatening the security and well-being of the people. By insisting that the ultimate earthly authority rests in their aggregate judgment, he is emboldening them to take on the responsibility of carefully assessing whether their government is furthering the public good. In the *Second Treatise*, Locke seeks to change the way his readers think about their place in the polity in order to inspire them to take matters into their own hands. He sets out to convince his contemporaries to understand themselves as permanent public judges, vigilantly assessing the actions of their leaders. He wants to show his readers the liberating possibilities of a politics based on probable judgment.

In the preface Locke states that the goal of the work is "to establish the throne of our great restorer, our present King William; to make good his title, in the consent of the people," which is "the only one of all lawful governments." Yet he also seeks "to justify to the world, the people of England, whose love of their just and natural rights, with their resolution to preserve them, saved the nation when it was on the very brink of slavery and ruin" (Preface, 137). In these few lines, Locke announces his support for a new monarch, yet he immediately circumscribes that support by insisting that his lawful title, or legitimacy, rests on the consent of the governed. The authority of William's crown, as well as that of any government, is derived from an original authority held by the people. Locke goes on to declare that he will justify the actual exercise of this authority. He will show that the people have a right to determine whether their government is fulfilling its proper task and, if they deem it necessary, have the right to rise up and replace a menacing ruler in order to preserve their natural rights and freedoms. Locke not only wants to justify William's title to the crown; he also wants to justify the people's title as the final judge of political legitimacy.

Although Locke directs his dual justification to the "world," we have reason to believe that he is not solely making his case before the court of international opinion. Indeed, it quickly becomes evident that he is writing primarily with a more local audience in mind. The context of the argument and the history of its publication reinforce this obvious point.[1] In the *Two Treatises,* Locke aims to justify the propriety of revolution to his countrymen. Yet political justification is intimately tied to ethical and intellectual transformation. The task of justification that lies at the heart of his account has certain parallels with the seventeenth-century practice of casuistry. In Stuart England, the practice of casuistry was employed to explain a particular set of actions by providing an account of how and why those actions are consistent with right reason and the proper care for one's soul.[2] In a similar way, Locke presents the *Two Treatises* as an explication of the proper conduct of a people who find themselves subjects of government. This approach has both backward- and forward-looking elements. Locke aims to explain why a people had a right to judge their government and actively resist what they saw as despotic excess. Yet he also hopes to teach his readers how they should continue to employ this judgment in the future.[3] He wants to instill in them a sense of their capacity for judgment as well as an understanding of how they should exercise that capacity properly.

In this way, the *Second Treatise* can be seen as a type of political pedagogy. In order to teach his readers to be active, critical, and perhaps even

---

[1] Of all the printings and reprintings of the *Two Treatises* during Locke's lifetime, all but one were published in his native tongue. A single edition of the *Second Treatise* by itself was published in French in 1691. For a comprehensive publishing history, see Laslett's introduction in Locke, *Two Treatises of Government,* 6–15.

[2] See Edmund Leites, "Casuistry and Character," in Leites, *Conscience and Casuistry.*

[3] For a discussion of the claim that Locke published the *Two Treatises* as a reminder to his countrymen of their continued responsibilities of judgment and thus also as a warning to William and Mary, see Charles D. Tarlton, "The Rulers Now on Earth: Locke's *Two Treatises* and the Revolution of 1688," *Historical Journal* 28, no. 2 (1985), 279–98.

revolutionary members of the polity, Locke sets out to convince them that they are able to make crucial determinations concerning the limits of political power. The success of this project rests on Locke's ability to inculcate a new way of thinking and speaking about judgment in matters of political controversy. Locke wants to resolve the problem of politics—a problem that emerges from the diversity of private judgment—by convincing his readers to embrace a common understanding of judgment that takes into account both its importance and its limitations. He seeks to reconstitute the way they view their own intellectual faculties in order to transform the way they conduct themselves in the political realm. As we have seen, Locke was concerned throughout his life with how individuals' beliefs and opinions shape their behavior. This is perhaps most clearly seen in the *Conduct of the Understanding*, which begins with the assertion, "The last resort a man has recourse to in the conduct of himself is his understanding" (CU 1). Locke goes on to state that the individual will is not only informed, but actually governed by the understanding: "Temples have their sacred images, and we see what influence they have always had over a great part of mankind. But in truth the ideas and images in men's minds are the invisible powers that constantly govern them" (CU 1). Here Locke describes in explicitly political language how the individual will is subject to the "invisible powers" of the mind. In the same way that the sacred images of holy shrines can captivate the individual intellect, the ideas that we have about ourselves and our polity can hold sway over our thoughts and actions.

It is this very concern for "the images of men's minds" that motivates Locke's earlier criticism of "the pulpit" for having "publicly owned" Filmer's doctrines of patriarchal power and "dangerously misled others" by teaching them to surrender their own faculties of judgment to the unquestionable authority of their rulers. Indeed, "there cannot be done a greater mischief to prince and people, than the propagating wrong notions concerning government" (Preface, 138). This is the reason that Locke is so serious about tearing down Filmer's intellectual edifice of patriarchy. Yet it is also the reason why he is determined to offer something else in its place. A stable and peaceful polity requires a common understanding of political authority.

In fact, Locke distinguishes between human beings and beasts by arguing that humans have the capacity to be governed by reason, while beasts are driven by their will alone. The internalized constraint of reason makes possible peaceful coexistence, while the boundless desire of will leads inevitably to violence. The establishment and maintenance of a stable polity thus requires the dissemination of reasonable notions concerning both the promise and the limits of government. If we are to avoid the conclusion that government is the "product only of force and violence" and thus "lay a foundation for perpetual disorder and mischief, tumult, sedition and rebellion," we must "find out another rise of government, another original of political power, and another way of designing and knowing the persons that have it, than what Sir Robert F. hath taught us" (2T 1). It is crucial to Locke that his readers gain a correct understanding of their role in the political sphere, because that understanding will govern their conduct of themselves and ultimately determine whether they can sustain a regime that will stave off perpetual disorder and preserve the rights and freedoms of the people (2T 3).

It is this effort to convey a common understanding of political power that leads Locke to replace the defunct and misleading vocabulary of absolutism with a new mode of discourse that is more tangible and durable. Having shown that Filmer's scriptural defense of patriarchy cannot serve as the foundation for a stable and just polity, Locke turns his attention to the "old way" of understanding government as the product of "the contrivance, and the consent of men" (1T 6). A legitimate polity does not simply result from an imposition of abstract principles, however certain their defenders might claim them to be. For Locke, the "original" of political power is the actual judgment of a particular people "making use of their reason to unite together into society" (1T 6). It is this judgment that also determines whether a government has exceeded its proper powers and betrayed its mandate to protect and secure the public good. Locke considers the establishment of civil government a fragile human solution to the profound problem of private judgment. Yet instead of trying to eliminate that problem completely, Locke seeks to mitigate its most dangerous consequences by instructing his readers how to be both free and rational. He invests the people with ultimate earthly authority because he believes that shared judgment of common, tangible experiences provides the most trustworthy and politically viable access to the laws that lie at the heart of a purposive and morally structured world.

Locke recognizes that a shared language is as necessary for the maintenance of long-term social bonds as a common currency is for long-term economic relationships. Yet the use of both words and coins brings with it new difficulties. In order to avoid manipulation and misuse, Locke attempts to shift the vocabulary of political justification from the metaphysical to the practical and recoin a language of judgment that can serve as "the great instrument, and common tie of society" (E III.i.1). He guides his readers from otherworldly heights of abstract speculation to the terrestrial concerns of physical experience. Locke sets out to convince his readers that their own disciplined judgment, based on the probable deliverances of the natural world, is adequate for the weighty task of recognizing their moral and political duties. By employing their best judgment, they will be able to "see and feel" the difference between legitimate government that must be obeyed and tyranny that should be resisted (2T 131). Although much of the argument of the *Second Treatise* is articulated within the abstract categories of natural law, Locke is far more interested in preparing his readers to make practical judgments in the world than in bestowing upon them a comprehensive ontological description of the source of their obligations. As Kirstie McClure puts it, "In the *Treatise,* it is not simply reason, but more specifically, reasoned judgment ... that becomes the core of the mode of political understanding that underlies both the theoretical 'original' of political power and the grounds of political actions."[4]

Whether it is employed by individuals in the state of nature, the executive in established government, or the body of the people during a constitutional crisis, the faculty of judgment based on visible and tangible experience is the animating force of our political life. It is the continuing exercise of the judgment that makes consensual politics possible. Of course Locke realizes that judgment does not always yield perfect results. Indeed, it is the failure of private judgment in the state of nature that necessitates government in the first place, and it is the failure of executive judgment within the structures of established government that compels the people to rise up and topple their oppressive rulers. Yet Locke insists that the only viable solution to the epistemological difficulties that afflict our political lives is to appeal to a shared standard of judgment based on our immediate, physical interaction with the world around us. Although this judgment will not provide us with absolute certainty in particular political situations, it will "shine bright enough for all our purposes" (E I.i.5). The account that Locke presents in the *Second Treatise* is a defense of a particular type of judgment as the natural right of free and equal individuals and an explanation of how the prudent exercise of that judgment can stave off political conflict and sustain a regime of relative stability and peace. He seeks to convince his readers that they will be able to navigate the complexities of self-government by making reasoned judgments concerning their own welfare and the welfare of the public as a whole.

The State of Nature as a Realm of Virtue and Convenience

Locke begins his defense of political judgment by describing the natural condition of human beings. "To understand political power right, and derive it from its original, we must consider what state all men are naturally in" (2T 4). The state of nature is a "state of perfect freedom" and of

---

[4] McClure, *Judging Rights,* 121.

"equality, wherein all the power and jurisdiction is reciprocal." It is the
condition of "men living together according to reason, without a common superior on earth, with authority to judge between them" (2T 4, 19).
At the outset of his argument, Locke seems to present the state of nature
as an abstract construct, a set of relations between hypothetical persons
defined in a particular way. This has led many commentators to interpret Locke's account as a thoroughly abstract moral argument. These
interpretations have generally fallen into two categories. The traditional
secular, liberal version stresses the concepts of liberty, equality, and contract as political ideals that find expression in the concept of the state of
nature.[5] More recent interpretations have emphasized the abstract theological relations between creator and workmanship that seem to set the
terms of the state of nature.[6] In either case the state of nature is assumed
to be a vehicle or metaphor that Locke employs in order to express certain independently grounded commitments. Dunn sums up this approach
by declaring that Locke's state of nature represents "neither a piece of
philosophical anthropology nor a piece of conjectural history." Indeed, it
holds "no transitive empirical content whatsoever."[7]

Yet these interpretations overlook Locke's repeated insistence that the
state of nature is something that actually exists in the world. He does
not simply appeal to this concept as a heuristic device used to clarify an
ideological position. Locke's account is very different from Kant's appeal
to the social contract as an "ideal" of reason or John Rawls's description
of a hypothetical original condition. For Locke, the state of nature is the
condition that "all men are naturally in" (2T 15). In an effort to persuade
his readers that the state of nature is not simply a philosophical abstrac-
tion but an historical and natural reality, Locke presents evidence from
ancient and modern history, the Bible, and traveler's tales. He points to
the founding of Rome, Venice, and Sparta, to accounts of interactions
between individuals in the wilds of America and on uninhabited islands,
and to the observable relations between the rules of independent governments (2T 14, 102–4, 115). Yet the energy that Locke devotes to providing historical examples is baffling to those who interpret the state of
nature as solely a moral concept. How does this extensive research add

[5] Grant, *John Locke's Liberalism*; Louis Hartz, *The Liberal Tradition in America* (New York: Harcourt, Brace, 1955); Schouls, *The Imposition of Method*, 195–99; Schouls, *Reasoned Freedom*, 19–22; Martin Seliger, *The Liberal Politics of John Locke* (London: Allen and Unwin, 1968), 83–105; A. John Simmons, "Locke's State of Nature," *Political Theory* 17 (1989).

[6] Forster, *John Locke's Moral Consensus*, 246–58; Harris, *Mind of John Locke*; Tully, *A Discourse on Property*; Dunn, *Locke: Past Masters*, 47; Dunn, *Political Thought of Locke*, 97–103.

[7] Dunn, *Political Thought of Locke*, 103.

anything to his argument? Does it really matter whether he can produce any of these examples? Locke himself concedes that historical evidence cannot demonstrate moral truths. He writes, "At best an argument from what has been to what should of right be, has no great force" (2T 103; see also 2T 179, 184, 186).[8] If this is true, it seems odd that Locke would bother to present such a wealth of historical evidence in order to defend his account. John Simmons writes, "Even if Locke were able to show none of these things, his moral concept of the state of nature would in no way be suspect."[9] On this reading, Locke's persistent concern with the historical instantiations of the state of nature seems to be irrelevant to the logical and moral coherence of his argument.

This easy dismissal of the historical, or natural, aspect of Locke's state of nature relies on a tidy division between moral and political argument on the one hand and the evidence of the natural world on the other. It is true that Locke himself makes this distinction in the *Essay* when he distinguishes between the abstract certainty of demonstrative logic and the less than certain deliverances of the signs of nature. Yet as we have seen, this tidy division quickly becomes fuzzy.[10] His insistence on the historical reality of the state of nature is evidence that this division is not as absolute as he initially maintains. In fact, his attempt to derive moral direction from his account of the state of nature shows that there is an important continuity between the two realms.[11] Locke is at pains to show his readers that the state of nature is *natural*; that is, he insists that it reflects the natural world in a way that makes it more substantial and more real than alternative accounts.

Locke is not simply trying to explicate the political implications of a certain set of agreed-upon axioms. He is trying to replace Filmer's scriptural history of political power with one that is more factual, more readily

---

[8] In the *First Treatise* Locke shows a deep suspicion of a particular type of historical argument that points to the existence of a practice in order to prove its moral validity. He presents lists of atrocities, including reports of parents castrating, selling, and even eating their children, to point out that the world is full of clearly immoral practices (1T 57–59, 106). Yet it is important to note that Locke is not rejecting all arguments that employ evidence from history and nature. He continues to appeal to the "patterns" of history and the "course of nature" in order to show that particular judgments are in conformity with the divine design (2T 108, 77, 89; see also E II.xxvi.2).

[9] Simmons, "Locke's State of Nature," 461.

[10] For a discussion showing that this distinction is already blurred in the *Essay*, see chapter 4.

[11] For interpretations that take into account the historical reality of the state of nature, see Myers, *Our Only Star*; Robert Goldwin, "Locke's State of Nature in Political Society," *Western Political Quarterly* 29 (1976), 126–35; Richard Ashcraft, "Locke's State of Nature: Historical Fact or Moral Fiction?" *American Political Science Review* 62 (1968), 898–915; Ashcraft, *Revolutionary Politics*, 97–122; Jeremy Waldron, "John Locke: Social Contract versus Political Anthropology," *Review of Politics* 51, no. 3 (1989), 3–28.

observable, and more obviously compatible with the available evidence. He wants to present a more authoritative account of the initial conditions of creation. Words such as "original," "beginning," and "infancy" all signal Locke's effort to compose an alternative history, and his repeated appeals to traveler's accounts and historical evidence reveal his desire to bolster his narrative with hard facts. The problem with Filmer's principles, Locke tells us, is that they "could not be made to agree with the constitution and order which God had settled in the world, and therefore must needs often clash with common sense and experience" (1T 137; see also 124, 153). In order for his alternative account to be plausible to his readers, it must be more than a demonstration following from arbitrary and abstract definitions. It must be a description of natural, palpable conditions that readers could potentially experience. While Locke recognizes that historical evidence alone cannot establish his account with certainty, he is convinced that such evidence can supply good reasons to accept the state of nature as a more plausible description of our natural condition than alternative accounts. It is the historical evidence, Locke writes, that reveals "how *probable* it is, that people ... are naturally free, and by their own consent ... submitted to the government" (2T 112; emphasis mine).[12]

Seen in this light, the state of nature takes on a very different character. It is not simply an abstract set of relations between juridically free persons, but an actual, persisting condition that lies just beyond the artificial barriers of government and civil society. Locke invites his readers to decide for themselves whether Filmer's biblical history is more or less accurate than his own account. He encourages his readers to look at the evidence of the external world and form their own judgments. The *Second Treatise*, despite its seemingly abstract character, confronts the problem of moral understanding from a decidedly practical standpoint. Locke wants to provide a solution to the problem of political authority that will resonate with the visceral experience of his readers.

The first thing that Locke tells us about the state of nature is that it is a condition in which all of the inhabitants are perfectly free and equal. All persons have an equal right to make choices about how they will conduct themselves "without asking leave, or depending on the will of any other man" (2T 4; see also 2T 7). We have the liberty to act and to acquire things that are conducive to our comfort and happiness without being impeded by another. In the *Essay* Locke defines freedom as our ability "to

---

[12] According to Ashcraft, "Locke's political thought is thus structured by a set of what *we* would regard as metapolitical beliefs and what *he* regarded as a number of prepolitical empirical observations derived from his experience or from the testimony of others." Ashcraft, *Revolutionary Politics*, 56.

act, or not to act, according as we shall choose, or will" (E II.xxi.27). In the state of nature, we find ourselves with an equal right to act without obstruction; we have a right to pursue our own convenience.

Yet Locke is quick to point out that this condition is also bounded by law. Although the state of nature is a state of freedom, it is not a state of license or boundless action (2T 6). It is constrained by the law of nature that "obliges every one" and "willeth the peace and preservation" of the species as a whole (2T 6, 7). This is not simply a claim about an abstract relation; Locke thinks that the obligatory force of natural law can be recognized and experienced in nature. He is also careful to point out that this law should not be seen as a curb on or impediment to the freedom of the individual, but as the condition of its possibility. It is a constitutive part of free activity. We are free, Locke teaches, only insofar as we recognize and conform our actions to the dictates of the natural law. This law "is not so much the limitation as the direction of a free and intelligent agent to his proper Interest, and prescribes no farther than is for the general good" (2T 57).[13] Thus we have an equal right or liberty to act in accordance with our private judgment of convenience, yet we also are equally obliged to conform our actions to the laws of nature or virtue. Locke initially presents the state of nature as one in which convenience and virtue go hand in hand. The natural condition of human beings is one that is governed by the laws and purposes of a morally structured cosmos. But the limits these laws set do not infringe upon the freedom and convenience of the individual. On the contrary, they make that freedom possible.

Yet here we face a contentious aspect of Locke's thought once again: how are inhabitants of the state of nature supposed to acquire knowledge of the injunctions of the law of nature? How are they supposed to know how they should constrain their actions? And how can they be assured that the right of convenience ultimately conforms to the law of virtue? At times Locke seems to suggest that the process of recognizing these moral rules is unproblematic. He even refers to "the great law of nature" at one point as embedded in the mind of each human being, "so plain was it writ in the hearts of all mankind" (2T 11). Yet we have good reason to view this formulation with skepticism. First, moralists and theologians in Locke's day often spoke of moral law as "writ in the hearts of all mankind." This commonplace phrase can be traced to a passage that would have been familiar to all of Locke's readers, found in Paul's letter to the Romans: "For when the Gentiles, which have not the law, do by nature the things contained in the law, these having not the law, are a law unto

---

[13] For a discussion of similar notions of freedom and self-restraint in the *Essay*, see chapter 4.

themselves: Which show the work of law written in their hearts."[14] While
many Thomist natural law thinkers such as Locke's "judicious Hooker"
used this phrase, other thinkers such as Pierre Gassendi (who shared
with Locke both empiricist reservations about Descartes and a commitment to a type of Christian Epicureanism) also spoke of moral law as
being "imprinted in the hearts of men."[15] Locke's fellow empirists such as
Gassendi certainly did not believe that human beings have innate moral
knowledge of the law of nature. The fact that they nonetheless fell back
on this stock phrase should lead us to be wary of reading too much into
Locke's use of it. More importantly, Locke himself explicitly and repeatedly denounced the claim that moral laws lie "open as natural characters
ingraven on the mind" (E I.iii.1). Indeed the entire first book of the *Essay*
is devoted to discrediting just this type of argument. Later in the *Second
Treatise*, Locke explicitly contradicts the claim that the moral law is "writ
in the hearts" by asserting that "the law of nature [is] unwritten" and is
"nowhere . . . found in the minds of men" (2T 136).

If we look carefully at the way Locke appeals to natural law throughout the *Second Treatise* it becomes evident that it is neither as immediately nor as effortlessly accessible as he first implies. In a passage immediately following the claim that the law of nature is "writ in the hearts
of all mankind," we find Locke adding the qualifier that the law is plain
to those who study it (2T 12). This law is only accessible to those "who
will but consult it" (2T 6). It turns out that the law of nature is not something already present in our hearts or minds, but something external to
us—and something that we often overlook. In a later passage, he goes so
far as to assert that the "greater part" of mankind is "ignorant for want
of study of it" (2T 123, 124).[16] Thus Locke is faced with a difficulty.
He requires natural law as something that provides boundaries for the
rights of individuals in the state of nature, yet he concedes that this law is
not immediately recognized as such. The law of nature seems to be both
present and absent in his account. This leads him to assert in the same
paragraph that the law of nature is "plain and intelligible to all rational
creatures" and also that the state of nature "wants an established, settled,
standard of right and wrong" (2T 124).

[14] Romans 2:14–15. See also Jeremiah 31:33.
[15] Pierre Gassendi, "The Discourses of Happiness, Virtue, and Liberty," in *Moral Philosophy from Montaigne to Kant*, ed. J. B. Schneewind (New York: Cambridge University Press,
1990), 366.
[16] In other texts Locke concedes that there are whole nations that live in ignorance of
natural law (LN 111; E I.iii.9), which he describes as "hidden and unperceived" (LN 111;
E I.iii.17, II.28.11). For this reason he can argue in *The Reasonableness of Christianity* that
ancient philosophers who devoted their lives to the task failed to discover the rule in its
entirety (RC 143, 149).

One way to explain, albeit not to solve, this difficulty is to point out how Locke equates natural law with the divine design of creation. The overarching purposes of the world are assumed to shape the very structure of our natural lives, yet they lie outside the reach of human comprehension. The glimpses that we do receive, however, are enough to guide our conduct in the world. Although he never completely rejects the possibility that both the content and the obligation of natural law could be demonstrated, Locke seems unworried about providing such a demonstration. Instead he slowly shifts his attention to the way in which our experience of the probable signs of nature reinforces a conviction that there is a moral structure to the world. He seems to assume that certain aspects of the law—such as our obligation to preserve ourselves (and others if doing so does not conflict with our own preservation)—simply become clear to us in the ordinary course of our lives. Locke speaks of a law of nature that is revealed in the natural world. These natural revelations must be deciphered if they are to provide adequate indication of what the law requires. In this way the law of nature is present to us in the same way that a text is. It is the moral message of the book of nature. This message is accessible to us, but does not simply reveal its own meaning. It takes effort and study to tease out all of the implications of the law of nature.

Yet since Locke states that an understanding of this law is a necessary precursor to the proper exercise of right, it is crucial that he show how cognizance of this law actually defines the bounds of natural liberty. It is not enough to point to the possibility of deciphering this law; he must show how individuals in the state of nature actually come to recognize the law and enforce it. This is one of the purposes of his account of the natural condition. In this state, he argues, the power to interpret and execute the law of nature is distributed equally among individuals. Since there is no earthly authority or common judge in the state of nature, there is neither a single authoritative interpretation of the law nor a centralized power to enforce that interpretation. The right and responsibility of interpretation and enforcement, what Locke calls the "executive power," falls on each individual equally. Thus Locke's state of nature is characterized not only by the natural drive to provide for one's own needs, but also by a capacity of judgment. And this capacity is distributed equally to everyone. It is significant that the executive power is not simply a recapitulation of the self-defense included in the general right to preserve oneself. The executive power is a right to interpret the law of nature and punish others for breaches of the law, even when one is not a victim. In the Locke's state of nature, each human agent judges and is judged by everyone else. He concedes that some will think that this is a "very strange doctrine," yet insists that it best reflects the exercise of power and

authority that we would experience in the world without earthly authority (2T 11).

Locke also tells us that this original condition of epistemic equality
is not, at least not initially, a state of conflict or confusion. In fact, he
describes it as a condition of fundamental harmony and agreement. The
natural state of the Lockean agent is one of confident assurance and
moral clarity. This is because there is an obvious and observable agreement between one's interests and one's duties. Actions emerging from an
individual determination of convenience reflect and reinforce the objective structure of law and right that demarcates properly human activities within God's design. In this initial state, before individuals formed
extended associations with one another or agreed upon artificial conventions of exchange, "right and conveniency went together," and an
act that was "dishonest" was also "useless" (2T 51). To act out of one's
own self-interest was to align one's conduct with the moral structure
of the natural world and thus secure and promote the natural law. This
is possible, Locke tells us in the *Essay*, because God "joined virtue and
public happiness together; and made the practice thereof, necessary to
the preservation of society and visibly beneficial to all" (E I.iii.6). This is
not surprising, given Locke's view of God as promulgating moral law in
order to promote this-worldly happiness.[17] Locke is at pains to show that
the initial state of nature is one in which the judgment of convenience or
happiness does not conflict with the moral law or the law of virtue.

The original complementarity of virtue and convenience is best illus-
trated by Locke's account of labor and property. In order to explain how
the existence of private right could have emerged from an original condition of common ownership, Locke introduces a theory of rightful acquisition based on individual exertion. He frames this discussion within the
very tangible and concrete experiences of self and labor. We find ourselves in such a condition, Locke argues, that our preservation requires
labor and the improvement of our surroundings. Since "every man has
a property in his own person," it is reasonable to allow that "the labour
of his body and the works of his hands ... are properly his" (2T 27).[18]
The creation of private property out of what was originally granted for
all in common is justifiable for reasons both of right and law, and of convenience and virtue. It is the right of the individual laborer to claim possession of what he adds his labor to, and it is certainly in his individual
interest to do so. Yet it is also consistent with the law of nature, insofar

---

[17] For a discussion of Locke's God, see chapter 5.

[18] For a more extensive discussion of Locke's account of property, see Alan Ryan, "Self-
Ownership, Autonomy, and Property Rights," *Social Philosophy and Policy* 11 (1994),
241–58; Simmons, *Lockean Theory of Rights*, chap. 5; Tully, *A Discourse on Property*.

as it requires the preservation of self and others, because private acquisition brings about general benefits. This is why Locke's somewhat optimistic predictions concerning the increased yield of cultivated land are important to his argument (2T 37). Privately owned farms in Devonshire, Locke implies, further God's purposes better than the wilds of America. For this reason we have both a right and a duty to enclose, improve, and cultivate land.

Yet Locke also claims that there are limits to this process of acquisition: "The same law of nature, that does by this means, give us this property, does also bound that property too" (2T 31). Here we see one of the crucial differences between Locke's view of property rights and the views of some of his most enthusiastic modern proponents. Locke insists that individuals do not have a right to use and abuse their property at will. Property is always held conditionally; individuals who acquire property through labor have a right to that property only insofar as they conform to the moral strictures of the law of nature. By acquiring property we extend our ownership beyond ourselves, but we also extend our responsibilities. These responsibilities, which Locke refers to as limitations or provisos, are easy to recognize and to fulfill because they are reinforced by the tangible standards of need and use. The first is that individuals should extract from the commons no more than they can use, since "nothing was made by God for man to spoil or destroy" (2T 31). The second proviso is that any one who acquires property by mixing labor with the natural world, must leave "enough and as good for others" (2T 27, 30, 36). Given the first proviso and the assumption of plenty that seems to underscore Locke's discussion at this point, an individual's acquisition of property simply does not infringe on another's ability to do the same. This type of limited acquisition that leaves enough and as good for others is "as good as taking nothing at all" (2T 33). Although Locke states that those who break these provisos depart from the law of nature and the law of reason and deserve punishment, it is difficult to imagine why anyone would want to transgress these provisos, since they are not only moral injunctions, but also rules of material convenience (2T 31).

Thus in Locke's account of property individuals initially have no difficulty recognizing the boundaries of natural right and natural law. Property acquisition does not harm others; it maintains a basic fairness between individuals; and it improves the lot of everyone. In this way the natural boundaries of property rights reflect a happy agreement between judgments of convenience and laws of virtue. With "property so established" there is "little room for quarrels or contentions" (2T 31). Individuals make determinations according to their own judgment of need, and those judgments ultimately lead to the benefit of every other individual. Thus there is "no reason for quarreling," "nor any doubt" as to the extent of a person's property, "no temptation" to accumulate beyond what is necessary for one's own use, "no room for controversy . . . nor for encroachment of the right of others" (2T 51). There is something obvious and transparent in human action here. The justice of one's conduct is "easily seen" by everyone. Under these conditions our judgment clearly conforms to the overarching moral structure of creation.

This account of the initial agreement of virtue and convenience in the state of nature need not require the utopian assumption that all will conduct themselves properly. Locke can concede that human freedom necessarily entails a potential for transgression without undercutting his account. Yet in this "simple poor way of living," transgressors can be recognized easily and punishments can be easily proportioned to the crime (2T 107). If someone steals a week's provisions, it is easy to remedy the situation by restoring the same amount to the victim. In this initial state of nature, goods have "an intrinsic value" that "depends only on their usefulness to the life of man" (2T 37). This value of an apple can be seen and felt by everyone and restitution can easily be made. By exercising their judgment, individuals are generally able to discern the outlines of right and propriety and correct any violations that might arise.

It would seem that such a collection of individuals, living according to their own private judgments, would indeed be able to achieve a relatively peaceful coexistence. The clarity and immediacy that Locke invests in human judgment lends plausibility to his characterization of the state of nature as one of "peace, good will, mutual assistance, and preservation" (2T 19). In the *Third Letter Concerning Toleration*, Locke develops this picture of the initial state of nature as a type of pastoral Eden in which "the rivers and woods afforded the spontaneous provisions of life" and no one had "enlarged desires after riches or power." Such a community could exist "without any municipal laws, judges, or any person with supremacy established amongst them." This is because they could settle all their private differences, if any arose, by the extemporary determination of their neighbors, or of arbiters chosen by the parties."[19] Here Locke links the experiential judgment of need and use with the rather complex matters of appropriation and punishment. In the natural condition, stripped of the artificial structures of government and the various conventions of society, convenience conforms to virtue, and the democratically distributed faculty of judgment ensures communal stability.

This account of the state of nature as a realm of moral clarity is important for Locke's larger project of authorizing judgment because it intro-

---

[19] John Locke, *The Third Letter Concerning Toleration*, in Locke, *Works of John Locke*, 6:225.

duces a type of natural reasoning based on visceral, tangible, and concrete experience in the natural world. The success of this judgment in recognizing and punishing transgressors in the state of nature bolsters Locke's claim that this democratically distributed faculty is also sufficient to discern the exercise of unlawful power in the civil condition. By presenting the state of nature as one in which virtue and convenience are initially in agreement, Locke can reassure his readers that an appeal to the judgment of the people will not necessarily entail the anarchic assertion of subjective will. In fact, the possibility of recovering order will rest on the willingness of individuals to reclaim the type of judgment that is naturally possessed in the original state. The appeal to judgment, then, represents a return to a lost orderliness and clarity, a condition Locke insists is natural to human beings.

From Moral Clarity to Epistemological Confusion

Given Locke's initial account of the state of nature as a realm of expansive freedom in which individuals live together in relative harmony, it is difficult to imagine why anyone would voluntarily leave such a condition and accept the inevitable constraints of civil society. The inconveniences that Locke mentions seem almost trivial compared with the obvious benefits that individuals enjoy. Yet we will see that these inconveniences turn out to be far more substantial than they first appear.[20]

It is significant that Locke does not trace the inconveniences of the state of nature to a constant threat of violence and misery or the inherent depravity of human beings. His account of the potential difficulties of the natural condition cannot be equated with either a Hobbesian state of war or a Calvinist fall of man. Although Locke often links conflict with bias and passion, he traces the primary cause of disruption in the state of nature to an epistemological uncertainty that unsettles the regular exercise of executive power. Men in the state of nature simply fail to make proper judgments concerning transgressions of the law of nature (2T 4, 13, 90, 127, 136). The impetus for entering into civil society is the desire "to avoid, and remedy those inconveniences of the state of nature,

---

[20] It should be noted that the term "inconvenience" had a very different connation in seventeenth-century England. According to the *Oxford English Dictionary*, an inconvenience was understood to be a condition in which there was "want of agreement; incongruity, disagreement; inconsistency with reason or rule." When Locke talks of the inconveniences of the state of nature, he is invoking this aspect of the word's meaning in order to draw attention to the epistemological confusion or incongruity that unsettles individual judgment and pushes men into society.

which necessarily follow from every man's being a judge in his own case" (2T 90). The difficulties of judgment transform the state of "peace, good will, mutual assistance and preservation" into an "ill condition" rife with "confusion and disorder" (2T 19, 127, 13).

The same condition that left "no doubt of right, no room for quarrel" (2T 39) is now described as one of conflict and disagreement. The law of nature, to which individual judgments and actions naturally conformed, becomes a contested moral standard that seems to do more to fuel disagreement than establish harmony. Locke writes that "the law of nature being unwritten, and so no where to be found in the minds of men, . . . serves not, as it ought to determine the rights, and fence the proprieties of those that live under it" (2T 136). The clear delineation of right and property suddenly becomes problematic. The happy agreement between the private judgment of convenience and the natural law gives way to a general inability to recognize and apply the law with sufficient clarity.

What happened? What could possibly have clouded natural judgment to such an extent that it could no longer serve as the facilitator of peaceful coexistence? For Locke the great confusion begins with the invention of money (2T 36). The most important and unsettling consequence of the introduction of a durable currency is not economic expansion or distributive inequality but epistemological confusion. Although the establishment of money does provide a shared medium through which exchanges can take place, it also distances individuals from the actual act of acquiring and producing property. Before money, judgments based on need and use were sufficient to conduct one's life in accordance with natural law. With the introduction of money, this direct experiential understanding is obscured. And this change brings about a crisis of probable judgment. Linking the emergence of conflict and disagreement in the state of nature with the introduction of money, Locke describes a condition with which his readers would have been very familiar. As Joyce Appleby notes, early economic relationships in England were intimately connected "to a social context where duties and rights were closely tied to the needs of security and survival. As long as the principal elements in the economic structure remained visible and tangible, the understanding of the system was the possession of the whole society."[21] Yet with the extensive growth of the economy and the increased importance of currency in the sixteenth and seventeenth centuries, the visible and tangible link to local markets and the visceral experience of dearth and abundance became increasingly

---

[21] Joyce Oldham Appleby, *Economic Thought and Ideology in Seventeenth-Century England* (Princeton: Princeton University Press, 1978), 25.

remote. The moral context of production and consumption was no longer immediately recognizable. Locke's description of the introduction of
money is aimed at capturing a change that his readers were experiencing
in their own lives.

Of course Locke also recognized that widespread acceptance, or "tacit
consent," of money brought about certain benefits. He knew that it was
vital for trade and that trade was crucial for national prosperity. The
combination of agriculture and money brought benefits to everyone in
society. The poorest in a society with currency are richer than the most
fortunate under primitive preagricultural conditions. Locke contrasted
the "needy and wretched" natives of North America with the laborers
of modern societies: "a king of a large and fruitful territory there feeds,
lodges, and is clad worse than a day labourer in *England*" (2T 41). Yet
in spite of this, Locke was far less sanguine about these improvements
than the confident champions of progress who would come after him. For
Locke every step forward involved loss. Increased production, money,
and technological advancement all brought blessings, but those blessings
were not without a cost. At several points in the *Second Treatise*, Locke
expresses nostalgia for a "golden age" before "vain ambition" and the
"desire of having more than men needed" (2T 111, 37). This earlier era
of moral clarity was a "poor but virtuous age" (2T 110). With the various
advances inaugurated by the invention of money, the simple virtue of that
age was eclipsed by an age of moral confusion.

Although his skill as an economic theorist is debatable, Locke's abiding
interest in the meaning and function of currency is generally recognized.
He was not only interested in understanding how money facilitates trade,
but he was also deeply concerned with the influence money could have
on the moral basis of human action.[22] The difficulty with money stems
from the fact that it is the product of imagination, the result of "fancy or
agreement . . . more than real use, and the necessary support of life" (2T
46). Money has no direct relationship to the visible and tangible needs
of human beings. "For as to money, and such riches and treasure," Locke
writes, "these are none of nature's goods, they have but a phantastical
imaginary value" (2T 184). It breeds a new type of greed that cannot be
confined by the concrete limitations of the natural world. In an effort
to forestall the development of this artificial delight in riches and finery,
Locke advises parents in *Some Thoughts Concerning Education* to avoid
rewarding a child's behavior with money (STCE 52, 151). Such actions
would only encourage "covetousness, and the desire of having in our
possession, and under our dominion, more than we have need of" (STCE

---

[22] See ibid., chap. 8, as well as Kelly's introduction to Locke, *Locke on Money*.

110; see also 103, 105). Those who are enthralled by the imaginary value of money are unable to make clear judgments based on the probable signs of nature:

> Let never so much probability hang on one side of a covetous man's reasoning, and money on the other; and it is easy to foresee which will out-weigh. Earthly minds, like mud walls, resist the strongest batteries: and though, perhaps, sometimes the force of a clear argument may make some impression, yet they nevertheless stand firm, keep out the enemy truth, that would captivate or disturb them. (E IV.xx.12)

Before the invention of money, the basis of property rights and the limits of the provisos were relatively easy to discern. Human agents in the state of nature could observe their rights and the rights of others and arrive at a proper judgment concerning the boundaries of propriety. Yet the invention of money brings about ambiguity and uncertainty. The durability of currency facilitates exchange and creates the possibility of possessing more than one needs, and this opens the door for temptation and covetousness. Yet it also obscures the original tangibility of the natural provisos, such as the spoilage limitation. When an individual is no longer limited by his immediate needs, he can begin to entertain less tangible desires and indulge in less publicly visible excesses. The obvious and recognizable correspondence between what one does and what one has is concealed. The invention of money removes the laborer from a direct relationship to and responsibility for the product of his or her exertions. Under these conditions it becomes increasingly difficult to see who is infringing on whom when land is enclosed and cultivated or resources are hoarded in times of need.

Yet even if transgressions of the natural law can somehow still be discerned after the invention of money, the task of punishment becomes increasingly complicated. Money complicates the previously intrinsic value of goods based on need and use, and makes it more difficult for individuals to determine proportional remedies for injuries incurred. In the original condition, the value of an object has a clear and observable connection to its usefulness. Yet with money, the value of an object can fluctuate over time. In one of his essays on currency reform, entitled "Some Considerations on Lower Interest," Locke writes, "It comes to pass that there is no manner of settled proportion between the value of an ounce of silver, and any other commodity: For either varying its quantity in that country, or the commodity changing its quantity in proportion to its vent [the proportion of buyers to sellers], their respective values change, i.e. less of one will barter for more of the other" (SCM 255). By obscuring "the intrinsic value of things" (2T 31), money makes it more difficult to make probable judgments concerning property and right. It unsettles the fixed or stable measure by which direct personal injuries such as theft might be equitably redressed without a stable authority.[23]

The introduction of money enables an expanding economy and a growing population that in turn leads to a rapid increase in the appropriation of land. The possibility of scarcity, which is noticeably absent from Locke's earlier discussion, suddenly becomes a problem. Were it not for the fanciful attachment to money and the "hopes of commerce," Locke writes, vast quantities of land "would not be worth enclosing." In the initial condition before money, "whatever was more than would supply the conveniences of life" would be returned "to the wild common of nature" (2T 48; see also 108). With the invention of money, however, the natural visceral measure of sufficiency is dissolved. The simple judgments that individuals could make in the initial stage are suddenly far more difficult: What if two neighbors both want to enclose the last remaining section of the commons adjacent to their properties? What if the first to do so deprives the other of sufficient property for subsistence? What type of restitution can be made? By whom and on what grounds should such judgments be determined?

Whatever answers we might offer to these difficult questions, one thing is clear. The invention of money creates conditions that disrupt the natural agreement of virtue and convenience. Without settled criteria for natural judgment, Lockean agents no longer inhabit a transparent world of clear moral boundaries. Instead they find themselves in a murky realm of controversy and uncertainty. Without a shared standard to determine the boundaries of property, everyone is "constantly exposed to the invasion of others" (2T 123). The difficulty is not simply one of defending the property of the "industrious and rational" from the covetous incursions of the "quarrelsome and contentious." Nor is it one of maintaining inequalities of possession that might result from varied rates of property acquisition. The primary threat to the peaceful coexistence of human agents in the state of nature is the epistemological confusion concerning the proper determination of natural rights and the appropriate application of natural law.

As unsettled as this condition is, it is still distinct from the state of war for Locke. In contrast to the state of nature, the state of war is characterized by the presence of intent to use "force without right" against another (2T 192). The difficulties involved in determining right need not necessarily lead to conditions in which someone declares "by word or action, not a passionate and hasty, but a sedate settled design, upon another

[23] In *Some Considerations,* Locke goes so far as to assert that in commercial society fueled by money, "there is no such intrinsic natural settled value in any thing." Locke, *Locke on Money,* 1:258.

man's life" (2T 16). Although the state of nature, even after the invention of money, is not necessarily a state of war, the dissolution of the link between virtue and convenience generates a much greater possibility that the types of transgressions that create a state of war will occur.

Under conditions of epistemic confusion, it becomes extremely difficult to recognize, define, or provide equitable punishment. Individual judgments of private convenience no longer bear a recognizable relationship with the convenience of the whole. Instead, they begin to take on the unmistakable odor of partiality. Locke recognizes that without a clear guide in meting out justice, "self-love will make men partial to themselves and their friends," while "ill nature, passion, and revenge will carry them too far in punishing others" (2T 13). They will act "with too much heat in their own cases," even as "negligence and unconcernedness will make them too remiss in other men's" (2T 125). The disordering of the criteria of natural judgment distances Lockean agents from the immediate experience of God's design and places them instead amidst a moral chaos of their own making.

Entrusting Judgment to a Shared Authority

Faced with the uncertainty brought about by the invention of money, Lockean agents join together in an effort to "avoid, and remedy the inconveniences of the state of nature, which necessarily follow from every man's being judge in his own case" (2T 90). They temporarily cede their natural right of judgment to a common authority in the hopes that this new authority will be able to interpret and enforce the natural law in a way that is both more public and more effective. In order for this condition to be an improvement over the state of nature, the common judge must be capable of providing a clearer and more obvious resolution to men's disputes than men themselves could arrive at on their own behalf. This rules out the institution of absolute monarchy, since it would not solve the problems of private judgment, but only exacerbate them. "If government is to be the remedy of those evils, which necessarily follow from men being judge in their own cases," Locke writes, "I desire to know what kind of government that is, and how much better it is than the state of nature, where one man commanding a multitude, has the liberty to be judge in his own case (2T 13). The absolute monarch is simply the institutionalization of the problem of private judgment that plagues the state of nature. The establishment of such a government cannot be seen as an improvement over the state of nature. In fact, the establishment of an absolute monarch does not constitute a government at all, but rather the entrenchment of the inconveniences of the natural condition.

The individual who accepts the rule of an absolute monarch is not a subject, but a slave (2T 91).

Locke tells us that the move out of the state of nature takes place when individuals transfer their right to judge and enforce the law of nature to a common authority. This transfer takes place in two stages. The first stage results from a unanimous decision to hand over the executive power of judging and enforcing the natural law to a common authority. This transfer establishes civil society, also called the body politic. The resulting entity, the "people," is thus prior to the government, and the government is answerable to it.[24] The second stage is accomplished by majority rule and sets up particular governmental institutions. It is important to note that, with the exception of absolute monarchy, Locke does not stipulate what type of government a people must choose. He leaves this determination to the judgment of the people taking into consideration their particular circumstances (2T 106, 107, 110–11). Once the majority chooses a government, individuals are obliged to suppress their own private judgments in cases of public controversy. The "known indifferent judge" that the commonwealth supplies is made possible by the ability of Lockean agents to relinquish their own judgment in matters in which an umpire government can more appropriately arbitrate disagreements.

Toward the end of the *Second Treatise*, Locke describes this process as a type of "trust" between the king and the people (2T 136, 139, 142, 167, 171).[25] At times this trust is discussed in a general way as a pattern of mutual expectations that must be maintained to sustain political society. Locke writes that "those, who liked one another so well as to join into society, cannot but be supposed to have some acquaintance and friendship together, and some trust in one another" (2T 107). Here we see that the original contract for Locke is not based exclusively on a series of individual promises, but on a general attitude of willing cooperation and trust. At other times Locke writes of this trust in a more explicitly legal manner, as a "fiduciary trust" between the king and the people (2T 156, 149). According to this model, the government is seen as a deputy that has been entrusted with powers of interpretation and application of the natural law. The people depute their right and obligation to judge

[24] Here Locke is implicitly rejecting the Hobbesian one-stage compact in which there is no body of the people independent of the sovereign.

[25] For various interpretations of the place of "trust" in Locke's theory see Govert den Hartogh, "Made by Contrivance and the Consent of Men: Abstract Principle and Historical Fact in Locke's Political Philosophy," *Interpretation* 17 (Winter 1989–90), 193–221; Joshua Foa Dienstag, *"Dancing in Chains": Narrative and Memory in Political Theory* (Stanford: Stanford University Press, 1997), 71; John Dunn, "'Trust' in the Politics of John Locke," in *Rethinking Modern Political Theory: Essays 1979–83* (Cambridge: Cambridge University Press, 1985).

individual cases concerning the boundaries of propriety to the government, and thus to the executive insofar as the executive requires a certain degree of discretion in order to fulfill its appointed task. In contrast to Filmer, the executive is a trustee of political power and not its owner. The people retain the right to reclaim it when the government itself becomes a threat to the property that it holds in trust.[26]

According to Laslett, "It is very difficult to make sense of what he says if you try to interpret the actions of people on breach of trust as those of defrauded beneficiaries under a formal trust."[27] Yet if we understand the right to judge for the public good as that which is placed in the trustee's hands, then the legalistic metaphor of fiduciary trust seems perfectly appropriate.[28] In fact, Locke's description of the relationship between people and government is more correctly thought of as a trust than a contract. In a contract the performance of one party binds the other, and any disagreements require independent arbitration. With a trust the original holder of goods confers a certain degree of power on a trustee or agent. The people, as the beneficiaries of the trust, retain ownership of a right to judge whether that trust is being properly carried out even though they believe that under normal conditions the trustee can more effectively and more beneficially make use of that power.

This effective management of the right of judgment rests on a government's ability to provide a trustworthy and steady standard of propriety in matters of public controversy. This is accomplished in part by the establishment of standing laws instead of temporary, arbitrary decrees. Laws can provide an important, public standard of justice when they are "settled, standing rules, indifferent, and the same to all parties" (2T 87). These laws are "not to be varied in particular cases, but to have one rule for rich and poor, for the favourite at court, and the country man at plough" (2T 142). Settled, standing rules are so important to Locke because they make the boundaries of right more visible and provide guidelines for proper punishment. Established, written laws can mitigate the uncertainty that is so unsettling to individuals in the state of nature. "For the law of nature being unwritten, and so no where to be found but

[26] John Dunn questions this legalistic interpretation as an imposition of an external category onto Locke's argument. He writes that "the metaphor of legal trust . . . was not original to him; and it carries little or no distinctive weight in his argument." Dunn, "Trust," 296. It is certainly true that this metaphor was in widespread use, especially during the trial and execution of Charles I, as Gough has shown. Gough, *John Locke's Political Philosophy*, chap. 7. Yet this historical evidence should actually strengthen the argument that legal language of fiduciary trust would resonate with Locke's audience.

[27] Locke, *Two Treatises of Government*, 130.

[28] For an innovative interpretation of the trust that is at stake here as one of common memory or history, see Dienstag, *Dancing in Chains*, 72.

in the minds of men," Locke writes, "they who through passion or interest shall miscite, or misapply it, cannot so easily be convinced of their
mistake where there is no established judge." For this reason "it serves
not, as it ought, to determine the rights, and fence the properties of those
that live under it." Given the practical difficulty of living according to
an unwritten law of nature, human beings enter society and establish
"standing Rules to bound it, by which every one may know what is his"
(2T 136). Thus the legislative, as well as the executive, serve to articulate
the natural law in a way that is more visible and effective by establishing
and ruling according to standing laws.

In addition to the existence of standing laws, Locke insists that an
avenue for appeal must be open to subjects to question decisions made
by the government and even challenge governmental actions themselves.
This requires that the executive be answerable to the law and that the
executive and the legislative be kept separate (2T 91, 205–7). In addition, the laws that apply to subjects should apply equally to rulers. The
possibility of a common judge—and thus the possibility of avoiding the
confusions of the state of nature—requires the establishment of the rule
of law (2T 93–94, 202).

Yet the civil government that Locke envisions as the remedy to the
inconveniences of the state of nature is not merely an arbiter of controversy. Nor is it simply a guarantor of a relatively stable realm in which parties and private interests can continue to do battle. Locke's understanding
of civil government is not laissez-faire. Instead he implies that the state
has a positive role to play in articulating public purposes, establishing
authoritative conventions, and making legislative judgments about what
policies best promote the interests of the public. The appropriate tasks of
government for Locke include those things that provide not only for the
preservation, but also for the prosperity of the commonwealth.[29]

Yet for Locke the interests of the public are limited to those things
that can be visibly or tangibly recognized as beneficial. Although he does
not explicitly discuss toleration in the *Second Treatise*, it is easy to see
how his argument in the *Letter Concerning Toleration* complements the
understanding of the proper responsibilities of government presented
here. He distinguishes between the finite, temporal, and public concerns
of this life and the infinite, eternal, and private concerns of the next.
The proper task of political power is to preserve "life, liberty, health,
and indolency of body" as well as material possessions (LCT 26). This
is best accomplished through the "impartial execution of equal laws" in

---

[29] For Locke's views on monetary and economic policy, see Locke, *Locke on Money*. For a
discussion of Locke's view of the responsibilities of government to promote the public good,
see Tully, *A Discourse on Property*.

order to secure property and punish lawbreakers. "All civil power, right, and dominion," he writes, "is bounded and confined to the only care of promoting these things: . . . it neither can nor ought in any manner to be extended to the salvation of souls" (LCT 26).[30]

The claim that civil authorities have no right to dictate religious beliefs or practices rests on two important limitations of the type of power that they exercise. First, the distinctive powers that are granted civil government "to give laws, receive obedience, and compel with the sword" mitigate the inconveniences of the state of nature, yet are neither appropriate nor effective in engendering a saving faith. Locke asserts that the performance of one's duties to God must carry an inward persuasion of conscience that can only be achieved through admonition and argument. "Penalties in this case are absolutely impertinent, because they are not proper to convince the mind. . . . It is only light and evidence that can change men's opinions." Genuine faith "can in no manner precede from corporal sufferings or any other penalties" (LCT 27).[31] Yet even if it were possible to compel belief, it would still be inappropriate. This is because rulers of commonwealths are not granted any special access to divine truths. Locke points out that while there is only one way to heaven, there are many princes with very different religious commitments. If salvation of souls were the concern of magistrates, one's ultimate fate would be bound up with whatever religion "either ignorance, ambition or superstition had chanced to establish" in one's country of birth. This is simply absurd, Locke argues, for it "ill suits the notion of a deity" that people "would owe their eternal happiness or misery to the place of their nativity" (LCT 28). While government created by the people is able to clarify some of the uncertainties of the state of nature, it is not able to supply a guaranteed passage to heaven for its subjects. Locke writes, "Neither

---

[30] As Eldon Eisennach puts it, the move out of the state of nature and into civil society is a process of rule learning through natural consequences. Eisennach, *Two Worlds of Liberalism* (Chicago: University of Chicago Press, 1992), 95.

[31] Jeremy Waldron, echoing Locke's tireless adversary Jonas Proast, has made the case that this argument in itself is not a convincing defense of toleration, since it is possible to coerce people into situations in which they can be persuaded through evidence and admonition into accepting a particular creed. This objection is not as fatal to Locke's project as Waldron supposes, however, since Locke bases his defense of toleration on a series of arguments instead of a single claim. One of the most important arguments, I would argue, is the claim that the proper scope of political judgment is limited to the visible, terrestrial matters of preservation and prosperity. Jonas Proast, *The Argument of the Letter Concerning Toleration Briefly Consider'd and Answered* (Oxford, 1690); Jeremy Waldron, "Locke: Toleration," in Mendus, *Justifying Toleration*. For a thorough commentary on Locke's several argumentative strains in the *Letter*, see Richard Vernon, *The Career of Toleration: John Locke, Jonas Proast and After* (Montreal: McGill-Queen's University Press, 1997); as well as Tarcov, "Foundations of Toleration."

the care of the commonwealth, nor the right enacting of laws does discover the way that leads to heaven more certainly to the magistrate, than
every private man's search and study discovers it unto himself" (LCT 36).
While princes might have more political power, they do not have special
insight into religious truth: "Neither the right, nor the art of ruling, does
necessarily carry with it the certain knowledge of other things, and least
of all of the true religion (LCT 36).[32] Since government is entrusted only
with performing those tasks that are conducive to the public good, and
it is unable to further the public good through imposition of religion, it
must limit itself to providing protection and benefits to human beings on
their earthly sojourn.

Of course this is not as simple as Locke's sharp dichotomy between
the business of government and the business of religion would suggest.
Certainly there are coercive measures that are appropriate to the tasks
of civil government that might inadvertently intrude on some religious
practices. For example, Locke maintains that it is appropriate for a commonwealth to prohibit the slaughter of livestock under certain conditions
of scarcity even if such a prohibition would force a religious individual
to refrain from sacrificing his calf. Here the magistrate's interpretation of
public interest takes precedence over individual religious freedom (LCT
41). In other words, Locke's defense of toleration rests on a claim concerning what the business of "true religion" is (LCT 36).[33] For Locke,
the proper interests of the church are purely spiritual and can be clearly
distinguished from the tangible and worldly interests of civil society. By
starting with this fundamentally theological assumption, Locke can insist
that "the chief characteristical mark of the true church" is toleration, and
that the purpose of political power is to limit the "injury done unto man's
neighbors and to the commonwealth" (LCT 23, 42). To attempt to leg-
islate or enforce laws that go beyond the proper civil concerns of injury,
peace, and preservation would be constitute a breach of trust since the
people have entrusted only their powers of judgment concerning what is
conducive to the public good. Thus the formation of limited government,
with its declared law, known judge, processes of adjudication and appeal,
and established power of executive punishment, is an attempt to mitigate

---

[32] Locke's insistence that princes do not have special insight into religious truth does not
mean that he thinks they will not try to claim special insight. In fact, he recognizes that there
is nothing more familiar than claims to certainty that serve "to palliate men's ignorance,
and cover their errours" (E III.x.14). Hannah Dawson implies that Locke's recognition that
individuals will misuse language to impose on others undermines his defense of toleration.
Yet Locke's point is not to refute toleration but to encourage it by pointing out the ways it
is subverted. See Dawson, "Locke on Language," 402.

[33] See Ingrid Creppell's chapter on the role of external and internal boundaries in *Toleration and Identity*.

the inconveniences of the state of nature by providing a common judge
that can make determinations concerning the visible and tangible benefits
of the people.

Prerogative, Public Good, and the Judgment of the People

Yet the formation of civil society and the establishment of government
does not completely resolve the problem of judgment that plagued
Locke's state of nature. The transfer of individually held powers of judgment and enforcement to a common authority does not result in the universal recognition of moral and political certainties in the public sphere.
The epistemological difficulty involved in interpreting the natural law
and applying it to particular cases of public disagreement remains an
inescapable aspect of civil life. Civil government does not provide a final
solution to the epistemological difficulties of the state of nature, only a
more convenient way to organize tentative and temporary responses to
that problem. It is for this reason that Locke places so much importance
on the prerogative power of the executive. He insists that the good of
the polity requires that a certain degree of discretion be granted those
who are entrusted with exercising the power of the state. There are some
things that simply cannot be "directed by antecedent, standing, positive
laws," and must instead be left to "the prudence and wisdom" of the
executive. In order to further the public good, Locke argues, a magistrate
will at times have to act beyond the letter of the law and occasionally
even in opposition to the positive, written statutes of a particular regime.
    However, this concession is especially disturbing considering that
one of the "inconveniences" that propelled individuals from the state
of nature into civil society was the absence of an "established, settled,
known law" (2T 124). For Locke one of the most important tasks of
government would seem to be the clarification of a contested natural law
through a written and durable body of statutes. "Government without
laws, is, I suppose, a mystery in politics, unconceivable to humane capacity, and inconsistent with human society" (2T 219; see also 94, 12). Yet in
spite of the weight that Locke places on settled and known law, he insists
that such laws do not eliminate the need for judgment.
    Judgment remains a crucial aspect of political power not simply
because positive, written law can be ambiguous or underspecified, but
because it is inadequate to fulfill the task that the people have entrusted
government. As Locke puts it, "Laws themselves should in some cases
give way to the executive power" in order to further the "good of the
society" (2T 159). There will be some cases in which law simply does not
provide rulers with the proper guidance to address novel situations and

still other cases in which "a strict and rigid observation of the laws may do harm" (2T 159). For these reasons it is important that the execute enjoy a prerogative power "to act according to discretion, for the public good, without the prescription of law, and sometimes even against it" (2T 160). Although Locke notes that the people retain the right to limit the executive prerogative by establishing specific positive laws in areas that might otherwise be left to executive discretion, he insists that government run entirely by standing laws is an impossibility (2T 164).

It is important to note that Locke is not in any way asserting that the executive will should thus be given an exalted status or that the magistrate should enjoy a type of boundless supremacy. This would be to endorse the arbitrary rule that is the primary target of the *Two Treatises*. Prerogative powers for Locke are not granted as a personal privilege, but rather as a means necessary to provide for the public good (2T 162–68). Yet by providing rulers with such far-reaching discretion in applying and interpreting the statutes of a polity, Locke seems to reintroduce many of the troubles that unsettled the epistemological clarity of the state of nature in the first place. From the perspective of the subject, an executive exercising prerogative by subverting written law and enforcing a particular interpretation of the law of nature would be difficult to distinguish from the type of imposition that government was established to avoid.

For example, Locke speaks of changing the terms of an election at two occasions in the *Second Treatise*. On the first occasion, he points out the inequity of the system of representation in his day due to the variable growth and decline of populations. It would be appropriate, he argues, if the executive would use prerogative power to adjust the electoral system, since it is in "the interest . . . as well as the intention of the people, to have a fair and equal representative" (2T 158). However, Locke later lists a series of hypothetical actions that an executive could take that would so alter the composition of the polity that "dissolution of government" could legitimately be "imputed to the prince" (2T 218). In one of those actions, "the electors or ways of election are altered without the consent and contrary to the common interest of the people" (2T 216). In the first instance the alteration of a system of representation makes the executive "an undoubted friend . . . to, and establisher of the government, and cannot miss the consent and approbation of the community" (2T 158). In the second, the prince is "justly to be esteemed the common enemy and pest of mankind" (2T 230).

The difference hinges on Locke's notion of the public good. Locke tells his readers that prerogative is "nothing but the power of doing public good without a rule" (2T 166). In his later writings on monetary policy, he reiterates this position, arguing that individual right is in some instances bounded by considerations of public well-being: "Private men's interests ought not . . . to be neglected, nor sacrificed to any thing but the manifest advantage of the public" (SCM 220). He also points to early political communities ruled by "godlike" princes "who cannot have too much prerogative" because they use such discretion to promote the interests of their subjects (2T 164). The difference between legitimate government and despotic control is that legitimate government acts in order to further public interests.

At this crucial point in his account, Locke leans quite heavily on the imprecise and certainly contested notion of public good. An appeal to the public good, in itself, cannot provide us with a standard to distinguish between the legitimate ruler and the tyrant. In the *Letter Concerning Toleration,* Locke points out that duplicitous leaders are apt to "colour their spirit of persecution and unchristian cruelty with a pretence of care of the public weal" (LCT 25). Doubtless all executives making changes to the franchise would claim that they were acting for the common good. Certainly Charles II would have said this. If discretionary power is not only the power to act but also the power to judge what is needed in a particular situation, then it would seem to include making a determination about what constitutes the public good in those situations. The point of granting an executive prerogative in the first place is to allow leaders the latitude to determine how best to serve the public, a task that rigorous application of law cannot achieve.[34]

It is important to note that although Locke allows for individual judgment of executive wrongdoing, it is the judgment of the people that ultimately gives the public good its concrete and tangible meaning. When a king appeals to prerogative in order to act against the public good, he is abusing a term that is held in common by his subjects. By subsuming an act that actually injures the public under the heading of prerogative, a ruler threatens to unsettle the steady, shared language of justification. He turns the common understanding of the word on its head. No longer is such a ruler interested in attempting to clarify and enact the judgment of the people. Instead of fulfilling the responsibilities of a trustee, the corrupt ruler becomes a tyrant ruling for his own benefit. Under such conditions the trust is dissolved and the people have the right and the duty to try to reclaim their stolen inheritance. They have a right to reclaim their authority to judge and enforce the law of nature.

In order to illustrate this difficulty we need only examine the way Locke appeals to James I to argue that a good monarch devotes his power and authority to further the common good. After quoting the monarch, Locke notes with approval that the "learned king, makes the difference

---

[34] For a more extensive discussion of prerogative, see Pasquale Pasquino, "Locke on King's Prerogative," *Political Theory* 26 (1998), 198–208.

betwixt a king and a tyrant to consist only in this, that one makes the law the bounds of his power, and the good of the public, the end of his government; the other makes all give way to his own will and appetite" (2T 200). By citing passages from a speech of James I, Locke is able to appropriate the comments of one of the most vehement defenders of divine right in order to bolster his argument in defense of revolution. Both Locke and James distinguish between legitimate prerogative and tyrannical excess by appealing to the intentions of the ruler and conse-quences of his rule. The nagging question, however, is who is to be the judge of whether the actions of the executive contribute to the public good. For James the only judge to whom monarchs must answer is God. Locke does not quote the passages in James's speech in which he states that God "doth . . . never leave kings unpunished when they transgress these limits."[35] Judgment and punishment of monarchs must be left to the wisdom and authority of God alone, for it is "sedition in subjects to dispute what a king may do in the height of his power."[36] Although Locke agrees that "princes . . . owe subjection to the laws of God and nature" (2T 195), he also insists that the limits of prerogative and thus the legiti-mate powers of the executive must also be defined and enforced in this world. For James I, God alone holds monarchs accountable. For Locke, "the people shall be judge" (2T 240).

Yet who exactly makes this determination? Although Locke at times seems to imply that this judgment is made individually, generally he argues that the "people as a body" determine when rulers have exceeded their proper powers. Dunn is surely mistaken when he writes, "The authority of the prerogative over the individual subject is precisely and exclusively what the individual recognizes it to be."[37] This is exactly the type of radical linguistic and political subjectivity that Locke tries to avoid throughout his career. Here we see why it is significant that he argues that the establishment of government takes place in two stages. When the magistrate is seen to abuse its trust, the right of judgment does not immediately fall back to individuals in the state of nature as it does with Hobbes, but to the people as a persisting entity. Locke writes, "The common question will be made, who shall be judge, whether the prince or legislator act contrary to their trust? . . . To this I reply, the people shall be judge; for who shall be judge whether his trustee or deputy acts well, and according to the trust reposed in him, but he who deputes him" (2T 240). When Locke writes that the people should be judge, he means that

[35] King James VI and I, *Political Writings*, ed. Johann Somerville (Cambridge: Cambridge University Press, 1994), 183.

[36] Ibid.

[37] Dunn, *Political Thought of Locke*, 155.

the community that constitutes the body of the people must arrive at a determination. As we have seen, Locke's distinction between the state of nature and civil society rests on the presence of a common authority. His entire political project of shaping a common language of judgment is aimed at providing his readers with epistemic criteria that can join them together as a people. When Locke says that "the people shall be judge," he means that civil society, and not individuals in the state of nature, should determine whether to resist a failed ruler (2T 240). A tyrant is said to be in "a state of war with the people, who have a right to reinstate their legislative" (2T 155). In the moment of revolution the people themselves are neither in the state of nature nor in the state of war with each other.[38] They retain the epistemological cohesiveness and unity that secures them from the inconveniences of the state of nature. Thus Locke writes that when the tyrant acts to put himself in "a state of war with his people, dissolve the government, and leave them to that defense, which belongs to every one in the state of nature," he is not necessarily saying that the people themselves are in a state of nature with each other, but only that they are as a body in a state of war with their ruler and have the defense that they would have in their natural condition.[39] Although members of society remain bound to each other, the king breaks his link with society and becomes a highwayman, a noxious beast who is "justly to be esteemed the common enemy and pest of mankind; and is to be treated accordingly" (2T 230). In this way resistance to the unlawful tyrant is modeled on the example of retribution against criminals (2T 9, 11, 16).

Locke's insistence that the people exist as an independent and incorporated entity with the power to judge and not simply as a disorganized multitude of private judgments is central to his understanding of the regenerative possibilities of revolution. For Hobbes, if the sovereign loses power and can no longer secure the safety of those who have joined society, citizens fall back into an anarchic world of fear and violence. For Locke, it is possible that the degeneration of a regime leaves society

[38] Locke appears to teach both that society can exist without government (2T 121, 211) and that society cannot exist without government (2T 205, 219). This apparent contradiction dissolves, however, if we interpret Locke's position as one in which society, or the people, exist independently only in a very few instances. The revolutionary moment is thus parallel to the majority decision that establishes the institutional framework or supreme power of government as individuals move out of the state of nature. The action sets up a new polity in the very moment that it abolishes the old one.

[39] Locke states that the "usual and almost only way" society is dissolved is by foreign conquest (2T 211), yet he also notes that civil society can be dissolved when the legislative is radically altered (2T 212). It seems that the distinguishing factor here is that as long as matters of public importance can be publicly deliberated and public judgments can be made, society remains intact. When public determinations can no longer be achieved, society dissolves into a state of nature in which there is no common authority.

intact to exercise its power of judgment and reestablish a more fitting government. Unlike Hobbes, Locke is convinced that his readers can and will exercise their judgment as a people with sober restraint and careful deliberation. His defense of the right of revolution rests on his assumption that the people will be able to form reasonable judgments about their condition.

Locke recognizes, however, that there will be objections to this somewhat shaky basis for legitimacy. He realizes that many will yearn for something more permanent and certain on which "to lay the foundation of government" than "the unsteady opinion, and uncertain humour of the people" (2T 223). Yet he remains adamant that there is no other foundation for legitimate government. Having shown in the *First Treatise* that a stable polity could not simply result from the imposition of a divinely ordained system of politics, Locke insists that the only other original or foundation of government is the "contrivance, and the consent of men" (1T 6). Locke believes that this teaching will not encourage "a busy head, or turbulent spirit" nor fuel frequent rebellion (2T 230, 224). This is because the opinions and humor of the people are not as unsteady as critics assert. The inhabitants of a Lockean regime are able to govern their leaders because they were first able to govern their own judgments. Here Locke is not only describing the way people will conduct their intellectual lives in practice, but is also encouraging his readers to conform to this model. It seems surprising that Locke should rely so much on judgment, given the unsettled nature of the state of nature in his account and the role that government plays in supplying the standards necessary for the proper ordering of right and propriety. Yet Locke is convinced that the people can be made to see the clear signs of tyranny and distinguish them from the ordinary defects of government.[40]

Locke's confidence rests on his belief that the judgment of the people is based on the hard currency of natural signs. The people determine the legitimacy of their rulers insofar as they "see and feel" infractions of their rights and threats to their well-being. For this reason the judgment of the people is not easily influenced by the passions and prejudices of a few. Although every polity will include "a raving mad man, or heady malcontent" and perhaps even "a few oppressed men" (2T 208), the people as a body will not be stirred by scattered calls for violent revolt. It is true "that the pride, ambition, and turbulency of private men have sometimes caused great disorder in commonwealths" (2T 208). Yet Locke remains convinced that the judgment of the people is more of a bulwark against chaos than an encouragement toward anarchy. This is because the people

---

[40] See Dunn, "Measuring Locke's Shadow," 277–78, on the centrality of judgment in Locke's vision of the precarious condition of human community.

"can think of things no otherwise than as they find and feel them" (2T 230). By attending to their senses, by reading the signs of nature and the patterns of experience, Lockean agents are able to form trustworthy judgments about the behavior and possible misbehavior of their rulers. Locke repeatedly emphasizes that the governed are able to recognize whether they are acting to promote the "peace, safety and public good" by referring to what they see and feel (2T 131). Whatever flatterers may say to convince them of the legitimacy of a regime, they cannot hinder subjects from "feeling" the burdens of despotic rule (2T 209). The improprieties of misrule will eventually become so great that the majority will "feel it" (2T 168). They will "see and feel" whether a governor "really means the good of his people" (2T 209). This process of forming judgments is slow and steady. It takes "a long train of abuses, prevarications, and artifices, all tending the same way," to "make the design visible to the people" (2T 225). When "the ill designs of the rulers become visible, or their attempts sensible," the people will arrive at a judgment "grounded upon manifest evidence" that their king has broken their trust and entered into a state of war with them (2T 230).

In such a case, Locke says, there is no judge on earth who can arbitrate between the people and their ruler. They must make their "appeal to heaven" (2T 21, 168, 176, 241). The way that Locke uses this traditional phrase, however, requires a bit of disentangling. King James also says that the only recourse an oppressed people have is an appeal to heaven. Yet for James, this means that subjects take solace in the fact that God will judge. They appeal to heaven through prayer and then wait for God to rectify the injustice.[41] This of course is not what Locke means by the phrase. For Locke, to appeal to heaven is to resort to violence. He defends his view by invoking the biblical figure of Jephtha as an example of someone who appeals to God's judgment by employing force. As Locke interprets the story, Jephtha seeks to clarify the will of the divine by entering into battle. This type of appeal to heaven is simply a recovery of the right to execute the law of nature, a right that everyone possesses in the state of nature. When a ruler abuses his prerogative and acts in a way that is contrary to the public good, he puts himself "into a state of war with his people" and leaves "them to that defense, which belongs to everyone in the state of nature" (2T 205). Since "in all states and conditions the true remedy of

---

[41] Seliger notes that Locke was able to transform "the traditional Christian view which restricted the appeal to heaven of the governed to mere prayer." Seliger, *Liberal Politics of Locke*, 63–64. Nathan Tarcov cites I Samuel 24:12 and 15, where the phrase "the Lord be judge" is invoked between subjects and ruler to mean that subjects should *not* take matters into their own hands. As we can see, Locke's use of a similar phrase is deployed for very different purposes. Tarcov, "Locke's *Second Treatise* and 'the Best Fence against Rebellion,'" *Review of Politics* 51 (1981), 198–217.

force without authority, is to oppose force to it," the people may choose to take up arms in order to free themselves from their oppressor and reestablish a government that can properly secure their rights (2T 163). To rise up against a tyrant, then, is to appeal "to the supreme judge, as Jephtha did" (2T 241).

Yet unlike Jephtha, the Lockean revolutionary is given no divine guarantee of success. What is striking about Locke's appeal to the people as judge is the deep uncertainty surrounding both the determinations that are made and the possibility of successful revolution. Although he points to the way general signs or patterns of behavior can be interpreted as abuse, Locke does not offer his reader a perfect way to delineate between tyranny and legitimate rule in the actual world. In the final chapter of the *Second Treatise*, "Of the Dissolution of Government," Locke lists a few guidelines for recognizing when government acts contrary to its trust, such as when the legislative is altered or when the executive or legislative "endeavors to take away, and destroy, the property of the people" (2T 212, 222). Yet Locke also notes exceptions to these rules, advocating the alteration of the legislature in paragraph 158 and the appropriation of property for the public good in paragraph 159. Thus tyranny cannot simply be determined by the application of unambiguous rules; it requires judgment in matters that are less than certain. For this reason, it is always possible that the people will judge incorrectly. God remains the only arbiter, and God's judgment is inaccessible to us in this moment of history (2T 242). And even if the people do manage to judge correctly, Locke offers no guarantee that justice will always triumph in battle (2T 21, 176). "For of such things," he writes, "who can tell what the end will be?" (2T 205). As Ruth Grant puts it, "To acknowledge a right of revolution is to acknowledge that there is no permanent solution to the political problem."[42]

Locke urges his readers not only to judge whether a wrong has been committed but also whether the time and conditions are conducive to a successful response (2T 13, 21, 87, 91, 179). Locke implies that there are situations in which it is simply not worth the risk, trouble, or cost to attempt to punish rulers who have exceeded their proper powers. An appeal to heaven is no small matter for Locke. Anyone who undertakes such an action "must be sure he has right on his side; and a right too that is . . . worth the trouble and cost of appeal, as he will answer at a tribunal, that cannot be deceived, and will be sure to retribute to every according to the mischiefs he hath created to his fellow subjects; that is, any part of mankind" (2T 176). In this context it is important to remember that Locke never tells his readers to revolt; he does not dictate to them what

---

[42] Grant, *John Locke's Liberalism*, 179.

they must do. Instead he presents an argument in defense of their right
to judge. In the end it is up to readers to decide whether the government has embarked on a course toward enslavement. Locke is confident
that the people will recognize what is happening to them and respond
appropriately, just as a passenger on a ship would eventually recognize
that their captain "was carrying him, and the rest of his company to
Algiers [a known slave market], when he found himself always steering
that course" (2T 210).

The message of the *Second Treatise* is unmistakable. Locke calls his
readers to begin the hard work of judgment. Do you live under the threat
of tyranny? Has there been a long train of abuses with a clear design to
oppress and defraud the people? Has the government put itself in a state
of war with the people? Ultimately the people themselves must determine the answers to these questions. It is only through the activity of
judging—as uncertain as it may be—that Lockean agents can come to
understand themselves as free beings. It is in this sense that Joshua Foa
Dienstag rightly points out that "Locke offers his readers a choice rather
than a creed."[43] To prove that we are rational and free persons and not
Filmerian slaves, we must reclaim what is naturally ours. We must take
up the difficult task of making determinations about the proper exercise
of political power under conditions of uncertainty. The success of Locke's
political project depends on the formation of citizens who seek to be
more than just obedient subjects or even zealous patriots. For Locke, as
for the liberalism that followed in his wake, truly consensual government
requires a willingness to exercise liberating judgment.

[43] Dienstag, *Dancing in Chains*, 73.

Conclusion

The Great Recoinage Revisited

LOCKE'S ATTEMPT to establish a stable and trustworthy monetary standard was nothing short of a fiasco. When the secretary of the Treasury proposed to stabilize the currency by lowering its silver content (or debasing) coins, Locke rejected the idea. He argued instead that coins should not represent anything other than the "intrinsick value" of their silver content. If the government abandoned the "natural" worth of coins, they would further undermine the trust that people have in their currency. Locke's dogged insistence that Parliament ensure the worth or trustworthiness of the currency by maintaining its weight led to the Great Recoinage of 1696. The process was expensive, chaotic, and generally unhelpful. Most contemporary economists believe that England would have been better off had Locke lost the argument and allowed the Treasury to debase the coin.[1]

Although Locke might have won the debate, his position has often puzzled contemporary readers. If Locke is viewed as a philosopher who recognizes that money is simply a sign and signs have conventional rather than natural values, his defense of the "intrinsick value" of silver is an inexplicable turn toward essentialism. By claiming that there must be an exact correspondence between the sign and its referent, Locke seems to contradict both the linguistic conventionalism that he advances in the *Essay Concerning Human Understanding* and the immediate evidence of history, since underweight coins had been circulating in England for decades. Faced with this inconsistency, Joseph Schumpeter laments, "It is a sorry picture that unfolds itself before the eyes of Locke's reader" as the great philosopher fails to understand the implications of his own arguments.[2] For Schumpeter, Locke's economic writings "stand in no relation to either his philosophy or his political theory" because Locke remains confined to traditional banalities when he addresses the currency crisis.[3] Similarly Joyce Oldham Appleby describes the victory of Locke's posi-

---

[1] See Thomas J. Sargent and François R. Velde, *The Big Problem of Small Change* (Princeton: Princeton University Press, 2002), 271–90; and Kelly's introduction to *Locke on Money*, 89–91.

[2] Joseph Schumpeter, *History of Economic Analysis* (New York: Oxford University Press, 1994), 285.

[3] Ibid., 113.

tion in 1696 as "the ironic triumph of mind over matter by one of the major architects of empiricism."[4] Blinded by the commitment to a mechanist natural world, Locke was unable to recognize the conventionality of money. His position on recoinage was the result of an outmoded belief in the natural worth of silver. Summing up the consensus view, John F. Chown describes Locke as "the greatest philosopher of his age but perhaps a rather muddled economist."[5]

Yet Locke's participation in the recoinage debates should not be dismissed as an obscure and perhaps even embarrassing case of intellectual overreaching. The concerns that animate his economic writings run through his philosophical and political writings as well. Locke's commitment to ensuring a stable, public vocabulary of judgment led him to advocate a Great Recoinage of public reasonableness. Here, as with the monetary crisis, Locke insisted that the new linguistic currency be tied to a standard that was more trustworthy than convention alone. Probable judgment must be stabilized by a standard that exists outside and beyond our individual will. As Locke puts it, "He that, with Archelaus, shall lay it down as a principle, that right and wrong, honest and dishonest, are defined only by laws, and not by nature, will have other measures of moral rectitude and pravity, than those who take it for granted that we are under obligations antecedent to all human constitutions" (E IV.xii.4). The judgments that humans make and the compacts that they form do not receive their legitimacy merely because they originate with us. The authoritative force of individual judgment derives from its grounding in nature and not just convention, *physis* and not merely *nomos*. The type of judgment that Locke hoped to disseminate rests on the assumption that there is a natural source, a substantive core from which emanates authoritative natural signs. However this ordering source is elusive; it exceeds our capacity to contain and comprehend it. Thus Locke appealed to the law of nature in a way that both assumes its existence and concedes the human propensity to confound and confuse such standards. He embraced the possibility of an overarching moral law while also resisting dogmatic claims concerning the specific content of that law. The type of judgment that Locke proposes as a standard of public reasonableness— judgment that involves disciplining one's assent according to the probable signs of nature—is an attempt to stabilize the linguistic currency of his contemporaries while also discouraging dogmatic appeals to the moral deliverances of nature.

This Great Recoinage of judgment produced quite durable results. Locke's linguistic reform was certainly more successful than his mon-

---

[4] Appleby, *Economic Thought and Ideology*, 236.
[5] John F. Chown, *A History of Money* (New York: Routledge, 1994), 63.

etary one. In fact, he established a standard that would become common currency in the eighteenth century. Clerics, journalists, politicians, academics, lawyers, and countless others who helped to shape political self-understanding in England, France, and America drew their inspiration from Locke's writings. His "reasonableness" set the agenda for an array of writers, including Paine, Jefferson, Burke, Hume, Bentham, Montesquieu, Voltaire, and Rousseau. Generations of religious thinkers, from scandalous deists such as John Toland and Matthew Tindal to pious theologians such as Jonathan Edwards, wrote in a distinctly Lockean idiom. His vocabulary also permeated the writing of essayists and novelists. Daniel Defoe, for example, often incorporated Locke's arguments word for word into his essays and stories. It seemed that everyone who wrote on politics, philosophy, religion, education, or economics in the eighteenth century was affected by the pervasive influence of Locke's ideas. His language of reasonable judgment became the intellectual currency of a burgeoning civil society. Today, three hundred years after his death, his formulations still influence how we speak and think about our political lives.

The continuing appeal of Locke's language rests in part on its resistance to rigid intellectual systems and in part on its emphasis on the liberating possibilities of disciplined, probable judgment. For Locke, it is our ability to make judgments under conditions of uncertainty that renders us free and equal individuals. We need not submit to a claim simply because it is made on behalf of custom, tradition, or hierarchy. In matters of the utmost importance, we can and should suspend our assent, evaluate whether it is warranted, and then accept or reject a proposition according to the available evidence. Locke equates this capacity with intellectual liberty, yet it plays a crucial role in his understanding of political liberty as well. In the same way that we experience intellectual freedom by stepping back from our social and religious context and assessing our beliefs, we experience political freedom by stepping back from our political institutions and practices and assessing whether they fulfill the purposes for which they were established. We realize our natural freedom by making judgments concerning the political structures we inhabit. For Locke, consent is not only the origin of political legitimacy, it is also the standard by which a regime continues to be measured. It is for this reason that the establishment of limited government is only a partial solution to the problem of politics. Although it is sensible to erect a polity characterized by representative government, the separation of powers, the rule of law, and religious toleration, these arrangements cannot guarantee that such a regime will remain just or stable. Those who seek to exercise power in violation of right will at times be able to manipulate the most carefully crafted structures and procedures. Institutions alone cannot eliminate the

possibility of political degeneration. Our ability to judge whether our
governors are acting in accordance with the public good is the final check
on despotism and the definitive sign of our natural liberty.

The plausibility of this account rests on a particular view of both the
limits and the possibilities of human understanding. Judgment is necessary because we are unable to eliminate partiality, fallibility, and uncertainty from our political lives. Yet it is possible because we are nonetheless
able to govern our thoughts in such a way as to collect evidence, discern
patterns, and make reasonable determinations. Locke's view of judgment
is neither radically skeptical nor wholly rationalist. He neither rejects the
possibility of rational justification nor asserts that warranted beliefs must
somehow involve a God's-eye view of the moral universe. The notion
of judgment that Locke endorses balances between these alternatives
because it involves adjudicating between moral principles and practical
experience. He insists on the existence of normative facts, yet is quick
to point out that our access to those facts is imperfect and incomplete.
Since our judgment aims at making reasonable decisions according to
transcendent principles, it cannot be reduced to immediate self-interest
or local convention. Yet since it must take into account the contingencies
of our everyday lives, its conclusions can never be absolutely certain. For
Locke, this type of judgment is appropriate for the "state of mediocrity"
in which we find ourselves. The candle that is set up within us cannot
replace the "twilight of probability" with the bright sunshine of comprehensive knowledge, yet it is sufficient for our purposes. We cannot, by
taking up the burdens of judgment, eliminate intellectual uncertainty or
political conflict once and for all. But we can work toward freedom, intellectual freedom from dogmatic imposition as well as political freedom
from despotic oppression.

Although Locke's account of reasonable judgment continues to shape
our self-understanding, it has not gone unchallenged. Many of Locke's
successors have sought to clarify or correct what they view as an unsat-
isfactory compromise between moral principles and prudential calculus.
In order to eliminate this tension, they have focused on one aspect of his
position and ignored or rejected the other. David Hume, for example,
jettisoned Locke's appeals to moral principle in order to achieve a thoroughgoing empirical or prudential theory. The philosophes, on the other
hand, disregarded Locke's reservations concerning the limitations of the
intellect and the contingencies of political life in order to achieve a comprehensive and logically compelling political knowledge. Although both
groups found support for their work in Locke's writings, their attempts
to purify his position led them to abandon the original liberating impulse
of his thought. For both Hume and the philosophes, the probable judgment that characterizes Lockean reasonableness and makes possible both

intellectual and political liberty was eclipsed by an epistemological dual-
ism that reduced justification to either the irrational realm of custom, cir-
cumstance, and passion or the very narrow and remote sphere of rational
demonstration. By briefly examining the ways in which Locke's vocabulary of judgment has been destabilized, we can better understand both its
intellectual vulnerability and its continued political importance.

To a great extent, Hume can be seen as a child of Lockean reasonableness. He embraced Locke's epistemological modesty as well as his
animosity toward those who claim to have special insight into moral and
political certainties. Following Locke's lead, Hume aimed his considerable wit at "enthusiastic" sectarians, "dismal" divines, and self-satisfied
system-builders. He ridiculed the hypocrisy and self-interest of those who
engage in metaphysical speculation in the same way that Locke derided
clerical pretension and epistemological arrogance. "A considerable part
of metaphysics," he wrote in *An Enquiry Concerning Human Understanding*, "is not properly a science, but [arises] either from the fruitless efforts of human vanity, which would penetrate into subjects utterly
inaccessible to the understanding, or from the craft of popular supersti-
tions, which being unable to defend themselves on fair ground, raise these
entangling brambles to cover and protect their weakness."[6] Hume joined
Locke in attacking those who seek to protect their privileged position or
impose their will by appealing to unquestionable and inscrutable systems
of morality.

Yet Hume departed from Locke in significant ways. Most importantly,
he rejected Locke's notion of probable judgment and thus denied it as
a source of political authority. Hume abandoned Locke's assumption
that the book of nature provides "legible characters of [God's] works
and providence" (E III.ix.23). Instead, he argued that the data we receive
from the external world comes to us without any discernible order at all.
The discrete impressions that we experience are always organized and
arranged in the mind by a force that exists prior to and apart from those
impressions. For Hume, that "gentle force, which commonly prevails" is
not reason but mental habit. It is habit or custom that leads us to perceive our experiences the way that we do, and those habits can never be
entirely transcended. Custom guides reason, not the other way around.

Hume's critique of Locke's notion of reasonable judgment led him
to reject many of the assumptions and arguments that underlie Locke's
political position. He denied Locke's claim that natural law can serve as a
standard for assessing political conduct. He dismissed Locke's notion of
natural rights and equality, his justification of prepolitical property, and

---

[6] David Hume, *An Enquiry Concerning Human Understanding*, ed. Thomas Beauchamp
(Oxford: Oxford University Press, 2001), I.11.

his argument that political authority is derived from the actual consent of the people. To Hume, the state of nature is a "philosophical fiction," a wholly "imaginary state" without justice or injustice, property, or any other qualities included in Locke's description.[7] It is "fruitless" to "seek in the laws of nature a stronger foundation for our political duties than interest and human conventions."[8] In fact, "those rules by which properties, rights, and obligations are determined, have in them no marks of a natural origin, but many of artifice and contrivance."[9] Hume stopped short of reducing justice itself to conventional agreement. He claims that there is "a sense of common interest," or sympathy, among all individuals that transcends particular agreements and sustains society through time.[10] Yet he nonetheless maintains, "The rules of equity or justice depend entirely on the particular state and condition, in which men are placed, and owe their origin, and existence to that utility which results to the public from their strict and regular observance."[11]

Having cut himself off from any source of transcendent moral principles, Hume tended to treat normative questions of legitimacy as descriptive questions of fact. This tendency seemed to foreclose the possibility of rational criticism and resistance. On Hume's account, the very existence of institutions and practices justifies them. When faced with the question of how to distinguish between legitimate and illegitimate government, Hume came to a very different conclusion than Locke: "Time alone gives solidity to their right, and operating gradually on the minds of men, reconciles them to any authority, and makes it seem just and reasonable."[12] Hume went on to claim, "Nothing causes any sentiment to have a greater influence upon us than custom."[13] He therefore concludes, "Time and custom give authority to all forms of government and all successions of princes; and power which at first was founded only on injustice and

[7] David Hume, *An Enquiry Concerning the Principles of Morals*, ed. Thomas Beauchamp (Oxford: Oxford University Press, 2006) III.1.14. See also David Hume, *Treatise of Human Nature*, ed. David Fate Norton and Mary J. Norton (Oxford: Oxford University Press, 2007), III.2.2, 8.

[8] Hume, *Treatise of Human Nature*, III.2.8.

[9] Ibid., III.2.6.

[10] Hume, *Principles of Morals*, Appendix III.7. On occasion, Hume suggests that human nature is "constant and universal." He argues that our moral distinctions stem from "some internal sense of feeling, which nature has made universal in the whole species." Hume, *Principles of Morals*, I.9. Yet it is difficult to see how he can justify this belief in "human nature" given his understanding of the self as a "bundle of impressions." Here he seems to be smuggling in generally accepted assumptions concerning human nature even though his own epistemological framework prohibits them. One could even say that he is reintroducing Locke's assumption of design, stripped of its explicitly theological framework.

[11] Hume, *Principles of Morals*, III.1.2.

[12] Hume, *Treatise of Human Nature*, III.2.10.

[13] Ibid.

violence, becomes in times legal and obligatory."[14] Since it is time and custom that authorize government, Hume counseled his readers to accept established authorities: "No maxim is more conformable, both to prudence and morals, than to submit quietly to the government, which we find established in the country where we hope to live, without enquiring too curiously into its origin and first establishment."[15] Hume's attempt to avoid what he saw as the inconsistencies at the heart of Locke's notion of judgment went hand in hand with his decidedly skeptical and conservative political position reminiscent of Montaigne's skeptical acquiescence. By arguing that human cognition is governed by habit and that legitimacy is solely the product of time and custom, he downplayed the role of critical judgment in politics. The Lockean notion of intellectual and political liberty based on the exercise of probable judgment was simply unavailable to Hume. Locke's call to exercise liberating judgment became for Hume an admonition to submit to custom and tradition.

Hume's attempt to isolate and refine the empirical elements of Locke's thought led him to place ethical and political deliberation outside of the realm of reasonable judgment. In contrast, philosophes such as Abbé de Condillac and Claude-Adrien Helvetius sought to extract the rationalist or transcendent aspects of Locke's position in order to place matters of public importance on the firm ground of certain knowledge. Dismissing the ambivalences of the *Essay* as "timidities" and "confusions," Condillac transformed Locke's cautious defense of probable judgment into a bold proposal for the establishment of an unassailable moral and political system. He argued that all knowledge rests on the single, unassailable foundation of "simple perceptions."[16] Similarly, Helvetius argued that "the senses never deceive us" because the "testimony of the senses" informs us of "the real forms of bodies."[17] By insisting that the sensations yield certain knowledge of the world, they assimilated Locke's language of reasonableness into a Cartesian quest for absolute certainty. They argued that individuals could attain scientific knowledge freed from the uncertainties and contingencies of political life by carefully collecting and arranging sensory perceptions.

In place of the "degrees of assent" that are so central to Locke's understanding of judgment, the philosophes reintroduced the Cartesian distinction between certain knowledge that is unequivocally true and all other assertions that are equally doubtful. Given this stark dichotomy, Locke's

[14] Ibid., III.2.11.

[15] Ibid., III.2.10.

[16] Etienne Bonnot de Condillac, *Essay on the Origin of Human Knowledge*, trans. Hans Aarsleff (Cambridge: Cambridge University Press, 2001), 7.

[17] Claude-Adrien Helvetius, *A Treatise on Man*, trans. W. Hooper, 2 vols. (New York: Burt Franklin, 1810), 1:14–15.

discussion of probability was pushed back into the shadows. Condillac made Locke's suggestion concerning the possibility of a moral science the focal point of his work, announcing, "one could reason in metaphysics and in the moral sciences with as much precision as in geometry."[18] In a similar vein, Helvetius wrote, "In geometry every problem not fully resolved may become the object of a new demonstration. It is the same in morality and politics."[19] Yet their goal was not simply to contemplate the demonstrative truths of morality and politics, but to apply them to every aspect of political life and make the world conform to the unquestionable deliverances of reason.

The philosophes and their technocratic successors soon discovered that this project of transformation would require more than simply the dissemination of moral proofs. Yet instead of moderating their rationalist aspirations, they speculated about bringing people in line with their systems through the deliberate contrivance of scientific legislators. Thinkers such as Helvetius and later Jeremy Bentham came to view the general public as a mass of passive material to be shaped and molded through legislation and education. They argued that leaders could bring about a truly rational society by strategically applying the findings of scientific knowledge. From this perspective, government becomes administration. It is not a matter of reciprocal judgment between ruler and ruled, but rather a unilateral application of reason by experts. Authority is not located in the hands of the people, but in the hands of the ideal legislator who is able to create a stable and happy social order. For the proponents of these theories of social change, the notion of Lockean judgment no longer played a role. The technocrats believed that experts could arrive at conclusions concerning the universal requirements of happiness and stability without having to venture into the murky world of probability, while citizens would have no need to think at all. When properly applied to society, the deliverances of reason would be so comprehensive and universally compelling that they would eliminate the need for individual judgment. Yet along the way they would also eliminate the possibility of genuine self-government.

In a certain sense, Locke's successors reintroduced the dangerous and destabilizing extremes that motivated his political project in the first place. One could argue, however, that they did so by emphasizing different aspects that are already present in Locke's own position. Hume's skepticism extended and deepened Locke's own epistemological suspicion of scholastic obscurities and enthusiastic assertions. The philosophes' hyperrationalism sought to articulate and apply the type of geometrically

---

[18] Condillac, *Origin of Human Knowledge*, 3.
[19] Helvetius, *A Treatise on Man*, 1:11.

certain science of morality that Locke flirted with at points in the *Essay*. However, these attempts to purify Lockean reasonableness led to the abandonment of the political aspirations that animate his position. They undermined Locke's common currency of judgment and opened the door to skepticism and fanaticism. Hume's rejection of probable judgment and his appeal to the authority of custom and tradition led him to counsel his readers to submit to whatever political power holds sway. On the other hand, the philosophes' desire to bring into being a perfectly rational and stable society eventually led them to view citizens as malleable material that must be continually molded and shaped by a small band of experts.

What is missing from both of these alternatives is Locke's central notion of the liberating power of probable judgment. For Locke, genuine freedom cannot be inherited through custom or tradition, nor can it be imposed by some all-knowing legislator. The freedom that defines us as human beings must be enacted by each individual through the arduous process of self-government. Ultimately, however, Locke does not provide us with a philosophically unassailable defense of this position. He does not resolve the tensions that characterize our political lives. Yet this is not his goal. He does not attempt to provide his readers with a comprehensive system of knowledge or establish each one of his claims on an unquestionable foundation of certainty. His aim is far more modest. He sets out to educate his readers in civic judgment so that we will be able to respond to urgent political dangers ourselves. Instead of assuming the presence of preconstituted, rational individuals, Locke seeks to shape his readers into the type of people who will be able to sustain stable and just institutions. To that end, he offers us a language of probable judgment that sidesteps both corrosive skepticism that ends in political acquiescence and dogmatic fanaticism that leads to irresolvable conflict. Ultimately it is an ability and willingness to employ probable judgment in matters of political contingency that distinguishes the freedom of self-government from the slavery of despotism.

References

Allison, Henry E. *Kant's Theory of Freedom*. Cambridge: Cambridge University Press, 1990.

Ames, William. *Conscience with the Power and Cases Thereof*. Norwood, N.J.: W. J. Johnson, 1975.

Appleby, Joyce Oldham. *Economic Thought and Ideology in Seventeenth-Century England*. Princeton: Princeton University Press, 1978.

Aquinas, Thomas. *Commentary on the Posterior Analytics of Aristotle*. Translated by Fabian R. Larcher. Albany, N.Y: Magi Books, 1970.

———. *Summa Theologiae*. Blackfriars ed. New York: McGraw-Hill, 1964.

Arendt, Hannah. *Between Past and Future*. New York: Penguin, 1968.

Aristotle. *Nicomachean Ethics*. Translated by Terence Irwin. Indianapolis: Hackett, 1985.

———. *Posterior Analytics*. Translated by Jonathan Barnes. Oxford: Clarendon Press, 1994.

Arnhardt, Larry. *Aristotle on Political Reasoning: A Commentary on the "Rhetoric."* DeKalb: Northern Illinois University Press, 1981.

Ashcraft, Richard. "Faith and Knowledge in Locke's Philosophy." In *John Locke: Problems and Perspectives*, edited by John Yolton. Cambridge: Cambridge University Press, 1969.

———. "Locke's State of Nature: Historical Fact or Moral Fiction?" *American Political Science Review* 62 (1968), 898–915.

———. *Locke's Two Treatises of Government*. London: Allen & Unwin, 1987.

———. *Revolutionary Politics & Locke's Two Treatises of Government*. Princeton: Princeton University Press, 1986.

Augustine. *Confessions*. Translated by Gillian Clark. Cambridge: Cambridge University Press, 1995.

Ayers, Michael. *Locke: Epistemology and Ontology*. 2 vols. New York: Routledge, 1993.

Bacon, Francis. *Novum Organum*. Edited by Lisa Jardine and Michael Silverthorne. Cambridge: Cambridge University Press, 2000.

Baumgold, Deborah. "Pacifying Politics: Resistance, Violence and Accountability in 17th Century Contract Theory." *Political Theory* 21, no. 1 (1993), 6–27.

Beiner, Ronald. *What's the Matter with Liberalism?* Berkeley: University of California Press, 1992.

Berkowitz, Peter. *Virtue and the Making of Modern Liberalism*. Princeton: Princeton University Press, 1999.

Black, Deborah. *Logic and Aristotle's Rhetoric and Poetics in Medieval Arabic Philosophy*. Leiden: Brill, 1990.

Blumenberg, Hans. *The Genesis of the Copernican World*. Translated by R. M. Wallace. Cambridge: MIT Press, 1987.

Bonelli, M. L., and William R. Shea, eds. *Reason, Experiment, and Mysticism in the Scientific Revolution*. New York: Science History Publications, 1975.

Boyle, Robert. *The Christian Virtuoso.* In *The Works of the Honorable Robert Boyle,* edited by Thomas Birch. London: Printed for A. Millar, 1744.

———. *Works of the Honourable Robert Boyle.* Edited by Thomas Birch. London: J. and R. Rivington, 1772.

Braithwaite, William Charles, and Henry Joel Cadbury. *The Beginnings of Quakerism.* Cambridge: Cambridge University Press, 1961.

Bramhall, John. "A Defence of True Liberty." In *Hobbes and Bramhall on Liberty and Necessity,* edited by Vere Chappell. Cambridge: Cambridge University Press, 1999.

Brown, Vivienne. "The 'Figure' of God and the Limits to Liberalism: A Rereading of Locke's *Essay* and *Two Treatises.*" *Journal of the History of Ideas* 60, no. 1 (1999), 83–100.

Burnet, Thomas. *Remarks Upon an Essay Concerning Humane Understanding in a Letter Address'd to the Author.* London: Printed for M. Wotton, 1697.

Button, Mark E. *Contract, Culture, and Citizenship.* University Park: Pennsylvania State University Press, 2008.

Byrne, E. F. *Probability and Opinion: A Study in the Medieval Pre-suppositions of Post-medieval Theories of Probability.* The Hague: Martinus Nijhoff, 1968.

Calvin, John. *Commentaries on the First Book of Moses, Called Genesis.* Edited by John King. Grand Rapids,: W.B. Eerdmans, 1948.

———. *Institutes of the Christian Religion.* Edited by Tony Lance and Hilary Osborne. Grand Rapids: Baker Book House, 1987.

Capp, B. S. "The Fifth Monarchists and the Popular Millenarianism." In *Radical Religion in the English Revolution,* edited by J. F. McGregor and Barry Reay. Oxford: Oxford University Press, 1986.

Caton, Hiram. *The Origin of Subjectivity.* New Haven: Yale University Press, 1973.

Chappell, Vere. "Locke's Theory of Ideas." In *The Cambridge Companion to Locke,* edited by Vere Chappell. Cambridge: Cambridge University Press, 1994.

Charron, Pierre. *Of Wisdom.* Translated by Samson Lennard. London: Edward Blount & Will, 1630.

Chillingworth, William. *The Religion of Protestants, a Sage Way to Salvation.* Oxford: Printed by Leonard Lichfield, 1638.

Chown, John F. *A History of Money.* New York: Routledge, 1994.

Cicero, Marcus Tullius. *The Nature of the Gods.* Edited by P. G. Walsh. New York: Clarendon Press, 1997.

Colie, Rosalie. "The Essayist in the *Essay.*" In *John Locke: Problems and Perspectives,* edited by John W. Yolton. London: Cambridge University Press, 1969.

Colman, John. *John Locke's Moral Philosophy.* Edinburgh: Edinburgh University Press, 1983.

Condillac, Abbé de. *An Essay on the Origin of Human Knowledge.* Gainesville, Fla.: Scholars' Facsimiles, 1971.

Coudert, Allison. "Forgotten Ways of Knowing: The Kabbalah, Language and Science in the Seventeenth Century." In *Shapes of Knowledge from the Renaissance to the Enlightenment,* edited by Donald Kelley and Richard Popkin. Dordrecht: Kluwer, 1991.

Courtenay, William J. "Nominalism and Late Medieval Religion." In *The Pursuit of Holiness in Late Medieval and Renaissance Religion*, edited by Charles Trinkhaus and Heiko Oberman. Leiden: Brill, 1974.

Cranston, Maurice. *John Locke: A Biography*. London: Longman, 1957.

Creppell, Ingrid. *Toleration and Identity: Foundations in Early Modern Thought*. New York: Routledge, 2003.

Curley, Edwin. *Descartes against the Skeptics*. Cambridge: Harvard University Press, 1978.

———. "From Locke's Letter to Montesquieu's Lettres." In *Renaissance and Early Modern Philosophy*. Malden, Mass.: Blackwell, 2002. 280–306.

Dagger, Richard. *Civic Virtues*. New York: Oxford University Press, 1997.

Daston, Loraine. *Classical Probability and the Enlightenment*. Princeton: Princeton University Press, 1988.

———. "Probability and Evidence." In *The Cambridge History of Seventeenth-Century Philosophy*. Edited by Daniel Garber and Michael Ayers. 2 vols. Cambridge: Cambridge University Press, 1998. 1108–44.

Dawson, Hannah. *Locke, Language and Early-Modern Philosophy*. Cambridge: Cambridge University Press, 2007.

———. "Locke on Language in (Civil) Society." *History of Political Thought* 26, no. 3 (2005), 397–425.

Dear, Peter. *Discipline and Experience*. Chicago: University of Chicago Press, 1995.

———. *Revolutionizing the Sciences*. Princeton: Princeton University Press, 2001.

den Hartogh, Govert. "Made by Contrivance and the Consent of Men: Abstract Principle and Historical Fact in Locke's Political Philosophy." *Interpretation* 17 (Winter 1989–90), 193–221.

Descartes, René. *The Philosophical Writings of Descartes*. Edited by J. Cottingham, R. Stoothoff, D. Murdoch, and A. Kenny. 3 vols. Cambridge: Cambridge University Press, 1984–91.

———. *Oeuvres de Descartes*. Edited by Charles Adam and Paul Tannery. 13 vols. Paris: Vrin, 1957–68.

Dewhurst, Kenneth. *John Locke (1632–1704), Physician and Philosopher: A Medical Biography*. London: Wellcome Historical Medical Library, 1963.

———. "Locke's Contribution to Boyle's Researches on the Air and on Human Blood." *Notes of the Royal Society of London* 17 (1962), 198–206.

Dienstag, Joshua Foa. *"Dancing in Chains": Narrative and Memory in Political Theory*. Stanford: Stanford University Press, 1997.

Drescher, Seymour. "On James Farr's 'So Vile and Miserable an Estate.'" *Political Theory* 16 (1988), 502–3.

Dunn, John. *Locke: Past Masters*. Oxford: Oxford University Press, 1984.

———. "Measuring Locke's Shadow." In John Locke, *Two Treatises of Government and a Letter Concerning Toleration*, edited by Ian Shapiro. New Haven: Yale University Press, 2003.

———. *The Political Thought of John Locke*. Cambridge: Cambridge University Press, 1969.

———. "'Trust' in the Politics of John Locke." In *Rethinking Modern Political Theory: Essays, 1979–83*. Cambridge: Cambridge University Press, 1985.

Eisenach, Eldon. "Religion and Locke's *Two Treatises of Government*." In *John Locke's Two Treatises of Government: New Interpretations*, edited by Edward Harpham. Lawrence: University Press of Kansas, 1992.

Ellis, Elizabeth. *Kant's Politics: Provisional Theory for an Uncertain World*. New Haven: Yale University Press, 2005.

Emerson, Ralph Waldo. "Representative Men." In *Collected Works*, edited by W. Williams and D. Wilson. Cambridge: Cambridge University Press, 1987.

Erasmus, Desiderius. "On Free Will." In *The Portable Renaissance Reader*, edited by James Bruce Ross and Mary Martin McLaughlin. New York: Viking Press, 1953.

Farr, James. "'Slaves Bought with Money': A Reply to Drescher." *Political Theory* 17 (1989), 471–74.

———. "'So Vile and Miserable an Estate': The Problem of Slavery in Locke's Political Thought." *Political Theory* 14 (1986), 263–89.

Faulkner, Robert. "Preface to Liberalism: Locke's *First Treatise* and the Bible." *Review of Politics* 67, no. 3 (2005), 451–72.

Ferreira, M. Jamie. "Locke's 'Constructive Skepticism'—a Reappraisal." *Journal of the History of Philosophy* 24 (1986), 211–22.

———. *Scepticism and Reasonable Doubt: The British Naturalist Tradition in Wilkins, Hume, Reid and Newman*. Oxford: Clarendon Press, 1986.

Feyerabend, Paul. "Classical Empiricism." In *The Methodological Heritage of Newton*, edited by Robert E. Butts and John W. Davis. Toronto: University of Toronto Press, 1970.

Figgis, John Neville. *The Divine Right of Kings*. New York: Harper & Row, 1965.

Filmer, Robert. *Patriarcha and Other Political Works of Sir Robert Filmer*. Edited by Peter Laslett. Oxford: Blackwell, 1949.

Flathman, Richard. *Reflections of a Would-Be Anarchist: Ideals and Institutions of Liberalism*. Minneapolis: University of Minnesota Press, 1998.

Forde, Steven. "What Does Locke Expect Us to Know?" *Review of Politics* 68 (2006), 232–58.

Foster, David. "The Bible and Natural Freedom in John Locke's Political Thought." In *Piety and Humanity: Essays on Religion and Early Modern Political Philosophy*, edited by Douglas Kries. Lanham, Md.: Rowman & Littlefield, 1997.

Forster, Greg. *John Locke's Politics of Moral Consensus*. Cambridge: Cambridge University Press, 2005.

Foucault, Michel. *The Order of Things*. New York: Random House, 1970.

Frame, Donald M. *Montaigne: A Biography*. San Francisco: North Point Press, 1984.

———. *Montaigne's Discovery of Man: The Humanization of a Humanist*. Westport, Conn.: Greenwood Press, 1983.

Frankfurt, Harry. *Demons, Dreamers and Madmen*. Indianapolis: Bobbs-Merrill, 1970.

Franklin, James. *The Science of Conjecture: Evidence and Probability before Pascal*. Baltimore: Johns Hopkins University Press, 2001.

Frei, Hans. *The Eclipse of Biblical Narrative: A Study in Eighteenth- and Nineteenth-Century Hermeneutics*. New Haven: Yale University Press, 1974.

Friedrich, Hugo. *Montaigne*. Translated by Dawn Eng. Berkeley: University of California Press, 1991.

Funkenstein, Amos. *Theology and the Scientific Imagination from the Middle Ages to the Seventeenth Century*. Princeton: Princeton University Press, 1986.

Galston, William. *Liberal Purposes: Good, Virtues, and Diversity in the Liberal State*. Cambridge: Cambridge University Press, 1991.

Garber, D., and S. Zabell. "On the Emergence of Probability." *Archive for History of Exact Sciences* 21 (1979), 35–53.

Gassendi, Pierre. "The Discourses of Happiness, Virtue, and Liberty." In *Moral Philosophy from Montaigne to Kant*, edited by J. B. Schneewind. New York: Cambridge University Press, 1990.

———. *Opera Omnia*. Stuttgart: Friedrich Frommann Verlag, 1964.

Gauthier, David. "Public Reason." *Social Philosophy and Policy* 12, no. 1 (1995), 19–42.

Gay, Peter. *The Enlightenment: An Interpretation*. New York: Random House, 1969.

Germino, Dante. *Modern Western Political Thought*. Chicago: University of Chicago Press, 1972.

Gibson, James. *John Locke*. London: H. Milford, 1933.

Gierke, Otto von. *Natural Law and the Theory of Society, 1500–1800*. Translated by Ernest Barker. Boston: Beacon Press, 1960.

Gillespie, Michael Allen. "Descartes and the Question of Toleration." In *Early Modern Skepticism and the Origins of Toleration*, edited by Alan Levine. Lanham, Md.: Lexington Books, 1999.

———. "Montaigne's Humanistic Liberalism." *Journal of Politics* 47, no. 1 (1985), 40–59.

———. *The Theological Origins of Modernity*. Chicago: University of Chicago Press, 2008.

Gilson, Etienne. *The Christian Philosophy of Saint Augustine*. Translated by L.E.M. Lynch. New York: Octagon Books, 1983.

———. *The Christian Philosophy of St. Thomas Aquinas*. Translated by L. K. Shook. New York: Random House, 1956.

———. *The History of Christian Philosophy in the Middle Ages*. New York: Random House, 1955.

———. *Reason and Revelation in the Middle Ages*. New York: C. Scribner's, 1938.

Gilson, Etienne, and Thomas Langan. *Modern Philosophy: Descartes to Kant*. New York: Random House, 1963.

Glucker, John. "*Probabile, Ver simile*, and Related Terms." In *Cicero the Philosopher*, edited by J.G.F. Powell. Oxford: Oxford University Press, 1995.

Goldwin, Robert. "Locke's State of Nature in Political Society." *Western Political Quarterly* 29 (1976), 126–35.

Gough, J. W. Introduction to John Locke, *Epistola de tolerantia*. Edited by Raymond Klibansky, translated by J. W. Gough. Oxford: Clarendon Press, 1968.

———. *John Locke's Political Philosophy: Eight Studies*. 2nd ed. Oxford: Clarendon Press, 1973.

Grant, Ruth. *John Locke's Liberalism*. Chicago: University of Chicago Press, 1987.

Gray, John. *Two Faces of Liberalism*. New York: New Press, 2000.

Grenberg, Jeanine. *Kant and the Ethics of Humility*. Cambridge: Cambridge University Press, 2005.

Grendler, Paul. "Pierre Charron: Precursor to Hobbes." *Review of Politics* 25 (1963), 212–24.

Grotius, Hugo. *The Truth of the Christian Religion*. Translated by John Clarke. Cambridge: J. Hall & Son, 1860.

Hackett, Jeremiah. "Roger Bacon on 'scientia experimentalis.'" In *Roger Bacon and the Sciences*, edited by Jeremiah Hackett. Leiden: Brill, 1997.

Hacking, Ian. *The Emergence of Probability: A Philosophical Study of Early Ideas about Probability, Induction and Statistical Inference*. London: Cambridge University Press, 1975.

Harnack, Adolf von. *Grundriss der Dogmengeschichte: Die Entstehung des Dogmas und seine Entwickelung im Rahmen der morgenländischen Kirche*. Freiburg: J.C.B. Mohr, 1889.

Harris, Ian. *The Mind of John Locke: A Study of Political Theory in Its Intellectual Setting*. Cambridge: Cambridge University Press, 1994.

———. "The Politics of Christianity." In *Locke's Philosophy: Content and Context*, edited by G.A.J. Rogers. Oxford: Clarendon Press, 1994.

Harrison, John, and Peter Laslett. *The Library of John Locke*. Oxford: Oxford University Press, 1965.

Harrison, Ross. *Hobbes, Locke, and Confusion's Masterpiece*. Cambridge: Cambridge University Press, 2003.

Hartle, Ann. *Michel de Montaigne: Accidental Philosopher*. Cambridge: Cambridge University Press, 2003.

Hartz, Louis. *The Liberal Tradition in America*. New York: Harcourt, Brace, 1955.

Helvetius, Claude-Adrien. *A Treatise on Man*. Translated by W. Hooper. 2 vols. New York: Burt Franklin, 1810.

Heyd, Michael. *"Be Sober and Reasonable": The Critique of Enthusiasm in the Seventeenth and Early Eighteenth Centuries*. Leiden: Brill, 1995.

Hill, Christopher. *Intellectual Origins of the English Revolution—Revisited*. Oxford: Clarendon Press, 2001.

Hobbes, Thomas. *The Elements of Law, Natural and Politic: Part I, Human Nature, Part II, De Corpore Politico; with Three Lives*. Edited by J.C.A. Gaskin. New York: Oxford University Press, 1994.

———. *Leviathan*. Edited by Richard Tuck. Cambridge: Cambridge University Press, 1991.

———. "Of Liberty and Necessity." In *Hobbes and Bramhall on Liberty and Necessity*, edited by Vere Chappell. Cambridge: Cambridge University Press, 1999.

———. *Man and Citizen: De Homine and De Cive*. Edited by Charles T. Wood. Indianapolis: Hackett, 1991.

Hooker, Richard. *Of the Laws of Ecclesiastical Polity*. Edited by Arthur Stephen McGrade. Cambridge: Cambridge University Press, 1989.

Horkheimer, Max. "Montaigne und die Funktion der Skepsis." In *Anfänger der Burgerlichen Geschichtsphilosophie*. Frankfurt am Main: Fischer Verlag, 1971.

Howell, Wilber Samuel. *Logic and Rhetoric in England, 1500–1700*. Princeton: Princeton University Press, 1956.

Hume, David. *An Enquiry Concerning Human Understanding*. Edited by Thomas Beauchamp. Oxford: Oxford University Press, 2001.

———. *An Enquiry Concerning the Principles of Morals*. Edited by Thomas Beauchamp. Oxford: Oxford University Press, 2006.

———. *A Treatise of Human Nature*. Edited by David Fate Norton and Mary J. Norton. Oxford: Oxford University Press, 2007.

Israel, Jonathan. *Radical Enlightenment: Philosophy and the Making of Modernity, 1650–1750*. Oxford: Oxford University Press, 2001.

Ivison, Duncan. *The Self at Liberty*. Ithaca, N.Y.: Cornell University Press, 1997.

Jacob, J. R. *Robert Boyle and the English Revolution*. New York: Bert Franklin, 1978.

James VI and I. *Political Writings*. Edited by Johann Somerville. Cambridge: Cambridge University Press, 1994.

Janowski, Zbigniew. *Cartesian Theodicy: Descartes' Quest for Certitude*. Dordrecht: Kluwer, 2002.

Jardine, Lisa. *Ingenious Pursuits: Building the Scientific Revolution*. London: Little, Brown, 1999.

Jolley, Nicholas. *Locke: His Philosophical Thought*. Oxford: Oxford University Press, 1999.

———. "Reason's Dim Candle: Locke's Critique of Enthusiasm." In *The Philosophy of John Locke: New Perspectives*, edited by Peter R. Anstey. New York: Routledge, 2003.

Josephson, Peter. *The Great Art of Government: Locke's Use of Consent*. Lawrence: University Press of Kansas, 2002.

Joy, Lynn Sumida. *Gassendi the Atomist: Advocate of History in an Age of Science*. Cambridge: Cambridge University Press, 1987.

Kahn, Victoria Ann. *Machiavellian Rhetoric: From the Counter-Reformation to Milton*. Princeton: Princeton University Press, 1994.

———. *Rhetoric, Prudence, and Skepticism in the Renaissance*. Ithaca, N.Y.: Cornell University Press, 1985.

Kant, Immanuel. *Critique of Pure Reason*. Translated by Paul Guyer and Allen W. Wood. Cambridge: Cambridge University Press, 1998.

———. *Political Writings*. Edited by Hans Reiss, translated by H. B. Nisbet. New York: Cambridge University Press, 1991.

Kargon, Robert Hugh. *Atomism in England from Hariot to Newton*. Oxford: Clarendon Press, 1966.

Keohane, Nannerl. *Philosophy and the State in France: The Renaissance to the Enlightenment*. Princeton: Princeton University Press, 1980.

King, Peter. *The Life and Letters of John Locke, with Extracts from His Journals and Commonplace Books*. New York: B. Franklin, 1972.

Koyré, Alexandre. *Descartes und die Scholastik*. Bonn: Bouvier Verlag Herbert Grundmann, 1971.

Koyré, Alexandre. *From the Closed World to the Infinite Universe.* Baltimore: Johns Hopkins Press, 1957.

Kraynak, Robert P. "John Locke: From Absolutism to Toleration." *American Political Science Review* 74, no. 1 (1980), 53–96.

Kroll, Richard W. F. *The Material World: Literate Culture in the Restoration and Early Eighteenth Century.* Baltimore: Johns Hopkins University Press, 1991.

Laski, Harold. *Political Thought in England: From Locke to Bentham.* London: Oxford University Press, 1950.

LaVaque-Manty, Mika. *Arguments and Fists: Political Agency and Justification in Liberal Theory.* New York: Routledge, 2002.

Lee, Henry. *Anti-Scepticism: Or, Notes upon each Chapter of Mr. Lock's Essay concerning Humane Understanding. With an Explication of all the Particulars of which he Treats, and in the same Order.* London: R. Clavel & C. Harper, 1702.

Leff, Gordon. *The Dissolution of the Medieval Outlook: An Essay on Intellectual and Spiritual Change in the Fourteenth Century.* New York: New York University Press, 1976.

Leibniz, G. W. *New Essays on Human Understanding.* Translated by Peter Remnant and Jonathan Bennett. Cambridge: Cambridge University Press, 1982.

Leites, Edmund. "Casuistry and Character." In *Conscience and Casuistry in Early Modern Europe*, edited by Edmund Leites. Cambridge: Cambridge University Press, 1988.

Lennon, Thomas M. *The Battle of the Gods and Giants: The Legacies of Descartes and Gassendi, 1655–1715.* Princeton: Princeton University Press, 1993.

Levine, Alan. *Sensual Philosophy: Toleration, Skepticism, and Montaigne's Politics of the Self.* Lanham, Md.: Lexington Books, 2001.

Locke, John. *The Correspondence of John Locke.* Edited by E. S. De Beer. 8 vols. Oxford: Clarendon Press, 1976.

———. "De Arte Medica." In Fox Bourne, *The Life of John Locke.* 2 vols. London: Harry S. King, 1876.

———. "A Discourse of Miracles." In *John Locke*, edited by I. T. Ramsey. Stanford: Stanford University Press, 1958.

———. *Drafts for the Essay Concerning Human Understanding, and Other Philosophical Writings.* Edited by P. H. Nidditch and G.A.J. Rogers. Oxford: Clarendon Press, 1990.

———. *An Essay Concerning Human Understanding.* Edited by P. H. Nidditch. Oxford: Clarendon Press, 1975.

———. *Essays on the Law of Nature.* Edited by W. von Leyden. Oxford: Clarendon Press, 1954.

———. *A Letter Concerning Toleration.* Edited by James Tully. Indianapolis: Hackett, 1983.

———. *Locke on Money.* Edited by P. H. Kelly. Oxford: Clarendon Press, 1991.

———. *A Paraphrase and Notes on the Epistles of St. Paul to the Galatians, 1 and 2 Corinthians, Romans, Ephesians.* Edited by Arthur William Wainwright. Oxford: Clarendon Press, 1987.

———. *Political Writings of John Locke.* Edited by David Wootton. London: Penguin, 1993.

————. *Questions Concerning the Law of Nature*. Edited and translated by Robert H. Horwitz, Jenny Strauss Clay, and Diskin Clay. Ithaca, N.Y.: Cornell University Press, 1990.

————. *The Reasonableness of Christianity as Delivered in the Scriptures*. Edited by George Ewing. Washington, D.C.: Regnery Gateway, 1965.

————. *Some Thoughts Concerning Education* and *Of the Conduct of the Understanding*. Edited by Ruth W. Grant and Nathan Tarcov. Indianapolis: Hackett, 1996.

————. *Two Tracts on Government*. Edited by Philip Abrams. London: Cambridge University Press, 1967.

————. *Two Treatises of Government*. Edited by Peter Laslett. Cambridge: Cambridge University Press, 1988.

————. *The Works of John Locke*. Oxford: Oxford University Press, 1823.

————. *Writings on Religion*. Edited by Victor Nuovo. London: Clarendon Press, 2002.

Luther, Martin. "The Appeal to the German Nobility." In *Documents of the Christian Church*, edited by Henry Bettenson and Chris Maunder. Oxford: Oxford University Press, 1999.

————. "The Babylonish Captivity of the Church." In *Documents of the Christian Church*, edited by Henry Bettenson and Chris Maunder. Oxford: Oxford University Press, 1999.

————. "Bondage of the Will." In *The Portable Renaissance Reader*, edited by James Bruce Ross and Mary Martin McLaughlin. New York: Viking Press, 1953.

————. "The Ninety-Five Theses, 1517." In *Documents of the Christian Church*, edited by Henry Bettenson and Chris Maunder. Oxford: Oxford University Press, 1999.

————. *Selections*. Edited by John Dillenberger. New York: Anchor Books, 1961.

Macedo, Stephen. *Liberal Virtues*. Oxford: Clarendon Press, 1990.

Machiavelli, Niccolò. *Discourses on Livy*. Translated by Harvey Mansfield and Nathan Tarcov. Chicago: University of Chicago Press, 1996.

————. *The Prince*. Edited by Quentin Skinner and Russell Price. Cambridge: Cambridge University Press, 1988.

MacIntyre, Alasdair. *After Virtue*. Notre Dame, Ind.: University of Notre Dame Press, 1984.

Macpherson, C. B. *The Political Theory of Possessive Individualism*. Oxford: Oxford University Press, 1962.

Marshall, John. *John Locke: Resistance, Religion and Responsibility*. Cambridge: Cambridge University Press, 1994.

————. "Locke, Socinianism, 'Socinianism,' and Unitarianism." In *English Philosophy in the Age of Locke*, edited by M. A Stewart. Oxford: Clarendon, 2000.

Martin, Julian. *Francis Bacon, the State, and the Reform of Natural Philosophy*. Cambridge: Cambridge University Press, 1992.

Marx, Karl. "Eighteenth Brumaire." In *Political Writings: Surveys from Exile*, edited by David Fernbach. New York: Random House, 1974.

McClure, Kirstie. *Judging Rights: Lockean Politics and the Limits of Consent*. Ithaca, N.Y.: Cornell University Press, 1996.

McGrade, Arthur S. *The Political Thought of William of Ockham: Personal and Institutional Principles*. Cambridge: Cambridge University Press, 1974.

McLachlan, H. John. *The Religious Opinions of Milton, Locke, and Newton*. Folcroft, Pa.: Folcroft Library Editions, 1974.

Mehta, Uday Singh. *The Anxiety of Freedom: Imagination and Individuality in Locke's Political Thought*. Ithaca, N.Y: Cornell University Press, 1992.

Milton, J. R. "Locke and Gassendi: A Reappraisal." In *English Philosophy in the Age of Locke*, edited by M. A. Stewart. Oxford: Clarendon Press, 2000.

Mitchell, Joshua. *Not by Reason Alone: Religion, History, and Identity in Early Modern Political Thought*. Chicago: University of Chicago Press, 1993.

Montaigne, Michel de. *Complete Essays*. Translated by Donald M. Frame. Stanford: Stanford University Press, 1958.

Myers, Peter C. *Our Only Star and Compass: Locke and the Struggle for Political Rationality*. Lanham, Md.: Rowman & Littlefield, 1998.

Nicholas of Cusa. *On Learned Ignorance: A Translation and an Appraisal of De Docta Ignorantia*. Translated by Jasper Hopkins. Minneapolis: A. J. Benning Press, 1981.

Nicole, Pierre. "On the Weakness of Man." In *John Locke as Translator: Three of the Essais of Pierre Nicole in French and English*, edited by Jean S. Yolton. Oxford: Voltaire Foundation, 2000.

Nuovo, Victor. "Locke's Theology, 1694–1704." In *English Philosophy in the Age of Locke*, edited by M. A. Stewart. Oxford: Clarendon Press, 2000.

Oakley, Francis. *Omnipotence, Covenant & Order: An Excursion in the History of Ideas from Abelard to Leibniz*. Ithaca, N.Y.: Cornell University Press, 1984.

Oberman, Heiko Augustinus. *The Harvest of Medieval Theology*. Cambridge: Harvard University Press, 1963.

———. *Luther: Man between God and the Devil*. New Haven: Yale University Press, 1989.

Ockham, William of. *Summa Logicae*. Edited by Philotheus Boehner. St. Bonaventure, N.Y.: Franciscan Institute, 1951.

O'Neill, Onora. *Constructions of Reason*. Cambridge: Cambridge University Press, 1989.

Origen. *Contra Celsum*. Translated by Henry Chadwick. Cambridge: Cambridge University Press, 1953.

Orwell, George. *1984*. San Diego: Harcourt Brace Jovanovich, 1984.

———. "Politics and the English Language." In *Shooting an Elephant, and Other Essays*. New York: Harcourt Brace, 1950.

Osler, Margaret. "John Locke and the Changing Ideal of Scientific Knowledge." *Journal of the History of Ideas* 31, no. 1 (1970), 3–16.

Ozment, Steven E. *The Age of Reform, 1250–1550: An Intellectual and Religious History of Late Medieval and Reformation Europe*. New Haven: Yale University Press, 1980.

———. "Mysticism, Nominalism, and Dissent." In *The Pursuit of Holiness in Late Medieval and Renaissance Religion*, edited by Charles Trinkhaus and Heiko Oberman. Leiden: Brill, 1974.

Pagel, Walter. *Paracelsus: An Introduction to Philosophical Medicine in the Era of the Renaissance*. New York: Karger, 1982.

Pangle, Thomas L. *The Spirit of Modern Republicanism: The Moral Vision of the American Founders and the Philosophy of Locke.* Chicago: University of Chicago Press, 1988.

Pascal, Blaise. *The Provincial Letters.* Translated by A. J. Krailsheimer. Harmondsworth: Penguin, 1967.

———. *Thoughts.* Translated by William Finlayson Trotter. New York: P. F. Collier & Son, 1910.

Pasquino, Pasquale. "Locke on King's Prerogative." *Political Theory* 26 (1998), 198–208.

Patey, Douglas Lane. *Probability and Literary Form: Philosophic Theory and Literary Practice in the Augustan Age.* Cambridge: Cambridge University Press, 1984.

Perez-Ramos, Antonio. *Francis Bacon's Idea of Science and the Maker's Knowledge Tradition.* Oxford: Oxford University Press, 1988.

Perkins, William. *William Perkins, 1558–1602, English Puritanist; His Pioneer Works on Casuistry: "A Discourse of Conscience" and "The Whole Treatise of Cases of Conscience."* Edited by Thomas F. Merrill. Nieuwkoop: B. De Graaf, 1966.

Pocock, J.G.A. "Enthusiasm: The Antiself of Enlightenment." In *Enthusiasm and Enlightenment in Europe, 1650–1850,* edited by Lawrence E. Klein and Anthony J. La Vopa. San Marino, Calif.: Huntington Library, 1998.

———. *The Machiavellian Moment.* Princeton: Princeton University Press, 1975.

Popkin, Richard. *The History of Scepticism from Erasmus to Spinoza.* New York: Humanities Press, 1964.

———. "The Role of Scepticism in Modern Philosophy Reconsidered." *Journal of the History of Ideas* 31 (1993), 501–17.

Rabieh, Michael S. "The Reasonableness of Locke, or the Questionableness of Christianity." *Journal of Politics* 53 (1991), 933–57.

Rahe, Paul. *Republics Ancient and Modern: Classical Republicanism and the American Revolution.* Chapel Hill: University of North Carolina Press, 1992.

Rasmussen, Douglas B., and Douglas J. Den Uyl. *Norms of Liberty: A Perfectionist Basis for Non-Perfectionist Politics.* University Park: Pennsylvania State University Press, 2005.

Rawls, John. "The Idea of Public Reason Revisited." In *The Law of Peoples.* Cambridge: Harvard University Press, 2001. 129–80.

———. *Political Liberalism.* New York: Columbia University Press, 1993.

———. *A Theory of Justice.* Cambridge: Harvard University Press, 1971.

Redwood, John. *Reason, Ridicule and Religion: The Age of Enlightenment in England, 1660–1750.* Cambridge: Harvard University Press, 1976.

Reedy, Gerard. *The Bible and Reason: Anglicans and Scripture in Late Seventeenth-Century England.* Philadelphia: University of Pennsylvania Press, 1985.

Riley, Patrick. *Will and Political Legitimacy.* Cambridge: Harvard University Press, 1982.

Rogers, G.A.L. *Locke's Enlightenment: Aspects of the Origin, Nature and Impact of His Philosophy.* Hildesheim: Georg Olms Verlag, 1998.

Romanell, Patrick. *John Locke and Medicine: A New Key to Locke*. Buffalo, N.Y:
Prometheus Books, 1984.

Rossi, Paolo. "Hermeticism, Rationality, and the Scientific Revolution." In *Reason, Experiment, and Mysticism in the Scientific Revolution*, edited by M. L.
Bonelli and William R. Shea. New York: Science History Publications, 1975.

Ryan, Alan. "Self-Ownership, Autonomy, and Property Rights." *Social Philosophy and Policy* 11 (1994), 241–58.

Ryle, Gilbert. "John Locke." In *Collected Papers*. Vol. 1. New York: Barnes &
Noble, 1971.

Sandel, Michael. *Liberalism and the Limits of Justice*. Cambridge: Cambridge
University Press, 1982.

Sarasohn, Lisa T. *Gassendi's Ethics: Freedom in a Mechanistic Universe*. Ithaca,
N.Y.: Cornell University Press, 1996.

Sargent, Thomas J., and François R. Velde. *The Big Problem of Small Change*.
Princeton: Princeton University Press, 2002.

Schaefer, David Lewis. *The Political Philosophy of Montaigne*. Ithaca, N.Y.: Cornell University Press, 1990.

Schmitt, C. B., Q. Skinner, E. Kessler, and J. Kraye, eds. *The Cambridge History of
Renaissance Philosophy*. Cambridge: Cambridge University Press, 1988.

Schneewind, J. B. *The Invention of Autonomy*. Cambridge: Cambridge University
Press, 1998.

Schochet, Gordon. *Patriarchalism in Political Thought*. New York: Basic Books,
1975.

Schouls, Peter A. *The Imposition of Method: A Study of Descartes and Locke*.
Oxford: Clarendon Press; New York: Oxford University Press, 1980.

———. *Reasoned Freedom: John Locke and Enlightenment*. Ithaca, N.Y: Cornell
University Press, 1992.

Schumpeter, Joseph. *History of Economic Analysis*. New York: Oxford University Press, 1994.

Schweber, Howard H. *The Language of Liberal Constitutionalism*. New York:
Cambridge University Press, 2007.

Schwoerer, Lois. *The Declaration of Rights, 1689*. Baltimore: Johns Hopkins University Press, 1981.

Seliger, Martin. *The Liberal Politics of John Locke*. London: Allen and Unwin, 1968.

Serjeantson, R. W. "Testimony and Proof in Early-Modern England." *Studies in
the History and Philosophy of Science* 3, no. 2 (1999), 195–236.

Shapin, Steven. *The Scientific Revolution*. Chicago: University of Chicago Press,
1996.

———. *The Social History of Truth: Civility and Science in Seventeenth-Century
England*. Chicago: University of Chicago Press, 1994.

Shapin, Steven, and Simon Schaffer. *Leviathan and the Air-Pump*. Princeton:
Princeton University Press, 1985.

Shapiro, Barbara J. *A Culture of Fact: England, 1550–1720*. Ithaca, N.Y.: Cornell
University Press, 2000.

———. *Probability and Certainty in Seventeenth-Century England: A Study of
the Relationships between Natural Science, Religion, History, Law, and Literature*. Princeton: Princeton University Press, 1983.

Shapiro, Ian. *The Evolution of Rights in Liberal Theory*. Cambridge: Cambridge University Press, 1986.

Shklar, Judith. *Ordinary Vices*. Cambridge: Harvard University Press, 1984.

Siegel, Jerrold. *The Idea of the Self: Thought and Experience in Western Europe since the Seventeenth Century*. Cambridge: Cambridge University Press, 2005.

Simmons, A. John. *The Lockean Theory of Rights*. Princeton: Princeton University Press, 1992.

———. "Locke's State of Nature." *Political Theory* 17 (1989), 449–70.

———. *On the Edge of Anarchy: Locke, Consent, and the Limits of Society*. Princeton: Princeton University Press, 1993.

Skerpen, Elizabeth. *The Rhetoric of Politics in the English Revolution: 1642–1660*. Columbia: University of Missouri Press, 1992.

Skinner, Quentin. *The Foundations of Modern Political Thought*. 2 vols. Cambridge: Cambridge University Press, 1978.

Soles, David E. "Locke's Empiricism and the Postulation of Unobservables." *Journal of the History of Philosophy* 23, no. 3 (1985), 339–69.

Spellman, W. M. *John Locke, British History in Perspective*. New York: St. Martin's Press, 1997.

———. *John Locke and the Problem of Depravity*. Oxford: Clarendon Press, 1988.

———. *The Latitudinarians and the Church of England, 1660–1700*. Athens: University of Georgia Press, 1993.

Spinoza, Baruch. *A Theological-Political Treatise*. Translated by Samuel Shirley. Indianapolis: Hackett, 1991.

Sprat, Thomas. *History of the Royal Society*. Edited by J. Cope and H. W. Jones. St. Louis: Washington University Press, 1958.

Starobinski, Jean. *Montaigne in Motion*. Translated by Arthur Goldhammer. Chicago: University of Chicago Press, 1985.

Stephen, Leslie. *The History of English Thought in the Eighteenth Century*. New York: G. P. Putnam's Sons, 1876.

Stevens, Jacqueline. "The Reasonableness of John Locke's Majority." *Political Theory* 24 (1996), 423–63.

———. *Reproducing the State*. Princeton: Princeton University Press, 1999.

Stewart, M. A. *English Philosophy in the Age of Locke*. New York: Oxford University Press, 2000.

Stout, Jeffrey. *Flight from Authority*. Notre Dame, Ind.: Notre Dame University Press, 1981.

Strauss, Leo. *Natural Right and History*. Chicago: University of Chicago Press, 1957.

Swift, Jonathan. "A Tale of a Tub." In *Gulliver's Travels and Other Writings*. Oxford: Clarendon Press, 1958.

Tarcov, Nathan. *Locke's Education for Liberty*. Chicago: University of Chicago Press, 1984.

———. "Locke's *Second Treatise* and 'the Best Fence against Rebellion.'" *Review of Politics* 51 (1981), 198–217.

Tarlton, Charles D. "A Rope of Sand: Interpreting Locke's *First Treatise of Government*." *Historical Journal* 21, no. 1 (1978), 43–73.

Tarlton, Charles D. "The Rulers Now on Earth: Locke's *Two Treatises* and the Revolution of 1688." *Historical Journal* 28, no. 2 (1985), 279–98.

Taylor, Charles. *Sources of the Self: The Making of the Modern Identity*. Cambridge: Harvard University Press, 1989.

Thomas, Keith. *Religion and the Decline of Magic: Studies in Popular Beliefs in Sixteenth and Seventeenth Century England*. New York: Oxford University Press, 1997.

Thucydides. *History of the Peloponnesian War*. Translated by Richard Crawley. New York: Modern Library, 1982.

Tierney, Brian. *The Crisis of Church and State, 1050–1300*. Englewood Cliffs, N.J.: Prentice-Hall, 1976.

Tocqueville, Alexis de. *Democracy in America*. Edited by J. P. Mayer, translated by George Lawrence. New York: Harper, 1969.

Todd, Margo. *Christian Humanism and the Puritan Social Order*. Cambridge: Cambridge University Press, 1987.

Toulmin, Stephen. *Cosmopolis: The Hidden Agenda of Modernity*. Chicago: University of Chicago Press, 1990.

Tuck, Richard. "Grotius, Carneades and Hobbes." *Grotiana* 4 (1983), 43–62.

———. "Hobbes and Descartes." In *Perspectives on Thomas Hobbes*, edited by G.A.J. Rogers and Alan Ryan. Oxford: Clarendon Press, 1988.

———. "Optics and Sceptics: The Philosophical Foundations of Hobbes's Political Thought." In *Conscience and Casuistry in Early Modern Europe*, edited by Edmund Leites. Cambridge: Cambridge University Press, 1988.

———. *Philosophy and Government, 1572–1651*. Cambridge: Cambridge University Press, 1993.

———. "Scepticism and Toleration in the Seventeenth Century." In *Justifying Toleration*, edited by Susan Mendus. Cambridge: Cambridge University Press, 1989.

Tully, James. *An Approach to Political Philosophy: Locke in Contexts*. Cambridge: Cambridge University Press, 1993.

———. *A Discourse on Property*. Cambridge: University of Cambridge Press, 1980.

Tyrrell, James *Patriarcha Non Monarcha. The Patriarch Unmonarch'd*. London: Printed for Richard Janeway, 1681.

Van Leeuwen, Henry G. *The Problem of Certainty in English Thought, 1630–1690*. Vol. 1. The Hague: Martinus Nijhoff, 1963.

Vernon, Richard. *The Career of Toleration: John Locke, Jonas Proast and After*. Montreal: McGill-Queen's University Press, 1997.

Vickers, Brian. *Occult and Scientific Mentalities in the Renaissance*. Cambridge: Cambridge University Press, 1984.

Voegelin, Eric. *The New Science of Politics*. Chicago: University of Chicago Press, 1987.

Voltaire. *Philosophical Letters; or, Letters Concerning the English Nation*. Edited by Ernest Dilworth. Mineola, N.Y.: Dover Publications, 2003.

Waldron, Jeremy. *Equality, Locke and God*. Cambridge: Cambridge University Press, 2002.

———. "John Locke: Social Contract versus Political Anthropology." *Review of Politics* 51, no. 3 (1989), 3–28.

———. *The Right to Private Property*. Oxford: Clarendon Press; New York: Oxford University Press, 1988.

Walker, Ralph. "Gassendi and Skepticism." In *The Skeptical Tradition*, edited by Myles Burnyeat. Berkeley: University of California Press, 1983.

Walker, William. *Locke, Literary Criticism, and Philosophy*. Cambridge: Cambridge University Press, 1994.

Wallace, W. A. "The Certitude of Science in Late Medieval and Renaissance Thought." *History of Philosophy Quarterly* 3 (1986), 281–91.

Walmsley, Peter. *Locke's Essay and the Rhetoric of Science*. Lewisburg, Pa.: Bucknell University Press, 2003.

Walzer, Michael. *Revolution of the Saints*. New York: Atheneum, 1968.

Webster, Charles. *From Paracelsus to Newton: Magic and the Making of Modern Science*. Cambridge: Cambridge University Press, 1982.

Weeks, Andrew. *Paracelsus: Speculative Theory and the Crisis of the Early Reformation*. Albany: State University of New York Press, 1997.

Welchman, Jennifer. "Locke on Slavery and Inalienable Rights." *Canadian Journal of Philosophy* 25 (1995), 67–81.

White, James Boyd. *Acts of Hope: Creating Authority in Literature, Law and Politics*. Chicago: University of Chicago Press, 1994.

Wilkins, John. *Of the Principles and Duties of Natural Religion: Two Books*. Edited by John Tillotson. London: Chiswall, Battersby and Brome, 1699.

Wolterstorff, Nicholas. *John Locke and the Ethics of Belief*. Cambridge: Cambridge University Press, 1996.

Wood, Neal. *The Politics of Locke's Philosophy: A Social Study of "An Essay Concerning Human Understanding."* Berkeley: University of California Press, 1983.

Woolhouse, R. S. *Locke: A Biography*. Cambridge: Cambridge University Press, 2007.

———. *John Locke*. Brighton: Harvester Press, 1983.

———. *Locke's Philosophy of Science and Knowledge*. Oxford: Basil Blackwell, 1971.

Wootton, David. Introduction to John Locke, *Political Writings*. London: Penguin, 1993.

Yaffe, Gideon. *Liberty Worth the Name: Locke on Free Agency*. Princeton: Princeton University Press, 2000.

Yolton, John. *Locke and the Compass of Human Understanding: A Selective Commentary on the Essay*. Cambridge: University Press, 1970.

———. *John Locke and the Way of Ideas*. London: Oxford University Press, 1956.

———. "Locke and Malebranche: Two Concepts of Ideas." In *John Locke: Symposium Wolfenbüttel, 1979*, edited by Reinhard Brandt. New York: Walter de Gruyter, 1981.

Zuckert, Michael. *Launching Liberalism: On Lockean Political Philosophy*. Lawrence: University Press of Kansas, 2002.

Zuckert, Michael. "Locke and the Problem of Civil Religion." In *The Moral Foundations of the American Republic*, edited by Robert Horwitz. Charlottesville: University Press of Virginia, 1986.

———. *Natural Rights and the New Republicanism*. Princeton: Princeton University Press, 1994.

Index